ROMANS

Smyth & Helwys Bible Commentary: Romans

Publication Staff

President
Cecil P. Staton

Publisher & Executive Vice-President
David Cassady

Vice-President, Editorial
Lex Horton

Senior Editor
Mark K. McElroy

Book Editor
P. Keith Gammons

Art Director
Jim Burt

Assistant Editors
Kelley Land

Smyth & Helwys Publishing, Inc.
6316 Peake Road
Macon, Georgia 31210-3960
1-800-747-3016

The paper used in this publication meets the minimum
requirements of American National Standard for Information
Sciences—Permanence of Paper for Printed Library Materials.
ANSI Z39.48–1984 (alk. paper)

Library of Congress Cataloging-in-Publication Data

Talbert, Charles H.
Romans / Charles H. Talbert.
p. cm. — (Smyth & Helwys Bible commentary, 24)
Includes bibliographical references and indexes.
ISBN 1-57312-081-2
1. Bible. N.T. Romans—Commentaries. I. Title. II. Series.

BS2665.53 .T35 2002
227'.1077—dc21

Library of Congress Control Number: 2002015327

SMYTH & HELWYS BIBLE COMMENTARY

ROMANS

CHARLES H. TALBERT

SMYTH&HELWYS
PUBLISHING INCORPORATED · MACON GEORGIA

ADVANCE PRAISE

Charles Talbert is a seasoned and trustworthy guide to this extraodinary epistle. His commentary captures the logic and ardor of its author. It is astute, vibrant, and relevant.

David E. Garland
Associate Dean of Academic Affairs
Professor of Christian Scriptures
George W. Truett Theological Seminary

Charles Talbert, perhaps the foremost Baptist biblical scholar of our day, has written an outstanding commentary on Paul's most important letter. His work will take its place alongside the classic Romans commentaries by Cranfield, Käsemann, Dunn, and Fitzmyer. The well-educated pastor will profit greatly from Talbert's magnum opus.

Mark Olson
Pastor, Thalia Lynn Baptist Church
Virginia Beach, Virginia

This commentary has the virtues of readibility and clarity combined with original scholarship and incisive interpretation. Anyone who ever teaches or preaches Paul's letter to the Romans must have it.

Sharyn Dowd
Associate Professor of Religion
Baylor University

CONTENTS

TO BETTY W. TALBERT
"SHE HAS BEEN A HELPER OF MANY
AND OF MYSELF AS WELL."

ABBREVIATIONS USED IN THIS COMMENTARY

Books of the Old Testament, Apocrypha, and New Testament are generally abbreviated in the Sidebars, parenthetical references, and notes according to the following system.

The Old Testament

Genesis	Gen
Exodus	Exod
Leviticus	Lev
Numbers	Num
Deuteronomy	Deut
Joshua	Josh
Judges	Judg
Ruth	Ruth
1–2 Samuel	1–2 Sam
1–2 Kings	1–2 Kgs
1–2 Chronicles	1–2 Chr
Ezra	Ezra
Nehemiah	Neh
Esther	Esth
Job	Job
Psalm (Psalms)	Ps (Pss)
Proverbs	Prov
Ecclesiastes	Eccl
or Qoheleth	Qoh
Song of Solomon	Song
or Song of Songs	Song
or Canticles	Cant
Isaiah	Isa
Jeremiah	Jer
Lamentations	Lam
Ezekiel	Ezek
Daniel	Dan
Hosea	Hos
Joel	Joel
Amos	Amos
Obadiah	Obad
Jonah	Jonah
Micah	Mic

Nahum	Nah
Habakkuk	Hab
Zephaniah	Zeph
Haggai	Hag
Zechariah	Zech
Malachi	Mal

The Apocrypha

1–2 Esdras	1–2 Esdr
Tobit	Tob
Judith	Jdt
Additions to Esther	Add Esth
Wisdom of Solomon	Wis
Ecclesiasticus or the Wisdom of Jesus Son of Sirach	Sir
Baruch	Bar
Epistle (or Letter) of Jeremiah	Ep Jer
Prayer of Azariah and the Song of the Three	Pr Azar
Daniel and Susanna	Sus
Daniel, Bel, and the Dragon	Bel
Prayer of Manasseh	Pr Man
1–4 Maccabees	1–4 Macc

The New Testament

Matthew	Matt
Mark	Mark
Luke	Luke
John	John
Acts	Acts
Romans	Rom
1–2 Corinthians	1–2 Cor
Galatians	Gal
Ephesians	Eph
Philippians	Phil
Colossians	Col
1–2 Thessalonians	1–2 Thess
1–2 Timothy	1–2 Tim
Titus	Titus
Philemon	Phlm
Hebrews	Heb
James	Jas
1–2 Peter	1–2 Pet
1–2–3 John	1–2–3 John
Jude	Jude
Revelation	Rev

Other commonly used abbreviations include:

BC	Before Christ
(also commonly referred to as BCE = Before the Common Era)	
AD	*Anno Domini* ("in the year of the Lord")
(also commonly referred to as CE = the Common Era)	
v.	verse
vv.	verses
C.	century
c.	*circa* (around "that time")
cf.	*confer* (compare)
ch.	chapter
chs.	chapters
d.	died
ed.	edition or edited by or editor
eds.	editors
e.g.	*exempli gratia* (for example)
et al.	*et alii* (and others)
f./ff.	and the following one(s)
gen. ed.	general editor
ibid.	*ibidem* (in the same place)
i.e.	*id est* (that is)
LCL	Loeb Classical Library
lit.	literally
n.d.	no date
rev. and exp. ed.	revised and expanded edition
sg.	singular
trans.	translated by or translator(s)
vol(s).	volume(s)

Selected additional written works cited by abbreviations include:

AB	Anchor Bible
ABD	*Anchor Bible Dictionary*
ACCS	Ancient Christian Commentary on Scripture
ANF	*Ante-Nicene Fathers*
ANTC	Abingdon New Testament Commentaries
BA	*Biblical Archaeologist*
BAR	*Biblical Archaeology Review*
CBQ	*Catholic Biblical Quarterly*
HTR	*Harvard Theological Review*
HUCA	*Hebrew Union College Annual*
ICC	International Critical Commentary
IDB	*Interpreters Dictionary of the Bible*
JBL	*Journal of Biblical Literature*

JSJ	*Journal for the Study of Judaism in the Persian, Hellenistic, and Roman Periods*
JSNT	*Journal for the Study of the New Testament*
JSOT	*Journal for the Study of the Old Testament*
KJV	King James Version
LXX	Septuagint = Greek Translation of Hebrew Bible
MDB	*Mercer Dictionary of the Bible*
MT	Masoretic Text
NASB	New American Standard Bible
NEB	New English Bible
NICNT	New International Commentary on the New Testament
NIV	New International Version
NovT	*Novum Testamentum*
NRSV	New Revised Standard Version
NTS	*New Testament Studies*
OGIS	*Orientis graeci inscriptiones selectae*
OTL	Old Testament Library
PRSt	*Perspectives in Religious Studies*
RevExp	*Review and Expositor*
RSV	Revised Standard Version
SBLSP	*Society of Biblical Literature Seminar Papers*
SP	Sacra pagina
TDNT	*Theological Dictionary of the New Testament*
TEV	Today's English Version
WBC	Word Biblical Commentary

AUTHOR'S PREFACE

The opportunity to write this commentary came to me in a round-about fashion. It was originally assigned to Robert Sloan when he was a member of the Baylor University Department of Religion. When Dr. Sloan became Dean of Truett Seminary and then President of Baylor, his administrative duties precluded his work on this project. It was at that time that Alan Culpepper asked me to undertake the task. It was an enterprise on which I was eager to work. When I began my teaching at Wake Forest University in 1963, I taught Romans on a regular basis for over a decade before moving on to other Pauline letters. When I joined the Baylor faculty in 1996, it was understood that my responsibilities were the Pauline and Johannine writings in the New Testament. This focus gave me an opportunity to join my research on Romans with the teaching of my doctoral seminars. A number of graduate students have made invaluable contributions to my work: Andy Arterbury, Eddie Ellis, Travis Frampton, Barbara Griswold, Derek Hogan, Galen Johnson, Annie Judkins, Pamela Kinlaw, Charles Ramsey, John Vast-Binder, Jeff Wilson, and Richard Young. Fellow learners, I thank you very much.

Working on Romans again has allowed me to try to come to terms with the numerous fresh perspectives on ancient Judaism that have emerged over the past generation and with their impact on Pauline studies. How my thinking on these issues has evolved may be seen in my presidential address before the Catholic Biblical Association in August, 2000, "Paul, Judaism, and the Revisionists," which has been published in the *Catholic Biblical Quarterly*, Volume 63 (January, 2001). It is this synthesis that serves as the presupposition for much of my reading of Romans. My intent has been to deal with Paul the Christian Jew and with his Jewish milieu with integrity. My readers will have to decide whether or not I have succeeded.

The editors have granted me the freedom to treat Romans as a theological document in the Connections sections and sidebar boxes as well as in the Commentary proper. For this I am deeply grateful. Paul's theological perspective is counter to the moralism that is the bane of most contemporary hermeneutics, teaching, and preaching, whether on the left or on the right. Not to have moralistic Connections and sidebars laid on top of an antimoralistic Commentary is clearly correct procedure.

I must express special gratitude to my wife, Dr. Betty W. Talbert, Director of Spiritual Formation at Truett Seminary, not only for her personal support of my efforts but also for her influence on my thought at points that should be obvious to the discerning reader. She should not be held accountable, however, for the many theological and ethical directions that are my responsibility alone.

Charles H. Talbert
Labor Day, 2001

SERIES PREFACE

The *Smyth & Helwys Bible Commentary* is a visually stimulating and user-friendly series that is as close to multimedia in print as possible. Written by accomplished scholars with all students of Scripture in mind, the primary goal of the *Smyth & Helwys Bible Commentary* is to make available serious, credible biblical scholarship in an accessible and less intimidating format.

Far too many Bible commentaries fall short of bridging the gap between the insights of biblical scholars and the needs of students of God's written word. In an unprecedented way, the *Smyth & Helwys Bible Commentary* brings insightful commentary to bear on the lives of contemporary Christians. Using a multimedia format, the volumes employ a stunning array of art, photographs, maps, and drawings to illustrate the truths of the Bible for a visual generation of believers.

The *Smyth & Helwys Bible Commentary* is built upon the idea that meaningful Bible study can occur when the insights of contemporary biblical scholars blend with sensitivity to the needs of lifelong students of Scripture. Some persons within local faith communities, however, struggle with potentially informative biblical scholarship for several reasons. Oftentimes, such scholarship is cast in technical language easily grasped by other scholars, but not by the general reader. For example, lengthy, technical discussions on every detail of a particular scriptural text can hinder the quest for a clear grasp of the whole. Also, the format for presenting scholarly insights has often been confusing to the general reader, rendering the work less than helpful. Unfortunately, responses to the hurdles of reading extensive commentaries have led some publishers to produce works for a general readership that merely skim the surface of the rich resources of biblical scholarship. This commentary series incorporates works of fine art in an accurate and scholarly manner, yet the format remains "user-friendly." An important facet is the presentation and explanation of images of art, which interpret the biblical material or illustrate how the biblical material has been understood and interpreted in the past. A visual generation of believers deserves a commentary series that contains not only the all-important textual commentary on Scripture, but images, photographs, maps, works of fine art, and drawings that bring the text to life.

The *Smyth & Helwys Bible Commentary* makes serious, credible biblical scholarship more accessible to a wider audience. Writers and editors alike present information in ways that encourage readers to gain a better understanding of the Bible. The editorial board has worked to develop a format that is useful and usable, informative and pleasing to the eye. Our writers are reputable scholars who participate in the community of faith and sense a calling to communicate the results of their scholarship to their faith community.

The *Smyth & Helwys Bible Commentary* addresses Christians and the larger church. While both respect for and sensitivity to the needs and contributions of other faith communities are reflected in the work of the series authors, the authors speak primarily to Christians. Thus the reader can note a confessional tone throughout the volumes. No particular "confession of faith" guides the authors, and diverse perspectives are observed in the various volumes. Each writer, though, brings to the biblical text the best scholarly tools available and expresses the results of their studies in commentary and visuals that assist readers seeking a word from the Lord for the church.

To accomplish this goal, writers in this series have drawn from numerous streams in the rich tradition of biblical interpretation. The basic focus is the biblical text itself, and considerable attention is given to the wording and structure of texts. Each particular text, however, is also considered in the light of the entire canon of Christian Scriptures. Beyond this, attention is given to the cultural context of the biblical writings. Information from archaeology, ancient history, geography, comparative literature, history of religions, politics, sociology, and even economics is used to illuminate the culture of the people who produced the Bible. In addition, the writers have drawn from the history of interpretation, not only as it is found in traditional commentary on the Bible but also in literature, theater, church history, and the visual arts. Finally, the *Commentary* on Scripture is joined with *Connections* to the world of the contemporary church. Here again, the writers draw on scholarship in many fields as well as relevant issues in the popular culture.

This wealth of information might easily overwhelm a reader if not presented in a "user-friendly" format. Thus the heavier discussions of detail and the treatments of other helpful topics are presented in special-interest boxes, or Sidebars, clearly connected to the passages under discussion so as not to interrupt the flow of the basic interpretation. The result is a commentary on Scripture that focuses on the theological significance of a text while also offering the reader a rich array of additional information related to the text and its interpretation.

An accompanying CD-ROM offers powerful searching and research tools. The commentary text, Sidebars, and visuals are all reproduced on a CD that is fully indexed and searchable. Pairing a text version with a digital resource is a distinctive feature of the *Smyth & Helwys Bible Commentary*.

Combining credible biblical scholarship, user-friendly study features, and sensitivity to the needs of a visually oriented generation of believers creates a unique and unprecedented type of commentary series. With insight from many of today's finest biblical scholars and a stunning visual format, it is our hope that the *Smyth & Helwys Bible Commentary* will be a welcome addition to the personal libraries of all students of Scripture.

The Editors

HOW TO USE
THIS COMMENTARY

The *Smyth & Helwys Bible Commentary* is written by accomplished biblical scholars with a wide array of readers in mind. Whether engaged in the study of Scripture in a church setting or in a college or seminary classroom, all students of the Bible will find a number of useful features throughout the commentary that are helpful for interpreting the Bible.

Basic Design of the Volumes

Each volume features an Introduction to a particular book of the Bible, providing a brief guide to information that is necessary for reading and interpreting the text: the historical setting, literary design, and theological significance. Each Introduction also includes a comprehensive outline of the particular book under study.

Each chapter of the commentary investigates the text according to logical divisions in a particular book of the Bible. Sometimes these divisions follow the traditional chapter segmentation, while at other times the textual units consist of sections of chapters or portions of more than one chapter. The divisions reflect the literary structure of a book and offer a guide for selecting passages that are useful in preaching and teaching.

An accompanying CD-ROM offers powerful searching and research tools. The commentary text, Sidebars, and visuals are all reproduced on a CD that is fully indexed and searchable. Pairing a text version with a digital resource also allows unprecedented flexibility and freedom for the reader. Carry the text version to locations you most enjoy doing research while knowing that the CD offers a portable alternative for travel from the office, church, classroom, and your home.

Commentary and Connections

As each chapter explores a textual unit, the discussion centers around two basic sections: *Commentary* and *Connections*. The analysis of a passage, including the details of its language, the history reflected in the text, and the literary forms found in the text, are the main focus of the *Commentary* section. The primary concern of the *Commentary* section is to explore the theological issues presented by the Scripture passage. *Connections* presents potential applications of the insights provided in the *Commentary* section. The *Connections* portion of each chapter considers what issues are relevant for teaching and suggests useful methods and resources. *Connections* also identifies themes suitable for sermon planning and suggests helpful approaches for preaching on the Scripture text.

Sidebars

The *Smyth & Helwys Bible Commentary* provides a unique hyperlink format that quickly guides the reader to additional insights. Since other more technical or supplementary information is vital for understanding a text and its implications, the volumes feature distinctive Sidebars, or special-interest boxes, that provide a wealth of information on such matters as:

• Historical information (such as chronological charts, lists of kings or rulers, maps, descriptions of monetary systems, descriptions of special groups, descriptions of archaeological sites or geographical settings).

• Graphic outlines of literary structure (including such items as poetry, chiasm, repetition, epistolary form).

• Definition or brief discussions of technical or theological terms and issues.

• Insightful quotations that are not integrated into the running text but are relevant to the passage under discussion.

• Notes on the history of interpretation (Augustine on the Good Samaritan, Luther on James, Stendahl on Romans, etc.).

• Line drawings, photographs, and other illustrations relevant for understanding the historical context or interpretive significance of the text.

• Presentation and discussion of works of fine art that have interpreted a Scripture passage.

Each Sidebar is printed in color and is referenced at the appropriate place in the *Commentary* or *Connections* section with a color-coded title that directs the reader to the relevant Sidebar. In addition, helpful icons appear in the Sidebars, which provide the reader with visual cues to the type of material that is explained in each Sidebar. Throughout the commentary, these four distinct hyperlinks provide useful links in an easily recognizable design.

Alpha & Omega Language

This icon identifies the information as a language-based tool that offers further exploration of the Scripture selection. This could include syntactical information, word studies, popular or additional uses of the word(s) in question, additional contexts in which the term appears, and the history of the term's translation. All non-English terms are transliterated into the appropriate English characters.

Culture/Context

This icon introduces further comment on contextual or cultural details that shed light on the Scripture selection. Describing the place and time to which a Scripture passage refers is often vital to the task of biblical interpretation. Sidebar items introduced with this icon could include geographical, historical, political, social, topographical, or economic information. Here, the reader may find an excerpt of an ancient text or inscription that sheds light on the text. Or one may find a description of some element of ancient religion such as Baalism in Canaan or the Hero cult in the Mystery Religions of the Greco-Roman world.

Interpretation

Sidebars that appear under this icon serve a general interpretive function in terms of both historical and contemporary renderings. Under this heading, the reader might find a selection from classic or contemporary literature that illuminates the Scripture text or a significant quotation from a famous sermon that addresses the passage. Insights are drawn from various sources, including literature, worship, theater, church history, and sociology.

Additional Resources Study

Here, the reader finds a convenient list of useful resources for further investigation of the selected Scripture text, including books, journals, websites, special collections, organizations, and societies. Specialized discussions of works not often associated with biblical studies may also appear here.

Additional Features

Each volume also includes a basic Bibliography on the biblical book under study. Other bibliographies on selected issues are often included that point the reader to other helpful resources.

Notes at the end of each chapter provide full documentation of sources used and contain additional discussions of related matters.

Abbreviations used in each volume are explained in a list of abbreviations found after the Table of Contents.

Readers of the *Smyth & Helwys Bible Commentary* can regularly visit the Internet support site for news, information, updates, and enhancements to the series at <**www.helwys.com/commentary**>.

Several thorough indexes enable the reader to locate information quickly. These indexes include:

- An *Index of Sidebars* groups content from the special-interest boxes by category (maps, fine art, photographs, drawings, etc.).

- An *Index of Scriptures* lists citations to particular biblical texts.

- An *Index of Topics* lists alphabetically the major subjects, names, topics, and locations referenced or discussed in the volume.

- An *Index of Modern Authors* organizes contemporary authors whose works are cited in the volume.

INTRODUCTION

The Apostle Paul, to whom thirteen letters in the New Testament are attributed, occupies a tenuous position within the canon of many modern people. In the nineteenth century his detractors were legion. None was more pointed than Ernest Renan. Near the end of his *The History of the Origins of Christianity, Book III: Saint Paul*,[1] Renan summarized his estimate of the apostle.

> After having been for three hundred years the Christian doctor in an eminent degree, thanks to orthodox Protestantism, Paul seems in our day near the end of his reign: Jesus, on the contrary, is more living than ever. It is no more the Epistle to the Romans which is the recapitulation of Christianity, it is the Sermon on the Mount. True Christianity which will last eternally comes from the Gospels, not from the Epistles of Paul. The writings of Paul have been a danger and a stumbling block, the cause of the chief faults of Christian theology. Paul is the father of the subtle Augustine, of the arid Thomas Aquinas, of the sombre Calvinist, of the bitter Jansenist, of the ferocious theology which condemns and predestinates to damnation.

The distaste of people like Renan for Paul in the nineteenth century has its parallels today. Paul is often dismissed both for his theology and for his ethics. On the one hand, his theology runs counter to the dominant cultural trends. For many persons it is easier to adapt the historians' Jesus to the norms of political correctness than Paul. His teaching about justification apart from law is often viewed as a doctrine directed against Judaism. If he abrogated the Law, then he abrogated Judaism, so the argument goes. The Paul who advocated a law-free gospel is, therefore, wrongly regarded as anti-Jewish. Consider the following rhetorical question (with an assumed answer of NO):

> Can a Paul who devotes his energies to the creation and maintaining of sectarian groups hostile to all non-members, and especially to the Jewish community from which in fact they derived, still be seen as the bearer of a message with profound universal significance?[2]

On the other hand, a misreading of Pauline positions on women and a correct reading of Paul's stance on homosexuality have gained him the hatred of many feminists[3] and prohomosexual advocates. Even those who do not openly oppose Paul often denigrate him by neglect.

Paul

The Apostle Paul is shown to have many faces as depicted throughout the history of art. In this painting by Velazquez, St. Paul is pensive and not overly invested in posing for a photo-op. In the various art depictions of Paul, he is almost always shown holding or somehow engaged with a book, which has become an attribute of his epistles.

Diego Rodriguez Velazquez. (1599–1660). *Saint Paul.* Museu d'Art de Cataluna. Barcelona, Spain. (Credit:Scala/Art Resource, NY)

Churches that follow the lectionary in their worship and preaching may become essentially Synoptic Gospel churches. The lectionary, which was touted as a means of avoiding a canon within a canon, in those cases ends up creating that very thing. Paul, along with the Gospel of John, is marginalized in some Christian preaching. In effect, Paul is excluded from the *de facto* canon. Paul's treatment today is in some ways analogous to that accorded to the Revelation to John: despised and/or ignored. In order for there to be a rehabilitation of the apostle Paul in contemporary churches, we must take the long view. The New Testament scholar, Ernst Käsemann, has categorized "the real" Paul's religious significance this way.

> This Paul remains confined in seven letters and for the most part unintelligible to posterity, not only to the ancient Church and the Middle Ages. However, whenever he is rediscovered—which happens almost exclusively in times of crisis—there issues from him explosive power. . . . It is never long, to be sure, until orthodoxy and enthusiasm again master this Paul and banish him once more to his letters. However, the church continues to preserve his letters in her canon and thereby latently preserves . . . the one who for the most part only disturbs her.[4]

The historian (Sydney Ahlstrom) has described Paul's theological influence this way: "Just as the European philosophical tradition, in Whitehead's famous phrase, consists of a series of footnotes to Plato, so Christian theology is a series of footnotes to St. Paul."[5] Looking back over the history of the church, as regards Paul's Roman epistle one can see that Paul's letter to the Romans has had remarkable renewing power in Christian history.[6]

Augustine (AD 354–430), struggling with his sexual addiction, at best could pray, "Give me chastity and continence, but not yet."[7] Then one day while reading Paul's letters, he heard a child chanting, "Take up and read; take up and read." Opening the book, the first thing his eyes fell upon were the words of Romans 13:13-14: "not in reveling and drunkenness, not in debauchery and licentiousness, not in quarreling and jealousy. But put on the Lord Jesus Christ, and make no provision for the flesh, to gratify its desires." Augustine puts his response thusly: "No further would I read; nor needed I; for instantly at the end of this sentence, by a light as it were of serenity infused in my heart, all the darkness . . . vanished away."[8] After his conversion in 386, he was baptized at Easter of 387. Paul's letter to the Romans had done its work.

(Martin Luther's) *Lectures on Romans* (1516) reflect the change that occurred in his life as a result of his encounter with Paul. Luther was accustomed to think of the righteousness of God as something to be feared. In his reading of Psalm 30, the phrase "in your righteousness deliver me" caused him to turn to Romans 1:16-17. Instead of the punitive righteousness of God, Luther now saw a reference to God's forgiving righteousness by which in mercy God makes us just. He says of his experience: "Then it seemed to me as if I were born anew and that I had entered into the open gates of

"The righteousness will live by faith"

Paradise. The whole Bible suddenly took on a new aspect for me."[9] Out of this encounter with Romans, the German Reformation was born. Of Romans, Luther said it is so important "that every Christian should know it word for word, by heart, (and) occupy himself with it every day, as the daily bread of the soul."[10]

In *John Wesley's Journal,* Wesley recounts his experience on 24 May 1738. He says that in the evening he

> went very unwillingly to a society in Aldersgate Street where someone was reading from Luther's preface to the Epistle to the Romans. About a quarter before nine, while he was describing the change which God works in the heart through faith in Christ, I felt my heart strangely warmed. I felt I did trust in Christ, Christ alone for my salvation: And an assurance was given me, that He had taken away my sins, even mine, and saved me from the law of sin and death.[11]

Once again Romans functioned as a catalyst for renewal.

While studying at the Orthodox Theological Seminary in Bucharest, Dumitru Cornilescu began his search for spiritual vitality. It led him to the study of the Scriptures. He determined to translate the Scriptures into Romanian. He began this project in 1916 and completed it within six years. This involved him in a study of Romans. As a result of this study he came to believe matters previously unknown to him. All are sinners; the wages of sin is death; sinners may be justified freely through Christ because of God's atonement in Jesus' blood. "I took this forgiveness for myself, " he said; "I accepted Christ as my living Saviour." From that point on, Cornilescu was assured that he belonged to God. His translation of the Scriptures (1921) became the standard Bible Society text for Romanians.[12]

In 1918 a young Swiss pastor named Karl Barth produced a commentary on Romans that reflected his encounter with the text of Paul's letter. In it he protested in the name of Paul against the premises of the liberal theology of his day. In the Preface to the second edition, he held up Calvin as a model for reading Romans.[13] Calvin, he said, set himself to rethink the whole material and to wrestle with it until the walls that separated the sixteenth century from the first became transparent. In this way, Calvin and the modern reader are brought face to face with the subject matter of the Scriptures: the Godness of God and the sinfulness of humanity. As a result of his encounter with Romans, Barth launched a major reorientation of theology in the twentieth century.

What can be illustrated with examples from noteworthy people in the church's history is confirmed by the experience of countless everyday Christians. The Pauline letter to the Romans has the potential to renew individuals, the church, and its theology.[14] A fresh reading of this seminal document holds the promise of new life. The experience of new life as a result of a reading of Romans offers the necessary legitimation of Paul's place in the canon. Such a reading begins with an attempt to situate Romans in its original historical context.

The Social Context of Romans

Knowledge of the history of the Jews in Rome is indispensable if one is to understand anything about the origins of Christianity in the city. We may begin in the second century BC. Judas Maccabeus sent envoys to Rome about 160 BC to establish an alliance and peace with the Romans,[15] a proposal agreed to by the Roman Senate.[16] Perhaps Jews were moving back and forth between Jerusalem and Rome by this time. The earliest Roman evidence for Jews in Rome comes from Valerius Maximus.[17] He said that in 139 BC the Praetor Hispalus expelled from Rome the Jews, the Chaldeans, and the Asiatic astrologers, that is, religious practitioners from the Orient. After 63 BC Pompey brought a great number of Jews, including a member of the ruling family, to Rome as captives.[18] In Cicero's time, Cicero defended one Flaccus against the charge that the Praetor had misappropriated funds of Asiatic Jews intended for the temple in Jerusalem. Roman Jews at that time were so numerous and influential that they tried to determine the outcome of the trial.[19] Cicero's defense utilized anti-Jewish prejudice. The number of Jews, he said, was large, they stuck together, were influential in political assemblies, and adhered to a barbarian superstition.[20] Julius Caesar sent a letter to the people of Parium about the Jews. In it he said that even in Rome Jews were not forbidden to assemble and live according to their religious customs.[21] At the death of Julius Caesar, Roman Jews provided an honor guard at his gravesite for several nights.[22] When Herod the Great died, more than 8,000 Roman Jews escorted the Palestinian legation that arrived in Rome to protest the rule of Archelaus.[23] Even if Josephus's numbers are exaggerated, they show the Jewish community was sizable by the end of the first century BC. Philo said that in the time of Augustus the Jews occupied the large section of Rome across the Tiber and that most were free Roman citizens.[24] [Roman Emperors]

Roman Emperors

Paul's ministry was carried out in the context of Roman imperial power. He would have lived as a Christian Messianist under four different emperors: Tiberius, Caligula, Claudius, and Nero. A list of Roman emperors from Augustus through Hadrian enables one to position Paul more accurately.

Augustus (27 BC–AD 14)

Tiberius (AD 14–37)

Caligula (AD 37–41)

Claudius (AD 41–54)—Priscilla and Aquila were among those expelled from Rome in AD 49. According to Acts 18:1-2, they came to Corinth and met Paul during this period.

Nero (AD 54–68)—Romans was written and Paul went to Rome in this period. Priscilla and Aquila were back in Rome at this point. Tradition locates the martyrdoms of both Peter and Paul in Nero's reign.

Galba, Otho, Vitellius (AD 69)

Vespasian (AD 69–79)

Titus (AD 79–81)

Domitian (AD 81–96)

Nerva (AD 96–98)

Trajan (AD 98–117)

Hadrian (AD 117–138)

Bust of Nero. AD 54–68. Marble. Ancient Corinth Archaeological Museum. Corinth, Greece. (Credit: Mitchell Reddish)

In AD 19 Tiberius expelled the Jews and the followers of Isis from the city.[25] Inscriptions nevertheless reveal many synagogues in the city, mostly using Greek. Inscriptional evidence indicates that there may have been ten to thirteen synagogues in Rome in the first century.[26] No single, controlling organization supervised the individual synagogues. This loose structure provided an essential prerequisite for Christian Judaism's early penetration of Rome. In AD 49 Claudius expelled the Jews because of their disturbance of the public order.[27] [Jewish Synagogues in Rome] As a result, Jewish Christians also had to leave the city. Aquila and Priscilla, for example, arrived in Corinth and there became coworkers with Paul.[28] In Nero's reign, the Jews returned to Rome in great numbers. Their influence increased, in part because Nero's wife, Poppaea, was friendly to them.[29] Nevertheless, Jews were generally objects of derision by the Romans. They were depicted as beggars,[30] fortune-tellers,[31] lazy folk,[32] people of superstition[33] and sexual lust,[34] with a tendency toward proselytism.[35] The Gentiles of Rome did not like the Jews.

The origins of Christianity in Rome are unclear. The association of Peter and Paul with the founding of the church by Irenaeus[36] is legend[37] but Christians certainly existed in Rome prior to the Claudian expulsion of AD 49. [Extracanonical Traditions about Paul.] The fourth-century commentator Ambrosiaster says that the Romans had early embraced the faith of Christ but in a Jewish form.[38] This fits with the evidence. After the expulsion of Jewish Christians in 49, only Gentile Christians remained in Rome. When Jewish Christians who had been expelled returned early in the reign of Nero, they found a dominant Gentile Christianity in place.

There is no reason to assume this Gentile Christianity was all of one type. Both Jewish and Gentile Christianity manifested significant diversity in the first century. Raymond Brown has argued that the NT reflects at least four types of Christians, distinguished by their attitudes towards the law. First, there were Jewish Christians and their Gentile converts who insisted on full observance of the Mosaic Law, including circumcision (e.g., Gal 2:4; Paul's opponents in Galatia; Acts 15:5). Second, there were the Jewish Christians and their Gentile converts who did not insist on circumcision but did require some Jewish observance, such as that related to food laws (e.g., those from James and Peter in Gal 2:11-14; James in Acts 15). Third, there were Jewish Christians and their Gentile converts who did not insist on circumcision and did not require observance of food laws (e.g., Paul's attitude toward his Gentile converts). Fourth, there were Jewish Christians and their Gentile converts who did not insist on circumcision, observance of the food laws, and who saw no abiding significance in the Jewish cult and feasts (e.g., the Hellenists in Acts 6:1-6; 6:8–7:60; Fourth Evangelist; Hebrews).[39] It is possible that the Roman Gentile Christians had representatives from each of these four options among them. They would not, of necessity, have been reduced only to a Gentile Christianity that shared the Roman disdain for Jews generally and adhered to position four. Those Jewish Christians who returned, moreover, were not all of the same stripe. Some, such as Priscilla and Aquila, had become Pauline-type Christians; others remained more in the mold of Christians

Jewish Synagogues in Rome

No remains of specific synagogues have been located within the city of Rome proper, although many are known to have existed. During the reign of Claudius (AD 41–54), extensive renovation was done to Rome's port at Ostia. Among the buildings that can be dated to this period is a Jewish synagogue. The earliest phase of the Ostia synagogue pictured here exhibits brickwork typical of Claudian-period construction. The edict of Claudius that expelled Jews from Rome may not have mandated their departure from all of Italy. Conceivably, Jewish Christians, including Priscilla and Aquila, may have met in this synagogue.

Ostia synagogue. (Credit: Scott Nash)

Extracanonical Traditions about Paul

Later Christian authors offered certain alleged information about Paul. Examples include the following:

- Jerome, in his *Commentary on Philemon*, says: "We have heard this story. They say that the parents of the Apostle Paul were from Gischala, a region of Judaea, and that, when the whole province was devastated by the hand of Rome and the Jews scattered throughout the world, they were moved to Tarsus, a town of Cilicia." The historicity of this tradition is possible but not certain. (Murphy-O'Connor)
- The *Acts of Paul* gives a legendary description of Paul's appearance: "a man small of stature, with a bald head and crooked legs, in a good state of body, with eyebrows meeting and nose somewhat hooked, full of friendliness." The historical value of this description is doubtful.
- A number of early Christian traditions claim Paul was beheaded under Nero (*Acts of Paul* 10; *Acts of Peter* 3.1; Tertullian, *Prescription against Heretics* 36; Eusebius, *Church History* 2.22.1-2; 2.25.5-8). This claim is widely regarded as historical.

True to the compositional excesses of Mannerism, this painting by Tintoretto captures the dramatic moment of beheading through the use of stark contrasts of light and shadow. The executioner's head is couched in the darkness of the cloud and his sword, moments from release, is aligned on the same plane as the head of Paul, which is, by contrast, radiant in light. Paul's armor is shown at the feet of the executioner. However, judging by the aura of light that bathes his head and the rays of light streaming down upon him, Paul is not naked as he has now put on the "armor of light" (Rom 13:12).

Jacopo Tintoretto. 1518–1594. *Decapitation of Saint Paul*. S. Maria dell'Orto. Venice, Italy. (Credit: Camerphoto/Art Resource, NY)

associated with James and were suspicious of Paul.[40] When Paul wrote Romans, therefore, at least three types of Christians were in the city: conservative Jewish and Gentile Christians (Brown's positions 1 and 2), Gentile Christians impatient with Jewish ways (Brown's position 4), and Pauline-type Christians from both Jewish and Gentile backgrounds (Brown's position 3).

These Christians were scattered in small house churches with no central governing authority.[41] Recent scholarship has identified at least five churches or cell groups reflected in Romans 16:[42] (1) 16:5a—the church in the house of Prisca and Aquila; (2) 16:10b—those who belong to the household of Aristobulus; (3) 16:11b—those in the household of Narcissus; (4) 16:14—the brothers; and (5) 16:15—the saints. And these were just the ones about which Paul had knowledge! They were, moreover, often in tension with one another.[43] Recognition of this elementary diversity allows the reader to make sense of the fact that Paul wrote to Gentile Christians (1:5-6, 13-15; 11:13; 15:15-16) on the one hand and the fact that much of his argument sounds as if it was addressed to Jewish and Jewish Christian people on the other. Some Gentile Christians could be Judaizing, while some could be impatient with Judaism.[44]

That Paul wrote Romans no one doubts. Who was this one called Paul? In the first place, he was a Jew. In Romans 11:1 he described himself as "an Israelite, a descendant of Abraham, a member of the tribe of Benjamin." In Philippians 3:5 he referred to being "of the people of Israel, of the tribe of Benjamin, a Hebrew born of Hebrews, as to the law a Pharisee." In 2 Corinthians 11:22, 24, he identified himself as a Hebrew, an Israelite, and of the seed of Abraham. From his letters it is clear that he was competent in Greek. He could use both the Hellenistic diatribe form of argument and Jewish methods of interpreting Scripture. In the second place, he had become a devotee of Christ when God's Son was revealed to him (Gal 1:15-16; 1 Cor 15:7; 9:1). He then became an evangelist, a missionary, and a church planter in areas untouched by the gospel (1 Cor 15:10; Gal 1:16; 2 Cor 10:16; Rom 15:18-20). In the third place, he remained a Jew. W. D. Davies has observed:

> In accepting the Jew, Jesus, as the Messiah, Paul did not think in terms of moving into a new religion but of having found the final expression and intent of the Jewish tradition within which he himself had been born. . . . He would not have conceived of himself as having ceased to be a Jew.[45]

How can this be? The many Judaisms that existed between the third century BC and the second century AD are often called Middle Judaism.[46] The genus Middle Judaism encompassed a variety of species: Pharisaism, Essenism, apocalyptic, mystical Judaism, Christian Messianists, and many more. As a result of the fall of Jerusalem to the Romans in AD 70 and again in AD 135, most of these species perished. The two forms of Middle Judaism that have survived to this day are rabbinic Judaism and Christianity. According to Alan Segal, both would

> consider themselves to be the heirs to the promises given to Abraham and Isaac and they are indeed fraternal twins emerging from the

nation-state of second commonwealth Israel. As brothers often do, they picked different, even opposing ways to preserve the family's heritage.[47]

Paul, then, fits into Middle Judaism before AD 70. He represents a form of Hellenistic Christian Messianic Judaism. His conversion, therefore, was from one form of Judaism (a nonmessianic Pharisaism with an apocalyptic-mystical cast to it) to another (Christian Messianism). Consequently, as James D. G. Dunn points out, "his writings can still be classified as Jewish literature."[48]

Many of the positions held by Paul were held by other Jews of the time. For example, other ancient Jews beside Paul did not regard circumcision as necessary for Gentiles to be saved (Josephus, *Antiquities* 20.2.3-4+34-48; the Noahide commands).[49] Others Jews did not regard literal observance of the ceremonial laws as necessary for God's people (Philo, *Migration of Abraham* 89–93). Other Jews did not believe ancestry/ethnicity guaranteed inclusion in the Israel to be saved (John the Baptist; Qumran). Other Jews did believe an individual's beliefs and behavior would determine one's inclusion/exclusion from God's people and the coming age (*m. Sanh* 10:1-4, read in its entirety). Other Jews did not make Moses central to Jewish identity (e.g., *History of the Rechabites* and *4 Baruch*, neither of which mentions Moses or the Law and both of which portray an optional religious authority). Daniel Boyarin asserts, "There is no reason, a priori, . . . why believing that Jesus was the Messiah would be considered as beyond the pale of rabbinic Judaism, any more than Rabbi Akiva's belief in Bar Kolchba as Messiah rendered him a heretic."[50] Nevertheless, his distinctive religious synthesis would have seemed "strange" to most other Jews.[51]

Two issues especially help clarify Paul's position within the Judaism of his time. First, the two forms of Judaism with which Paul was involved were very different in their anthropological assumptions.[52] The anthropology underlying Pharisaism/rabbinic Judaism was optimistic. Humans, it was assumed, have free will. Its soteriology, therefore, was synergistic. Salvation depends partly on good works.[53] Paul's anthropology, at least for the time after he became a Messianist and probably before, was pessimistic. Humans, he contended, did not have free will in the area of soteriology. His soteriology, therefore, was *sola gratia* (by grace alone). Good works arose out of God's action in and through the Christian. This difference did not mean Paul rejected Judaism. He did not see himself as ceasing to be Jewish but as having found the true form of Judaism. His argument in Romans operates within Judaism and contends for a specific understanding of what the Scriptures of Israel really teach.

Second, Paul's relation to non-Christian Judaism has been understood in a variety of ways. (1) Judaism was legalistic; Paul was right in recognizing and opposing it. (2) Judaism was not legalistic; Paul or his interpreters got it wrong. The apostle either did not oppose Jewish legalism, or, if he did, he was misrepresenting ancient Judaism. (3) Judaism was not legalistic but some Jewish adherents got it wrong and were legalists (e.g., *4 Ezra*; *T. Abr.*; *Ap Zeph*) ; Paul was right about the latter group. (4) Middle Judaism was diverse. (a) Some were legalistic (e.g., Gentiles had to be circumcised in order to become Jews = part of God's people; cf. Josephus, *Antiquities* 20.17-48). (b) Many were synergistic. They advocated covenantal nomism. A Jew got into the covenant by God's grace but remained in the covenant, and got in the New Age beyond the resurrection, by works of the Law (e.g., 1 QS; *2 Bar* 41, 42, 51; *m. Sanh* 10:1-4). (c) Some held to *sola gratia* (by grace alone) insofar as both Gentile and Jew were concerned (e.g., LXX Jer 38:31-34; LXX Isa 2:1-4 and Tob 14:6-7; *Ap Abr*). This piety held that one not only got in by grace but also remained in the people of God by grace and ultimately got into the New Age beyond the resurrection by grace. I regard the fourth position to be the most accurate of this group. It will be the position of this commentary that Paul criticized (a) and (b) in the name of (c). His critique was an intra-Jewish argument. There was one genus: Judaism. Within that genus, a number of species were in tension with one another over who represented the true tradition with reference to the Scriptures of Israel. Paul was an example of one of those species of Middle Judaism. His critique was also an intra-Christian argument. The diversity of non-Christian Judaism about the role of the Law was reflected in early Christian messianic Judaism as well. Paul, then, was also a critic of Christian messianists who fell into categories (a) and (b).

Paul wrote Romans at the end of his mission in the Aegean area just as he was about to embark on a journey to Jerusalem with the collection for the saints there.[54] [Pauline Chronology] The letter was likely sent from Corinth or its environs.[55] Paul's secretary was one Tertius.[56] It was probably delivered by Phoebe.[57] The letter is now generally considered to be a unity. Chapter 16 is believed by most to belong with 1–15 as an integral part of the letter.[58] When Paul wrote Romans, he had to address the various types of Christians in Rome. Romans 1:5-6, 13; 11:13-32; chapter 14; and 15:15-16 reflect Gentile Christians who are independent of Paul's perspective. Romans 14:2,3,5,21 reflect Jewish and Gentile Christians of a different mind from Paul. Romans 16:3,5 reflect Christians of a Pauline persuasion, whether Jewish or Gentile Christian.

The Stated Aims of Romans

In Romans Paul had at least three stated aims. The first was that Paul wrote to get the Roman Christians to pray for him as he went to Jerusalem (15:30). Two things in particular were requested. He asked for prayer that he "may be delivered from the unbelievers in Judea" (15:31a). He also asked the Romans to intercede that "my service for Jerusalem may be acceptable to the saints" (15:31b). So when Paul wrote Romans he was thinking especially of the collection visit he was undertaking in order to demonstrate the unity of Gentile and Jewish Christians in one church. Paul's second stated aim was his desire to impart some spiritual gift to strengthen the Roman Christians (1:11-12; 15:15-16). This spiritual gift was doubtless his gospel, which offered a basis for the unity of Gentile and Jewish Christians in the church. The third stated aim was to get the Roman Christians to speed him on his way to Spain (15:24). This, of course, would not have been possible if the various types of Jewish and Gentile Christians in Rome were not united. These three stated aims in writing indicate that Romans was written both because of Paul's own plans and because of needs in the Roman church. A consensus seems to be building, moreover, that the main need in the Roman church addressed by Paul was that of resolving the disunity between Jews and Gentiles. If so, then the spiritual gift Paul wanted to impart was his gospel, which was to be the basis of unity for the Roman congregations.

These occasions functioned as catalysts for Paul's letter. The argument of Romans, however, was determined by the logic of the gospel as Paul had thought it out during his Aegean mission. In this sense Romans is a summary of Paul's mature thought insofar as it applied to the Roman occasion. This means, on the one hand, that Romans has relevance beyond the specific occasions that evoked the letter. For example, insofar as sin affects Jew and Gentile alike, it is a human problem. Insofar as Christ saves Jew and Gentile alike, he is a universal savior. This means, on the other hand, that Romans does not offer a summary of all of Paul's teaching but only of those points that were called for by the letter's occasions. Romans, then, is an occasional letter but with universal applicability—not either-or but both-and.

Pauline Chronology

Establishing an exact chronology of Paul's life is difficult. The one fixed point is provided by an inscription found at Delphi that refers to Gallio, the proconsul of Achaia.

Tiberius Claudius Caesar Augustus Germanicus, 12th year of tribunician power, acclaimed emperor for the 26th time, father of the country, sends greetings to [_____]. For long have I been well-disposed to the city of Delphi and solicitous for its prosperity, and I have always observed the cult of the Pythian Apollo. Now since it is said to be destitute of citizens, as my friend and proconsul L. Iunius Gallio recently reported to me, and desiring that Delphi should regain its former splendour, I command you to invite well-born people also from other cities to come to Delphi as new inhabitants, and to accord them and their children all the privileges of the Delphians as being citizens on like and equal terms. For if some are transferred as colonists to these regions. . . .

From the inscription it is possible to date Gallio's service either to AD 50–51 or 51–52. Then attention is called to Acts 18:12, which says: "When Gallio was proconsul of Achaia, the Jews made a united attack on Paul and brought him before the tribunal." Putting the two pieces of evidence together makes it likely that Paul came before Gallio in 51. If so, all other dates are derived from reasoning backward and forward from 51. This does not lend itself to scholarly agreement. One possible schema, given by Karl Donfried, is as follows.

Conversion of Paul (AD 33)
First missionary journey (AD 47–48)
Apostolic conference in Jerusalem
  (AD 49)
Paul's arrival in Corinth (AD 50)
Paul leaves Corinth (AD 51 or 52)
Paul arrives in Ephesus (AD 53)
Paul leaves Ephesus (AD 56)
Paul's arrival in Corinth (AD 56)—the
  time of the writing of Romans
Paul's arrival in Jerusalem (AD 57)
Paul before Festus (AD 59)
Paul's arrival in Rome (AD 60)

Translation of Gallio inscription taken from Jerome Murphy-O'Connor, *St. Paul's Corinth* (Wilmington: Michael Glazier, 1983), 141-42.

Karl P. Donfried, "Chronology," (*ABD*; New York: Doubleday, 1992), 1.1016.

Gallio Inscription
A group of nine fragments on an inscription found at Delphi and housed in the Delphi museum that refer to the proconsul Gallio mentioned in Acts 18:12. (Credit: Charles H. Talbert)

The Literary Presentation of Romans

Romans opens and closes as an ancient letter would. The opening in 1:1-15 contains the usual A to B, greeting (expanded by Paul's explanatory material), and a prayer (also expanded). The closing in 15:14–16:27 contains the summing up, the greetings, the exhortations, and the liturgical ending that one expects from Pauline letters. A number of attempts have been made to determine exactly what kind of letter Romans is: an ambassadorial letter[59] or a letter essay,[60] for example. So far none has gained a consensus. Romans is so complex that no one epistolary classification describes it.[61] [First Page of Romans in Erasmus's Greek New Testament of 1524]

Romans is also a rhetorical act. Within the letter envelope is a long sustained argument running from 1:16 to 15:13 that some scholars think conforms to the rules of ancient rhetoric. Romans, it is argued, is a deliberative speech, one that seeks to persuade. It contains at least an *exordium* (1:1-12), a *narratio* (1:13-15), a *propositio* (1:16-17), a *confirmatio* (1:18–15:13), and a *peroratio* (15:14–16:23) as the ancient handbooks dictated.[62] Comparison of the proposals of various scholars' suggestions reveals great diversity of opinion about what parts of Romans belong to what categories of ancient rhetoric. Again, Romans' argument is so complex that it cannot be forced into artificial categories. Indeed, the *Rhetorica ad Herrennium* 3.16 says that often the rules stated in the ancient rhetorical handbooks do not apply to a good speech. A speech using deliberative rhetoric, for example, often did not include all parts of other rhetorical forms. The precise rhetorical divisions of Romans are as yet unagreed upon by interpreters. Perhaps this is because the species and organization of ancient rhetoric, woodenly applied, are not appropriate to analyze the Pauline epistles.[63]

Romans 1:16–15:13 is most definitely an extended argument. There is general agreement on its thought units, save one. The parenetic section runs from 12:1–15:13. The doctrinal section covers 1:18–11:36. This doctrinal section consists of three parts. Chapters 9–11 are clearly a unit. Chapters 1–8 fall into two units. The basic issue is where the break comes between the two parts. Some argue for chapters 1–4 and 5–8 as the two units. Others prefer chapters 1–5 and 6–8. Still others contend that the break comes at the end of 5:11, yielding 1:18–5:11 and 5:12–8:39. In this commentary preference is given to the break at 5:11.

General agreement exists that the theme of Romans is given in 1:16-17. Less agreement exists about what that theme is. Is it the righteousness of God? Is it that the righteous shall live by faith? Is it salvation? Is it universalism (to Jew and Greek; to all who believe)? Is it the gospel? Probably all of the above make up the theme of Romans. If these components are focused in any way, it is likely that Romans is about the gospel of the righteousness of God revealed in the faithfulness of Jesus that issues in salvation for all who believe. This focus of Romans is on the relationship between Jews and Gentiles in salvation history, but it is not to be reduced to that. It is above all concerned about how God's saving activity deals with the guilt and power of sin in the lives of humans and how that

First Page of Romans in Erasmus's Greek NT of 1524

 First page of Romans, taken from the Greek New Testament of 1524, edited by Jacob Ceporinus. (Credit: Baylor University Rare Books Collection)

saving activity issues in Christian communal unity and ethical behavior in the world.[64] An outline of the letter as a whole might look like this:

1:1-7 Salutation
1: 8-15 Prayer form

1:16-17 Thesis: the gospel of God's righteousness
1:18–15:13 Argument
  1:18–8:39 God justifies
    1:18–5:11 From the human condition to God's remedy to the
        role of the Law to ultimate salvation
    5:12–8:39 From the human condition to God's remedy to the
        role of the Law to ultimate salvation
  9:1–11:36 God is righteous
  12:1–15:13 God's righteousness in human behavior: what slavery
        to righteousness (6:19) looks like
    12:1–13:14 General parenesis
    14:1–15:13 Specific parenesis
15:14–16:27 Letter closing

The audience addressed in 1–8 consisted probably of Gentile
Christians who thought in Jewish categories. While some of this
section is a debate with non-Christian Judaism, it is not necessary
that Jews or Jewish Christians were the intended audience of the
debate. The Gentile Christians were almost certainly originally
God-fearers. They would have known the law (e.g., 7:1) and would
have understood non-Christian Jewish objections to Paul's gospel.
The audience in chapters 9–11 was composed of Gentile
Christians; in chapters 12–15 probably both Jewish and Gentile
Christians of diverse persuasions were intended. The purpose
pursued in 1–8 is the destruction of Jewish presumption and objections, in 9–11 it is the overturning of Gentile pride, and in 12–15
it is opposition to mutual arrogance. The theological base for the
argument is the good news of the righteousness of God revealed in
Jesus Christ. In 1–8 God justifies all who believe, in 9–11 God is
righteous/faithful to the covenant promise, and in 12–15 God's
people are called to show what being a slave of righteousness
looks like.

Underlying the argument of Romans was a wider world view and
belief system on which Paul drew.[65] It may be inferred from his
writings from the period of the Aegean mission. In order rightly to
interpret Paul the thinker, it is necessary to understand what this
wider world view was. What was it? Simply put, Paul read his
Scriptures, the Scriptures of Israel, in a way that valued certain
covenants and not others.[66] Paul made no mention of the
covenants with Noah (Gen 9:8-17), Phinehas (Num 25:10-13),
Joshua (Josh 24), Josiah (2 Kgs 23), and Ezra (Ezra 9–10; Neh
9–10).The covenant with David was not central to Paul's thought,
although it was echoed in the oral tradition taken up in Romans

1:3-4 ("descended from David according to the flesh") and in the quotation from Isaiah 11:10 in Romans 15:12 ("The root of Jesse shall come, he who rises to rule the Gentiles; in him shall the Gentiles hope"). Paul saw the promise to David fulfilled in the reign of Jesus after the resurrection (1 Cor 15:20-28). Three covenants of the Scriptures of Israel received significant attention in Paul's letters: (1) the covenant with Abraham, (2) the covenant through Moses, and (3) the new covenant of Jeremiah 31. Of the three covenants that play significant roles in Paul's letters, two were highly valued, while the third's importance was minimized by the apostle. The construct that makes the most sense out of the various things Paul said about the covenants throughout his letters may be summarized as follows. (1) The covenant with Abraham furnished Paul a scriptural way to argue that justification through faith had been God's plan all along for Jew and Gentile alike. (2) The Law (Mosaic covenant) was a temporary phase in God's dealings with the covenant people. In spite of its just requirements, it was impotent because of human sin. With the coming of Christ, the Law (Mosaic covenant) had come to an end as a part of ongoing salvation history. (3) The Mosaic covenant had been replaced in salvation history by the prophesied New Covenant of Jeremiah 31 in which God enables the people's faithfulness to the relationship. This way of reading the Scriptures of Israel underlies all of Paul's thought in Romans.

Paul's thought in this regard is seen most clearly when set against the backdrop of Middle Judaism. The covenants were variously valued by different groups in Middle Judaism. For example, the *Psalms of Solomon* refer to the covenant with Abraham (9:9-10; 18:3) and to the Mosaic covenant (10:4), but the covenant central in their thought is the Davidic one (e.g., *Pss Sol* 17 and 18). The new covenant of Jeremiah 31:31-34, moreover, was absent from Second Temple Judaism, except for Qumran and Christian Messianic Judaism. At Qumran, new covenant (CD-A 6.18-19; 8.20-21; CD-B 19.33-34; 20.11-13; 1QpHab 2.3) was used interchangeably with other expressions such as "covenant of God," "this covenant," "covenant of the everlasting community," and others.[67] Qumran did not set "new covenant" in opposition to "old covenant." Rather "new covenant" was used over against "broken covenant." So, at Qumran, "new" referred to the restoration of the law, which CD saw fulfilled in the coming of the Teacher of Righteousness.[68] The Covenanters, then, saw the new covenant as a return to the original intentions of the Mosaic Torah.[69] (This trajectory continues into the earliest rabbinic exegetical use of

Jeremiah 31:31-34. *Sifra* on Leviticus, edited in the third century AD, juxtaposes Jeremiah 31 with Leviticus 26:9 in order to clarify the latter v.. The result is a reading in which the promise to maintain the covenant in Leviticus 26 is identified with the making of the new covenant in Jeremiah 31.[70])

Among the early Christian Messianic Jewish references to the new covenant are: Gal 4:21-31 (?); 1 Cor 11:25; 2 Cor 3:6,14; Rom 7:6; 11:27; Heb 8:6-13; and Luke 22:20. Some less reliable manuscripts of Mark 14:24 add "new" before covenant. A similar situation applies in Matthew 26:28. In both cases, the "new" was likely added to make explicit what is implicit in the best texts. The reference in John 13:34 to a "new commandment" assumes a new covenant; the "new song" of Revelation 5:9 also assumes a new deliverance/covenant. Christian Messianic Judaism saw the old Sinai covenant as defective and inefficacious.[71] Paul, then, fit into Christian Messianic Judaism's way of thinking about a new covenant that replaced an old, defective one. In addition, he focused on the Abrahamic covenant as a basis for Gentile inclusion in God's people. Although the term "new covenant" is not used in Romans, it is part of the world view Paul assumed in this epistle. In chapters 1–4 , 9–11, and 15 the covenant with Abraham furnishes the substructure of the argument. In chapters 5–8 it is the New Covenant that functions as the unarticulated matrix of thought that must be understood in order rightly to interpret the argument.

In constructing his arguments, Paul used a number of conventional devices. He frequently employed the diatribe form[72]; the citation of traditional material such as creeds and hymns and Old Testament proof texts is frequent[73]; parallelism and chiasm often shape the material.[74] Any reading of Romans that expects a fruitful harvest will be attuned to the tactics of the Pauline argument. [Chiasm and Diatribe]

CONNECTIONS

How Can Occasional Writings Function As Scripture?

Scholars spend a great deal of effort attempting to describe the original historical situation out of which a biblical writing arose. This is important because the original meaning of what was said is determined by the context in which the words were used. Words do not have an inherent meaning; they mean what they mean in context. In order to determine what the words of a biblical text

Chiasm and Diatribe

A Make the heart of this people fat,
   B and their ears heavy,
      C and shut their eyes;
      C' lest they see with their eyes,
   B' and hear with their ears.
A' and understand with their hearts, and turn and be saved.

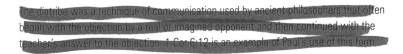

   Paul's opponents are cited first: "All things are lawful for me."
   To which the apostle responds: "But not all things are beneficial."

Both chiasm and diatribe are found frequently in Paul's letters.

---

originally meant, it is necessary to set these words in their original cultural and historical context. Once this is done, the question arises: how does this text with this response to this original situation function as normative for Christians in our time and place? Without trying to be exhaustive, one may note two different ways of using such an occasional writing.

On the one hand, sometimes what the biblical text said becomes relevant because the occasion that was its catalyst is analogous to our own occasion. If we have the same problem, then the word spoken to that problem originally is relevant for us now. Similarity in occasion, then and now, leads to relevance of the word spoken then for the present.

On the other hand, sometimes the occasion that evoked the text is not analogous to our own situation. What then? In such circumstances, one may ask about the general theological and ethical structures that underlie the historical argument. Even if the occasion of the text in its original setting is not ours, the theological substructure of the text's argument can be relevant as a substructure for our dealing with our particular occasion. The view of God, of Christ, of human sin, of salvation, and of the Christian life style all are relevant regardless of occasion.

Take the case of Romans, for example. Romans was written to deal with the particular historical problem of the relations between Jewish and Gentile Christians in Rome. (1) The *function* of Paul's gospel was to unify Jewish and Gentile Christians in Rome. (2) The *content* of his gospel was a theology that placed Jew and

~~Gentile on an equal footing; both in their sin and in their salvation.~~
Sometimes a modern situation corresponds to Paul's original one.
In such a case, Romans speaks directly. Most of the time, modern
situations are different from the original one. Romans still speaks.
Although the content of Paul's gospel was elaborated in a particular
cultural context, its applicability goes far beyond the original
milieu, as Christian history has amply demonstrated.

NOTES

[1] (London: Mathieson & Co., n.d.), 302.

[2] Francis Watson, *Paul, Judaism and the Gentiles* (Cambridge: Cambridge University Press, 1986), 180-81.

[3] Richard A. Horsley, *1 Corinthians* (ANTC; Nashville: Abingdon, 1998), dedicates his commentary "To the many many women. . . who suffered because of what 'Paul' wrote and how that was used."

[4] Ernst Käsemann, "Paul and Early Catholicism," *New Testament Questions of Today* (Philadelphia: Fortress, 1969), 249-50.

[5] Cited by Wayne Meeks, ed., *The Writings of St. Paul* (NY: W. W. Norton, 1972), 435.

[6] For a history of the interpretation of Romans from earliest times to the present, see R. Morgan, "Romans, Letter of," in *Dictionary of Biblical Interpretation*, ed. John H. Hayes (2 vols.; Nashville: Abingdon, 1999), 1.411-22

[7] *Conf.* 8.7 (*The Confessions of Saint Augustine*, trans. E. B. Pusey [NY: Pocket Books, 1957], 140)

[8] *Conf.* 8.12 (*The Confessions of Saint Augustine*, 147-48).

[9] Preface to *Lectures on Romans*.

[10] Luther, *Commentary on Romans*, xiii.

[11] *The Journal of John Wesley: A Selection*, ed. Elisabeth Jay (London: Oxford University Press, 1987), 34-35.

[12] John Stott, *Romans: God's Good News for the World* (Downers Grove: InterVarsity, 1994), 22-23.

[13] *The Epistle to the Romans* (trans. E. C. Hoskyns; London: Oxford University Press, 1933), 7.

[14] Robert Morgan, *Romans* (NT Guides; Sheffield: Sheffield Academnic Press, 1995), 14, observes: "Religious art and music. . . have drawn almost nothing from this epistle."

[15] 1 Macc 8:17-22.

[16] 1 Macc 8:25.

[17] *Factorum et dictorum memorabilium* 1.3.3.

[18] Josephus, *Ant* 14.77, 79; *J.W.* 1.155, 157.

[19] *Flacco* 67-69.

[20] *Pro Flacco* 66-67.

[21] Josephus, *Ant* 14.214-15.

[22] Suetonius, *Jul.* 36 (*Lives of the Twelve Caesars*).

[23] Josephus, *Ant* 17.61.

[24] Philo, *Embassy* 155-56.

[25] Tacitus, *Annals* 2.85; Suetonius, *Tib.* 36 (*Lives of the Twelve Caesars*).

[26] James D. G. Dunn, *Romans 1–8* (WBC; Dallas: Word, 1988), xlvi.

[27] Suetonius, *Claud.* 25.4 (*Lives of the Caesars*).

[28] Acts 18:2.

[29] Josephus, *Life* 3.

[30] Juvenal, *Sat*.2.11.

[31] Juvenal, *Sat*.6.541-44.

[32] Juvenal, *Sat.* 14.105.

[33] Persius, *Sat.* 5.184.

[34] Tacitus, *Hist.* 5.5.

[35] Juvenal, *Sat*.14.96-102.

[36] Irenaeus, *Haer*. 3.1.1; 3.3.2-3.

[37] Oscar Cullmann, *Peter: Disciple, Apostle, Martyr* (NY: Meridian Books, 1958), 72-157.

[38] Ambrosiaster, *Ad Romanos*.

[39] Raymond E. Brown, "Further Reflections on the Origins of the Church of Rome," in *The Conversation Continues: Studies in John and Paul*, ed. R.T. Fortna and B. R. Gaventa (Nashville: Abingdon, 1990), 98-115.

[40] Cf. Acts 15; 21:20-21; Gal 2:12; Rom 3:8.

[41] E.g., 16:3-5a; 16:15; 16:14; 16:10; 16:11, etc.

[42] Reta Halteman Finger, *Paul and the Roman House Churches* (Scottdale PA: Herald Press, 1993), following Peter Lampe, contends Paul greets five groups.

[43] This reconstruction is influenced by the seminal work of Wolfgang Wiefel, "The Jewish Community in Ancient Rome and the Origins of Roman Christianity," in *The Romans Debate: Revised and Expanded Edition*, ed. Karl P. Donfried (Peabody MA: Hendrickson, 1991), 85-101.

[44] This seems a better explanation than that the Gentile Christians addressed in Romans continued to be involved in the Jewish synagogues, remaining within them, as is claimed by Mark D. Nanos, "The Jewish Context of the Gentile Audience Addressed in Paul's Letter to the Romans," *CBQ* 61 (1999): 283-304.

[45] W. D. Davies, "Paul and the People of Israel," *NTS* 24 (1977-78): 20. C. K. Barrett says of Paul's conversion: "This did not mean an abandonment but it did mean a rethinking of Judaism." ("The Development of Theology in the New Testament," in *Jesus, Paul and John*, ed. Lo Lung-kwong [Hong Kong: Theology Division, Chung Chi College, 1999], 37.)

[46] Gabriele Boccaccini, *Middle Judaism: Jewish Thought 300 B.C.E. to 200 C.E.* (Minneapolis: Fortress, 1991), 7-25.

[47] Alan F. Segal, *Rebecca's Children: Judaism and Christianity in the Roman World* (Cambridge: Harvard University Press, 1986), 179.

[48] James D. G. Dunn, "Who Did Paul Think He Was? A Study of Jewish-Christian Identity," *NTS* 45 (1999): 175.

[49] See the evidence assembled by Neil J. McEleney, "Conversion, Circumcision and the Law," *NTS* 20 (1974), especially 328-33.

[50] Daniel Boyarin, *Dying for God: Martyrdom and the Making of Christianity and Judaism* (Stanford: Stanford University Press, 1999), 17.

[51] Alan F. Segal, *Paul the Convert* (New Haven: Yale University Press, 1990) provides us with a modern, sympathetic Jewish reading of Paul. He concludes: "Paul's letters record the thinking of a Pharisee who has converted to a new, apocalyptic, mystical, and—to many of his contemporaries—suspiciously heretical form of Judaism" (xii). His conversion experience carries him from one variety of Judaism to another.

[52] Timo Laato, *Paul and Judaism: An Anthropological Approach* (Atlanta: Scholars Press, 1995).

[53] Timo Eskola, *Theodicy and Predestination in Pauline Soteriology* (Tübingen: Mohr Siebeck, 1998), 162, 272, 296.

[54] Rom 15:25-27.

[55] Rom 16:1, 23 (cf. 1 Cor 1:14; 2 Tim 4:20); Acts 20:2-3.

[56] Rom 16:22. Secretaries functioned in different ways in antiquity: (1) the author gave a secretary the general ideas and the secretary composed the piece; (2) the author dictated the piece and the secretary took it down in short hand and later wrote it out in longhand; (3) the author dictated the piece and the secretary wrote it out in longhand. Tertius would likely have functioned in terms of categories (2) or (3).

[57] Rom 16:1-2.

[58] Harry Gamble, *The Textual History of the Letter to the Romans* (Grand Rapids: Eerdmans, 1977).

[59] Robert Jewett, "Romans as an Ambassadorial Letter," *Interpretation* 36 (1982): 5-20.

[60] Martin Luther Stirewalt, Jr., "The Form and Function of the Greek Letter-Essay," in *The Romans Debate*, 147-74.

[61] Brendan Byrne, *Romans* (SP 6; Collegeville: Liturgical Press, 1996), 16.

[62] Robert Jewett, "Following the Argument of Romans," in *The Romans Debate*, 265-77.

[63] So Stanley E. Porter, "The Theoretical Justification for Application of Rhetorical Categories to Pauline Epistolary Literature," in *Rhetoric and the New Testament*, ed. S. E. Porter and T. H. Olbricht (Sheffield: JSOT, 1993), 100-122.

[64] Cf. Douglas J. Moo, *The Epistle to the Romans* (Grand Rapids: Eerdmans, 1996), 28, who argues strongly against the thesis associated with Krister Stendahl and his followers that Romans was only an occasional letter devoted to establishing Jewish and Gentile Christian unity in Rome.

[65] N. T. Wright, "Romans and the Theology of Paul," in *Pauline Theology, Volume III: Romans*, ed. David M. Hay and E. Elizabeth Johnson (Minneapolis: Fortress, 1995), 30-67, especially 31-34, and *The New Testament and the People of God* (Minneapolis:

Fortress, 1992), 268-79, sees this assumption system located in the alleged belief of many first-century Jews that the Babylonian exile of Israel continued into their own day. So Israel's promised forgiveness of sins and restoration from exile were yet to come. Paul, then, claimed the hour of fulfillment had arrived in Jesus' death and resurrection. This view is suspect not only because many believed the exile was over (e.g., Baruch 4:36; 5:5-9; Judith 4:1-5; 5:17-19; Josephus, *Ant.* 4.314;10.112-113;11.1-4; *m. 'Abot* 1.11) but also because Paul makes no explicit reference to it.

[66] Charles H. Talbert, "Paul on the Covenant," *RevExp* 84 (1987): 299-313.

[67] Susanne Lehne, *The New Covenant in Hebrews* (Sheffield: JSOT Press, 1990), 43.

[68] Ellen Juhl Christiansen, *The Covenant in Judaism and Paul* (Leiden: Brill, 1995), 129-30.

[69] Lehne, *New Covenant*, 58.

[70] Richard S. Sarason, "The Interpretation of Jeremiah 31:31-34 in Judaism," in *When Jews and Christians Meet*, ed. Jakob J. Petuchowski (Albany: SUNY Press, 1988), 99-123.

[71] Lehne, *New Covenant*, 59, 78.

[72] Stanley Kent Stowers, *The Diatribe and Paul's Letter to the Romans* (Atlanta: Scholars Press, 1981).

[73] A. M. Hunter, *Paul and His Predecessors* (Philadelphia: Westminster, 1961).

[74] Ian H. Thompson, *Chiasmus in the Pauline Letters* (Sheffield: Sheffield Academic Press, 1995); John Breck, *The Shape of Biblical Language: Chiasmus in the Scriptures and Beyond* (Crestwood NY: St. Vladimer's Seminary Press, 1994); Nils W. Lund, *Chiasmus in the New Testament* (reprint of 1942 edition; Peabody MA: Hendrickson, 1992); John W. Welch, *Chiasmus in Antiquity: Structures, Analyses, Exegesis* (Hildesheim: Gerstenberg, 1981).

THE CONVERSATION BEGINS

1:1-17

COMMENTARY

Romans is a concentrated theological and ethical argument (1:18–15:13) enclosed in a letter envelope (1:1-17; 15:14–16:27). In 1:1-17 one finds the letter's opening. Ancient letters reflected a stereotyped form: salutation, prayer, body of the letter, and the closing. Romans 1:1-17 provides a salutation and a prayer.

The normal salutation of a Greek letter was A to B, greeting. For example, a letter of 168 BC opens: "Isias to Hephaestion her brother, greeting."[1] Acts 23:26 reads: "Claudius Lysias to his Excellency the governor Felix, greeting." Xenophon, *Ephesian Tale* 2.5, has: "From his mistress to the fair Habrocomes, greeting." First Maccabees 10:25 has: "King Demetrius to the nation of the Jews, greeting." Christian usage of this simple formula is reflected in Acts 15:23 and James 1:1. Paul adapted the formula to his ends. [Secretaries and Coauthors]

In Romans 1:1-6 the 'A' component omits any reference to cosenders (as in 1 Cor 1:1; 2 Cor 1:1; Gal 1:2; Phil 1:1; Col 1:1; 1 Thess 1:1; 2 Thess 1:1; Phlm 1); otherwise it is expanded. This

---

Secretaries and Coauthors

Paul did not personally put his letters on paper. Like most ancient authors, he used a secretary, and Rom 16:23 indicates that Tertius was the secretary for this letter. In Gal 6:11 Paul wrote: "See with what large letters I have written to you with my own hand." This shows that he did not write the rest of the letter with his own hand. The same applies for 1 Cor 16:21; Phlm 19; 2 Thess 3:17; Col 4:18. By the 1st century BC a system of shorthand was used (Plutarch, *Cat Man* 23.3-5, attributes its importation from Greece to Rome to Cicero; Seneca, *Ep* 90:25; Martial, *Epigrams* 14.208). This allowed dictation to proceed at a pace that did not impede the author's train of thought (Quintilian, *Institutio Oratoria* 10.3.20). The secretary's role varied. He could simply copy down what was dictated. Or, he could be allowed to make minor changes in the form or content of the letter when preparing the final text (Cicero, *Fam* 16.17.1). Or, he could be trusted to create a letter's content. He would be told to create a suitable letter and to send it in his employer's name (Cicero, *Att* 11.5; 6.6.4). In this case, the secretary is a virtual coauthor. Indeed, in antiquity some letters were written in one's own name, some jointly with others (Cicero, *Att* 11.5.1). In the Pauline corpus coauthors are mentioned in the case of Galatians (all the brethren with me); 1 Thessalonians (Silvanus and Timothy); 1 Corinthians (Sosthenes); 2 Corinthians, Philippians, and Philemon (Timothy), 2 Thessalonians (Timothy and Silvanus); Colossians (Timothy). No coauthors are mentioned for Romans, Ephesians, 1 & 2 Timothy, and Titus. The mention of coauthors indicated that the author consulted with his companion(s) and then did the dictation himself.

Rembrandt's Paul

In this representation of Paul, the artist shows no awareness of the likelihood that Paul probably had a secretary actually write his letters. Paul seems transfixed and thoughtful in the act of receiving and transmitting the "13th" gospel. Following a pattern that goes back to the 9th century, Paul is depicted in a mode similar to that of the Gospel writers—receiving and simultaneously transmitting the word of God.

Rembrandt van Rijn. 1606–1669. *The Apostle Paul.* 1633. Kunsthistorisches Museum. Vienna, Austria. (Credit: Erich Lessing/Art Resource, NY) allowed Paul to identify himself to a church he did not found and had not visited but which he hoped would help him on his Spanish mission. According to vv. 1-6, who is Paul? He referred to himself in three ways. First, he is a servant of Christ Jesus (v. 1; cf. Gal 1:10; Phil 1:1). In the OT, the expression "servant of the Lord" was often used of individuals who served God in special ways: Moses (2 Kgs 18:12); Joshua (Judg 2:8); David (2 Sam 7:5); the prophets (Amos 3:7; Zech 1:6). Paul understood himself this way. He was one in service of a higher authority. Other early Christian authors spoke of their dedication to Christ in the same way (Jas 1:1; 2 Pet 1:1; Jude 1:1).

Second, Paul describes himself as a called one (*klētos*; cf. 8:30— "He called"). In Pauline thought "to call" is a technical term for the choice of a person by God for salvation. In the LXX "to call" is an equivalent of "to choose" (e.g., Isa 41:9). Paul did not use "call" in relation to a specific vocation or station in life. "Calling" in Paul everywhere refers to the call to salvation. One who has been called is a Christian.[2] Exactly how the servant who has been called serves God is made clear in the next self-designation.

Third, he presented himself as an apostle set apart for the gospel of God (v. 1; cf. Gal 1:15). In his letters, Paul used apostle for two different groups. He spoke of apostles of Christ (Gal 1:1; 1 Cor 9:1-2; 15:7, 9; Rom 16:7) and apostles of churches (2 Cor 8:23; Phil 2:25). The latter type is sent forth by a church to be its representative, usually in business matters. The former type is sent forth by Christ himself as his ambassador, normally for evangelistic purposes. Paul classified himself as an apostle of Christ. He was one who had seen the risen Lord and had received a commission. Paul's commission was to preach the gospel of Christ among the Gentiles (Gal 1:16). This understanding of apostle of Christ is akin to what Epictetus said about the true Cynic. The Cynic knows himself to be a messenger (*angelos*), a scout (*kataskopos*), and a herald (*kēryx*) of God (*Dissertations* 3.22.69) because he is divinely sent (*apostaleis*), as was Diogenes (1.24.6). Indeed, the ultimate presupposition for genuine Cynicism is awareness of being divinely sent (*apo tou Dios apestaltai, Dissertations* 3.22.23). Of course, when late first-century Gnostics such as Menander, the disciple of Simon Magus, claimed that they were sent (*apestalmenos*), other criteria were called for—such as having been with Jesus all of his public ministry (cf. Acts 1:21-22). But in Paul's time and mind, an apostle of Christ was one who had seen the risen Lord and had been sent on a mission of evangelization.

Although Paul's letters were a part of the New Testament canon from its earliest stages, his apostleship was variously regarded by early Christians. (1) In some circles he was ignored. Focus was on the Twelve alone (e.g., Rev 21:14; *Didache*; *Ep Barn* 8:3; Justin, *1 Apology* 39, 50). (2) In other instances, Paul was appropriated by heretics (e.g., Marcion [Tertullian, *Against Marcion* 1.19.4, says Marcion's radical separation of Law and Gospel was derived primarily from the writings of Paul]; Valentinus [Clement of Alexandria, *Stromata* 50.7]; Apocalypse of Paul [NHL][3]; Basilides [Origen, *Commentary of Romans* 5.2; Hippolytus, *Refutation of All Heresies* 7.14-15; 7.25.5; 7.26.3]; the Naassenes [Hippolytus, *Refutation of All Heresies* 5.2, says this group claimed to derive their entire secret knowledge from Romans 1:20-27]; Sethians [Hippolytus, *Refutation* 5.14]; Justinian heretics [Hippolytus, *Refutation* 5.22]; Simonians [Hippolytus, *Refutation* 6.9]; Ophites [Irenaeus, 1.30.13]; Marcosians [Irenaeus, 1.19.1]; Tertullian, *Prescription of Heretics* 23.5-24.5-6, mentions an unnamed group that based their teachings on the revelation Paul received in his ascent into heaven mentioned in 2 Corinthians 12:2-4 and that disparaged the other apostles [23.3, 5]); the Nag Hammadi document *On the Resurrection* 45.24-28, says: "Already you have the resurrection" and quotes Paul as support; the Encratite, Cassianus, interpreted the sowing to the flesh of Galatians 6:8 as the transmission of seed in sexual intercourse and used the saying as an argument to prove the sinfulness of any type of sexual intercourse [Jerome on Gal 6:8]. Tertullian, *Prescription Against Heretics* 23, summarized the situation when he said, "Very great is the use which they [the heretics] make of him [Paul]." This misuse left Paul in need of rehabilitation in the larger church. Irenaeus, *Against Heresies* 4.41.4, said:

> It is necessary to subjoin . . . the doctrine of Paul, . . . to examine the opinion of this man, and to expound the apostle, and to explain whatsoever [passages] have received other interpretation from the heretics, who have altogether misunderstood what Paul has spoken, and to point out the folly of their mad opinions; and to demonstrate from that same Paul, from whose [writings] they press questions upon us, that they are indeed utterers of falsehood, but that the apostle was a preacher of the truth, and that he taught all things agreeable to the preaching of the truth.

The fact that Paul was in some cases the heretics' apostle explains the caution in using him displayed by the early fathers, Hegesippus, Papias, and Justin.[4]

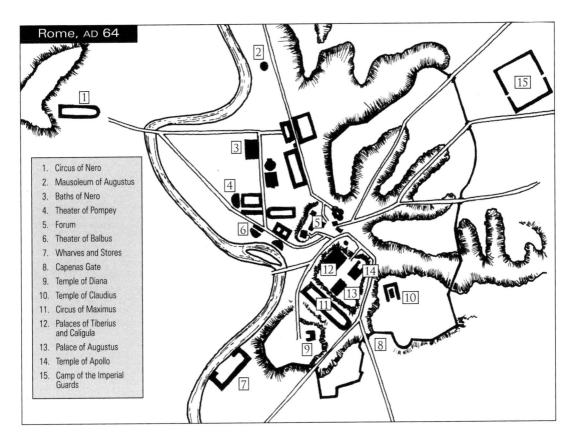

Rome, AD 64

1. Circus of Nero
2. Mausoleum of Augustus
3. Baths of Nero
4. Theater of Pompey
5. Forum
6. Theater of Balbus
7. Wharves and Stores
8. Capenas Gate
9. Temple of Diana
10. Temple of Claudius
11. Circus of Maximus
12. Palaces of Tiberius and Caligula
13. Palace of Augustus
14. Temple of Apollo
15. Camp of the Imperial Guards

(3) In still other circles Paul was reviled. References to him from these groups are hostile (e.g., Acts 21:21 recounts a hostile view of Paul by some Jewish Christians; the Ebionites [Epiphanius, *Panarion* 30.16.6-9, said they slandered Paul; Eusebius, *Church History* 3.27.4, says they thought the letters of Paul ought to be rejected wholly; Irenaeus, *Against Heresies* 3.15.1]; the Cerinthians [Epiphanius, *Panarion* 28.5.1-3, said they broke with Paul because he did not accept circumcision; Irenaeus, *Haer* 1.26.2; 3.15.1]; the Severiani [Eusebius, *Church History* 4.29.5, said they blasphemed Paul and rejected his epistles]; the Elkesites [Eusebius, *Church History* 6.39, said they rejected the Apostle entirely]; the Jewish Christian Ps-Clementine *Recognitions* 4.35, rejected any apostleship, like Paul's, based on visions and limited apostleship exclusively to the Twelve; an unknown Jewish Christian sect known from an Arabic manuscript of the tenth century contended that Paul encouraged the Romans to practice a religion opposed to the religion of Christ.[5]) All of these abusers of Paul were Jewish Christians of one stripe or another. The opposition of certain types of Jewish Christians to Paul's apostleship began in the first century and continued for several centuries. In spite of the variety of less than positive responses to Paul's apostleship, by the late second

St. Paul Holding a Book

This early Byzantine ivory depicts an interpretation of St. Paul that is character-ized by its abstracted body—stiff, frontal, and reflecting very little naturalism. The iconic attribute for Paul—the book—is blatantly signified as Paul holds it up and points to it while appearing to be spiritually focused as suggested by his inward-looking eyes. Though Paul's authority as an Apostle of God (Christ) is evident, this depiction also shows an affinity with imperial Byzantium and blurs the distinctions between imperial authority and the kingdom of God.

The scalloped shell that is placed inside the arch under which Paul stands is not simply a decorative embellishment. This use of shell motifs suspended above a prominent person has its origins in Roman art of the 5th century. These motifs were used in the so-called consular diptychs.

With Paul, the shell motif no longer refers to imperial power or prestige but now refers to the Lordship of Christ and Paul as his "consular." It is thought by some that the halo that would later become a standard convention to signify the holiness of Christ and the disciples has its origins in the consular nimbuses, originally associated with imperial Rome.

Saint Paul Holding a Book. Byzantine. Ivory. c. AD 600. Musee du Moyen Age (Cluny). Paris, France. (Credit: Erich Lessing/Art Resource, NY)

century Paul's letters were an integral part of the New Testament canon and his authoritative role for the main stream church was secured. He became the thirteenth apostle and his gospel, even if not often understood, was held in high esteem.

It is this gospel that defines Paul's apostleship. What is it? There were competing views of the gospel in Mediterranean culture. In the LXX 2 Kingdoms 18:25 (= 2 Sam 18:25), David says that if the runner is alone, then good news (*euangelia*) is in his mouth. Here gospel is good news about political fortunes. In an inscription of 311 BC the citizens of the city of Skepsis in northwest Asia Minor paid honor to Antigonus I for his deeds. An altar, a cultic image, sacrifices, and an athletic contest were instituted. The inscription read: "Besides this, the city is to offer thanksgiving sacrifices for the *euangelion* (gospel) sent by Antigonus" (= a letter guaranteeing the freedom and autonomy of the Greek states). Here too the good news is about political freedom.[6] Lucretius in his *On the Nature of the Universe*, at the beginning of Book 5, praised his master, the philosopher Epicurus. Lucretius spoke of Epicurus's gospel (*euangelion*), which had been broadcast through the length and breadth of empires and which brought solace to human minds. Here gospel is a philosophic doctrine. A resolution passed by the Provincial Assembly of Asia Minor regarding Caesar Augustus said that Augustus's birthday was for the whole world the beginning of the gospel (*euangelion*) concerning him.[7] Here the good news is about the imperial peace. In *Psalms of Solomon* 11:1 the "voice of one bringing the gospel" is the announcement of the ingathering of the scattered people of Israel to Jerusalem in the End Time. Here good news is about eschatological, but this-worldly, salvation for Israel. Clarification was necessary about the meaning of gospel.

Paul's gospel is clarified here in two ways. First, it was announced beforehand through God's prophets in the holy Scriptures (v. 2; cf. 1 Cor 14:3-5). That is, Paul's gospel has its roots in Israel's Scriptures (Sirach, prologue, speaks about the Law, the prophets, and the other books of our fathers; Josephus, *Against Apion* 1.38-40, referred to twenty two books: five of Moses, thirteen prophetic books, and four of hymns to God and precepts for conduct; 4 Ezra 14:45 mentions twenty four books to be made public; Luke 24:44 speaks about the Law of Moses, the prophets, and the psalms).

Second, the gospel concerns God's son, Jesus Christ our Lord (vv. 3a, 4b). [Jesus as Son of God] At this point Paul included three pre-Pauline oral traditions about Christ that he and his readers had in common. Verse 3a offers the first: Jesus is God's son. "Jesus is the Son of God" was among the earliest Christian christological

---

Jesus as Son of God

One way Paul spoke about Jesus was as Son of God. This title was not unique to Paul among early Christians (cf. Mark 1:11; 9:7; 12:6; John 1:34,49; 3:18; 1 John 3:8; 5:12; Heb 1:2; 4:14; Rev 2:18). Prior to Paul (AD 30–50) at least three pictures of Jesus circulated among the Christian Messianists. (Fuller) A two-foci christology focused on Jesus' authoritative messenger of repentance during his earthly life and on his role as messianic judge at the parousia. An exaltation christology focused on Jesus' resurrection as his exaltation to the role of heavenly ruler. An epiphany christology focused on the heavenly one's descent from the realm of spirit to the realm of flesh and his subsequent ascent back to the realm from which he had come. Echoes of all three are found in Paul's letters: the two-foci christology with its emphasis on Jesus as returning messianic judge (e.g., 1 Thess 1:9-10); the exaltation christology with its emphasis on the risen Jesus as heavenly ruler (e.g., Rom 1:3-4); and the epiphany christology with its emphasis on preexistence and divine sending (e.g., Rom 8:3; Gal 4:4). In Paul's letters the three originally independent pictures of Jesus merge into a new whole that encompasses all of the foci of the others (preexistence, heavenly reign, parousia) and subordinates them to Jesus' death (e.g., Rom 8:32-33; Gal 2:20). In Paul, Son of God shares with other christological titles a focus on Jesus as mediator of salvation. More than any other title, Son of God emphasizes the relation of Christ to God.

How might the Roman auditors of Paul's letter have heard his assertion that Jesus was son of God? Although "son of God/son of the Most High" was seemingly a Messianic title at Qumran (4Q246; 4Q174), the expression is found mainly in pagan usage. Several examples suffice. After the official deification of Caesar in 42 BC, Octavian began to call himself officially *divi filius* (son of a god). From 27 BC until AD 3, Augustus's official name in Greek documents included *theou huios* (son of god). Tiberius's adopted son, Germanicus, referred to himself in an edict as "son of the god Augustus" (Tiberius). The earliest documented title of the high priest of the imperial cult in the Roman province of Asia is "high priest of the goddess Roma and of Emperor Caesar Augustus, son of God" (Collins). From Paul's time, a votive inscription for Nero on a marble slab at Magnesia on the Maeander calls Nero "Son of the greatest of the gods, Tiberius Claudius" (Deissmann). Given the political context of the Roman readers of Paul's letter, it would have been difficult not to have heard Jesus as a rival to Caesar.

R. H. Fuller, *The Foundations of New Testament Christology* (NY: Charles Scribner's Sons, 1965). See especially the diagrams on pages 243-50.

A. Y. Collins, "Mark and His Readers: The Son of God among Greeks and Romans," HTR 93 (2000): 85-100.

Adolf Deissmann, *Light from the Ancient East* (4th ed.; New York: Harper & Brothers, 1922), 347.

confessions (1 Thess 1:9-10; Gal 4:4-5; Acts 8:37; Heb 4:14; 1 John 4:15). Verses 3b-4a , the second, are also widely regarded as such an oral tradition: "the one being born of the seed of David according to flesh" (cf. 2 Tim 2:8; Ign *Smyr* 1.1; Rom 9:5) and "the one being appointed son of God with power according to spirit of holiness from the resurrection of the dead" (cf. Acts 13:33; Ign *Smyr* 1.1). Like other oral traditions taken up by Paul elsewhere in his letters, this material reflects a rhythmic style, a preference for participles over finite verbs, and employs language and concepts that are not usual in Paul's letters. For example, "Son of David" is used only here in the undisputed letters; the verb *horizein* (to appoint) is used only here in Paul; the Semitic phrase "spirit of holiness" is not Paul's usual way of speaking (cf. *T. Levi* 18:11); the contrast between flesh and spirit is used in a non-Pauline way but in a way like that found in other traditional passages (1 Tim 3:16; 1 Pet 3:18); the association of Jesus' sonship with the resurrection is unlike Paul in his letters but like Acts 13:33, which probably also reflects pre-Pauline tradition. Although it is not possible to define exactly the boundaries of the unit, it is likely that vv. 3-4 reflect oral tradition used by Paul. The point of this tradition is that Jesus was exalted at his resurrection to a level of power and authority he did not have previously.[8]

The third pre-Pauline tradition, Jesus Christ our Lord, comes at the very end of v. 4. The confession, "Jesus is Lord," seems to have been among the first honorific ways of speaking of Jesus (Rom 4:24; 1 Cor 8:6; 12:3; Phil 2:11). So Paul clarified his gospel with three traditional statements about Jesus, establishing common ground with the Roman congregations who did not know him personally. By including them he was saying: this is what we have in common.

It was through this Jesus Christ about whom the tradition spoke that Paul received his gift (*charin*) of apostleship (v. 5a). In v. 1 Paul designated himself *klētos apostolos* (a called apostle or, as suggested above, a called one, an apostle). How do these two statements fit together? First,

Augustus Caesar

Julius Caesar had been made a god after his death, and Augustus, while never claiming to be a god himself, widely advertised himself as the son of a god. (*Gardner's Art through the Ages*, Vol.1-264) He also promoted the cult of emperor as divine by building a temple to the Divine Julius. Accordingly, this Prima Porta statue of Augustus also points to the emperor's deification, though never proclaimed while he was alive.

Augustus Prima Porta. c. AD 100. Marble. Braccio Nuovo. Vatican Museums. Vatican State. (Credit: Scala/Art Resource, NY)

consider Paul's usage of "call." We have seen that in Pauline usage "to call" is a technical term for the choice of a person by God for salvation (Rom 8:28-30). The caller is God (Rom 9:11; Gal 5:8). The calling is to God's kingdom and glory (1 Thess 2:2) or to salvation (Rom 8:28-30). The basis of the calling is the grace of God (Gal 1:6,15). The background for this meaning is the LXX's use of "to call" as an equivalent of "to choose" (Isa 41:9; 42:6; 48:12, 15; 51:2). In fact, in Paul "calling" refers everywhere to the call to salvation (Rom 11:29; 1 Cor 1:26; Phil 3:14). The deutero-Pauline Ephesians 4:1 makes it explicit: "I beg you to lead a life worthy of the calling to which you have been called." The apostle did not use "call" in relation to a specific occupation or station in life. It is improper, therefore, to interpret "a called one, an apostle" as one who has been called to be an apostle (as the NRSV). This is reinforced by the observation that Paul viewed apostleship as a spiritual gift. First Corinthians 12:28, in context, seems to require this conclusion. The deutero-Pauline Ephesians 4:11-12 makes it explicit. One of the risen Christ's gifts to the church is apostles. Hence the translation "gift of apostleship" seems appropriate, as does the translation "a Christian, an apostle."

Paul's apostleship, moreover, had as its aim the obedience of faith (= the obedience that is faith; cf. Rom 10:16; 15:18) among the Gentiles (v. 5b). The majority of Roman Messianists whom Paul was addressing in this letter belonged to the Gentiles (v. 6a). They too had been called to belong to Jesus Christ (v. 6b). The one who wrote was an apostle to Gentiles; the ones who read were converts out of the Gentiles. There was, therefore, to be a bond between Paul and the Gentiles among the Romans. Everything in vv. 1-6 identifies Paul as someone who had much in common with the readers. Besides being mainly Gentiles, who were they?

The 'B' component of the salutation identifies the readers geographically ("in Rome," v. 7) and spiritually. [Sending a Letter] They are "beloved of God" (Deut 33:12; Neh 13:26; Dio Chrysostom 3.60; Plutarch, "Numa") and they are "called saints" (v. 7;

Sending a Letter

In antiquity a postal system like our modern one did not exist. The emperor Augustus was the first to set up a regular postal service in the west (Suetonius, "Augustus," 49). It was a relay system similar to the early American Pony Express. This imperial system carried only official correspondence, however. Individuals had to make their own arrangements. Most of the time, this meant sending a letter depended on the availability of a traveler going in the right direction (Cicero, *Att* 2.12.2,4). In such circumstances, this sometimes meant that letters were never received (Cicero, *Att* 2.13.1). If the bearer of the letter did deliver it, that person could supplement its contents with verbal information (*PColZen* 1.6). Paul fortunately had a coterie of people about him who could serve as his postal service (e.g., 2 Cor 2:4—Titus; 2 Cor 8:6—Titus; Col 1:7; 4:7-9—Ephaphras, Tychicus, Onesimus; Rom 16:1-2—Phoebe).

1 Cor 1:2). Again, the notion of calling is related to that of being a Christian. The term "saints" is to be read against an OT background where the term is commonly used of Israel as God's people (Deut 7:6; 33:3; Ps 50:5), of the faithful remnant of Israel (Isa 4:3), or of the faithful Israelites of the Maccabean period (Dan 7:18, 21-22). Paul regularly described believers as saints (Rom 8:27; 12:13; 15:25; 1 Cor 6:1-2). Other early Christian writers did the same (e.g., Acts 9:13,32; Heb 6:10; *Did* 4:2; 16:17; *1 Clem* 46:2; 56:1; Ign *Smyr* 1.2). In the NT the term designates neither a moral nor a mystical state. It refers rather to those who are set apart (= holy) for God.

The greeting is shaped in a distinctive way. Paul did not use the simple "greeting." Instead he combined "Grace to you and peace" (1 Thess 1:1) with "from God our Father and the Lord Jesus Christ "(1 Cor 1:1). This makes his greeting a distinctively Christian one. Alternate combinations included "greeting and good peace" (2 Macc 1:1) and "mercy and peace be with you" (*2 Bar* 78:2; Gal 6:16; Jude 2; Polycarp, *Phil,* preface).

The salutation is followed by prayer. [The Form of Ancient Letters] Traditionally prayer was offered at the beginning of a literary, rhetorical, or philosophical effort in Mediterranean antiquity. In Plato's *Euthydemus* 275c5-d2, Socrates says, "I must begin my description as the poets do, by invoking the Muses." In Plato's *Timaeus* 27b8-d4, Socrates says Timaeus should speak, after duly calling upon the gods. In 27c, Timaeus replies, "All men, Socrates, who have any degree of right feeling, at the beginning of every enterprise, whether small or great, always call upon God." Plato himself, in *Epistle* 8, 353a1-2, said we should always offer prayer to

---

The Form of Ancient Letters

 An ancient letter was made up of an address, a prayer form, a body, and a closing. Paul's letters adapted the usual form. They usually looked like this:

Address: A to B, Greeting

Prayer form: Thanksgiving (in all the Pauline letters except Galatians, 1 Timothy, and Titus)
Petition/Intercession (not in 1 Corinthians, 2 Corinthians, Galatians, 1, 2 Timothy, and Titus)

Body: (includes both doctrinal and ethical material: e.g., Rom 1:16–11:36 = doctrinal; 12:1–15:12 = ethical)

Closing: Greetings (not in Galatians, Ephesians, 2 Thessalonians, 1 Timothy)
Peace-wish (not in 1 Corinthians, Colossians, 1, 2 Timothy, Titus, Philemon)
Grace-benediction (in all the Pauline letters)

At the same time that the Pauline letters reflect the conventional letter form of antiquity, each one is adapted, sometimes in surprising ways, to serve the letter's purpose.

the gods when we begin to speak or think. Iamblichus, *On the Pythagorean Life* 1.1, said that at the start of any philosophical investigation it was the custom to invoke God. Indeed culturally, prayer was the way to begin any undertaking. Xenophon had Critobulus tell Socrates: "Well, Socrates, I think you are right when you bid me try to begin every undertaking with the gods' help" (*Oeconomicus* 5.20). That ancient Greek letters began with a prayer is a reflection of this cultural expectation. In Isias's letter to Hephaestion from about 168 BC, following the greeting, she said: "If you are well . . . , it would be as I am continually praying to the gods."[9] Second Maccabees 1:11 offers an example of a thanksgiving in a non-Christian Jewish letter. Only in Galatians did Paul omit a prayer of thanksgiving. There, because he was so angry, he inserted a double curse instead (Gal 1:8, 9). In Romans 1:8 there is a prayer of thanksgiving. "I thank my God through Jesus Christ for all of you." "The exalted Christ is understood here as filling the role elsewhere in Judaism already attributed to archangels (Tob 12:12; *1 Enoch* 9:3; 99:3; 104:1; *T. Levi* 3:5; 5:6-7; *T. Dan* 6:2) and already to the patriarchs by Philo (*Praem* 166; cf. *2 Enoch* 7; 53:1)."[10] In 1:9-17 the prayer shifts to petition: "asking that somehow by God's will I may now at last succeed in coming to you" (v. 10).

Verses 11-17 provide the basis for Paul's desire expressed in his petition. Why did he want to come? He wanted to share some spiritual blessing with them so they might be mutually encouraged (vv. 11-12). In fact he had often wanted to come to Rome but had thus far been prevented (v. 13). Because he was under obligation to Gentiles of all kinds, he had wanted to preach also in Rome (vv. 14-15). [Roman Forum in AD 64] This need not be understood as exclusively proclamation that evokes faith for the first time. The obedience of faith involved more than simply an initial response. Why did he preach generally? He preached because the gospel is God's power unto salvation to every one who has faith (v. 16). It has this power because in it the righteousness of God is revealed (v. 17). As his conclusion to the basis for his petition in v. 10 Paul has in vv. 16-17 come to a statement of the theme of the letter: the gospel of the righteousness of God that results in salvation for all who believe. Any hope of understanding Romans' argument depends on one's ability to grasp what Paul meant by the righteousness of God.

Attempting to understand Paul's teaching about "righteousness" and "justification" requires readers first to recognize that they are dealing with one concept, not two. Both the adjective and the

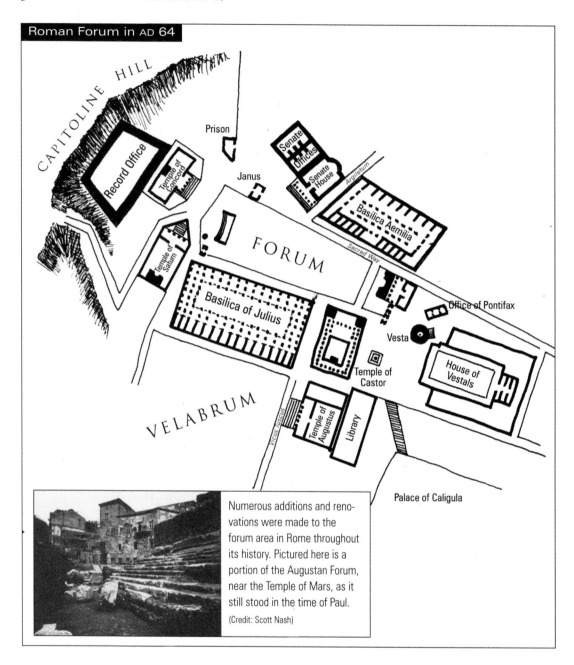

Roman Forum in AD 64

CAPITOLINE HILL

Record Office

Temple of Concord

Prison

Janus

Senate Offices

Senate House

Argiletum

Basilica Aemilia

Sacred Way

FORUM

Temple of Saturn

Basilica of Julius

Office of Pontifax

Vesta

Temple of Castor

House of Vestals

VELABRUM

Vicus Vicus

Temple of Augustus

Library

Palace of Caligula

Numerous additions and renovations were made to the forum area in Rome throughout its history. Pictured here is a portion of the Augustan Forum, near the Temple of Mars, as it still stood in the time of Paul.

(Credit: Scott Nash)

noun on the one hand and the verb on the other come from the same root: *dikaios* (righteous), *dikaiosynēs* (righteousness), *dikaioun* (to justify). The view that God's righteousness has to do with the enforcement of moral standards among humans while God's justification of the sinner has to do with forgiving the ones who have violated those moral standards is eliminated. The revelation of God's righteousness and God's justifying the sinner are the same thing.

Scholars are virtually unanimous about two things. First, Paul's usage is not to be understood against the background of classical literature. In Aristotle, the Greek *dikaioun* with a personal object almost invariably is applied to someone whose cause is unjust. It thus bears the negative meaning "to punish." In Cicero, the Latin *iustificare* means "to condemn the sinful man." That the early Luther understood the righteousness of God in these terms explains why he did not regard the revelation of God's righteousness as good news. Second, scholars are united in affirming that the Pauline usage of the terms for righteousness must be understood against the background of Paul's Bible, the LXX, in which the meaning of the Greek *dikaioun* was determined by the Hebrew Bible that lay behind it. At the same time, evidence from Qumran and other noncanonical literature may be used to support the line of interpretation opened up by the LXX.

In the LXX, righteousness is a covenant term. One is righteous if he/she fulfills the demands or responsibilities of the relationship. One is unrighteous is he/she does not fulfill the responsibilities of the covenant relation. This means that Paul was using a relational concept.

How were the *dikai* cognates used of God in the LXX? Four things may be said. First, God is righteous. This means God is faithful to the covenant. Several examples illustrate this. In Nehemiah 9:8 for God to be righteous means God fulfills the covenantal promise to Abraham. In Isaiah 45:21 that God is righteous is synonymous with "God is savior." LXX Psalm 114:5 (= 116:5) says God is merciful and righteous. The Psalmist was brought low and God saved him. Psalm 128:4 (=129:4) says that the righteous Lord has done away with sinners who have warred against Israel. For God to be righteous is for God to be faithful to the covenant (cf. *Jub* 1:5-6).

Second, God's righteousness refers to God's covenant faithfulness. Several illustrations show this to be so. For example, God's righteousness consisted in acts that saved Lot from destruction (Gen 19:19). In the MT the term is *ḥesed* (covenant love). In Judges 5:11, God's righteousness is seen in acts that enable Israel's military victory over her foes. In LXX 1 Kingdoms 12:7 (= 1 Sam 12:7) God's righteousness is equated with saving deeds on behalf of Israel from the Exodus generation to the time of Samuel. In LXX Psalm 30:1 (= 31:1) God's righteousness is deliverance of the individual Israelite. In LXX Psalm 50:14 (= 51:14) it is rescue of the individual Israelite from blood-guilt. In Isaiah 45:23 it is fulfillment of God's words. In Isaiah 46:13; 51:5, 8, it is God's salvation of the Babylonian exiles. In 4 Ezra 8:36, it is God's showing mercy to those without a store of good works. In all of these references, God's righteousness is seen as covenant loyalty.

Third, it is said that God is justified by humans. This means that God is recognized and acknowledged to be faithful in covenant relationships. Two examples suffice. LXX Isaiah 42:21 says God has taken counsel in order to be justified. In Sirach 18:2 we hear that the Lord alone will be justified. Here the emphasis is upon humans' recognizing that God is faithful.

Fourth, God justifies. This means making humans beneficiaries of righteousness. For example, LXX 3 Kingdoms 8:31-32 (= 1 Kgs 8:31-32) and Isaiah 53:11 say that God recognizes and rewards the righteous Israelite. LXX Esther 10:3 I (= RSV 10:12) says God justifies/rescues people from extermination. LXX Isaiah 50:8 indicates that when justifying God vindicates people in the face of their enemies. LXX Isaiah 43:25-26 defines God's justifying activity as blotting out people's sins after they have confessed. LXX Isaiah 45:26 says God's justifying activity means delivering people from bondage to the nations.

Fifth, God's righteousness can be given to humans. This may have two very different connotations. On the one hand, LXX Psalm 71:1-2 (= 72:1-2) asks God's righteousness be given to the king so that the king can judge righteously. Here the gift of God's righteousness to a human is couched in the language of enablement. God enables the king to act as God acts. This is the equivalent of "to make righteous" by means of being "given righteousness." The same emphasis is found outside the LXX in the *Epistle of Aristeas* 280. There God gives the king a crown of righteousness thereby enabling the king to act justly. On the other hand, LXX Baruch 5:2 exhorts readers to cast about themselves a garment of righteousness from God (*tēs para tou theou dikaiosynes*); 5:9 speaks about a "righteousness from Him" (*dikaiosynē tē par' autou*). In context the statements refer to God's eschatological salvation. To be clothed with God's righteousness means to experience the salvation that comes from God. This is the equivalent of "being justified." Finally, moving again outside the LXX, it is not clear how *T. Levi* 18:14 should be taken. There "and all the saints shall be clothed in righteousness" comes at the end of a section that deals with eschatological salvation. It could mean the saints are beneficiaries of God's righteousness in terms of their circumstances or it could mean that the saints have been transformed personally by God's righteousness. It may very well be that both meanings are present. In any case, there are instances where God gives humans righteousness. When this is so, it is in the context of divine enablement of humans.

There are similarities between some of these LXX examples and the use of the Hebrew equivalents in the Qumran scrolls. For example, 1 QS XI.3 says, "with His righteous acts He cancels my sin"; 1 QS XI.14 says, "in His righteousness He will cleanse me from the sin of humans." First QH XII.37 says that through righteousness God atones for sin and cleanses humans of their fault.

A summary of the findings so far clarifies the use of the *dikai* cognates in ancient Judaism when they were used of the relations between God and humans. (1) The declarative, courtroom component, while present (LXX Isa 50:8), is minimal. (2) There is no significant difference between the meaning associated with the noun and the verb. For example, both speak of God's righteousness and God's justifying activity not only as removal of guilt but also deliverance from bondage or oppression (noun—LXX Ps 50:14 guilt; Isa 46:12-13; 51:5, 8 bondage; verb—Isa 43:25-26 guilt; Isa 45:26 bondage). (3) There is not only a granting of a new status as a result of the removal of guilt (LXX Ps 50:14; Isa 43:25-26; 1 QS XI.3; 1 QH XII.37) but also a transformation of humans by means of divine enablement (LXX Ps 71:1-2; 1 QS XI.14; 1 QH XII37). (4) The connotations of the terms shift depending upon whether the humans are deemed righteous or unrighteous. If the former, then to be justified means to have one's righteousness (= faithfulness to the covenant) recognized and rewarded (LXX 3 Kgs 8:32; Isa 53:11). If the latter, then to be justified means to have one's guilt removed (Isa 43:25-26) and to be delivered from one's bondage (Isa 45:26). (5) There is a recognition in some places that human righteousness (= acts reflecting covenant faithfulness) is dependent on divine enablement (= God's giving righteousness or covenant faithfulness to humans (LXX Ps 71:1-2; *Ep Aris* 280). With this perspective, it is time to turn to Paul's usage of the *dikai* terms.

The *dikai* cognates are used of God in Paul's letters in much the same way that they are in Paul's Bible. Paul could say that God is righteous (Rom 3:26). He could also speak of God's righteousness (Rom 1:17; 3:5; 3:21, 22, 25, 26; 10:3). He said God is justified by humans (Rom 3:4-5). God also justifies or does not justify humans (Rom 2:13; 3:20, 24, 26, 28, 30; 4:5; 5:1, 9; 6:7; 8:30, 33; Gal 2:16, 17; 3:8, 11, 24). Paul could also speak of a righteousness from God (*ek*—Phil 3:9; *apo*—1 Cor 1:30; a free gift—Rom 5:17).

How should these references to God's righteousness in Paul's letters be understood? The *dikai* cognates in Paul are used (1) for a quality of God (= God's covenant fidelity, so Rom 3:5, 25, 26); (2) for divine activity (= God's saving activity, so Rom 1:17; 3:21, 22); and (3) for a condition granted by God to humans (= God's gift of righteousness, so Rom 5:17; 10:3; 2 Cor 5:21; Phil 3:9).

When the verbal form "to justify" appears in Paul, both God and humans may be the object. On the one hand, as in the LXX God may be justified by humans (= shown as righteous, acknowledged as faithful, so Rom 3:4-5). On the other hand, humans are justified or not justified by God. Sometimes, to be justified means to be declared or acknowledged as righteous by God and rewarded (Rom 2:13; 3:20; 8:33-34; 1 Cor 4:4; Gal 2:16; 3:11). At other times, to be justified means to be granted a new status or condition as a gift from God (Rom 3:24, 26, 28, 30). At still other times, to be justified means to be freed or released from sin's power (Rom 6:7). A corollary to these meanings is the idea of divine enablement expressed in terms of receiving a righteousness from God (Phil 3:9) or being made righteous (Rom 5:19).

Such a survey of meanings of the *dikai* cognates both in Paul's Bible and in his letters makes clear that the Reformation debates about whether being justified means being declared righteous or made righteous have been transcended. It is no longer a matter of either-or, either declarative or effective, but rather both-and, both declarative and effective. "Those whom God has vindicated he also changes."[11] In Paul, God who is righteous (= faithful) reveals His righteousness (= saving acts), resulting in justification (= salvation) of people. Of what does that salvation consist? In Romans, one sees it involves at least (1) acquittal/forgiveness of guilt, so that one is at peace with and able to stand before God at the Last Day; (2) freedom from sin's power and enablement to be faithful to God; (3) freedom from legalistic religion; (4) freedom from death's ultimacy; (5) participation in the people of God made up of Jew and Gentile who are justified through Christ; and (6) involvement in a distinctive lifestyle that reflects a transformed mind.

To suggest such a range of meanings for one cluster of words—without courting the charge of incoherence—requires that one describe the fabric of thought incorporating the diverse elements. (1) Paul and his Bible assume a covenantal/relational way of thinking. (2) One is righteous if one if faithful to the covenant/relationship. (3) One's righteousness is one's faithfulness to the covenant/relationship. (4) God's faithfulness/righteousness can be variously understood. On the one hand, if one thinks in terms of Deuteronomic theology, then God is required by righteousness to justify/vindicate the righteous Israelite (like a judge who vindicates the person who is in the right). Here one's being justified is having one's righteousness recognized and rewarded. Here the language of justification arises out of a courtroom context. On the other hand, if one thinks in terms of exilic theology, where unrighteous Israelites are assumed, then righteousness/faithfulness requires God to make sure the covenant endures and to ensure that the divine promises are fulfilled. In this context, the language of justification arises out of the context of God's promise to Abraham. Here being justified is having one's guilt covered and one's bondage broken and being restored to a right relation with God. (5) God's righteousness is something people need in order to relate rightly to each other and to God. For example, the king needs to be given God's righteousness in order to judge rightly. Also, Jerusalem needs to be clothed with God's righteousness in order to experience salvation. (6) The Last Judgment is viewed in terms of a judicial setting. There God's righteousness is the vindication of the righteous. There God is a just judge. Within history, however, when dealing with unrighteous people, God's righteousness is a synonym for showing mercy, being long suffering, compassionate, true, and for taking away iniquity, unrighteousness, and sins (LXX Exod 34:6-7). Here God is a gracious savior doing for humans what they cannot do for themselves.

In v. 17 Paul states that the righteousness of God is revealed in the gospel. If by "righteousness" he means the saving activity of God, what does he mean by the expression "through/out of faith for faith" (*ek pisteōs eis pistin*)? Numerous options have been proposed: from the faith of the OT to the faith of the NT; from the faith of the preacher to the faith of the hearer; from the faithfulness of God to the faith of humans; from the faithfulness of Jesus for the faithfulness of humans; from one degree of faith to another, that is, growth in faith; a rhetorical expression meaning "faith from first to last." Given our discussion of God's righteousness as God's faithfulness, it seems that a paraphrase of "through/out of either God's or Jesus' faithfulness for the faith of humans" is preferable.

Paul's statement in v. 17a concludes with an OT proof text in v. 17b: "as it is written, *ho de dikaios ek pisteōs zēsetai.*" This citation from Habakkuk is variously understood and translated. The MT seems to say: "the righteous man by his faithfulness shall live." This reading is also found among the Dead Sea Scrolls (1QpH 8:1-40; 8HevXIIgr 17.29-30). The LXX manuscripts contains multiple readings. Some manuscripts (S, B, Q, V, W) have "the righteous one out of my faithfulness shall live." Others (A, C) have "my righteous one shall live by faith." One late secondary witness

(MS 763) has "the righteous one by faith shall live." This might have been influenced by Paul. Hebrews 10:38 has "my righteous one out of faithfulness shall live." Romans 1:17 and Galatians 3:11 read: "the righteous one out of faithfulness shall live." The central issue is: who is the righteous one?

In any number of contexts, "the righteous one" is a title for the Christ. In the Jewish document *1 Enoch* there are at least two references to the Messiah as the Righteous One. *First Enoch* 38:2-3 speaks about the Righteous One who appears at the End Time when sinners shall be judged for their sins and driven from the face of the earth. *First Enoch* 53:6 also refers to the Righteous One who appears when Satan is chained and the kings of the earth are destroyed. This, then, was a traditional messianic title in the first century. In the NT there are several such references. Acts 3:14 has Peter say: "But you denied the Holy and Righteous One, and asked for a murderer to be granted to you." In Acts 7:52, Stephen says: "Which of the prophets did not your fathers persecute? And they killed those who announced beforehand the coming of the Righteous One, whom you have now betrayed and murdered." In Acts 22:14, Ananias says to Paul: "The God of our fathers appointed you to know His will, to see the Righteous One and to hear a voice from his mouth." First Peter says that Christ died "the Righteous for the unrighteous." First John 2:1 speaks about our advocate with the Father, "Jesus Christ the Righteous." If "the Righteous" is taken as a title for Christ in v. 17b, then "from faith to faith" should be understood as "from the faithfulness of Jesus to human faith." If so, then both parts of the verse would agree. The OT proof text would then confirm the faithfulness of Jesus in the quotation from Habbakkuk. "The Righteous One shall live by faith."

A secondary issue is the relation of "out of faith" to the rest of the OT quotation. Does it go with "shall live" or with "the Righteous One"? If Paul had intended to associate "out of faith" with "the Righteous One," he would have written *ho de ek pisteōs dikaios* (Rom 10:6). This he did not do. So one should translate: "The Righteous One (= Christ) shall live out of (his) faithfulness." This has the virtue of using *ek pisteōs* (out of faith) in the same way in both parts of the verse.

The translation of 1:17 that results from these discussions is this. "For the righteousness of God (= God's saving activity) is being eschatologically revealed in the gospel (= the life, death, and resurrection of Jesus) out of the faithfulness of Christ for the faith of humans, as it has been written, "The Righteous One (= Christ)

shall live out of his faithfulness." Such a rendering of Romans 1:16-17 raises the question of how the faithfulness of Christ is to be understood in Paul.

Paul used two different expressions when relating "faith" and "Christ." Sometimes he spoke of faith in Christ. In Galatians 2:16, for example, he talked about faith in (*eis*) Christ. It is this meaning that is implicit in Romans 1:16: "salvation to every one who has faith." At other times, Paul used another expression: *pistis Iēsou Christou* (faith of Jesus Christ), Rom 3:22; Gal 3:22; *pistis Iēsou* (faith of Jesus), Rom 3:26; *pistis Christou Iēsou* (faith of Christ Jesus), Gal 2:16; *pistis Christou* (faith of Christ), Gal 2:16; Phil 3:9; *dia tēs pisteōs autou* (through his faith), in the deutero-Pauline Ephesians 3:12. An important question to ask is whether "faith in Christ" and "faith of Christ" mean similar or different things.

If "faith of Christ" is taken as an objective genitive, it would mean the faith of which Christ is the object and it would be synonymous with "faith in Christ." If "faith of Christ" is taken as a subjective genitive, it would mean the faith of which Christ is the subject, that is, Christ's faith. In this case, the two expressions would have different meanings. Faith in Christ—the act of a believer—would be different from the faith of Christ—Christ's own activity. Interpreters are divided on how to read the evidence?

Pistis (faith), followed by a genitive either of a person or a personal pronoun, has the potential to be either an objective or a subjective genitive. Examples of a subjective genitive usage include: (1) *pistis* (faith) followed by a genitive pronoun (Rom 1:8—the faith of you all = your faith; 1:12; 4:5; 1 Cor 2:5; 15:4; 15:17; 1 Thess 1:18; 3:2; 3:5; 3:7; 3:10; Phlm 6; the deutero-Pauline Colossians 1:4); (2) *pistis* (faith) followed by a genitive of person (Rom 3:3—faithfulness of God = God's faithfulness; Rom 4:12, 16—faith of Abraham = Abraham's faithfulness); 1 Macc 14:35—faith of Simon = Simon's faith; Josephus, *Life* 84—faith of the people of Galilee = Galileans' loyalty). Examples of the objective genitive include: 2 Thess 2:13, faith of truth = belief in the truth; Acts 3:16a, faith of his name = faith in his name; Mark 11:22, faith of God = faith in God; Josephus, *Antiquities* 19.16, faith of God = faith in God. There are also many debatable passages. In Philippians 1:27, "faith of the gospel" may mean faith in the gospel or it may be an epexegetic genitive meaning "faith, namely the gospel." It is probably the latter. In Colossians 2:12 the genitive could mean you were raised with Christ through faith in the working of God or through the faithfulness of God's working? It is probably the latter. In Revelation 14:12 the "faith of Jesus" could mean faith in Jesus or the faithfulness of Jesus? It is likely the latter. In Revelation 2:13 the genitive could be taken to mean faith in me or my faithfulness? It is probably the former. The evidence is divided. Furthermore, it does not matter whether or not an article is used in the genitive. According to ancient stylistic rules, one could write either way (with or without an article), and the two alternatives were equivalents.

Ancient translations from the Greek often illuminate thorny interpretive issues such as this one. Although the evidence of the Vulgate is ambiguous, the early versions (Latin, Coptic, and Syriac) translated "faith of Christ" as a subjective genitive, Christ's faithfulness. Among the early English versions, Wycliffe (1380) and the KJV (1611) followed suit. In fact the evidence seems to show that Luther was the first to make it an objective genitive, faith of which Christ is the object, faith in Christ.

Although the linguistic and translational evidence slightly favors the subjective genitive, the faithfulness of Christ, the deciding factor is how either position fits into Paul's theology generally. The debate focuses on two main issues. (1) Is a focus on Christ's faithfulness characteristic of Paul's theology? Some interpreters contend that although the notion of Christ's faithfulness is found elsewhere in Christian writings (Jas 2:1; Heb 2:17; 3:2; 12:2; Rev 2:13; 14:12), it runs counter to the main thrust of Paul's theology in which Christ is presented as an object of faith. Others argue that this position does not eliminate the Pauline emphasis on "faith in Christ." The two emphases stand side by side and complement one another. Note how this works in Galatians 2:16, for example: "a person is not justified on the basis of works of the law but through the faithfulness of Christ, so we have believed in Christ Jesus in order that we may be justified on the basis of the faithfulness of Christ and not on the basis of works of law." In Romans 3:21-22, moreover, the text reads: "Now apart from law God's saving activity is being revealed, a saving activity through the faithfulness of Christ for all who believe (in him)" (cf. Phil 1:29; Col 2:5 where faith is *in* Christ).

(2) Does the faithfulness of Christ have a necessary function in Pauline theology? Opponents of the rendering "faithfulness of Christ" contend that they can see no reason for it. It offers, they say, nothing necessary to Pauline thought. Indeed, proponents of "faith of Christ" are not yet agreed exactly as to how the phrase functions in the context of Pauline thought. Some see it as a support for a soteriology in which Jesus is example or model. So we are to have faith as Jesus had faith. So Luke Johnson wants to

replace faith in Christ with faith of Christ. Why? Johnson agues that faith in Christ would be inconsistent with Paul's whole argument, since it would claim that one had to be a Christian in order to have access to God. Then the particularity of the Christian religion would simply replace the particularity of Judaism, providing an expanded but, in principle, equally restricted range of accessibility to God.[12] Johnson's reading is clearly not Paul's view (cf. Gal 2:16; Phil 1:29; Col 2:5), but this line of reasoning may explain why some scholars want to avoid the translation "Christ's faithfulness."[13]

Others who accept the subjective genetive connect it to a soteriology in which Jesus is mediator: faith in the one who was himself faithful. This fits Pauline theology generally, suiting Paul's concern in the avoidance of works righteousness. Leander Keck has noted, "At stake here is emancipation from a subjectivist reading of justification, according to which its basis is either our 'works' or our believing."[14] What follows is an attempt to show how Christ's faithfulness fits into Pauline thought overall, assuming a soteriology in which Jesus is mediator and not merely example.

Paul's thinking is "covenant thought." Of the three covenants mentioned in the LXX that play significant roles in Paul's letters, two are highly valued. They are the covenant with Abraham (Gen 12, 15, 17) and the new covenant of Jeremiah 31. The third, the covenant through Moses (Exod 24), is minimized. We may collect Paul's statements on these three covenants and synthesize them into the following framework. First, through the Abrahamic covenant Paul used Scripture to argue that justification through faith had been God's plan all along for both Jew and Gentile. Second, by giving priority to the covenant with Abraham, Paul could argue that the Law (the Mosaic covenant) was a temporary phase in God's dealings with His people. It was just, but because of human sin, it was powerless to save, and only functioned to expose sin. With the coming of Christ, the Law came to an end as part of ongoing salvation history. Third, God has replaced the Mosaic covenant with the prophesied new covenant of Jeremiah 31. In this covenant God gives the people what they need to remain faithful to the relationship. That is, their righteousness (= faithfulness) is from God. When Paul wanted to make the point that Christian soteriological reality had been a part of God's plan from the beginning and includes the nations, he worked with the Abrahamic covenant and its relation to the Mosaic Law. When he wanted to emphasize the soteriological reality that human faithfulness to God in the covenant relationship depends on God, he worked with the new covenant of Jeremiah 31.

The "faith of Christ," understood as "Christ's faithfulness," functions in a twofold way in this covenantal thinking: one in relation to the Abrahamic covenant and the other in relation to the new covenant. In relation to the Abrahamic covenant, the faith of Christ fulfills the promise to Abraham and his seed. Christ's faithfulness shows him to be the seed of Abraham (Gal 3:16). People of faith who belong to Christ, Gentiles included, are Abraham's offspring (Gal 3:29). They are blessed with Abraham who had faith (Gal 3:6-9). Christ's faithfulness makes him a part of the Abrahamic covenant and guarantees the inclusion of the Gentiles in God's promise.

In relation to the new covenant of Jeremiah 31, Christ's faithfulness enables human faithfulness in the relation to God. It is important first to see that Paul used a number of expressions that are virtual synonyms when speaking about Christ's relation to God. The "faith of Christ" (Rom 3:22,26; Gal 2:20), the "obedience of Christ" (Rom 5:19; Phil 2:8), the "righteous act of Christ" (Rom 5:18), Christ's dying to sin (Rom 6:10) all speak of Christ's dying on the cross as an act of faithfulness/obedience/ righteousness towards God and therefore as his death to sin. He died rather than sin.

It is important to see, second, that the transfer of Christ's faithfulness/obedience/righteousness to believers is spoken of in several different ways as well. Sometimes Paul used the language of indwelling. Either Christ (Gal 2:20) or the Spirit (Gal 5:25; Rom 8:14) or the spirit of Christ (Rom 8:9-10) or God (Phil 2:12-13) indwells the believer(s) and lives through him/her/them enabling covenant fidelity. Such thinking is prefigured in language about David (LXX 1 Kgs 16:13; Josephus, *Ant* 6.165-96) and Elisha (LXX 4 Kgs 2:13). It is seen in Christian writings after Paul: in *Hermas, Mandate* 12:3, and Ignatius, *Ephesians,* 15:3. At other times, Paul used the language of transformation through vision (2 Cor 3:18). As one beholds the glory of the Lord (Christ), he/she is transformed from one degree of glory into another. Such thinking may be seen in later Christian writings in 1 John 3:2 and *Epistle to Diognetus* 2:5. It is prefigured in Philo, *Moses* 1.158-59, *1 Enoch* 71, and is also found in the Hermetica 13:3; 10:6; 4:11. On still other occasions, Paul spoke in terms of being clothed in the garments/qualities/person of another (Gal 3:27; 1 Thess 5:8). When one is clothed with Christ, one is changed into another person and becomes endued with the Christ's qualities. This way of thinking is prefigured in LXX Numbers 20:23-28; LXX 3 Kingdoms 19; and LXX 4 Kingdoms 2:13; LXX Baruch 5:2; *2 Enoch* 22; *Biblical Antiquities* 20:2-5. In the last of these texts, Joshua is told by God to clothe himself in Moses' garments and promised that he would be changed and become another man. In these and other ways, Paul conceptualized how Christ's faithfulness is transferred to those who believe in him. On occasion the apostle may say that the risen Lord lives in and through the believer with the same faithfulness that he manifested in the days of his flesh (Gal 2:20). At other times he said the believer is clothed with Christ, which makes the believer a new person endued with Christ's own fidelity. On still other occasions he spoke about how the Lord who is contemplated by the believer transforms the believer into a new creature. It is in this sense that the righteousness (covenant faithfulness) from God is given to believers through the faithfulness of Christ. It is in this sense then that Paul could say that Christ is our righteousness (1 Cor 1:30). It is because of his faithfulness in the days of his flesh that the risen Lord can now enable such faithfulness in his people who have faith in him.

Viewed in this way, Paul's soteriology is clearly relational, not juridical. There is no legal fiction transacted in the heaven that leaves the human self on earth untouched and untransformed. At the same time, any righteousness that a human may manifest belongs not to him/her but to the Lord who grants His righteousness to that human. There is human transformation by the Risen One who in the days of his flesh was faithful/obedient/righteous to the point that his death was a death to sin. It is this dimension of Christian soteriology that makes Christian preaching "good news" and "power" unto salvation. Viewed in this way, there is a central place in Pauline soteriology for the "faith of Christ," understood as "Christ's faithfulness."

CONNECTIONS

What is the significance of contending that Romans 1:1 should be translated "Paul, a servant of Jesus Christ, a called one, an apostle " instead of "a called apostle"? Far from being a trivial point of punctuation, it has to do with whether or not Paul is to be understood as an ethical progressive or an ethical reactionary. How so?

There are three possible meanings of Paul's "call" terminology. One meaning is clear, the other two are debated. First, scholars agree that in Paul's letters "to call" can be used as a technical term for the choice of a person by God for salvation (Rom 8:28-30; 9:11; Gal 5:8; 1:6,15; 1 Thess 2:2; 2 Thess 2:13). The background for this meaning is the LXX's use of "to call" as an equivalent of "to choose" (e.g., Isa 41:9). In Paul "to call" is a synonym for "to justify," "to reconcile," "to redeem," and other salvation terms. About this there is no debate.

Second, on the basis of Hebrews 5:4 where a priest is said to be called to his office, and Acts 13:2 and 16:10 where Paul and his helpers are said to be called to a certain missionary task, the expression *klētos apostolos* in Romans 1:1 and 1 Corinthians 1:1 has often been taken to mean that Paul was called to be an apostle. If so, then "to call" may refer, in Paul as well as elsewhere, to the divine summons to an office or to a special work. In 1 Corinthians 12:27-30, however, apostleship is understood as a spiritual gift, analogous to the gifts of healing or tongues (cf. Eph 4:8, 11 for the same view). In Romans 1:5 this seems to be Paul's view as well. If so, then Paul does not understand his apostleship to be the result of God's call but as the result of a spiritual gift. This would set Paul apart from Hebrews and Acts in their use of the same terminology. Moreover, it is as easy to translate *klētos apostolos* as either "a Christian apostle" or "a called one, an apostle."

Third, since *hē klēsis* is sometimes used in nonbiblical literature to mean "station in life," "position," "vocation," certain interpreters try to read 1 Corinthians 7:20 in this way (e.g., RSV and NAB, "every one should remain in the state in which he was called"; NRSV, "Let each of you remain in the condition in which you were called"; NIV, "Each one should remain in the situation which he was in when God called him"; the Net Bible, "Let each one remain in that situation in life in which he was called," and footnote 6 explains: "calling here stands by metonymy for a person's circumstances when he becomes a Christian."). The context in 1 Corinthians 7 speaks about circumcision and slavery. Interpreted as many propose, the text presents Paul as an advocate of the status quo in social relations: "If you were a slave (= your calling/station in life) when you became a Christian, stay a slave (= remain in your calling/station in life) because it is irrelevant whether or not you are slave or free." "Calling" does not have this meaning in 1 Corinthians 1:26; it does not have this meaning anywhere else in the Pauline corpus. In the letters of Paul, "calling" always refers to the call to salvation (Rom 11:29; 1 Cor 1:26; Phil 3:14; 2 Thess 1:11; Eph 1:18; 4:1, 4; 2 Tim 1:9). If so, then Paul's point in 1 Corinthians 7 is that whether you are slave or free, remain in your calling to be a Christian (= be a good Christian regardless of your circumstances).

When the apostle gives his two guidelines in 7:17 for Christian living what he is saying is: (1) lead the life the Lord has assigned to you (= live in line with your spiritual gifts), and (2) lead the life to which God has called you (= live in line with your calling to be a Christian). In vv.18-24 Paul makes two main points. First, one's social circumstances in this life (e.g., whether one is circumcised or whether one is a slave) are not ultimately significant. What has ultimate significance is keeping the commandments of God. So if one is not able to better one's social circumstances, it is not ultimately significant in one's relation to God. Second, if one is able to better those social circumstances, that is fine so long as one is faithful to the relation to God. If you are able to gain your freedom, he says to the Christian slaves, "make the most of your freedom" (so RSV; TEV; NIV; NEB; not as the NRSV translates, "make use of your present condition").[15]

If Paul uses "calling" of the call to be a Christian only, then some clarity can be gained about his theology and ethics. When he speaks of one's being called, what is meant is the person has been called to be a Christian. That is, "call" is a salvation term. When he speaks of a called one, an apostle, he is referring to a Christian whose apostleship is the result of a spiritual gift. When he exhorts slaves who have become Christians and have a possibility of obtaining their freedom to remain in the calling to which they have been called, Paul is merely asking that they remain Christians when they become free. Seen in this light, Paul is no ethical reactionary but an ethical progressive. He stands not for an hierarchical status quo but rather for improvement of human circumstances when that is possible. What he asks in the midst of this social improvement is that those who better themselves remain followers of Christ. The KJV's ambiguity offers the best translation of 1 Corinthians 7:17 and 20, if we remember that "calling" always refers in Paul to the call to be a Christian: "as the Lord has called every one, so let him walk"; "Let every man abide in the same calling wherein he was called." This is not an exhortation to maintain the social status quo but an admonition to avoid apostasy if and when one gains upward social mobility.

Traditonal Language for God?

One of the most sensitive issues confronting Christians today is that of the traditional language for God. Some Christians are

God as Father in the Pauline Corpus

God is called Father throughout the thirteen letters associated with Paul's name; in two letters God is addressed as Father.

- God is the Father (Rom 6:7; 1 Cor 8:6; 15:24; Gal 1:3; Phil 2:11; 1 Thess 1:1; Eph 2:18; 3:14; 5:20; 6:23; Col 1:12; 3:17; 2 Thess 1:2; 1 Tim 1:2; 2 Tim 1:2; Titus 1:4).
- God is the Father of our Lord Jesus Christ (Rom 15:6; 2 Cor 1:3; 11:31; Eph 1:3; 1:17; Col 1:3).
- God is our Father (Rom 1:7; 1 Cor 1:3; 2 Cor 1:2; Gal 1:4; Phil 1:2; 4:20; 1 Thess 1:3; 3:11; 3:13; Phlm 3; Eph 1:2; 4:6; Col 1:2; 2 Thess 1:1; 2:16).
- Christians pray to "Abba, Father" (Rom 8:15-16; Gal 4:6).

In Romans, the focus is on God as Father of Jesus (15:6) who gives Jesus an inheritance, life from the dead (6:4). When we are identified with Jesus and pray "Father," it is the Spirit testifying that we, both Jews and Gentiles (1:7), are children of God and fellow heirs with Christ (8:15). We may anticipate sharing the same inheritance (life from the dead).

Marianne Meye Thompson, "Mercy upon All: God as Father in the Epistle to the Romans," in *Romans and the People of God*, ed. S. K. Soderlund and N. T. Wright (Grand Rapids: Eerdmans, 1999), 203-16.

---

offended by Trinitarian language (Father, Son, and Holy Spirit) and by the Lord's Prayer (Our Father). This language, it is felt, has been used to support patriarchy, subjugate women, and deprive them of their full participation in home and church. There is no doubt that the language has at times functioned in this way in the history of the church and continues to do so in the present. As a result, some Christians have called for a replacement of the traditional language for God, deleting all references to God as Father. A more basic question to be faced is whether or not the Father language for God originated in biblical times out of the same motives that have driven its oppressive use in later history. I hold that it did not. [God as Father in the Pauline Corpus]

Let us look first at two very different views of religious language operative in Christian churches in our time: (1) a relational view and (2) a political view. (1) The relational view of religious language assumes that such speech arises out of reflection on an ongoing relationship between God's people and God. It is analogous to speech that arises out of a durable human relationship such as marriage. For example, John Doe has been married to Jane Doe for over thirty years. It is a durable personal relationship. As a result of the ongoing relationship John can say certain things. He can say something about Jane (e.g., Jane is the most interesting person I have ever known). He can say something about himself (e.g., I am a different man today than I was before we married. I have been changed.). He can say something about the relationship between the two of them (e.g., Life together is unpredictable but never dull.). Such talk arises out of his reflection on the relationship.

On the basis of an ongoing relationship John simply confesses what is: about Jane, about himself, and about the nature of the relationship between them. This is confessional language. By analogy, Paul can speak of Jesus' role in the relationship (e.g., Jesus is Lord/Messiah/Son of God), of himself in terms of the relationship (e.g., I am not the man I was before I met Christ; I have been changed/ justified/saved.), and of the nature of the relationship between himself and Christ (e.g., It is by grace through faith; it is one in which God always has the initiative and I always do the responding.). This is simple confessional religious language. It confesses what Paul senses to be the case about the role of Jesus in the relationship, about what has happened to him as a result of the relationship, and about the nature of the relationship between them.

God the Creator

Here, the fatherly aspect of God is emphasized as God, the Creator, is depicted separate and apart from Creation though invested in it.

Genesis. Frontispiece depicting the Creation from the Luther Bible. 1534. Colored Woodcut. (Credit: Art Resource)

(2) An understanding of religious language as political assumes that religious language is a projection of the organization of human relationships on earth onto the canvas of heaven. Such language functions to buttress the social status quo. If so, then any change in the human social order demands a corresponding change in the way one speaks of the heavenly world. Moreover, if one wishes a change in the human social order, this can be facilitated by a change in the language used of heavenly reality. For example, if God is spoken of in masculine terms (e.g., Father), this is a projection onto heaven of a patriarchal social system on the human level. If the social order either is egalitarian or if an egalitarian social structure is what one hopes for, then the language for God must also be egalitarian (e.g., either Mother as well as Father, or some name that avoids gender altogether, like God). It is assumed that Father language for God is a reflection of the patriarchal world in which the Bible was written.

In the crassest terms, the Bible was written by men so God is male! This language is political, that is, it is all about power in relationships.

While it is true that sometimes in antiquity the depictions of the gods were indeed a projection of earth's social order onto heaven, the gendered descriptions of God/gods do not seem so to be. On the basis of the assumptions of a political view of religious language that holds calling God Father is a projection of a patriarchal social system, then where one finds worship of a goddess, the social order should be matriarchal, and where one finds worship of male and female deities together, the social order should be egalitarian. The correlation does not hold! In antiquity even where a female deity is worshipped, the social order remains patriarchal; where one finds both male and female deities worshipped, the social order remains patriarchal. This disparity is enough to falsify the assumptions of a political view of religious language, especially as it relates to gender issues.

The relational view of religious language assumes that deity transcends sexuality. The biblical God is neither male nor female. Yet God is still sometimes spoken of in Scripture in gendered terms. Sometimes in the Bible God is spoken of in feminine terms: e.g., Isaiah 42:14—God says, "I will cry out like a woman in travail"; 49:15—God asks: "Can a woman forget her suckling child. . . ? Even if these may forget, yet I will not forget you"; 66:13—God says: "as one whom his mother comforts, so I will comfort you'; Luke 13:34b—Jesus says: "How often would I have gathered your children together as a hen gathers her brood under her wings."). When this is so, it is always as *simile*. God is compared to a mother but is never named Mother. This distinction is fundamental. At other times in the Bible God is spoken of in masculine terms: both with simile (e.g., Isaiah 42:13—"The Lord goes forth like a mighty man, like a man of war he stirs up his fury") and metaphor (e.g., Isaiah 63:16—"Thou art our Father, . . . thou, O Lord, art our Father, our Redeemer from of old is thy name"; 64:8—"Yet, O Lord, thou art our Father; we are the clay, and thou art the potter"; Mark 14:36—Jesus prays: "Abba, Father"). In the Bible God is both compared to a male (*simile*) and addressed as Father (*metaphor*).

Why does the Bible reserve a masculine metaphor for God? Two reasons stand out. The first reason grows out of ancient Israel's experience. The prophets would not speak of God with a female metaphor because such language results in a basic distortion of the nature of God and His relation to the creation. Creation by a feminine deity was understood as a birthing process, and the world was understood as an extension of God. This is pantheism (the world is divine), not theism (the world is created by God but is radically other than God). Israel knew that God acted like a mother as well as like a father. Israel, therefore, occasionally spoke of God as like a mother (simile). Israel did not use the feminine metaphor for God, however, because she wanted to guarantee that the qualitative distinction between God the creator and the creation be clearly maintained. Since God relates in personal ways, neuter language would not do. Since creation must be distinguished from the Creator, feminine metaphor would not do. Israel spoke of God as Father not to say He was male but to maintain the otherness of God from the created order at the same time that He was spoken of as personal.

The second reason grows out of the practice of Jesus. The canonical Jesus not only spoke of God as Father (Mark 13:32), he also spoke to God as Father (Mark 14:36; John 11:41; 12:27). Before Easter he taught his disciples to address God as Father (Luke 11:2; Matt 9:13), a practice his disciples continued after Easter (Rom 8:15-16; Gal 4:6). After Easter he taught his disciples to baptize in the name of the Father, the Son, and the Holy Spirit (Matt 28:19-20). For Jesus before Easter, the name of God was Father; for Jesus after Easter, the name of God was Father, Son, and Holy Spirit. In the New Testament, God is called Father and addressed as Father because Jesus knew God as Father and taught his disciples so to address God. Father is God's name.[16] This name is made known as revelation by Jesus, God's son.

The traditional language for God, then, assumes a deity who transcends sexuality and not only signals the qualitative distinction between the Creator and the creation but also speaks of God in terms of God's revealed name. Since Father language for God did not originate for oppressive reasons, it is inappropriate to use it that way today. It is also inappropriate to reduce Father language for God to political rhetoric and to violate the legitimate reasons for its use, whether it be to avoid pantheism or to respect the Other's revealed name.

NOTES

[1] George Milligan, *Selections from the Greek Papyri* (Cambridge UK: Cambridge University Press, 1927), 8-9.

[2] For a fuller discussion of "calling" in Paul's letters, see Charles H. Talbert, *Reading Corinthians*, rev. ed. (Macon GA: Smyth & Helwys, 2002) 40-41.

[3] Elaine H. Pagels, "The Valentinian Claim to Esoteric Exegesis of Romans as Basis for Anthropological Theory," *Vigiliae Christianae* 26 (1972): 241-58, offers examples of Valentinian exegesis and concludes that the Valentinians claim not to present any new doctrine but rather to expound the theology of election and grace they claim to find in Paul.

[4] C. K. Barrett, "Pauline Controversies in the Post-Pauline Period," *NTS* 20 (1974): 229-45.

[5] S. Pines, "The Jewish Christians of the Early Centuries of Christianity according to a New Source," *Proceedings of the Israel Academy of Sciences and Humanities* 2 (1968): 237-310 (esp. 263-64).

[6] OGIS 6.10-34; ET in Hans-Josef Klauck, *The Religious Context of Early Christianity* (Edinburgh: T. & T. Clark, 2000), 255.

[7] Frederick W. Danker, *Benefactor* (St. Louis: Clayton Publishing House, 1982), 217.

[8] Thomas R. Schreiner, *Romans* (Grand Rapids: Baker, 1998), 42.

[9] Milligan, *Selections from the Greek Papyri*, 9.

[10] James D.G. Dunn, *Romans 1–8* (WBC; Dallas: Word, 1988), 1.28.

[11] Thomas Schreiner, *Romans*, 67.

[12] Luke T. Johnson, *Reading Romans* (NY: Crossroad, 1997), 63.

[13] Douglas J. Moo, *The Epistle to the Romans* (Grand Rapids: Eerdmans, 1996) p.225, n.29, says to translate "faith of Christ" means "one must interpret Jesus more as the 'pattern' for our faith than as the object of our faith."

[14] L. E. Keck, "Jesus in Romans," *JBL* 108 (1989): 454.

[15] Charles H. Talbert, *Reading Corinthians*, rev. ed. (Macon GA: Smyth & Helwys, 2002) 40-42.

[16] For a full argument along these lines and key bibliography on both sides, see Charles H. Talbert, "The Church and Inclusive Language for God?" *PRS* 19 (1992): 421-39.

THE HUMAN CONDITION, PART ONE

1:18-32

The background against which Paul spoke about the covenant loyalty and the saving activity of God (= God's righteousness) in Jesus Christ is his depiction of the human condition. In 1:18–3:20 his argument leads to the conclusion: "None is righteous, no, not one." This includes Jews as well as Gentiles. In an argument that assumes a Jewish frame of reference, the apostle made his case. In 1:18-32 he spoke about the sin of the Gentiles, something every Jew would grant, as would Gentiles who had been God-fearers before they became Christian Messianists (cf. 1 Pet 1:14, 18; 4:3-4). In 2:1–3:2 he dealt with the sin of Jews, a matter about which persuasion is needed. What is argued in 1:18–3:20 is the equal status of Jew and Gentile under sin (cf. Rom 11:30-32).

Philosophers in antiquity regarded it as their duty to make their audiences aware of their ills first of all. Epictetus, *Discourse* 3.23.23-38, said:

> I invite you to come and hear that you are in a bad way, and that you are concerned with any thing rather than what you should be concerned with, and that you are ignorant of the good and the evil, and are wretched and miserable." That's a fine invitation! And yet if the philosopher's discourse does not produce this effect, it is lifeless and so is the speaker himself.[1]

Paul's auditors would have expected a diagnosis of human ills to begin his argument.[2]

Horace, *Ars Poetica* 191-92, laid down a rule of dramatic art. A god, he said, must never be introduced into the action unless the plot has got so tangled that only a god could unravel it. Both the apostle and his readers would have regarded a description of such a tangle as necessary before the introduction of God's saving activity in 3:21-31. A diagnosis is a necessary precursor to a cure. Romans 1:18–3:20 provides that needed diagnosis.

An outline of the argument of 1:18-32 assists a reading of the passage:

The Unrighteousness of the Gentiles (1:18-32)
I. Statement of the principle being argued (vv. 18-21)
  A. Wrath is being revealed (v. 18)
  B. Why?
    1. A revelation has been made (vv. 19-20)
    2. The revelation has been rejected (v. 21)
II. Three illustrations of the principle (vv. 22-24, 25-27, 28-32)
  A. First illustration (vv. 22-24)
    1. Rejection of the revelation (vv. 22-23)
    2. Consequences (v. 24)
  B. Second illustration (vv. 25-27)
    1. Rejection of the revelation (v. 25)
    2. Consequences (vv. 26-27)
  C. Third illustration (vv. 28-32)
    1. Rejection of the revelation (v. 28a)
    2. Consequences (vv. 28b-32)

The passage may be read in light of the outline. We begin with Paul's statement of principle.

COMMENTARY

God's wrath is being revealed against "all ungodliness and wickedness of those who by their wickedness suppress the truth" (v. 18). "Wrath of God" is found in Romans 1:18; 12:19; [Col 3:6; Eph 5:6]. "Wrath" is employed in Romans 2:5, 8; 3:5; 4:15; 5:9; 9:22; 12:19; 13:4-5; 1 Thess 1:10; 2:16; 5:9; [Eph 2:3]. In speaking about God's wrath Paul deviated from some ancient Jews who did not believe God could be associated with wrath (*Ep Arist* 254; Philo, *Unchangeableness of God* XI.51). In Paul, what does the expression mean? God's wrath is His "holy hostility to evil."[3] Always, when applied to God, wrath describes how God acts. It is personal but not emotional (cf. Rom 1:18; 2:5, 8). This activity of God is sometimes described as an eschatological expectation (Rom 2:5, 8; 5:9; 12:19; 1 Thess 1:10; 5:9). In this Paul was like certain other Jews of his time (*1 Enoch* 90:18; 91:7, 9; *Sib Or* 4.159-61). At other times Paul described God's wrath as a present reality (Rom 1:18; 13:4-5; 1 Thess 2:16). In this respect Paul was like some other Jews of his period (LXX Bar 1:13; 1 Esdr 8:21; 9:13; 1 Macc 3:8; *T. Reub* 4:4). Both the present and the eschatological activity of God are universal in scope (Rom 1:18; 2:5-6). God's wrath is

Sinners in the Hands of an Angry God

Excerpt from Sermon: *The bow of God's wrath is bent, and the arrow made ready on the string; and justice directs the bow to your heart, and strains at the bow: and it is nothing but the mere pleasure of God, and that of an angry God, without any promise or obligation at all, that keeps the arrow one moment from being made drunk with your blood.*

Jonathan Edwards (1703–1758) was a great American revivalist, theologian and missionary. The sermon was delivered during a meeting in Enfield, Massachusetts, in 1741 with the headline: "Sinners in the Hands of an Angry God." In the sermon, the wrath of God is described as if hanging over the heads of humankind, just moments from unleashing its fury.

Sinners in the Hands of an Angry God, Repent. Title page of the sermon by Jonathan Edwards. 1741. Rare Books Division. The New York Public Library. (Credit: Astor, Lenox, and Tilden Foundation)

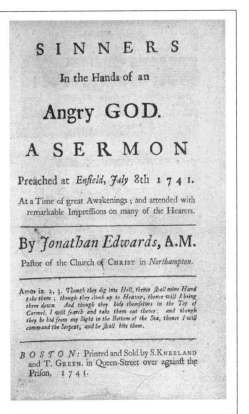

directed against the ungodliness (the vertical dimension) and wickedness (the horizontal dimension) of humans (Rom 1:18; 2:8).

The content of the present aspect of eschatological wrath in Romans 1:18-32 is given in vv. 24, 26, and 28: "and God gave them up." The language echoes that of the LXX Psalm 105:41 (*paredōken autous*). The thought is typically Jewish. For example, Ezekiel 23:28-30 has God say: "I will deliver you (*egō paradidōmi se*) into the hands of those whom you hate . . . and they shall deal with you in hatred . . . and leave you naked and bare, and the nakedness of your whorings shall be exposed." Here idolatry results in Israel's being given up to a punishment that fits the crime. The nakedness of her whoring/idolatry results in her being given up to nakedness at the hands of enemies. Wisdom of Solomon 11:15-16 says: "In return for their foolish and wicked thoughts, which led them astray to worship irrational serpents and worthless animals, you sent upon them a multitude of irrational creatures to punish them, so that they might learn that one is punished by the very things by which one sins." Again the punishment fits the crime. *Jubilees* 21:22 says: "Be careful not . . . to commit a mortal sin before God . . . so that He will deliver you into the power of your sin." In the *T. Gad* 5:10 we hear: "By whatever human capacity anyone transgresses, by that he is also chastised." Two later rabbinic statements are similar. The first, *m. 'Abot* 4.2, reads: "Every fulfillment of duty is rewarded by another, and every transgression is punished by another." The second, *b. Sabbat* 104a teaches: "Whoever strives to keep himself pure receives the power to do so, and whoever is impure, to him is it (the door of vice) thrown open." God's wrath, then, takes the form of God's giving humans up to the chaos for which we have voted.

The content of the future aspect of God's wrath in Romans 2:5-10 is the last judgment with its punishments (fury, tribulation, distress) for those who do not obey the truth (cf. 2 Thess 1:5-12).

What is the relation between God's righteousness and God's wrath? Some think God's wrath is a part of God's righteousness. If so, then Romans 1:18 (God's wrath is being revealed) continues the thought of 1:16-17 (God's righteousness is being revealed). [Revelation] If so, God's covenant faithfulness (= righteousness) includes God's punishing activity. Others, however, think that God's wrath is contrasted with God's righteousness. Two main

---

Revelation

Revelation is a key concept in Rom 1:17-19. In 1:17 Paul says God's righteousness is revealed in the gospel. In 1:18 he says God's wrath is revealed against human godlessness and unrighteousness. In 1:19 he says God's eternal deity and power have been revealed. The idea of revelation deserves a closer look.

In the history of Christian thought there have been two very different ways of viewing revelation.

- On the one hand, revelation has sometimes been understood as the communication of a body of knowledge. Some part of this knowledge could be obtained or verified by the light of reason, while the rest was supplemental to what could be so obtained or verified by reason and had to be taken on trust. Acquisition of this body of information was analogous to the two ways a school child might obtain the correct answer to a math problem. He/she could work it out for himself/herself or he/she could take it on trust from the teacher or textbook. Revelation here is seen as the communication of an object, information. This information both overlaps what can be known by reason and goes beyond it. What goes beyond reason must be accepted on the basis of trust in the authority that passed it on.

- On the other hand, others have understood revelation in the context of a personal relationship. It is not the revelation of an object, a body of knowledge, but of a subject, God. It is not so much information about God that is revealed but God's self. It is self-disclosure, analogous to the disclosure of one's self to another human being. Revelation is from Subject to subject. It is also of Subject to subject. There is a cognitive element to this self-disclosure but the self-disclosure is not propositional. Reflection on the self-disclosure brings the cognitive components to verbal self-expression. Propositions express the response of human witnesses to divine events. It is analogous to a wife's disclosure of herself to her husband in the context of an ongoing relationship, marriage. He, in turn, can reflect on the relationship and speak conceptually about her.

When Paul spoke about God's revelation in Rom 1:17-19, revelation there is not propositional. It is God's self-disclosure through acts in the world, in human history, and in human hearts. What is provided humans, said Paul, is not mere knowledge about but knowledge of God's self. This is what is called knowledge by acquaintance as distinct from merely conceptual knowledge. (Baillie) In Romans, "revelation" describes a personal relationship rather than the communication of information.

John Baillie, *The Idea of Revelation in Recent Thought* (NY: Columbia University Press, 1956), while dated, still offers the clearest statement of the two options. See especially p. 47.

arguments support this latter position. First, v. 18 begins with a *gar* (for) that indicates a new section is beginning. Second, in Paul's Bible passages such as LXX Micah 7:9 indicate that Jewish thought made a distinction between the two. "I will bear the wrath of the Lord because I have sinned against Him, until He justifies . . . and leads me into the light. . . . I shall see His righteousness and my enemy will see." Also, LXX 3 Kingdoms 8:31-32 contrasts God's condemning the wicked and justifying the righteous. In such texts, God's wrath and righteousness are distinguished from one another. Hence, in Romans 1 it is best to see God's righteousness as saving activity and as distinguishable from God's wrath that is resistance to evil.

Paul argues that God's wrath results from human willful disobedience. Verses 19-20 say that humans generally possess a knowledge of God. "Ever since the creation of the world His eternal power and divine nature, invisible though they are, have been understood and seen through the things He has made." This knowledge is available to all people in all times and all places. So humans generally are without excuse for our idolatry. Nevertheless, this knowledge has been suppressed. Verse 21 says: "though they knew God, they did not honor Him as God or give thanks to Him, but they became futile in their thinking." This rejection of knowledge of God provokes God's wrath. [Karl Barth on the Wrath of God]

In Romans 1:20 Paul said of the Gentiles: "they knew God." How? Romans 1:20 says that ever since the creation God's eternal power and divine nature have been seen through the things God made. In 1:19 he said: "what can be known about God is plain to them, because God has shown it to them." An ancient auditor might have understood these statements in at least four ways.

First, in Mediterranean antiquity there was belief in the possibility of human reason's climbing the ladder from the world or the self to God. This position is often called natural theology. The Greco-Roman philosophical tradition held to such a natural theology (Plato, *Timaeus* 28A-30C, 32A-35A; Aristotle, *de mundo* 6.397b-399b). Cicero, *Tusculan Disputations* 1.29.70, contended that when humans behold the heavens and the earth, they cannot doubt that some being is over them, some author, some governor

Karl Barth on the Wrath of God

The wrath of God is the judgment under which we stand in so far as we do *not* love the Judge; it is the "No" which meets us when we do *not* affirm it; it is the protest pronounced always and everywhere against the course of the world in so far as we do *not* apprehend it; it is our boundedness and corruptibility in so far as we do *not* acknowledge their necessity. The judgment under which we stand is a fact, quite apart from our attitude to it. Indeed, it is the fact most characteristic of our life. Whether it enters within the light of salvation and of the coming world depends upon the answer we give to the problem of faith. But it is a fact, even should we choose the scandal rather than faith (1.16).

Karl Barth, *The Epistle to the Romans* (New York: Oxford Univ. Press, 1933), 43.

Heavenly Ladder

The instruction to the monks, as illustrated by the icon, reads: *"Good monks climb steadily heaven-wards toward perfection, bad monks are dragged to Hell by black devils."* Though framed by a hierarchy of ascending stages moving upward from the world and closer toward God, this ascent is based more upon the life of faith and the quest for a heavenly vision rather than the ascent of reason.

Johannes Klimax (c. 570–649) was the abbot of Saint Catherine's of Alexandria on Mt. Sinai. He was the author of the work *Klimax tou Paradeisou* or *Ladder of Paradise*. Addressing the monastic life, Klimax stresses that the passions are to be confronted and controlled before anyone embraces the contemplative way of living. The ladder represents the monastic journey through a series of thirty steps that ultimately lead to a mastery of the passions and a realization of the heavenly vision.

Heavenly Ladder. Illustration on an instruction to monks by abbot Johannes Klimax. c. 1100. St. Catherine Monastery. Mount Sinai. Sinai Desert, Egypt. (Credit: Erich Lessing/Art Resource, NY) of so stupendous a work of construction. Although humans cannot see God, they nevertheless can recognize deity from divine activity. This position, Cicero said, was that of Plato and Aristotle. There was, moreover, within Judaism a variation of the natural theology of the pagan world. Some Jews believed that one could reason from either nature or human nature to God. They believed, furthermore, that some Gentiles did this but others did not. For example, Wisdom of Solomon 13:1-9 claims pagans ought to have reasoned from the things made to their maker but have not done so. Philo, *On Rewards and Punishments* 43-46, spoke of admirable men who through contemplation of His works had ascended by reason, as if by some ladder reaching to heaven, to form a conception of the Creator. In his *On Abraham* 17.77-79, he said that Abraham reasoned from the world to its cause. In 33.185 he said that Abraham claimed that by contemplating the things that are seen one can arrive at a correct knowledge of God. In 35.195, Philo contended that knowledge of God also derives from contemplation of the human self. Likewise in the *Migration of Abraham* 35 reason's inference comes from the order and rule seen within humans themselves. Josephus, *Antiquities* 1.154-56, told how Abraham reasoned from the world to God. The later *Genesis Rabbah* 38.13 also tells how Abraham discovered the existence of God by reasoning back to a first cause. Some streams of early Christianity also fit into this stream of thought. Acts 14:15-17 says that there are signs in the natural world that witness to God. Whether or not they have been seen and received is not mentioned explicitly. The context of the speech (vv. 12, 13, 18) seems to indicate that the Gentiles had not attained a knowledge of God. Acts 17:27 says God made humans "that they should seek God, in the hope that they might feel after Him and find Him." Verses 29, 30a, 23 seem to indicate that rather than finding the Creator, the Gentiles worshiped the creation instead. They did not attain a knowledge of God. The emphasis in both speeches is on the fact that the Gentiles did not infer God's existence from the external world of nature.

A second option in antiquity proposed that belief in deity is innate in all humankind. Two examples suffice. Cicero, *Laws* 1.8.4 said: "There is no race so highly civilized or so savage that even if it does not know what sort of god it ought to have, yet thinks that it ought to have one." Dio Chrysostom, in his *Twelfth Discourse* 39, held that a conception of the nature of the gods, especially the highest one, is innate in all humans.

A third option is associated with certain circles of Hellenistic Judaism. These Jews held that knowledge of God came not from human reason's climbing the ladder to God but from God's self-revelation. *Sibylline Oracles* 3.8-45, especially 15-16, for example, says: "He Himself, eternal, revealed Himself as existing now, and formerly and again in the future." Philo (*Abr.* 80) says that it is impossible that people should themselves apprehend the truly Existent, "did not He reveal and manifest Himself." If humans know God, it is because of God's self-disclosure.

A fourth option is found in still other circles of ancient Judaism. Here it was held that knowledge of God comes in a two-step process. First, human reason is used to dispense with the plausibility of idols. Second, a divine disclosure is made to the seeker. Three documents illustrate this position. In *Jubilees* 12:16-24 Abraham infers God from looking at the stars. Then he prays and God answers with a promise. In *Testament of Job* 2–5 Job reasons that idols cannot be the creator of the heavens and the earth. Then his inference is confirmed by a revealing angel. In *Apocalypse of Abraham* 1–7 Abraham reasons that idols are not God for fire and water are greater. But beyond fire and water there is One. He prays and asks for a revelation of the true God. This happens.

An auditor of Romans who heard 1:20 might have thought Paul was speaking in terms of the ancient world's natural theology, where knowledge of God is the consummation of an upward ascent of the rational mind. Romans 1:19, however, says plainly that what can be known about God has been shown to humans by God: "For what can be known about God is plain to them, because God has shown it to them." This statement is closer to the point of view represented by *Sibylline Oracles* 3:15-16 than to any other of the options. In other words, Paul seems to have been speaking in terms of a general revelation rather than a natural theology. The general revelation has been mediated through "the things made" since the creation of the world, and consists of God's eternal power and divine nature (v. 20) and some moral sense (v. 32). In Paul's view, humans know God not by natural theology but by a general revelation apart from the revelation in Christ.[4] In this context in Romans, such a general revelation functions as an aid to the demonstration of human responsibility before God.

We can see the difference between Paul's approach and an argument from natural theology by taking notice of Wisdom of Solomon 13:1-9. There Gentiles fall short of the knowledge of God because they remain immersed in the world. Their ignorance is a deficiency caused by their failure to climb the ladder of reason all the way up from the knowledge of the creation to the Creator. For Wisdom of Solomon, knowledge of God is the consummation of

Similarities between Paul and the Wisdom of Solomon

In Rom 1 there are indications that Paul was indebted to the theological structure of thought found in the Wisdom of Solomon. The following chart illustrates the similarities between them.

A Jewish appraisal of the pagan world involves the following:

Idolatry is the source of all evil	Rom 1:22-23	Wis 14:12
Since God can be known, humans are without excuse	Rom 1:20	Wis 13:8
Idolatry results in immorality	Rom 1:24-27	Wis 14:22-27
Such immorality involves sexual perversion	Rom 1:24-27	Wis 14:24-26
A list of vices describes Gentile corruption	Rom 1:29-31	Wis 14:23-26
Idolatry leads to a corrupt mind	Rom 1:28,32	Wis 14:22b
Immorality contains within it its own punishment	Rom 1:27	Wis 14:31;16:24

A Jewish appraisal of the Jewish situation involves the following:

Gentile behavior is awful, but Jews do not behave like that	Rom 2:1	Wis 15:1-6, esp. v. 2

an upward ascent of the rational mind. The same perspective is found in Acts 14 and 17. [Similarities between Paul and the Wisdom of Solomon]

In Romans 1:18-32, however, Paul assumed that every individual already knows the truth about God due to a general revelation (1:19). Ignorance, then, is not due to the failure to reason one's way to knowledge of God, but is a consequence of a determined effort "to suppress the truth" that is already known (1:18, 21). The Gentiles, then, are not deficient but knowingly ignorant. This is because Paul assumed universal knowledge of God due to God's general revelation. Emil Brunner put Paul's perspective plainly.

> [T]here is no human existence without a relation to God. The pagan religions testify to this, too. They would not exist if God did not at first and inescapably declare Himself to everyone since the dawn of humanity in His works, in nature and history. The denial of such a "general revelation" preceding the historical revelation of grace in Jesus Christ can appeal neither to Paul nor the Bible at large.[5]

The principle stated by Paul in vv. 18-21 is that God's wrath is revealed because humans—or most of them—have rejected God's self-revelation. What follows are three illustrations of this principle in vv. 22-24, 25-27, and 28-32. To these illustrations we now turn.

The first illustration follows the order: rejection of the revelation, punishment. In vv. 22-23, Paul said humans "exchanged the glory of the immortal God for images resembling a mortal human being or birds or four footed animals or reptiles" (cf. Ps 106:20; Jer 2:11). This is human rejection of God's general revelation. In v. 24, the apostle stated the consequence. "Therefore God gave them up (= God's wrath) in the lusts of their hearts to impurity, to the degrading of their bodies among themselves." As the result of idolatry, God gives humans up to immorality.

Hellenistic Judaism contended that idolatry was the essence of the human predicament, not fate as ancient pagans believed. The pagan position can be seen in Apuleius's *Metamorphoses*. There, Lucius's problem was that he had been under the cruel dominion of Fortune/Fate, which had driven him through many dangerous experiences. Hence Lucius's salvation was expressed as "hostile fate has no power over those whose lives had been claimed by the majesty of our goddess" (= Isis, so *Metamorphoses* 11.15). If the human plight is bondage to Fate, then salvation is deliverance from Fate by a powerful deity. In contrast, the Hellenistic Jewish *Joseph and Aseneth* sees the predicament of Aseneth as her idolatry. By it she was cut off from the living God and therefore existed in a state of darkness, death, and destruction. She was not bound by Fate but defiled by idolatry. Hence, Aseneth's salvation was found in renouncing her idols, worshipping the God of Israel, and sharing in this life in the food and hence the immortality of the angels in Paradise. The apostle Paul stood with Hellenistic Judaism in diagnosing the human predicament as idolatry: worshipping something God made instead of the Creator. This happens when God's general revelation is rejected.

Idolatry, moreover, leads to immorality. This was also a stock belief of Hellenistic Judaism. Wisdom of Solomon 14 states the case clearly: "For the idea of making idols was the beginning of fornication, and the invention of them was the corruption of life" (14:12). Verse 27 repeats the idea: "For the worship of idols . . . is the beginning and cause . . . of every evil." Exactly how idolatry leads to immorality is stated in vv. 22-26.

> Then it was not enough for them to err about the knowledge of God.
> . . . whether they kill their children in their initiations, or celebrate secret mysteries, or hold frenzied revels with strange customs, they no longer keep either their lives or their marriages pure, but they treacherously kill one another, or grieve one another by adultery, and all is a raging riot of murder, theft and deceit, corruption, faithlessness, tumult, perjury, confusion over what is good, forgetfulness of favors, defiling of souls, sexual perversion, disorder in marriages, adultery and debauchery. (cf. *Sib* Or 3.764-66)

Paul stood with Hellenistic Judaism in affirming that idolatry leads to immorality (cf. 1 Cor 10:6-8). If the essence of sin is idolatry, one fruit of sin is immorality. God's wrath is expressed by giving idolatrous humans over to immorality. [Godlessness]

The second illustration comes in vv. 25-27. Again the order is: rejection of revelation, punishment. In v. 25 Paul stated the problem. "They exchanged the truth about God for a lie and worshipped and served the creature rather than the Creator." Once the general revelation is rejected, idolatry reigns. Humans worship and serve something God has made rather than the God who made it. Verses 26-27 sketch the consequences. "For this reason God gave them up (= God's wrath) to degrading passions."

> **Godlessness**
>
> According to William Barclay, godlessness "is the total disregard of God; it is treating God as if He did not exist. It is not atheism, for atheism does not believe that there is a God. Godlessness knows that there is a God—and totally disregards Him; it is therefore even worse than atheism."
>
> William Barclay, *The Mind of St. Paul* (NY: Harper & Brothers, 1958), 191.

The immorality is described in sexual terms. "Their women exchanged natural intercourse for unnatural, and in the same way also the men, giving up natural intercourse with women, were consumed with passion for one another. Men committed shameless acts with men and received in their own persons the due penalty for their error." Several separate issues arise from this statement about homosexual practice.[6]

First, both female (v. 26) and male (v. 27) homosexual practices are described. The OT does not mention female homosexual practices but postbiblical Jewish sources denounce such acts (*Ps-Phocylides* 192; *Sifra on Lev* 18:3 describes marriage between women as a practice of Canaanites and Egyptians; *b. Sabb* 65a; *b. Yebam* 76a; possibly Philo, *Spec* 3.51; *Sacr* 100; *Her* 274; *Virt* 21[7]). Female homosexual practice was mentioned by pagan sources of our period (Plautus, *Truculentus* 262-63; Seneca the Elder, *Controversiae* 1.2.23, referred to a man who caught his wife and another woman in bed together and killed them both; Ovid, *Metamorposes* 9.758, mentioned a girl who loved another, who yet knew "nature does not will it"; Martial, *Epigrams* 7.67.1-3, spoke about a woman who was sexually aggressive towards girls and battered eleven in a day; Iamblichus's novel *Babyloniaka* tells of the love of Berenike for Mesopotamia, with whom she slept and whom she then married; Lucian, *Dialogi meretricum* 5.2; *Amores* 28; Plutarch, *Lycurgus* 18). Women who had sexual relations with other women were increasingly becoming a matter of concern to male authors in the late republican and early imperial Roman period.[8] Juvenal, *Satires* 6.306-13, was typical when he treated it with disgust. The Socrates of both Plato (*Symposium* 217-19) and of

Xenophon (*Memorabilia* 2.1.32) condemned homosexual copulation. Socrates had an absolutist rejection of all genital relations between males. Plato, *Laws* 1.2 [636B-C] spoke of sexual relations between men and between women as "contrary to nature" [a different perspective from that in Plato's *Symposium*].

The OT rejects male homosexual practice generally (Lev 18:22; 20:13). This rejection is continued in postbiblical Jewish sources (e.g., Wis 14:26; *Ep Arist* 152; Philo, *On Abraham* XXVI.135-36; *Special Laws* 2.XIV.50; *Ps-Phocylides* 190-91; Josephus, *Against Apion* 2.25 + 199; *Sib Or* 2.73; 3.185-87,594-600,763; 5.386-433; *2 Enoch* 10:4; *T. Levi* 14:6; 17:11; *T. Naph* 4:1).

The early church fathers continued the opposition (Aristides, *Apology* 17, against both male and female homosexual practice; Polycarp, *Philippians* 5.3; *Apocalypse of Peter*, where hell includes both male and female homosexual practitioners; cf. Syriac version of the *Acts of Thomas* 6.55; *Apocalypse of Paul* 39; Tertullian, *De Corona* 6.1; *On the Resurrection of the Flesh* 16.6; Clement of Alexandria, *Paidagogos* 2.10.83.3; 3.3.21.3; Chrysostom, *Homily 4 on Romans*).

Homosexual marriages were known and condemned as well (e.g., *Sifra on Lev* 18:3; Suetonius, "Nero," told with disgust how Nero castrated the boy Sporus and married him with all the usual ceremonies, including a dowry and a bridal veil, took him to his house and treated him as his wife). Paul belonged to the larger stream of ancient thought that was opposed to homosexual practice. His "indictment seems to include all kinds of homosexual practice, female as well as male, and was not directed against one kind of homosexual practice in distinction from another."[9]

Second, Paul described homosexual practice as unnatural or against nature (v. 26-27). In this he shared the views of some pagans and of Hellenistic Judaism. For example, Plato, *Laws* 1.2 [636B-C] said same-sex relations were "contrary to nature"; Ovid, *Metamorphoses* 9.758, had a girl involved in same sex love say "nature does not will it"; Ps-Lucian, *Erotes* 19, said female homoeroticism is contrary to nature. The view was unanimous in Hellenistic Judaism. Philo, *On Abraham* XXVI.135, spoke about men, discarding laws of nature, lusting after one another. In *Special Laws* 2.XIV.50, he talked about men lusting unnaturally. *T. Naphtali* 3:4 said: "Do not become like Sodom, which departed from the order of nature." *Ps-Phocylides* 190 exhorted the readers not to transgress sexually the limits set by nature. Josephus, *Against Apion* 2.25 + 199, said the law "owns no other mixture of sexes but that which nature has appointed. . . . It abhors the mixture of a

Bacchanal

Bacchanal refers to the drunken revelry of Bacchus, the Roman god of wine, and his hedonistic entourage. While the Romans officially banned the cult of Bacchus in 186 BC, Roman banquets frequently involved drunken sexual activity, a feature often criticized by ancient writers such as Plutarch.

Andrea Mantegna. 1431–1506. *Bacchanal with the Tub.* Drawing. c. 1400. Gabinetto dei Disegni e delle Stampe. Uffizi, Florence, Italy. (Credit: Alinari/Art Resource, NY)

male with a male." *Second Enoch* 10:4 regards homosexual practice as a sin against nature. This Jewish contention was continued by the early fathers. Polycarp, *Philippians* 5.3, for example, said that those given to unnatural vice would not share in the kingdom of God. Clement of Alexandria, *Stromateis* 2.12.55 and 7.10.59, said women who married women acted contrary to nature. For him, the Genesis creation narratives laid the framework for understanding nature as gendered. John Chrysostom's *Fourth Homily on Romans* treats both male and female homoeroticism as unnatural. In all of these sources, the conviction is that God's intention in creation (Genesis 1–2) was a union of heterosexual partners and that only after the Fall (Gen 3) did homosexual practice enter human history. Plato, *Leg* 636b,c, regarded intercourse that is according to nature as that which leads to procreation. Philo, *Abr* 137, took the same position. These two references are representative of antiquity. Intercourse that is according to nature is that with the possibility of begetting children. In both of these senses, Paul would have regarded homosexual practice as unnatural.

Third, Paul linked homosexual practice with idolatry. In Hellenistic Judaism the same link was made. Two examples suffice. In Wisdom of Solomon 14:26 "sexual perversion" is listed as one of the fruits of the worship of idols. *Sibylline Oracles* 5.386-433 links homosexual practice with idolatry. Recognizing the Creator and acknowledging God's order in creation leads to proper sexual practice. To "suppress the truth" about God and the divine intention in creation leads to disorder in human sexuality. This includes both disorder in heterosexual relationships and the disorder of homosexual practice. For Paul and the Judaism from which he came, idolatry was the root of sexual disorders.

Fourth, Paul said that as a result of homosexual practice men "received in their own persons the due penalty for their error" (v. 27b). This refers not just to "permanent uncontrollable desire to enagage in the activity in question"[10] but rather to disease, both physical and psychological. Philo, *On Abraham* XXVI.136, said that when men discard the laws of nature and lust after one another, their practices result in disease. In *Special Laws* III.37, Philo contended that men who engage in homosexual practice waste away in both their souls and their bodies. In ancient Judaism, sexual sins of all kinds, heterosexual as well as homosexual, were believed to be sins against one's own body/self (Prov 5:11, in context; 6:32; 1 Cor 6:18; cf. Musonius Rufus's assertion that the man who has intercourse with *hetairae* [prostitutes] sins against himself, for a pagan version of the same conviction).[11] Wisdom of Solomon 16:24 states the assumptions of Hellenistic Judaism. "For creation, serving you who made it, exerts itself to punish the unrighteous, and in kindness relaxes on behalf of those who trust in you." Human behavior that runs counter to God's order in creation pays a price at the hands of the very natural order that is violated. Why? Because it is God's world and it cooperates with God's purposes and resists those who do not cooperate. *T. Gad* 5:10 puts it this way: "by whatever human capacity anyone transgresses, by that he is also chastised." The same sentiment is found in the pagan world. Epictetus, *Discourses* 3.11.1, said: "There are certain punishments, assigned as it were by law, for those who are disobedient to the divine dispensation." The philosopher spoke about the law of nature which, when violated, issues in punishment. Similarly, Paul did not speak about direct divine retribution. He said, "God gave them up" to their misguided desires. As a result, the natural world, when violated, exacts its toll. In Paul's second illustration idolatry has again resulted in immorality. God's wrath is seen as God's giving humans who have acted unnaturally in their worship over to unnatural sexual practices and the diseases that result.

The third illustration also follows the order: rejection of the revelation (v. 28a), punishment (vv. 28b-32). The rejection of God's revelation is described here as "since they did not see fit to acknowledge God." The consequences of such behavior are described as "God gave them up to a debased mind and to things that should not be done." Whereas formerly God's giving humans up consisted only of sensuality, now it includes much more. The "things which should not be done" are listed in vv. 29-31; the debased mind is illustrated in v. 32. In vv. 29-31 Paul included a catalog of vices.

Seven Deadly Sins

Christian tradition developed a catalog of vices known as the Seven Deadly Sins, as indicated in the wheel scene by Bosch. The particular sins are (clockwise from top): gluttony, sloth, lust, pride, wrath, envy, and avarice.

Hieronymus Bosch. 1450–1516. Center piece from *The Seven Deadly Sins.* Museo del Prado. Madrid, Spain. (Credit: Erich Lessing/Art Resource, NY)

> They were filled with every kind of wickedness, evil, covetousness, malice. Full of envy, murder, strife, deceit, craftiness, they are gossips, slanderers. God-haters, insolent, haughty, boastful, inventors of evil, rebellious toward parents, foolish, faithless, heartless, ruthless.

Such catalogs of vices are found elsewhere among philosophers (Plato, *Gorgias* 525; *Republic* 4.441c), in Judaism (Wis 14:23-26; Philo, *Sac* 32; 4 Macc 1:26-27; *T. Levi* 14:5-8; CD 4.17-18; 1 QS 4.9-11), and in early Christian sources (Gal 5:19-21; 1 Cor 5:9-11; 6:9-10; Rom 13:12-14; Mark 7:21-22; Rev 21:7-8; 1 *Clem* 35:5; *Ep Barn* 20:1; *Did* 5:1). Enough difference exists in the contents of the various lists to show that there was no standard catalog of vices that Paul was taking over. He was using a standard form with his own content. Romans 1:29-30, like Galatians 5:19-21, deals with vices that go beyond sensuality into antisocial attitudes and behavior directed towards both humans and God. Such immoral behavior, said the apostle, results from idolatry. But that is not all. In v. 32 Paul spoke about the debased mind that results from idolatry. "They know God's decree, that those who practice such things deserve to die—yet they not only do them but even applaud others who practice them." This was a sentiment expressed in Paul's Jewish tradition. Isaiah 5:20 refers to those who "call evil good and good evil, who put darkness for light and light for darkness, who put bitter for sweet and sweet for bitter!" *T. Asher* 6:2, in speaking about the two-faced, uses similar language. "The two-faced are doubly punished because they both practice evil and approve of others who practice it." Wisdom of Solomon 14:22 says of idolaters involved in immoralities: "they call such great evils peace." The same sentiment can be found in the pagan Seneca, *Epistle* 39.6. Nevertheless, 1:32 implies that some knowledge of God remains even after a person has suppressed it.

In Romans 1:18-32, Paul assumed humans (Gentiles) were worshiping beings, acting beings, and thinking beings. He talked about us in a way that shows how sin affects all three levels of the self. When humans worship the creature/creation rather than the Creator, that is idolatry. What begins at the level of what one worships inevitably passes over into the area of how one behaves. The result is immorality. Furthermore, what has affected one's worship and one's behavior eventually corrupts one's reason. [The Effects of Sin on Human Relations] The result is that idolaters who are also immoral attempt either to justify their own behavior or to applaud others who join them in their immorality. Quimby has noted, "Rationalization is the art of putting fine-sounding excuses on wrong actions, and 'fine' reasons for bad purposes."[12]

The Effects of Sin on Human Reason

Emil Brunner has said:

The nearer anything lies to that center of existence where we are concerned with the whole, that is, with man's relation to God and the being of the person, the greater is the disturbance of rational knowledge by sin; the farther away anything lies from this center, the less is the disturbance felt, and the less difference is there between knowing as a believer or as an unbeliever.

For example, the social sciences (psychology, sociology, economics, anthropology) deal directly with the center of our existence and so are more subject to rational distortion than the natural sciences and math. A Christian can profitably employ a "hermeneutics of suspicion" (= a reading that asks what is assumed and who stands to profit by the stated positions) especially when evaluating the claims of the social sciences because of this fact of fallenness.

Emil Brunner, *Revelation and Reason* (Philadelphia: Westminster, 1946), 383.

Fallen humans are natural spin doctors! For Paul, the surest sign of original sin was our infinite capacity for rationalization.[13] The Stoic philosopher Seneca bemoaned this circumstance. He said, "We push one another into vice. And how can a man be recalled to salvation when he has none to restrain him and all mankind to urge him on" (*Epistle* 41)? From Paul's point of view, humans are corrupted totally. This does not mean humans are as bad as we can be but rather that a human's entire selfhood is affected by sin. Human depravity means total in extent not total in degree. There is no part of a human (Gentile) self that is untouched.

There was no one Jewish view of Gentiles in Mediterranean antiquity. Some Jews regarded the Gentiles as "aliens from the commonwealth of Israel, strangers to the covenants of promise, having no hope, and as without God in the world" (Eph 2:12; cf. *Jubilees* 15:26; *t. Sanh* 13:2, citing R. Eliezer about AD 100). Other Jews believed that there were some righteous Gentiles. Although not converts to Judaism, these Gentiles will have a place in the world to come (*t. Sanh* 13:2, citing R. Joshua about AD 100; cf. Rom 2:15-16). Still others thought that some Gentiles could either become proselytes to Judaism (Jdt 14:10) or be included among the eschatological pilgrims who respond to God's saving vindication of Israel in the eschatological future (Isa 2:2-4; Tob 13:11; 14:5-7). In Romans 1:18-32, Paul was assuming what most likely was the most common view of Gentiles among ancient Jews, the first of our list. Gentile life is described entirely in negative terms (cf. Eph 2:12). Idolatry, immorality, and a debased reason characterize the Gentiles. With this depiction most ancient Jews would have agreed. The Gentiles are, of course, unrighteous.

By contrast, ancient Jews often said of themselves: "but we will not sin, because we know that you acknowledge us as yours. For to know you is complete righteousness" (Wis 15:2). Since Paul had been following the structure of the thought of Wisdom of Solomon 13–14 in Romans 1:18-32, it is not surprising that he followed Wisdom chapter 15 in Romans 2. Such an attitude of Jewish pride presented Paul his challenge in Romans 2:1–3:20.

CONNECTIONS

Natural Theology and General Revelation

Romans 1:18-32 raises a number of questions for the modern reader. The first is obviously the issue of the possibility of a knowledge of God outside the revelation in Israel and in Jesus. Proofs for the existence of God achieved a climax in the philosophical-theological system of Thomas Aquinas.[14] The five arguments of Thomas may be summarized. (1) Since motion exists, a First Mover must be assumed. (2) Since things are caused, a First Causer must be assumed. (3) Since contingent things exist, a necessary being must be assumed. (4) Since varying degrees of perfection exist, an infinitely perfect being must be assumed. (5) Since things show evidence of design, a designing intelligence must be assumed. The first four arguments are various forms of the cosmological argument since they argue from the world to God. The fifth is a form of the teleological argument since it argues from design in the world to a designing intelligence. To the cosmological and teleological arguments traditional theism has added two others: the ontological and the moral. The ontological argument was expressed clearly by Anselm. He contended that the idea of something "than which nothing greater can be conceived" includes within itself the existence of the object. Otherwise it would not be "greater than which nothing can be conceived." Hence God, who by definition is "greater than which nothing can be conceived," exists. Immanuel Kant's moral argument is found in his *Critique of Pure Reason*. Believing moral experience (= an absolute and universal experience of obligation to respect persons) beyond doubt, Kant asked upon what basis is this moral experience intelligible? Three things: freedom, immortality, and God. Modern scholars, however, tend to discount the traditional arguments for the existence of God. Natural theology is highly suspect to modern intellectuals.

Paul, however, was not arguing for natural theology. He rather spoke of general revelation. General revelation has four main characteristics.[15] First, it is general because it is made to everyone everywhere. Special revelation is made to particular people in particular times and places (Israel and Jesus). Second, it is made through the natural order: the world and the human self. Special revelation involves the history of Israel and the incarnation. Third, it is continuous. It has gone on since the creation of the world. Special revelation comes to completion in Jesus and scripture. Fourth, it reveals God as Creator. Special revelation reveals God as Savior.

John Baillie's old book, *Our Knowledge of God*, is a classic statement of Paul's position.[16] Baillie asked if there is a human consciousness that has never been invaded by the divine. He then replied:

> It is clear to me that I cannot find such a consciousness by going back to the beginnings of my own experience. No matter how far back I go, . . . I cannot get back to an atheistic mentality. . . . My earliest memories have a definitely religious atmosphere. They are already heavy with 'the numinous.'[17]

This awareness of God, moreover, he said, contained within it a sense of obligation.[18] Baillie's reflections are a modern statement very much like that of Paul in Romans 1.

This theological treatise's thesis is reinforced by the field work of psychiatrist Robert Coles. In his *The Spiritual Life of Children*,[19] from his field work all over the world, with Jewish, Christian, Islamic, Hopi, and secular children, Coles has offered evidence that all children have a sense of God. They often communicate with God, sometimes have visionary experiences, and frequently reflect on God and life. Coles has called children "pilgrims" who are trying to figure out what it all means and where it all leads. Often as they age, the culture suppresses what is so natural to the young. This sounds remarkably like Romans 1:18-32.

Paul did not think that this natural consciousness of God is saving knowledge. It is, however, the beachhead on which the gospel can land with its saving message. There was, moreover, for Paul enough knowledge of God and the divine will derived from general revelation to hold humans responsible for our idolatry, immorality, and rationalization.

Discerning Religions and Gods

What is religion? What are religions? Lesslie Newbigin has suggested the following:

> [Religion consists of] all those commitments that . . . have an overriding authority over all other commitments and provide that framework within which all experience is grasped and all ideas judged.[20]

What is a god? Bruce C. Birch and Larry L. Rasmussen have spoken of our functional deities. "[O]ur lives take shape in keeping with our functional deities (the objects of most basic trust and loyalty). And our social world is already alive with these 'gods' as we enter it."[21]

If our gods are our centers of value and our religion consists of our overriding commitments, then one's real religion/deity may not be his or her stated religion. A person's covert religion must be distinguished from his or her overt religion. One may, for example, be a professing Christian but a practicing secularist or polytheist. Moreover, one may be totally unaware, at the conscious level, of one's true religion and deities.

In these terms, it is possible to say that western culture is idolatrous because it is, like the Gentile world of Romans 1:18-32, polytheistic. We have multiple centers of value or functional deities that are the recipients of our commitments in a variety of areas of our lives.

Human Sexuality

Another area of concern raised by Romans 1:18-32 is Paul's claim that sexual excess and perversion are due to idolatry and represent God's giving humans over to what we have voted for: idolatrous sexuality. There are four main attitudes toward sex in society.[22] The first holds that sex is vile. So flee it; abstain. The second maintains that sex is necessary, yet debasing. So be embarrassed about it when you, of necessity, engage in it. The third contends that sex is the be-all and end-all of life. So revel in it with no restraints. Push the boundaries! The fourth believes sex is God's good gift to be used joyously and responsibly as the Creator intended: within heterosexual marriage. So enjoy it God's way. Clearly in Romans 1:18-32 Paul saw Gentile practice reflecting attitude three. It is the attitude assumed in virtually all of Western mass media. Modern North Americans tend to think of the self as a helpless victim of the body's desires, "desires we imagine as plotted in the genes, born with the body, and knowing its objects when it sees them—irreducible, nonnegotiable, 'natural,' built-in desires."[23] From Paul's perspective, when a culture loses its focus on God, it obsesses about sex. Obsession about sex is an indicator of an individual's or a society's suppression of the knowledge of God. Promiscuity and perversion result with STDs and psychological and social damage following in their wake. Peter Kocan's poem, "AIDS, Among Other Things," relates Romans 6:23 powerfully to the issue at hand.[24]

Perhaps the most perplexing sexual issue raised by Romans 1:18-32 is the matter of Paul's attitude towards homosexual practice. It is without a doubt negative. Is that value judgment normative for contemporary Christians? In order to answer that question, one must first answer a prior question. What role does the ethical material in the Bible play in the construction of a normative Christian ethic for today? How is such material to be used in constructive Christian ethics? The rule of thumb that controls all reading is: read a text in its context. Taking this admonition seriously, we say that one should read the Bible's ethical material in the context of the total biblical plot.

What is that plot? The Bible tells a story that runs from Creation through the Fall to the Covenant with Abraham and Israel, to Christ, to the Church, and ultimately to the Consummation. If one reads the Bible's references to homosexual practice in this context, certain interpretations result. First, according to the story of creation (Gen 1–2) God's intention in creation is that humans be equal as persons but different as sexual beings. These different sexual beings, male and female, are intended for one another and are to become one flesh. It is only after the Fall (Gen 3) that homosexuality is mentioned (Lev 18, 20). When it is mentioned, it is regarded negatively. This would be because such practice runs counter to God's intention in creation. Jesus never mentioned homosexuality. This is likely because it was regarded so negatively in his Jewish context that it presented no problem that he had to address. Paul, in the period of the Church, while working in the Gentile world in which homosexual practice was widespread, did address it. When he did, the practice was always regarded negatively. Indeed, at no point in the Bible is the practice ever spoken of other than in negative terms. Reading Paul's words in Romans 1 in the context of the total biblical plot indicates that what he had to say reflected God's intention in creation and that homosexual practice reflects the Fall.[25] A second question may be raised about Paul's view on homosexuality. Can it really be said to be against nature or to be unnatural? Why is there sexual differentiation among humans? Viewed biologically, sexual differentiation and sexual practice exist for the propagation of the species. In order to ensure their use, such activity is pleasurable. In order to provide care for the young, sexual desire is continual in humans. This encourages the partners to stay together year round. Repeated sexual contact over time also bonds the two partners together. Again, this encourages them to stay together year after year. Staying together is necessary for the care of the human young, who mature slowly. Speaking biologically, all of this is to ensure the perpetuation of the species. If so, then sexual liaisons that do not function with at least this potential run counter to nature. No sexual ethic can stray too far from the biological roots of sexual differentiation and practice.[26] If the biological roots of human sexuality are taken seriously, what can be said about people whose orientation seems to be only towards the same sex? Did God create them that way? The debate over whether or not a person is born homosexual is scientifically undecided. There is not conclusive evidence either way. If, for the sake of argument, one assumes that it might be possible for a person to be born with a homosexual orientation, what then? Given the argument so far, the logic of Paul's thought is that the orientation is a flaw, much like tendencies toward alcoholism, dwarfism, or sociopathology with which people are born, and the practice is a sin insofar as it deviates from God's intention in creation. In 1 Corinthians 6:9-11, moreover, Paul assumed that the practice could be cured by radical conversion.

Modern Christians who seek to adhere to the biblical values expressed by Paul will neither celebrate homosexual practice nor single it out as the only sin expressing human fallenness. Furthermore, if homosexual acts are wrong, those committing them are sinners, like the rest of us, who are in need of a Savior. So Christians are called to show Christ's love to them, not a radical intolerance. While acknowledging that the Bible regards all sexual activity outside of a permanent heterosexual marriage as sin, Christians must also confess that we are all sinners being saved by grace. Whereas Christians should love and welcome all sinners, we cannot, however, affirm and condone all actions and ways of life. The church is a place of transformation, discipline, and learning, not merely a place to be indulged.

Balancing the welcome of sinners and the maintenance of God's standards is perhaps the most difficult task of the church in all times and places. Alexander Pope (1688–1744), *An Essay on Man*, Epistle II, line 217, pointed to a reason why.

Vice is a monster of so frightful mien,
As to be hated needs but to be seen;
Yet seen too oft, familiar with her face,
We first endure, then pity, then embrace.

Perhaps that is why Paul in 1 Corinthians 5 called for the expulsion of the sinful man who gloried in his sin by the community of Christ that was beginning to glory with him.

Wolfhart Pannenberg has contended that a church that has "ceased to treat homosexual activity as a departure from the biblical norm . . . would stand no longer on biblical ground but against the unequivocal witness of scripture." Such a church "would thereby have ceased to be one, holy, catholic, and apostolic."[27]

NOTES

[1] Abraham J. Malherbe, *Moral Exhortation: A Greco-Roman Sourcebook* (Philadelphia: Westminster, 1986), 123.

[2] This fact renders the hypothesis of a non-Pauline interpolation unnecessary. Contra W. O. Walker, Jr., "Romans 1:18–2:29: A Non-Pauline Interpolation?" *NTS* 45 (1999): 533-52, especially 540-41.

[3] John Stott, *Romans: God's Good News for the World* (Downers Grove: InterVarsity, 1994), 72.

[4] Bo Reicke, "Natürliche Theologie nach Paulus," *Svensk Exegetisk Arsbok* 22/23 (1957–1958): 154-67.

[5] Emil Brunner, *The Letter to the Romans* (Philadelphia: Westminster, 1959), 17.

[6] For a fuller statement regarding homosexuality in relation to 1 Corinthians 6:9-11, see Charles H. Talbert, *Reading Corinthians* (Macon GA: Smyth & Helwys, 2002), 22-26.

[7] Holger Szesnat, "Philo and Female Eroticism," *JSJ* 30 (1999) 140-47.

[8] J. P. Hallett, "Female Homoeroticism and the Denial of Roman Reality in Latin Literature," *Yale Journal of Criticism* 3 (1989): 209-27.

[9] James D. G. Dunn, *Romans 1–8* (WBC; Dallas: Word, 1988), 1.65.

[10] As is claimed by Brendan Byrne, *Sacra Pagina, 6: Romans* (Collegeville: Liturgical Press, 1996), 70.

[11] Bruce N. Fisk, "*Porneuein* as Body Violation: The Unique Nature of Sexual Sin in 1 Corinthians 6:18," *NTS* 42 (1996): 540-58.

[12] Chester Warren Quimby, *The Great Redemption* (NY: Macmillan, 1950), 59.

[13] Merold Westphal, "Taking St. Paul Seriously: Sin as an Epistemological Category," in *Christian Philosophy*, ed. Thomas P. Flint (Notre Dame IN: University of Notre Dame Press, 1990); Stephen K. Moroney, "How Sin Affects Scholarship: A New Model," *Christian Scholar's Review* 28 (1999): 432-51.

[14] Thomas Aquinas, *Summa Theologica*, Part I, Question 2, Third Article.

[15] John Stott, *Romans*, 73.

[16] John Baillie, *Our Knowledge of God* (NY: Charles Scribner's Sons, 1939).

[17] Baillie, *Our Knowledge*, 4.

[18] Ibid., 4-5, 182-83.

[19] Robert Coles, *The Spiritual Life of Children* (Boston: Houghton Mifflin Company, 1990).

[20] Lesslie Newbigin, *The Open Secret: An Introduction to the Theology of Mission* (Grand Rapids: Eerdmans, 1978), 160.

[21] Bruce C. Birch and Larry L. Rasmussen, *Bible and Ethics in the Christian Life* (Minneapolis: Augsburg Publishing House, 1976), 87.

[22] Quimby, 47.

[23] Margaret R. Miles, "Disney Spirituality: An Oxymoron?" *Christian Spirituality Bulletin* 7 (1999), 17.

[24] Robert Atwan & Laurance Wieder, eds., *Chapters Into Verse: Volume 2: Gospels to Revelation* (NY: Oxford University Press, 1993), 268-69 (selected from *Freedom to Breathe*, 1985, and used by permission of Collins/Angus & Robertson Publishers).

[25] A helpful statement of the biblical perspective on homosexual practice may be found in Richard B. Hays, *The Moral Vision of the New Testament* (San Francisco: Harper, 1996), 379-406. Stanley Grenz, *Sexual Ethics: An Evangelical Perspective* (Louisville: Westminster John Knox, 1997), offers a clear affirmation of the Pauline perspective and a critique of writers of a different persuasion. John Nolland, "Romans 1:26-27 and the Homosexuality Debate," *Horizons in Biblical Theology* 22 (2000): 32-57, offers a wide ranging critique of the latest prohomosexual arguments. The best single treatment of the issue is Robert A. J. Gagnon, *The Bible and Homosexual Practice: Texts and Hermeneutics* (Nashville: Abingdon Press, 2001).

[26] Walter Burkert, *Creation of the Sacred: Tracks of Biology in Early Religions* (Cambridge: Harvard University Press, 1998), argues the thesis that religions follow biological preconditions.

[27] In an article in *Church Times* of June 21, 1996, cited by R. T. France, "From Romans to the Real World: Biblical Principles and Cultural Change in Relation to Homosexuality and the Ministry of Women," in *Romans and the People of God*, ed. S. K. Soderlund and N. T. Wright (Grand Rapids: Eerdmans, 1999), 249, n. 20. France's article is a hermeneutical justification for ordaining women while declining to endorse homosexual practice.

THE HUMAN CONDITION, PART TWO

2:1–3:20

In his pursuit of his conclusion that "all are sinners" Paul, in Romans 1:18-32, argued a case that the average Jew would uphold: Gentiles are ungodly and unrighteous. They are idolaters, immoral, and have corrupted minds. Paul must then argue a harder case: Jews also stand under God's judgment. Remember, Paul was following the argument of Wisdom of Solomon 13–14 in Romans 1:18-32. Then he moved to Wisdom of Solomon 15:2 where the Jews said: "We will not sin, because we know you acknowledge us as yours." This part of Paul's argument runs from 2:1–3:20. Remember, although the written argument is with the non-Christian Jew, the auditors were mostly Gentile Christians in Rome (1:5-6, 13-15). An outline of the argument makes following it easier.

COMMENTARY

The Unrighteousness of the Jew, 2:1–3:20

I. The self-righteous Jews who act as Gentiles do will not escape divine judgment (2:1-3)
   A. The principle (2:2)
   B. The application (2:1,3)
II. The presumptuous Jews who take God's kindness for granted will also receive wrath at the judgment because God is impartial (2:4-11)
   A. The principle (2:4-5)
   B. The basis (2:6-11)
III. Gentile and Jew alike will be judged (2:12-29)
   A. The principle (2:12-13)
   B. The application (2:14-29)
      1. Those without the law (2:14-16)
      2. Those under the law (2:17-29)

a. those who know the law but disobey it (vv. 17-24)

b. those who are physically but not inwardly circumcised (vv. 25-29)

IV. Jewish objections answered, using a diatribe form (3:1-20)

A. Objection One (3:1-2)

B. Objection Two (3:3-4)

C. Objection Three (3:5-6)

D. Objection Four (3:7-8)

E. Objection Five (3:9-20)

The argument must be traced, following the various parts of this outline.

The first step of Paul's argument comes in 2:1-3. In form, it moves from an indicting statement (v. 1), to a confession of common knowledge (v. 2), to a rhetorical question (v. 3). In content, it consists of a principle (v. 2) and an application (vv. 1, 3). What is the apostle's point? The self-righteous Jews who act as Gentiles do will not escape divine judgment. In v. 2 Paul said: "We know (cf. 3:19; 7:14; 8:22, 28) that God's judgment on those who do such things is in accordance with truth." "Such things" is a reference back to 1:32's "such things" (= 1:19-31). The reference is to the behavior of the Gentiles. That behavior merits judgment. This principle is common knowledge. Verse 1 draws the inference: "Therefore you have no excuse (cf. 1:20), whoever you are, when you judge others; for in passing judgment on another you condemn yourself, because, you, the judge, are doing the very same things" (cf. 1:29-31). Then comes the incredulous question in v. 3: "Do you imagine, whoever you are, that when you judge those who do such things and yet do them yourself, you will escape the judgment of God?" Of course, the implied answer to this rhetorical question is: No! You will not escape judgment if you are doing such things, not even if you are a Jew. The *Psalms of Solomon* 15:8 reflects the same sentiment. "Those who act lawlessly shall not escape the Lord's judgment." John the Baptist took a similar stand (Matt 3:7-10). Paul, then, was using a typically Jewish argument[1] against self-righteous but lawless Jews (cf. Matt 7:1-2). He said thereby: when judged by your own standards, you do poorly.

The second part of Paul's argument comes in 2:4-11. In form this unit consists of two rhetorical questions (v. 4a; v. 4b), an indicting statement (v. 5), and a section of tradition organized in a concentric pattern (vv. 6-11). In content, the apostle stated a principle (vv 4-5) and followed it with its basis (vv 6-11). What is the point? Paul said that the presumptuous Jew who takes God's kindness for granted (cf. Wis 15:1-2) would also receive wrath at the judgment because God is impartial (= fair). The principle comes in v.s 4-5. "Or do you despise the riches of His kindness and forbearance and patience (by continuing to behave as the Gentiles do when there is no immediate judgment for such behavior)? Do you not realize that God's kindness is meant to lead you to repentance?" [Repentance] The equation of God's patience with the suppression of God's wrath was a Jewish commonplace (*2 Bar* 21:20). The concern is that this not be taken as God's weakness. Wisdom of Solomon 11:23 says to God: "But you are merciful to all . . . and you overlook people's sins, so that they may repent." *Testament of Abraham* 10:18 says God puts off a sinner's death until he turns again and lives. Of course, failure to profit from God's kindness leads to disaster. Sirach 5:4-7 speaks of the Lord's being slow to anger but also exhorts: "Do not delay to turn to the Lord, nor postpone it from day to day, for suddenly the wrath of the Lord will go forth, and at the time of punishment you will perish." So in v. 5 Paul said: "By your hard and impenitent heart you are storing up wrath for yourself on the day of wrath (cf. Zeph 1:15, 18; 2:2-3), when God's righteous judgment will be revealed."

The basis for the claim that judgment will come upon such presumptuous behavior comes in v.s 6-11. The material is presented in a concentric pattern.

> a. God will repay everyone according to his deeds (v. 6)
>   b. Eternal life for those who do good (v. 7)
>   c. Wrath (cf. 1:18) and fury for those who disobey (v. 8)
>   c'. Distress and anguish for those who do evil (v. 9)
>   b'. Glory, honor, and peace for those who do good (v. 10)
> a'. There is no partiality with God (v. 11)[2]

There are many parallels to the idea that God will repay everyone according to his deeds. Sirach 35:13 says: "The Lord is the one who repays." Psalm 62:12 reads: "You repay to all according to their work" (cf. Prov 24:12; Jer 25:14; Lam 3:64). In the *Testament of Abraham*, chapters 12–13, we hear that all people are judged by their deeds. *First Enoch* 95:5 ("you shall be rewarded in accordance

Repentance

AΩ One way of speaking about conversion in the New Testament is by the use of the term repentance. Its roots are in the Scriptures of Israel (e.g., Isa 1:27; Jer 3:12-14, 22). Post biblical nonmessianic Judaism continued the practice (e.g., Sir 17:24-26; *Jub* 5:17-18; *Pss Sol* 9; *T. Gad* 5:3-8). John the Baptist made repentance central to his ministry (Mark 1:4; Matt 3:2; Luke 3:8). Jesus continued John's emphasis with modifications (Matt 4:17; Luke 5:32; Mark 1:15; Luke 24:47). In the Acts of the Apostles, both Peter (2:38; 5:31) and Paul (17:30-31; 26:20) make repentance central to their preaching. The Pauline corpus does not often use the term (e.g., Rom 2:4; 2 Cor 12:21; 2 Tim 2:25). Other terms, such as faith, replace it. Hebrews knows the concept (6:6, 6), as does 2 Peter (3:9) and the Revelation to John (2:5, 16, 21, 22; 3:3, 19). When talking about conversion by means of the term repentance, what is emphasized is a change of mind and an about-face in direction.

with your deeds"), 100:7 ("you shall be recompensed according to your deeds"), and *2 Baruch* 54:21 ("At the end of the world, a retribution will be demanded with regard to those who have done wickedly in accordance with their wickedness") continue the theme.

Jewish literature also portrays God as an impartial judge. The *Testament of Job* 4:7 has God say: "the Lord is impartial—rendering good things to each one who obeys." In 43:13 we hear: "Righteous is the Lord, true are His judgments. With Him there is no favoritism. He will judge us all together." *First Enoch* 63:8 says: "Our Lord is faithful in all His works, His judgments, and His righteousness; and His judgments have no respect of persons." *Second Baruch* 44:4 says: "He whom we serve is righteous and . . . our Creator is impartial." Again, Paul carried on his argument against the self-righteous Jew on the basis of generally accepted Jewish assumptions and convictions.

For the text to say, then, that God will judge all people according to their works is to say that God is impartial. In no sense was Paul here contradicting his conviction expressed elsewhere that no one is able to stand before God at the judgment on the basis of works. This passage is not discussing how Paul believed one is justified before God. Its point is that, on Jewish assumptions, Jews will be judged in the same impartial way as Gentiles: on the basis of their deeds. This is the basis for the claim made in v. 5 that the presumptuous and lawless Jew would meet wrath on judgment day. God judges impartially (= fairly. Cf. *Ep Barn* 4:12).[3]

The apparent contradiction between Paul's claim that no one is justified by (*ek*) works and the contention in this text that all are judged on the basis of (*kata; dia*) their works may be resolved if one notes the prepositions used by the apostle in the two statements. On the one hand, when Paul said "no one will be justified by works of law" (Rom 3:20; Gal 2:16) his language was *ex ergon nomou*. The *ek* expresses instrumentality, not evidential basis. So Paul was saying that the means of justification is not works of law. On the other hand, when he said those who do the law will be justified or that one will be judged on the basis of his/her deeds (Rom 2:7, 12, 13; cf. Rom 2:10; 1 Cor 4:3-5; 2 Cor 5:10), Paul spoke about the basis of final justification. It is deeds done in the body. The law, then, is not a sufficient instrument of salvation. It cannot transform the self imprisoned by sin. Only the faith(fulness) of Jesus Christ can do that (Gal 2:16; Rom 3:22). It is Christ's faithfulness lived out in believers that enables their transformation.

The judgment, however, is on the basis of (*kata*) one's transformation or lack thereof as evidenced by the deeds done in the body.[4]

The third of these sections on the unrighteousness of Jews is found in 2:12-29. It begins with a statement of principle in vv. 12-13. "All who have sinned apart from the law will also perish apart from the law, and all who have sinned under the law will be judged by the law." [Perish] Why? "For it is not the hearers of the law who are righteous in God's sight, but the doers of the law who will be justified" (cf. Jas 1:22-24; Matt 7:24-27). This was, again, a widespread Jewish conviction. Leviticus 18:5 cites the words of God: "You shall keep my statues and my ordinances; by doing so one shall live: I am the Lord." In *m. 'Abot* 1:17 we hear: "not the expounding [of the Law] is the chief thing but the doing [of it]."

What follows is an application of this general principle to both Gentiles and Jews. The application to Gentiles comes in 2:14-16; the application to Jews in 2:17-29. Verses 14-16 speak about Gentiles. "When Gentiles, who do not possess the law, do

Perish

AΩ "To perish" is an expression used in Scripture of the negative outcome for those who are not in line with God's will.

- The outcome for Israel if the people forsake God after entrance into the land of promise (Deut 4:26; 8:19-20 [= a synonym of destroy]; 30:18)
- The end of the ungodly/wicked whether individuals (Pss 1:6; 37:20) or nations (Isa 60:12)
- The result of God's wrath (Ps 2:12), of God's rebuke (Ps 80:16), of God's fierce anger (Jonah 3:9)
- The opposite of being saved (1 Cor 1:18; 2 Cor 2:15; 4:3; 2 Thess 2:10) and of eternal life (John 3:15, 16; 10:28)
- The outcome of the Last Judgment for those who do not repent (2 Pet 3:9) or follow the light they have (Rom 2:12)

Dieric Bouts. 1415–1475. *The Fall of the Damned.* c. 1450. Oil on wood. Musee de Beaux-Arts. Lille, France. (Credit: Erich Lessing/Art Resource, NY)

instinctively (= by nature) what the law requires (cf. 4 Ezra 3:36), these, though not having the law, are a law unto themselves. They show that what the law requires is written on their hearts." These statements pick up what Paul had already said in 1:32: "They know God's decree, that those who practice such things deserve to die." How would ancient Mediterranean peoples have heard such a claim?

There were essentially two options. On the one hand, there was the Stoic teaching about natural law. Cicero said: "Law is the highest reason implanted in Nature, which commands what ought to be done and forbids the contrary. This reason, when firmly fixed and perfected in the human mind, is law" (*De legibus* 1.6.18). This natural law contained what was deemed appropriate or seemly. It was followed by the Sage or wise man. Paul's language "by nature" (2:14) echoes this teaching, as does the phrase "the things not fitting" (1:28). In Epictetus, *Discourses* 1.15.4; 1.26.15; 2.18, we find the concept of an internal "governing principle" that acts as an inner guide to right behavior, even when that behavior is contrary to society's norms. Certain Jews had adapted this mindset to their own thought. For example, Philo knew the Stoic teaching and repeated it. "The Sage, being himself a law and an unwritten statue" (*On Abraham* 46+276); "right reason is an infallible law engraved not by this mortal or that, and thus perishable, nor on lifeless scrolls or stellae, and thus lifeless, but by immortal nature on the immortal mind" (*Every Good Man Is Free* 7+46). "This world . . . has one polity and one law, and this is the word of nature, dictating what must be done and forbidding what must not be done" (*On Joseph* 6+29). *On the Creation*, 143, claims that the right reason of nature is the guide to life. What Philo did that was Jewish was to claim that the patriarchs such as Abraham realized the ideal of the Sage and fulfilled the law of nature so that they were "living law." The earliest men obeyed the unwritten principle of legislation that is according to nature (*On Abraham* 1+5). In 3+16, Philo spoke of an unwritten self-taught law that nature had implanted in humans. This belief was held more widely than Philo. Josephus, *JW* 4.6.3+382, said the Zealots, by not burying the dead, canceled "both the laws of their country and the laws of nature." *First Enoch* 5:4, which belongs to the Book of Watchers (= *1 Enoch* 1–36) and is dated to perhaps 200 BC, speaks about the "law of the Lord." It is in the context of Enoch's words about how nature follows God's decree. Yet humans have not "observed the law of the Lord." This is neither the Noachic laws nor the law of Moses, both of which were unknown in the time of Enoch. It is rather a reference to the law of nature that applies to all humanity.

On the other hand, there were the Noachic laws. Some streams of Judaism held to the belief that certain laws were given by Noah to his sons and grandsons. For these laws the Gentiles were responsible. This belief was based on Genesis 9:3-6 (v. 4—do not eat flesh with its blood in it; v. 6—do not shed a person's blood). In the pre-Christian *Jubilees* 7:20, we hear that Noah gave the commandments that he knew to his grandsons as a guide for doing justice. They were: (1) cover the shame of the flesh; (2) bless the Creator; (3) honor your father and mother; (4) love your neighbor; (5) avoid fornication; (6) avoid pollution; (7) avoid injustice. The earliest form of these laws among the rabbis occurs in the Tosefta (early 3rd century AD) in Tractate '*Aboda Zara* 8.4-6 (also *b. Sanh* 56b). The list of laws includes: (1) set up courts of justice; (2) no idolatry; (3) no blasphemy; (4) no fornication; (5) no bloodshed; (6) no thievery; (7) do not eat limbs cut from living animals. Other rabbinic versions include more than seven such commandments. This stream of thought influenced the Hellenistic Jewish *Ps-Phocylides* (1st century BC—1st century AD). This writing belongs to a type of Jewish propaganda that did not seek proselytes but aimed merely to raise the level of ethical consciousness and behavior among the Gentiles. In *Ps-Phocylides* the seven commandments mentioned in *t. Aboda Zara* 8.4-6 are reflected (so they are earlier than the Tosefta). They are: (1) referred to in *Ps-Phocylides* 9-12, 86; (2) and (3) referred to in *Ps-Phocylides* 8,54; (4) referred to in *Ps-Phocylides* 4,32,58; (5) referred to in *Ps-Phocylides* 3,177-83; (6) referred to in *Ps-Phocylides* 6,18,135-36;154; (7) referred to in *Ps-Phocylides* 147-48. Indeed, at least twenty five lines reflect ideas that are found in the Noachic laws. All claim a universal validity independent of Jewish particularities.

Some Jewish references are difficult to place in either the one or the other category, natural law or Noachic commands. *Second Baruch* 57:2 says that in the time of Abraham the unwritten law was in force and that Abraham kept that law. Remember, Abraham was a Gentile. *Sibylline Oracles* 4.24-39 specifies rules that are incumbent on Gentiles but that are not tied to Jewish particularities. It is not clear whether the minority belief in certain Jewish circles that there were or would be some righteous Gentiles (*t. Sanh* 13.2) was connected with either Natural Law or Noachic Law. If they were righteous, these Gentiles would be doing the law on some basis other than a knowledge of the Torah. References such as these may have belonged to one or the other of the streams of

Conscience

AΩ Conscience in Paul is morality's inner voice. There are at least two major ways the term is used.

- First, it refers to the human capacity that either condemns or recommends one's fitness before God. As in Wis 17:11 and the *T. Reub* 4:3, Rom 2:15-16 mentions Gentiles who at the last judgment experience a painful awareness of wrongdoing. At the same time, passages such as 2 Cor 1:12; 1 Tim 1:5; 3:9; 2 Tim 1:3 (and Acts 23:1; 24:16 in Paul's mouth; cf. 1 Pet 3:16) speak about one's having a good or clear conscience. That is, the absence of inner pain is a testimony of the absence of wrongdoing. In Rom 2:15-16 Paul held out the possibility that some Gentiles at the last judgment would experience the absence of inner pain.
- Second, conscience can refer to the moral repository of moral convictions that legislates actions in accord with God's will. Here conscience helps determine correct acts ahead of time. Just as in Epictetus, *Dissertations* 3.22.94 and Josephus, *Against Apion* 2.218, Paul in 1 Cor 8:7, 10, 12 and 10:27 used the term in this way. It should be noted that here the conscience that guides can be weak or strong. This meaning of conscience is not found in Romans.

---

thought in antiquity. In either case, they show that a pervasive belief existed among ancient Jews as well as pagans that all people had some elemental knowledge of morality for which they were responsible.

Within such a milieu, how would ancient auditors have heard Paul's statements? An ancient auditor from a pagan milieu would have heard the Stoic terminology and thought immediately of that position on natural morality. A Hellenistic Jew would have heard it in a similar way, although one mediated through Hellenistic Jewish authors. Since there was no linguistic link to the Noachic commandments, there is no indication that an auditor would have considered that as a basis for Paul's words in Romans 2:14-16. In any case, both Paul and Jubilees used such knowledge on the part of Gentiles to establish their culpability.

Since the Gentiles who do not have the Torah do have a law written on their hearts, they are responsible for their deeds and their conscience bears witness either for or against them. This is true now and will be so on the day of judgment when "God, through Jesus Christ, will judge the secret thoughts of all" (v. 16; cf. *1 Enoch* 49:4; 61:7). [Conscience]

Ancient Jews often thought of some mediator acting on behalf of God at the last judgment. *First Enoch* 45:3-6 mentions Enoch as judge; 11 Q Melchizedek says it will be Melchizedek; and the *Testament of Abraham* specifies Abel as judge. Paul, as a Christian Messianist, offered his community's mediator: Jesus Christ (see 2 Cor 5:10; Matt 25:31-46; John 5:28-29; Acts 17:31; Heb 9:28; 12:23-24; Jas 5:8-9; Rev 20:11-13). When Christ comes as judge at the last day, the Gentiles will be judged on the basis of the light they had. They are responsible because there is a law written on their hearts. "All who have sinned without the law (Torah) will also perish without the law" (v. 12a). What about the Jew?

In his statement of principle, Paul had said: "all who have sinned under the law will be judged by the law" (v. 12b). This principle is now applied to Jews in Romans 2:17-29. The application falls into two parts: vv. 17-24 and vv. 25-29. In v.s 17-24 the focus is on the Jews as those who possess the law (cf. Sir 24:23), know the law, and are able to function as teachers of the law (vv. 17-20; cf. Sir 24:27). *Second Baruch* 48:22-24 reflects Jewish belief that since they possess the law, they are better than non-Jews in God's sight. It was a Jewish conviction that they were guides to the blind (Isa 42:7; *1 Enoch* 105:1; *Sib Or* 3.194-95; Josephus, *Against Apion* 2.291-95). Yet these same people, for all their knowledge of the law, do not keep it (vv. 21-24). "While you preach against stealing, do you steal" (v. 21b; cf. Exod 20:15)? "You that forbid adultery, do you commit adultery" (v. 22a; cf. Exod 20:14; *Ps Sol* 8:10!)? "You that abhor idols, do you rob temples" (v. 22b; Chariton's *Chareas and Callirhoe*, 1.7.6; 1.10.4, shows pagan abhorrence for such activity; for such practice or alleged practice by Jews, see *Ps Sol* 8:11; Josephus, *Antiquities* 18.3.5+81-84; *JW* 5.13.6+562; *Against Apion* 1.26+249; 1.35+318; *Antiquities* 4.8.10+207 prohibits such behavior)? "You that boast in the law (cf. Sir 39:8), do you dishonor God by breaking the law" (v. 23; cf. Isa 52:5; *T. Naph* 8:6)? The apostle assumed that the answer to all these rhetorical questions is yes: yes, they steal, commit adultery, rob temples, and dishonor God. Paul's target was Jewish assurance of a position of privilege because of their possessing the law.[Jew]

In v.s 25-29 the focus is on circumcision as a sign of Jewishness. Physical circumcision was, for Jews, a sign of the covenant (Gen 17:10-11; *Jub* 15:28) and was central to Jewish identity (1 Macc 1:48, 60-61; 2:46; 2 Macc 6:10). No one could be counted as belonging to the people of God without it (*Jub* 15:25-34; Josephus, *Antiquities* 13.257-58,318). Later rabbis could say: "No person who is circumcised will go down to Gehenna" (*Exodus Rabbah* 19 [81c]). At the same time, there was within Judaism the notion of the circumcision of the heart. "Circumcise, then, the foreskin of

Jew

AΩ Prior to the Maccabean period *Ioudaios* (Jew) had been a name used by foreigners for persons belonging to Judea. From the 2d century BC, the name was accepted and used by the Jews themselves as a self-designation in place of the older "Israelite" and "Hebrew." So used, it functioned to distinguish Jew from non-Jew (cf. Rom 1:16; 2:9-10; 3:9, 29; 9:24; 10:12; Gal 2:14-15; 3:28). The national religion was correspondingly called *Ioudaismos* (Judaism) (2 Macc 2:21; 8:1; 14:38). Hence, by Paul's time, "Jew" would have been a label accepted with pride by his contemporaries (cf. 4 Ezra 6:55-59). In Rom 2:17 Paul used Jew in this sense. Later, in writings such as the Acts of the Apostles and the Gospel of John, "Jew" came to mean, for the most part, establishment synagogue Judaism that was normally hostile to Christian Messianic Judaism.

Circumcision of Christ

The Jewish ritual of circumcision on the eighth day of an infant's life symbolizes the covenant relationship between God and Israel and the baby's participation in the continuing unfolding of creation.

Bartolomeo Veneto. 1502–1530. *The Circumcision.* Oil on wood. Louvre. Paris, France. (Réunion des Musées Nationaux/Art Resource, NY)

your heart, and do not be stubborn any longer" (Deut 10:16). "Moreover, the Lord your God will circumcise your heart and the heart of your descendants, so that you will love the Lord your God with all your heart and with all your soul" (Deut 30:6). "Circumcise yourselves to the Lord, remove the foreskin of your hearts, O people of Judah and inhabitants of Jerusalem" (Jer 4:4). "All the house of Israel is uncircumcised in heart" (Jer 9:26b). "I shall cut off the foreskin of their heart and the foreskin of the heart of their descendants" (*Jub* 1:23). In 1QpHab 11:13 the interpretation of Habakkuk 2:16 runs: "Its interpretation concerns the Priest whose shame has exceeded his glory because he did not circumcise the foreskin of his heart." This distinction between literal and spiritual circumcision had a variety of results. Philo knew Jews in Alexandria who dispensed entirely with physical circumcision. They believed circumcision was rather a matter of inward reality. It involved "the excision of pleasure and all passions, and the putting away of sacrilegious opinion" (*On the Migration of Abraham* 92). This spiritualizing tendency reflected a widespread Greco-Roman tendency. It affirmed that externals were not as important as what is on the inside (Horace, *Satires* 2.3.159-62; Ovid, *Amores* 3.4.4;

Musonius Rufus XII; Seneca, *De Beneficiis* 4.14.1; Dio Chrysostom 69.8). Philo himself could agree that "he shows himself most clearly that he is a proselyte who is not circumcised in foreskin but in pleasure, desires, and other passions of the soul" (*Questions and Answers on Exodus* 2.2, fragment on Exod 22:21). Nevertheless, Philo insisted that literal circumcision be retained (*Migration of Abraham* 92-93; *Special Laws* 1.1+6). It is this distinction between physical and spiritual circumcision that Paul employed in v.s 25-29. "For a person is not a Jew who is one outwardly, nor is true circumcision something external and physical. Rather a person is a Jew who is one inwardly, and real circumcision is a matter of the heart—it is spiritual and not literal" (vv. 28-29; cf. 1 Cor 7:19). Of course, in 3:1 Paul allowed a place for literal circumcision for the ethnic Jew. This, however, is only on the basis of historical priority. It has no soteriological value in the era of Christ.

In v.s 17-29 Paul has made two points. First, Jewish obedience to the law has not matched Jewish knowledge of the law (cf. 7:14-24 where the "I" values the law but is unable to obey it). Second, the Jew's circumcision has been only physical and not spiritual. With both points the apostle has applied the principle, all who have sinned under the law will be judged by the law" (v. 12b), to Jews. Jews, as well as Gentiles, stand under God's impartial judgment. Note that Paul's argument here has exposed, not Jewish ethnic exclusiveness, but Jewish disobedience to God.

In Romans 3:1-20 Paul answered Jewish objections to his argument in 2:1-29. The answers came in the context of a diatribe form with a series of five questions raised by Paul's imaginary dialogue partner, which likely reflected real arguments the apostle had experienced in his missionary activity (vv. 1, 3, 5, 7-8a, 9a). The first two, together with their Pauline answers, deal with the issue of Jewish advantage (vv. 1-4). The next two, together with their Pauline responses, address the issue of implicit antinomianism in Paul's positions (vv. 5-8). The fifth question returns to the first concern expressed, that of Jewish advantage (v. 9a).

We begin with v.s 1-4 and the question of Jewish advantage. Paul's imaginary Jewish opponent raises a first question: "Then what advantage has the Jew? Or what is the value of circumcision" (v. 1)? These questions grew out of Paul's assertions in 2:9-10, 12-13 where the apostle had asserted God's impartiality. Judgment would be for both Jew and Greek; blessing would be for both Jew and Greek. Both would be judged on the basis of their doing or not doing the law. If that is so, then what advantage is it to be a Jew instead of a Gentile? Paul replied: "Much in every way. For in the first place, the Jews were entrusted with the oracles of God" (v. 2; cf. 9:4-5). The reference is to the Scriptures of Israel (Heb 5:12; 1 Pet 4:11). Jews knew God's will. The Jewish dialogue partner then raises a second question: "What if some (Jews) were unfaithful? Will their faithlessness nullify the faithfulness of God" (v. 3; cf. 1 Cor 1:9; Deut 7:9; 32:4; Isa 49:7; Philo, *Sacrifices* 93)? This question grew out of Paul's argument in 2:17-29. There the apostle contended that Jews, although they knew the law and were circumcised, did not obey the law. They were unfaithful. Would their violation of the law's demands destroy the covenant relation with God? Paul responded: "By no means! . . . let God be proved true" (v. 4a). He cited an OT proof text to buttress his argument (= Ps 51:4). Human faithlessness does not nullify God's faithfulness (see Ps 89:2, 33-34). Jews had the advantage of possessing the Scriptures and of being related to a God who is faithful. These issues will be addressed more fully in chapters 9–11.

In v.s 5-8 questions about possible antinomianism arise. In v. 5 the Jewish interlocutor asks: "But if our injustice serves to confirm the justice of God, what should we say? That God is unjust to inflict wrath on us?" If human wickedness brings about a manifestation of God's righteousness, a good thing, then why should we be judged for our sin? This is a false inference from v. 3b and moreover a specious one. Paul answered with a wave of the hand. "Then how could God judge the world" (v. 6)? Such a specious question's implied answer would deprive Judaism of one of its most prized tenets: God will judge the world, punishing evil and rewarding virtue. This is unthinkable. The next question is a variant on the previous one. It also is a false inference from the answer in v. 3b. "If through my falsehood God's truthfulness abounds to His glory, why am I still being condemned as a sinner? And why not say, 'Let us do evil so that good may come'" (vv. 7-8a)? This is mere sophism, and Paul did not argue against it but rather dismissed it for what it was worth. "Their condemnation is deserved" (v. 8b). The alleged antinomian implications of his claims about God's faithfulness in the face of human faithlessness are dismissed. They will, however, be addressed more fully starting at Romans 6:1.

The fifth question from Paul's dialogue partner returns to the issue of Jewish privilege. "What then? Are we any better off" (v. 9a)? The apostle's answer runs from v. 9b to v. 20. "No, not at all; for we have already charged that all, both Jews and Greeks, are under the power of sin" (v. 9b). To support his contention, Paul again appealed to Scripture. What follows in v.s 10-18 is a catena of ten quotations. Such collections of proof texts aimed at demonstrating some point are characteristic of non-Christian Jews (e.g., CD 5:13-17; 4QFlorilegium; 4 Ezra 7:22-24) and Christian Jews alike (1 Pet 2:6-8; Heb 1:5-14; Justin, *Dialogue* 27.3). All the texts cited in Romans 3:10-18 testify to human sinfulness. (1) With v. 10b, compare Ecclesiastes 7:20 and Psalm 14:3b; (2) with v. 11, compare Psalm 14:2; (3) with v. 12, compare Psalm 14:3a; (4) with v. 13a, compare Psalm 5:9; (5) with v. 13b, compare Psalm 140:3; (6) with v. 14, compare Psalm 10:7; (7) with v. 15, compare Proverbs 1:16 and Isaiah 59:7a; (8) with v. 16, compare Isaiah 59:7b; (9) with v. 17, compare Isaiah 59:8; and (10) with v. 18, compare Psalm 36:1b. Cannot these scriptural quotations be taken to refer to Gentiles only and not Jews? Paul prevented that inference by saying: "Now we know that whatever the law says, it speaks to those who are under the law" (v. 19a). These scriptural quotations are directed to the Jew. Why? So that the whole world may be held accountable to God. The evidence for Gentile godlessness and wickedness is abundant. But Scripture also says what Paul has argued in 2:1-29. Jews, whom Paul has charged with knowing the Law but disobeying it, stand under God's judgment. The fact is that all humans, Jew and Gentile, are sinners. This leads to Paul's conclusion. "'No human being will be justified (= recognized as righteous and rewarded for it) in His sight' (Ps 143:2) by deeds prescribed by the law" (v. 20a).

Here for the first time we encounter a key phrase in Paul's argument: "works of the law" or, as the NRSV puts it, "deeds prescribed by the law." Romans 3:20, 28; 9:32 (in some manuscripts) and Galatians 2:16; 3:2, 5, 10, contain the expression "works of the law." Romans 3:27; 4:2, 6, 32, contain the abbreviated expression "works." What do these expressions mean in Paul's letters? There are two major alternatives. On the one hand, some think "works of the law" are all the things prescribed or required by the Mosaic Law. On the other hand, others hold that "works" are limited to ethnic identity markers of Jews such as circumcision, food laws, and observance of the sabbath. The background of this difference of opinion is helpful in understanding the issues.

In the late 1970s and the early 1980s, E. P. Sanders argued that Palestinian Judaism in the time of Paul was not legalistic in nature but rather reflected "covenantal nomism." Legalism, he said, is a structure requiring observance of the law to "get in" God's people. This did not characterize ancient Judaism because Jews believed they got in the covenant by God's grace. Sanders's alternative, covenantal nomism, holds that ancient Judaism was a structure in which the law was obeyed in order to "stay in" the covenant. This was the posture of ancient Palestinian Judaism of Paul's time. Such a description of ancient Judaism, if true, raises questions about Paul's statements about Judaism. Were there really any Jews like Paul claimed, that is, who were legalistic? James D. G. Dunn has assumed Sanders's depiction of Judaism and has attempted to describe Paul in a way that is compatible with it. Paul, he has said, was not hostile to legalism because there was not any. Rather Paul's opposition was to Jewish particularism and ethnicity. "Works of law," he thinks, referred to ethnic identity markers. Paul was then opposing a people of God understood in ethnic terms. Read in this way, the issue in Paul is not grace versus legalism but universalism versus ethnic particularism.

Jewish literature from antiquity illustrates how widespread was the notion that salvation— defined as membership in God's people or participation in the Age to Come— depended on obedience to the law. We begin with the question of the admission of *Gentiles*. In ancient Judaism there were basically two avenues by which Gentiles could facilitate their entrance into God's people and/or the Age to Come. The first was by becoming a proselyte. In the case of native-born Israelites, circumcision was a response to the grace of election. They were "in" unless they gave evidence of being apostate. In the case of Gentiles, proselytes had to bear the burden of proof to show that they accepted the covenant and intended to keep the law. That is, they had to take a human initiative to align themselves with the elect people—by works of the law. Ancient sources reflect this.

The Mosaic Law
The central role of Torah in Jewish life is clearly evident in the great care and veneration given to Torah scrolls themselves. Often produced at great cost and preserved at great risk, the scrolls embody the Jewish trust in the instruction of God given unto the people of Israel.

Illustration by Barclay Burns

Josephus said that many Greeks "have agreed to adopt our laws" (*Against Apion* 2.123). He also said that Moses took measures regarding Jewish customs

to throw them open ungrudgingly to any who elect to share them. To all who desire to come and live under the same laws with us, he gives a gracious welcome, holding that it is not family ties alone which constitute relationship, but agreement in principles of conduct. (*Against Apion* 2.209-10)

The ethical emphasis in what is said here is obvious. A Gentile's ethical convictions relate him/her to the Jews and apparently have the same importance as racial origin. What seems clear from Josephus's statements is that a Gentile "got in" the people of God by works of the law.

Justin's *Dialogue with Trypho* offers further, if later, evidence. In chapter 8, after Justin has told Trypho about his conversion to Christ, his Jewish dialogue partner tells Justin that his profession is empty. Trypho then gives his prescription for salvation to Justin.

> If, then, you are willing to listen to me . . . , first be circumcised, then observe what ordinances have been enacted with respect to the Sabbath, and the feasts, and the new moons of God; and, in a word, do all things which have been written in the law: and then perhaps you shall obtain mercy from God.[5]

Here a Jew addresses a philosopher who has been converted to Christ. Trypho seems to be calling for Justin to become a proselyte. This would be accomplished by works of the law. This sounds like what Sanders has called legalism. One "gets in" by works of the law. Also, note how, in addition to what Dunn has called "ethnic identity markers" (circumcision, sabbath observance, holidays), Trypho expects "all things written in the law."

The case of Izates makes concrete what the previous statements have said in general terms. In *Antiquities* 20.17-41, Josephus told of the conversion to Judaism of Izates of Adiabene through the witness of a Jewish merchant named Ananias. This Ananias told Izates that circumcision was unnecessary for him to be a Jewish convert. Later, in 20.42-48, another Jew named Eleazar came from Galilee and told Izates that, according to the law, circumcision was necessary. Izates thereupon complied and was circumcised. In the case of Eleazar, in order for a proselyte to "get in" the people who would get the the Age to Come, he had to be circumcised. This is what is normally called legalism.

The second avenue by which a Gentile might enter the Age to Come was by being a "righteous Gentile," that is, a Gentile who keeps the law. In Romans 2:10, 14-15, in the context of an argument that operates with non-Christian Jewish logic, Paul spoke of Gentiles who do by nature what the law requires and who receive glory, honor, and peace before God at the last judgment. The initiative of these righteous Gentiles receives approval from God in the last judgment. This sounds like legalism.

From the period before AD 70 two non-Christian Hellenistic Jewish documents speak the same way. *Testament of Abraham,* written in Greek probably in Egypt in the first century, makes no distinction between Jew and Gentile. The sins mentioned are specifically Jewish. Everyone is judged by the same standard—whether the majority of his/her deeds are good or evil. Both Jew and Gentile get into heaven by having a majority of their deeds be righteous. *Apocalypse of Zephaniah*, written probably before AD 70 outside of Palestine, makes no mention of covenant or election. All people, Jew and Gentile, are judged on the basis of their deeds, which are written down throughout their lives by angels. The good and evil are weighed in balance at the judgment. Both documents display what has normally been called legalism.

4 Ezra 3:36, from Palestine after AD 70, completes a complaint made by Ezra to God about the fate of God's people. What other nation has been as mindful of the commandments as Zion? God may find individual Gentiles who have kept God's commandments but no nations besides Israel. In the Tosefta, *Sanhedrin* 13.2, there is a debate between two second-century rabbis, Rabbi Joshua and Rabbi Eliezer. Eliezer contends that none of the Gentiles has a portion in the World to Come. To which Joshua responds that if scripture had said "The wicked shall return to Sheol—all the Gentiles," he would agreed with Eliezer. Since scripture says, however, "All the Gentiles who forget God," it indicates that there are righteous people among the nations of the world who have a portion in the World to Come. In *Sifra*, Parashat Ahare Mot, Pereq 13.15, Rabbi Jeremiah asks a rhetorical question. How can one know that even a Gentile who keeps the law is beloved of God? The argument that unfolds runs like this: the law was given to humans; those who keep it and are righteous enter the Age to Come; therefore, even a Gentile who keeps the Torah will enter the Age to Come. This, of course, is what has traditionally been labeled legalism.

What about the ethnic Jew? How does such a one "get in" the Age to Come? We can get a sense of what hellenistic Jews believed by returning to two documents, both pre-70, which speak to the issue. *Testament of Abraham's* soteriology for Jews is the same as it is for Gentiles. Everyone is judged by the same standard—whether or not the majority of his/her deeds are good or evil. The Jews, as well as the Gentiles, get into heaven by having a majority of their deeds be righteous. *Apocalypse of Zephaniah* makes no mention of covenant or election. The patriarchs are mentioned but only as examples of pious men. Angels write down the good deeds of the righteous and the evil deeds of the wicked. At the judgment they are weighed in balance. Every person is judged on the basis of earthly deeds. In both of these sources, "getting in" the Age to Come is a matter of righteous behavior, not election. This is what has traditionally been called legalism.

Turning now to Palestinian Judaism, we may begin with the rabbis. There are two foci in rabbinic soteriology: election and obedience. E. P. Sanders has understood them sequentially: "getting in" by election and "staying in" by obedience. Friedrich Avemarie, however, has argued that the two foci represent two models instead of two stages.[6] Some sources place the emphasis on election, others on obedience. Sanders's favorite text is found in the Mishnah: "All Israelites have a share in the World to Come, for it is written: 'Thy people shall all be righteous; they shall inherit the land forever" (*m. Sanh* 10:1). Here the emphasis is on election. The initial assertion ("All Israelites have a share in the World to Come"), however, is qualified by its supporting scripture citation ("The people shall all be righteous"). Furthermore, what follows qualifies "all Israelites." There are some who have no share in the World to Come: for example, those who deny the resurrection, those who deny the law's heavenly origin, and others. Indeed *m. Sanhedrin* 10:1-4 sets out a long list of exceptions to "all." These presumably are those whose behavior constitutes apostasy. Even with the exceptions, however, the focus is still probably on election. Nevertheless, there is even here no entry into the Age to Come apart from one's obedience to the law. This is soteriological synergism, legalistic covenantal nomism.

Other Palestinian Jews insisted on salvation by obedience to the law. John the Baptist is a case in point. Mark 1:4 and Luke 3:3 say John preached a "baptism of repentance for the forgiveness of sins." Taken alone, this sounds like a call for an atoning activity done within a covenantal nomistic context so as to "stay in" the people of God who would survive the last judgement. Matthew 3:8-10 and Luke 3:8-9, however, say John told his Jewish auditors to bear fruit that befits repentance, not to presume on their ethnicity/election, and that without this fruit their election would not enable them to survive the fire of the last judgment. Here Jews must do more than avoid apostasy. They must actively seek the atonement of repentance and then act obediently. Descent from Abraham, taken alone, is soteriologically ineffective.[7] This is a synergistic, legalistic covenantal nomism.

The Rule of the Community at Qumran (1QS) starts with the assumption that obedience to what God commanded through Moses and the Prophets has not been actualized by most of those born Jews (1:2-3). The community that will carry out all that God

Qumran

Qumran, at the northwest tip of the Dead Sea, is the place where the Dead Sea Scrolls were found when, in 1947, a young Bedouin shepherd wandered into a cave looking for a lost animal. Caves 4 and 5 near the settlement above Wadi Qumran in the Jordan Valley contained more than 40,000 fragments of ancient writings, including commentaries on many biblical books. They reflect a monastic form of Judaism possibly linked with the Essenes, a sectarian Jewish movement in Palestine at the time of Jesus.

(Credit: Tony W. Cartledge)

commands (1:16-17) will be made up of Jews who "freely volunteer to carry out God's decrees" (1:7; 5:1, 22; 6:13). These are those selected by God for an everlasting covenant (4:22). Those who enter the community swear by an oath to revert to the Law of Moses with all its decrees (5:8). These members are to have their spirits tested with respect to their deeds in the law by the community year after year (5:20-24; 6:18). Here again, ethnicity/election/God's grace is soteriologically ineffective. An ethnic Jew must choose to enter the community that will carry out the obedience to the Law of Moses that God expects. Only these will "get in" the Age to Come.[8] Here again, one encounters a synergistic, legalistic covenantal nomism.

The Qumran document, 4QMMT, confirms the reading of 1QS. 4Q398 [4QpapMMTe] fragment 2, column II (= 4QMMT 111-118) uses the expression "works of the law." It sees such observance as paying off at the end of time: "It shall be reckoned to you as in justice when you do what is upright and good before him." At best, this is legalistic covenantal nomism.

In 4 Ezra we find a Palestinian Jewish document that is clearly legalistic. In 4 Ezra the covenants no longer exist (4:23). Humans have scorned God's Law, denied the covenants and have not performed God's works (7:24). Humans are so full of sin (7:68; 8:35) that they will have nothing to say in the judgment (7:73). This judgment of God is drawing near (8:61). Those who will be saved will be able to escape on account of their works (9:7), while those who have received the law and have sinned will perish (9:36). Here human sin has nullified the covenant (= election has been canceled). Henceforth, judgment will be strictly according to one's works. Only a very few will be saved. In this structure, a Jew enters the Age to Come on the basis of works of law. This is, indeed, what has been traditionally called legalism.

Second Baruch 41 speaks both about some of God's people who have rejected the covenant and law and about some who have fled for refuge beneath God's wings (vv. 3-4). In chapter 42, God says that those who have embraced the covenant will receive the good things while those who have abandoned it will receive the judgment (vv. 2-3). Verse 5 seems to imply that Gentiles who proselytize to Judaism will gain the benefits of the New World while v. 4 indicates that Jews who go off and mingle with foreigners will not. Here it is not one's position in the covenant people conveyed by birth that yields life in the New World but obedience to the law. *Second Baruch* 51 speaks of those who at the last judgment have been "justified through obedience to my law" (v. 3). These will be transformed so that they will look like the angels (v. 5). "Those who have been saved by their works, whose hope has been in the law" (v. 7) shall see marvels. They shall be made like the angels (v. 10) and will experience Paradise (v. 11). Here one enters the New World by works of law. Those whose obedience to the law is real will be justified. Again, in *2 Baruch* we see operative a synergistic, legalistic covenantal nomism.

This ethos of legalism and synergism had ancient roots. Genesis 26:2-5 indicates God that acted favorably toward Isaac *because of* Abraham's obedience. Jubilees 15:3-4 has the Lord tell Abraham to be pleasing before Him and He would, *as a consequence*, make a covenant with him and multiply his descendants. Sirach 44:19-21 says the blessing on Abraham was *due to* his obedience. CD 3:2 asserts that Abraham was counted a friend of God *because* he kept God's commands. In all of these references to Abraham, the prototype of Jewish life, the emphasis is on human obedience as a cause of divine recognition.

Sanders's categories of "getting in" and "staying in" are grossly misleading. Why? Because "staying in" in Paul's time was for the purpose of "getting in," that is, getting into the New Age beyond the resurrection. By obeying the law, one "stayed in" God's covenant in hopes of "getting in" the New Age. Paul would have rightly regarded this as a legalistic/synergistic structure.[9]

Timo Eskola has argued that the soteriology of ancient Judaism was synergistic; that is, God and humans cooperate for human salvation. Once covenantal nomism is set in an eschatological context, he said, it becomes legalistic nomism. How so? One may be a part of God's people by grace, but in order to stay in the people and in order to enter the New Age beyond the Last Judgment, one must obey the law. Obedience is the condition for eschatological salvation. If legalism means that keeping the law is the way to gain eschatological salvation, then in an eschatological framework covenantal nomism becomes legalistic nomism. So the soteriology is synergistic. By God's grace one gets in the people, but by human effort/obedience to the law one gets into the Eschatological Age beyond the Last Judgment. It is this synergistic, legalistic, covenantal nomism against which Paul fights.[10]

There was in fact a law-observant mission to the Gentiles in early Christianity?[11] In the second century the Ascent of James (in Ps-Clementine *Recognitions* 1.42) and the Preachings of Peter (in Ps-Clementine *Homilies*, Epistle of Peter to James, 2) testify to this. In addition, Justin in *Dialogue* 47, referred to hardline Jewish Christians who evangelized for circumcision and sabbath observance. Furthermore, when Ignatius, in *Philadelphians* 6-8, spoke of those who "propound Judaism to you" he was likely referring to Jewish Christians. The New Testament shows that this movement existed in the first century. Acts 15:1, 5, tells of believers from the party of the Pharisees who claimed that "Unless you are circumcised according to the custom of Moses, you cannot be saved." Acts 21:20 refers to thousands of Jewish believers who were zealous for the law. Confirmation comes from the genuine epistles of Paul. Philippians 3:2-11 implies such, and Galatians confirms it. Galatians depicts the false preachers as Christians (1:6-9), as Jewish (5:3,12; 6:12), and as outsiders who had only recently come into the Galatian churches (1:6). Their position was that the Galatians could only be justified by the law/legalism (5:4) and/or can only be perfected by works of law/covenantal nomism (3:3).

Given the evidence for the existence of "legalistic" and "synergistic"structures in the religion of at least some ancient Jews, it should be no surprise that some converts to the Jesus movement would have brought that ethos with them into the Christian Messianist movement. Paul, then, likely tangled with two groups of legalists: some non-Christian Jews and some Jewish Christians. Given the evidence, it should be no surprise to find passages in Paul's letters in which "works of the law" are understood more broadly than circumcision, food laws, and sabbath observance (see Gal 3:10; Rom 2:17-24; 3:20; 4:6-8). As noted above, many Jewish writings—Hellenistic and Palestinian, pre- and post-70—understand salvation "legalistically, and use "works of the law" with a broad range of meanings. For example, at Qumran the expression "works of law" appears with the broader meaning (1QS 5.21; 6.18; 4QFlor frags 1-3, col II 2; 4QMT [found in multiple fragments; one, 4Q398 {4QpapMMTe}in frag 2, col II {= 4QMMT 111-118} 3, speaks of "works of the Torah" and in 7, says "it will be reckoned to you as righteousness" when one does what is upright before God. This suggests that when Paul spoke about Judaism the way he did, he reflected concrete reality. Paul's use of "works of law" to mean "all the required demands of the Mosaic law" would have been reflecting a position of legalism or synergistic nomism or both that characterized certain strains of ancient non-Christian Judaism and/or certain streams of early Christian Judaism. If so, then the crux of the issue for Paul was indeed grace versus legalism and not universalism versus ethnicity/particularism. In this respect, at least, the Reformation reading of Romans is to be preferred to that of modern revisionists.

The law cannot justify, Paul said, because "through the law comes the knowledge of sin" (3:20a). The law's function is to make sin known (Rom 7:7,13). If in 2:13 Paul had said that the doers of the law would be justified, in 3:20 he made it clear that no one can do the law. If not, then no one will be justified thereby. With this final word, the apostle's first main section of his argument is complete. The human condition is clear. All are unrighteous, both the Gentile and the Jew (cf. 1:16; 2:9-11; 3:9; 3:22; 3:29; 9:23-24; 10:12; 11:32).

CONNECTIONS

Works of Law

In order to be able to understand Paul's aversion to works of the law, it is necessary to grasp three basic structures of thought involving religious law. The three may be called "legalism," "covenantal nomism," and "new covenant piety." Each needs to be described in turn.

Legalism is a structure in which there are three movements in a certain order. First, God gives the Law, making the divine will known to humans. Second, humans obey God's Law. When they obey the law, they do so as a means of gaining a relationship with God. Third, after humans have obeyed God's Law, God then responds by entering into a covenant relation with them. If the Old Testament story were told in these terms, it would run something like this. Movement One: God appeared to Moses in the wilderness, saying, "Come up into Mount Sinai. I want to give you my law." So Moses went up into the mountain and received the Law. Movement Two: Then God said: "Take this law into Egypt. Say to the Hebrew slaves, 'This is God's law. If you will keep God's law, then He will be your God and you will be His people. And He will deliver you from your Egyptian bondage and give you the land of Canaan.'" Movement Three: So Moses did as the Lord had commanded. The Hebrew slaves accepted God's Law and obeyed it. As a result, God "bared His mighty arm" and delivered them from their bondage, entered into a covenant with them, and brought them to the promised land. It is this type of view of Israel's history that lay behind the part of the theology of Paul's opponents in Galatia. These opponents said: "We have been justified by works of law." In other words, they had received the Law, had obeyed the Law, and God had responded by entering into a relationship with them. This was obviously not Paul's position. The apostle opposed legalism. He saw it as antithetical to justification by grace through faith. Legalism absolutizes human moral resources and constitutes idolatry, sin (cf. Gal 3:3).

Covenantal nomism is the name for another position that also has three movements in a certain order. First, out of grace God grants a covenant relationship with Himself to humans. Second, within the context of the covenant relation already granted, God gives the Law. The law functions as a guide for humans as to what pleases and displeases the God with whom they already have a relationship. Third, when humans obey the law, they do so out of gratitude for what God has already done for them. If the Old Testament story is told in these terms, it would sound like this. God appeared to Moses in the wilderness and said to him: "Go into Egypt and say to Pharoah, 'Let my people go.'" So Moses went into Egypt and God "bared His mighty arm" and brought the Hebrew slaves out of the land of bondage to Sinai. At Sinai the people were given the Law in order that they could know what pleased and displeased God. When Israel obeyed the Law, they did so out of gratitude for what God's bringing them out of the land of Egypt, out of the house of bondage. In Paul's time, certain opponents claimed that they had been justified by grace through faith. Now, however, it was necessary to complete their relation with God by obeying the Law (Gal 3:2-3). This they would do out of gratitude for what God had already done for them. So they began with a faith response to God's grace, but they continued/matured by obeying the law. This obedience to the law was deemed necessary if one wanted to stay in God's people. Staying in God's people was necessary if one wanted to enter the New World beyond the resurrection and last judgment. This Paul opposed. He opposed it because it made the part of the Christian life after conversion dependent upon human effort and initiative. This he viewed as idolatry, the essence of sin (cf. Gal 3:3)!

The third option is that of new covenant piety. This structure also has three movements in a certain order. First, out of grace God grants a relationship with humans. Second, within the context of that relationship that is already established God gives the law of Christ (Gal 6:2; 1 Cor 9:21). This law of Christ consists of both tradition and the Spirit's leading. The tradition consists of the parts of the Old Testament that have been filtered through Jesus and of various early Christian traditions (e.g., Jesus' words, deeds, death, and resurrection) passed down through the churches before Paul. The Spirit given to believers indwelt them (Rom 8:9) and offered guidance not only for interpreting the tradition (2 Cor 3:16-17; cf. John 14:26; 16:14-15) but also for daily life (Gal 5:25; cf. John 16:13). This law of Christ functions as a guide for what pleases and displeases the God with whom one already has a relationship. Third, when believers obey the law of Christ, they do so because they are enabled by the indwelling God (Phil 2:12-13), Christ (Gal 2:19-20; Rom 8:10), Spirit (Rom 8:9,11). This structure is that of the new covenant prophesied by Jeremiah 31:31-34 and Ezekiel 36:26-27. It assumes that God not only takes responsibility for granting the covenant but also for enabling human faithfulness as well. In this structure one not only begins the Christian life by God's grace and enablement but also continues in the very same way. If one follows the law of Christ, it is because grace enables it through God's own presence and power in the believer's life. This, of course, is Paul's own position.

Looking at Paul's views overall, one can see that he opposes not only legalism but also covenantal nomism. He regards both of these structures as depending on "works of the law" as a means of salvation. What they both demand, humans are not able to achieve. He is an advocate of new covenant piety because it offers what humans desperately need. We need God to do for us what we cannot do for ourselves, to save us!

The two positions with which Paul struggled are like mirrors in which we see ourselves. Over and over again we propose that humans gain a relation to God by moral actions, by inner attitude, by religious experience, or by human effort and initiative. These are works of the law. Over and over we propose that now that we have been saved by grace we move on to the maturity of charitable service and advanced spiritual disciplines in order to gain God's favor at the last judgment. This is works of the law. We find the apostles' guidance in his new covenant piety. Therein everything depends upon the divine initiative and enablement. From start to finish, the Christian life is by grace through faith.

Sin

For most people, "sin" means actions that violate some social norm, usually associated with a church body's views. Paul's views are different. Luke Timothy Johnson has noted:

> [A]s Paul speaks of it, sin is not a moral category but a religious one. . . . Immorality may be a result and symptom of sin, but it is not itself sin. . . . As Paul uses the concept, sin has to do . . . with the breaking of a human relationship with God. In this sense, the opposite of sin is not virtue but faith.[12]

That is why Paul starts with idolatry. Idolatry is at the heart of sin. Sins, of course, are understood by Paul in moral terms: sensuality and injustice and advocacy of evil. What make these matters "sins" is that they are against God. In what sense? In each case, the behavior runs contrary to God's will for the creation and the creature. Hence, it is against God. The roots of sin are in idolatry; its fruits are seen in immorality and the rationalization of it. Modern culture has rejected the vocabulary of sin or sins (= something that is against God) because modern culture is practically atheistic (that is, it operates as if God did not exist).

For Paul, sin is something we choose that then becomes our prison. For him, we are responsible for our idolatry and our behavior. Modern culture, however, has all but lost any sense of personal responsibility. Individuals are viewed as victims of their collectives. Hence, when society encounters something that is truly bad (e.g., two high school students on a rampage, shooting a host of other students and teachers), it finds it almost impossible to talk about it except in banalities. The behavior must have been due to social or psychological causes. It was symptomatic of our culture's Male Identity Crisis; it was because the individuals were poor, fatherless, abused; it was because they were not part of the in-crowd at school; it was because society made guns available to them. Always personal responsibility is forgotten in the assignment of social and psychological blame. For Paul, such individuals chose idolatry and chose immorality and chose a corrupt mind before they became prisoners to them. The fact is: most people do not act this way (i.e., killing classmates and teachers at school), even those with the same collective influences. Why? There is an element of personal choice involved. Some people choose to act this way.

The Birth of the Idol

While precise description of this surrealist work defies reason, it aptly depicts the disjointed human perspective that leads to the "birthing" of idols. Typical of the surrealist movement, stark images are juxtaposed with other vivid images, clear in their depiction but refusing to reveal a clear, concise overall meaning. In this painting the fullness of creation may be seen with the creation symbolized in the form of a tumultuous sky and a frothing ocean—infinite in its proportions. A human-shaped form is shown extending out of the ocean (birthed from the ocean) in the direction of the viewer. This symbol of human creation functions as some sort of gangplank / diving board on which a hybrid form stands vertical. Perhaps this hybrid form, which is composed of a bedpost and a dangling, disembodied arm, is the human concoction that we call an idol. To the left, there is a mirror, amongst several empty frames, which may be seen as another expression of the human "concoction" and its narcissistic aspirations.

Rene Magritte. 1898–1967. *La Naissance de l'Idole (The Birth of the Idol).* 1926. Oil on canvas. (Credit: Photothèque R. Magritte-ADAGP/Art Resource, NY/©2002 C. Herscovici, Brussels/ARS, NY))

To label the acts as sin or sins implies two things: first, the acts are against the Creator, and second, the actors are personally responsible for their deeds. Pauline thought lends a corrective to the practical atheism and the avoidance of personal responsibility that dominate our culture.

NOTES

[1] E. P. Sanders, *Paul, the Law, and the Jewish People* (Philadelphia: Fortress, 1983), 123-35, contends that the treatment of the law (salvation is dependent on obedience to the law) cannot be harmonized with any of the things Paul said about the law elsewhere. It is likely a synagogue sermon taken up and used by Paul.

[2] Kendrick Grobel, "A Chiastic Retribution-Formula in Romans 2," in *Zeit und Geschichte: Dankesgabe an Rudolf Bultmann*, ed. E. Dinkler (Tübingen: Mohr [Siebeck], 1964), 255-61.

[3] Kent L. Yinger, *Paul, Judaism, and Judgment according to Deeds* (Cambridge: Cambridge University Press, 1999).

[4] Charles Cosgrove, "Justification in Paul: A Linguistic and Theological Reflection," *JBL* 106 (1981): 653-70.

[5] *ANF* 1.198-99.

[6] Friedrich Avemarie, "Erwählung und Vergeltung zur optionalen Struktur Rabbinischer Soteriologie," *NTS* 45 (1999): 108-26; and *Tora und Leben: untersuchungen zur Heilsbedeutung der Tora in der frühen rabbinischen Literatur* (Tübingen: Mohr-Siebeck, 1996).

[7] Dale C. Allison, "Jesus and the Covenant: A Response to E. P. Sanders," in *The Historical Jesus: A Sheffield Reader*, ed. C. A. Evans and S. E. Porter (Sheffield: Sheffield Academic Press, 1995), 61-82.

[8] Ibid.

[9] Timo Eskola, "Paul, Predestination and Covenantal Nomism—Re-assessing Paul and Palestinian Judaism," *Journal for the Study of Judaism* 28 (1997): 390-412.

[10] Timo Eskola, *Theodicy and Predestination in Pauline Soteriology* (Tübingen: Mohr Siebeck, 1998).

[11] J. Louis Martyn, *Theological Issues in the Letters of Paul* (Nashville: Abingdon, 1997), 7-24.

[12] Luke Timothy Johnson, *Reading Romans* (NY: Crossroad, 1997), 46.

THE DIVINE REMEDY IN RELATION TO THE LAW

3:21–4:25

If Romans 1:18–3:20 drew a picture of the human condition, 3:21–4:25 depicts the divine remedy and speaks about its relation to the law. The universal sinfulness of humans, Jew and Gentile alike, is dealt with by the righteousness of God. This divine remedy is apart from law but fulfills the law. [Names in Paul's Letters] This section, 3:21–4:25, is organized around a "principle-example" pattern. Romans 3:21-31 states the principle; 4:1-25 provides the example. An outline of the section offers assistance in reading.

Names in Paul's Letters

ΑΩ Paul used the Greek word *nomos* is two very different ways. On the one hand, the dominant use of the term is for the Torah (= the Jewish Scriptures/the Old Testament).

- the whole Torah—Rom 3:19
- some part of the Torah
  - the Pentateuch—Rom 3:21b
  - the Decalogue—Rom 13:8-10
  - a particular law—Rom 7:2-3; 7:7
  - the essence of the Torah—Rom 8:4
- Torah as shorthand for the Mosaic covenant of obligation—Gal 3:21; Rom 3:21a; 10:4

On the other hand, Paul sometimes used *nomos* to mean something like "principle," "claim," or "purpose." (Cf. Rom 3:27; 7:23,25; 8:2) Only the context can determine which meaning is appropriate in each case.

I. The Principle (3:21-31)
  A. The righteousness of God apart from law (3:21-26)
  B. The implications of the righteousness apart from law (3:27-31)
    1. Opponent (v. 27a) // Paul (v. 27b)
    2. Opponent (v. 27cd) // Paul (vv. 27e-29a)
    3. Opponent (v. 29b) // Paul (v. 30)
    4. Opponent (v. 31a) // Paul (v. 31b)
II. The Example (4:1-25)
  A. The Righteousness of Abraham was a gift through faith (4:1-12)
    Introduction: Opponent (vv. 1-2a) // Paul (vv. 2b-3)
    1. Abraham's righteousness was a gift (vv. 4-5)
    2. Abraham's righteousness consisted of forgiveness (vv. 6-8)
    3. Abraham's righteousness came while he was a Gentile/uncircumcised (vv. 9-12)
  B. The Promise to Abraham was from grace through faith (4:13-25)
    1. The promise rests on grace (vv. 14-17a)

2. The promise is appropriated by faith (vv. 17b-25)
   a. Abraham (vv. 17b-22)
   b. Application to Christians (vv. 23-25)

The argument may be clarified by following this outline in the remarks that follow.

COMMENTARY

Romans 3:21-26 presents the righteousness of God that is apart from law. This is the divine remedy for the human condition. There are two major interpretive problems in this passage. First, was Paul here using a piece of oral tradition from Christians before him? How does the thought develop in the text? Second, what does Paul's term *hilastērion* (translated in the NRSV as "sacrifice of atonement") in v. 25 mean? The first problem must be addressed before anything else is done because it affects one's reading of the entire passage.

A number of scholars have argued for Paul's use of a pre-Pauline oral tradition in 3:24-25.[1] A variety of reasons have been offered:

(1) In this section, it is alleged, there are a number of words not normally used by Paul: *apolytrōsis* (in the sense of "redemption" [NRSV] already attained), *protithesthai* (translated in the NRSV as "put forward"), *hilastērion* (NRSV—"sacrifice of atonement"), *haima* (NRSV—"blood"), *dikaiosynē* (NRSV—"righteousness" in the sense of a divine attribute), (*paresis* (NRSV—"passed over"), *progegonota* (NRSV "previously committed"), *hamartēmatōn* (NRSV—"sins"). (2) The use of a participle at the beginning of v. 24 is awkward (*dikaioumenoi*, NRSV—"justified"). (3) There is one view of the effects of the Christ-event in vv. 24-26a and another in v. 26b.

These arguments have not gone unchallenged. (1) Redemption already attained is Pauline (1 Cor 1:30; [Col 1:14; Eph 1:7]). *Protithēmi* is found in Romans 1:13 with the sense of "purposed," a meaning that is entirely possible in 3:25. "Blood" used for Christ's cross is found in Romans 5:9; 1 Corinthians 10:16; 11:25-26; (Col 1:14,20; Eph 1:7; 2:13), not always in traditional material. To claim "righteousness" as a divine attribute is opposed to "righteousness" as a divine activity is a specious argument. The two are but parts of the same conceptual whole. The One who is righteous

AΩ **The Logic of Romans 3:21-26**

- In vv. 21-22a, 24b, the key idea is the "righteousness of God." Several things are said about it.
  - It is apart from Law.
  - It is witnessed to by the law and the prophets.
  - It is through the faithfulness of Christ for all who believe.
  - It is through the redemption in Christ Jesus.
- In vv. 22b-24a, the point is that since all have sinned, all must be justified by God's grace. There is no distinction between Jew and Gentile.
- In vv. 25-26 the focus is on Christ Jesus. Several things are said about him.
  - What? Within the divine purpose, Christ is God's dwelling place.
  - How? Christ's obedience unto death purified his selfhood from sin.
  - Why? God acted this way to prove the divine righteousness (= God is both righteous and the one who justifies).

(= faithful to the covenant) is the One who acts for our salvation. *Hamartēma* (NRSV—"sin") is also found in 1 Corinthians 6:18. This leaves only three *hapax legomena*: *hilastērion* (NRSV—"sacrifice of atonement"), *paresis* (NRSV—"passed over"), and *progegonotōn* (NRSV—"previously committed"). Given the distinctive topic treated, three such terms seem hardly enough to demand pre-Pauline oral tradition to explain them.

(2) The question about the awkwardness of the beginning of v. 24 can be explained by a careful examination of the syntax of the passage. Romans 3:21-26 can be read as a single sentence wrapped around an inserted remark.[2] [The Logic of Romans 3:21-26] A translation with appropriate punctuation follows:

But now apart from law,
the righteousness of God has been manifested,
  being witnessed to by the law and the prophets:
the righteousness of God *through* (*dia*) the faithfulness of Jesus Christ for all who believe
  (for there is no distinction,
  for all have sinned and fallen short of the glory of God,
  with the result that all are being justified freely by His grace)
[the righteousness of God] *through* (*dia*) the redemption in Christ
  Jesus,
whom God purposed as the locus of divine presence through his faithfulness in his blood,
  for a proof of His righteousness
    because of the passing over of former sins in the kindness of
God,

for a proof of His righteousness in the present
  unto His being righteous
  and the One justifying the one who lives out of the faithfulness
of Jesus.

This passage follows the pattern: righteousness of God (v. 21), righteousness of God (v. 22), *dia* (NRSV, "through"—v. 22), *dia* (NRSV, "through"—v. 24), proof of His righteousness (NRSV, "show" His righteousness—v. 25), proof of His righteousness (v. 26). While there may very well be traditional material behind vv. 21-26, such an hypothesis is not necessary to make sense of the syntax and thought of the sentence. Our task, in any case, is to interpret the final form of the text.

(3) The claim that the effects of Christ's death in vv. 24-26a are different from those in v. 26b is strained. In both segments Christ's death results in forgiveness of sins, however understood. Since the arguments for Paul's use of a pre-Pauline oral tradition in vv. 24-25 are so weak, it seems better to focus on the text as we have it. To that task we now turn.

"The righteousness of God has been disclosed" (v. 21). Righteousness here means God's covenant faithfulness seen in saving activity. This saving activity is both "apart from law" and "attested by the law and the prophets" (v. 21). [Law and the Prophets] On the one hand, God's saving activity is quite separate from any demand for "works righteousness." This point continues the statement of v. 20: "No human being will be justified by deeds prescribed by the law." On the other hand, God's saving activity is in line with the witness of the Scriptures of Israel. This latter point will be the object of concern in 3:31–4:25. This saving activity of

---

Law and the Prophets

 The "law and the prophets" is one way the Scriptures of Israel were spoken of in the 1st century AD by both nonmessianic and Christian messianic Jews.

- Law and the prophets referred to the whole of Israel's Scriptures (Matt 5:17; 7:12; 11:13; 22:40; Luke 16:16; John 1:45; Acts 24:14; 28:23; cf. 4 Macc 18:10; 2 Macc 15:9)
- Similar expressions were "Moses and all the prophets" (Luke 24:27); "the law of Moses, the prophets, and the Psalms" (Luke 24:44); "the law, the prophets, and the other books of our fathers" (Sirach, prologue)
- They were taught to children by responsible parents (4 Macc 18:10; 2 Tim 3:15 [cf. 2 Tim 1:5])
- They were read in the synagogue on the Sabbath (Acts 13:15)
- They were believed by Christian Messianists to have had their prophecies fulfilled in and by Jesus (Luke 24:27; Acts 28:23; John 1:45; Rom 3:21)

God has been manifested "through the faithfulness of Jesus Christ" (v. 22). At this point the alternate reading in the NRSV footnote is to be preferred. Taking the genitive "faith of Christ" as "faithfulness of Christ" does not exclude the Pauline focus on faith in Christ. That comes next. The righteousness (= saving activity) of God that is manifest in Christ's faithfulness is for "all who believe," that is, in Christ. In Galatians 2:16 we see yet another reference to the faithfulness of Christ followed immediately by faith in Christ, the one reference complementing the other. The faith of Christ does not eliminate faith in Christ in Paul (cf. Phil 1:29; Rom 10:14).

The emphasis on "all" who believe in Christ being recipients of God's saving activity (v. 22a) is matched by an emphasis on "all" having sinned (v. 23a). This echoes the argument of 1:18–3:20. The point is contained in a parenthesis (vv. 22b-24a) inserted into the larger sentence. "Since all have sinned and fall short of the glory of God (cf. *Apoc Moses* 21:6), they are now justified by His grace as a gift." There is no distinction. This harks back to the earlier section of the argument. It functions to keep the point already established before the readers' minds: universal sinfulness. Paul's point would have been shared by other Jews in the first century. For example, 4 Ezra 7:46 asks: "For who among the living is there that has not sinned, or who among men that has not transgressed thy covenant?" In 8:35 the statement is made: "For in truth there is no one among those who have been born who has not acted wickedly, and among those who have existed there is no one who has not transgressed." At the same time, the parenthesis reiterates another point: "justified by His grace as a gift." This also picks up the theme that no one will be justified "by deeds prescribed by the law" (v. 20). God's saving activity is "apart from law" (v. 20). Justification here is probably to be understood as acquittal, release from guilt, forgiveness (cf. 4:7-8).

The original sentence resumes in 24b: "through the redemption that is in Christ Jesus." If the righteousness of God is manifested through the faithfulness of Jesus Christ (v. 22), it is also manifested through "the redemption" in Christ Jesus (v. 24b). Redemption had multiple connotations in antiquity. It could be used for the liberation of Israel from Egypt (LXX Exod 6:6; Ps 110:9), of Judah's return from exile (LXX Isa 51:10-11; 52:3-9), for what God would do for Israel at the end of days (LXX Ps 129:7-8), for redeeming a slave (LXX Exod 21:8; Lev 25:25), for the emancipation of war prisoners (*Ep Arist* 12:35), and for the sacral manumission of slaves (Josephus, *Ant* 12.2.3+27). All of these various usages have in common "liberation from enslavement."[3] In all of the usages involving a divine subject, the meaning is "the salvation of God's people." Elsewhere Paul could say that Christ is our redemption (1 Cor 1:30) and that we look forward to the redemption of our bodies (Rom 8:23; cf. Eph 4:30). Either Paul or a Paulinist said: "in him we have redemption, the forgiveness of our sins" (Col 1:14; Eph 1:7). The saving activity of God manifested through the faithfulness of Christ is experienced as a redemption. In the context of 3:21–4:25, redemption is most likely to be understood here also as forgiveness of sins (cf. 4:6-8). [Karl Barth on the Righteousness of God Manifested through Faithfulness in Christ]

Karl Barth on the Righteousness of God through Faithfulness in Jesus Christ

The faithfulness of God is the divine patience according to which he provides, at sundry times and at many divers points in human history, occasions and possibilities and witnesses of the knowledge of his righteousness. Jesus of Nazareth is the point at which it can be seen that all the other points form one line of supreme significance. He is the point at which is perceived the crimson thread which runs through all history. Christ—the righteousness of God himself—is the one theme of this perception. The faithfulness of God and Jesus the Christ confirm one another. The *faithfulness of God* is established when we meet the Christ in Jesus.

Karl Barth, *The Epistle to the Romans* (New York: Oxford Univ. Press, 1933), 94.

The very mention of the name, Christ Jesus (v. 24b), causes Paul to speak about the saving activity of God in Christ in yet another way. "Whom God purposed (cf. 1:13) as a *hilastērion*" (NRSV—sacrifice of atonement; fnt—a place of atonement) through Jesus' faithfulness in his blood. Jesus' faithfulness is his obedience unto death ; his blood is his cross. Clearly his faithfulness is demonstrated by his death, but what does *hilastērion* mean? At this point the second major problem in this sentence must be addressed.

English translations reflect a variety of understandings of the meaning of *hilastērion* in Romans 3:25: KJV—a propitiation; NASV—as a propitiation; Moffatt—as the means of propitiation; RSV—as an expiation; NAB—as an expiation; NEB—as the means of expiating sin; Centenary—as an offering of atonement; NIV—as a sacrifice of atonement (fnt—as the one who would turn aside his wrath, taking away sin); Goodspeed—as a sacrifice of reconciliation; NJB—as a sacrifice of reconciliation. Two issues are reflected in these translations:

(1) Scholars debate whether "propitiation" or "expiation" is the appropriate translation of *hilastērion*. Propitiation implies that the sacrifice effects a change in God's disposition towards humans. Expiation implies that the sacrifice effects a change in humans. The choice between the two is difficult because the evidence is mixed.

A. The verb (*hilaskesthai* and variants) is often used with God as the object. When this is so, the term carries the idea of "acting in such a way as to cause God's wrath to cease and His mercy to be manifest" towards humans. (1) Pagan usage reflects this meaning

(Homer, *Iliad* 1.386; Strabo, *Geography* 4.4.6). (2) The LXX sometimes uses the term in the same way. For example, 4 Kings 5:18—*hilasetai kyrios*, the Lord will be propitiated toward your servant when he enters a pagan temple (= be merciful in this matter); 4 Kings 24:4—*ouk kyrios hilasthēnai*, the Lord would not be propitiated (= caused to cease from His wrath because of the sins of Manasseh); Esther 4:17h—*hilasthēti* to your inheritance, Lord; do not destroy Israel (= cease from your wrath); Lamentations 3:42—we have sinned and you have not been propitiated, *hilasthēs* (= caused your wrath to cease); Daniel 9:19—Lord, *hilasthēti*, be propitious (= be merciful). (3) Josephus, *JW* 5.19, also reflected this usage. He spoke about propitiating the God who has devastated you.

The adjective can take over the meaning of the verb both in the LXX and outside of it. (1) 4 Maccabees 17:22—Through the blood of the martyrs and their atoning death, *hilastēriou thanatou* (= propitiatory death), God saved Israel (= His wrath turned to mercy). (2) Josephus, *Antiquities* 16.182, also has this usage: *hilastērion mnēma* (= a propitiatory memorial).

B. *Hilaskesthai* can sometimes be used with God as the subject. When this is so, the meaning is something like "to show mercy, to pardon, to forgive," and expiation is the focus. (1) The LXX often uses the verb forms this way. For example, LXX Psalm 24:11—For your name's sake, O Lord, also *hilasē* (= be merciful) to my sin, for it is very great; LXX Psalm 64:3—The words of transgressors have overpowered us, but would you *hilasē* (=be merciful to/pardon) our sins; LXX Psalm 77:38—But He is compassionate and *hilasetai*

Christ as Redeemer

In this painting the atoning sacrifice of Christ is directly addressed in the most dramatic of ways. To the right of Christ stand John the Baptist, Lucas Cranach, and Martin Luther. John is pointing out to these stalwarts of the Reformation that Christ is the sacrificial Lamb. The atoning aspect of the blood of Christ is graphically portrayed as blood issues forth from the side of Christ and in a direct stream arcs onto the head of Cranach. The viewer is led to understand the saving atonement of Christ who suffered for us while we were yet sinners. Cranach is literally being anointed in this gift of sacrifice. To the left of the cross, Christ is shown treading upon death and the devil. In the background, the law is shown to be at work as the commandments are held up in judgment of an individual who is being pursued by death. In this understanding, there is no grace or atoning sacrifice for humankind's sin—only the judgment of the Law. This previous understanding is also being redeemed as seen in the foreground—the old life has gone, and a new life has begun.

Lucas Cranach. *Christ as Redeemer with Martin Luther, Lucas Cranach, and John the Baptist.* 1552–1555. Weimar.

(=will forgive) their sins and will not destroy them; LXX Psalm 78:9—Help us, O God our savior; for the glory of your name, deliver us; *hilasthēti* (=be merciful) to our sins, for your name's sake; LXX Sirach 5:6—Do not say, "His mercy is great, He will *exilasetai* (= forgive) the multitude of my sins. (2) The same usage is found in Luke 18:13. The publican prayed, "O God, *hilasthēti* (=be merciful) to me, a sinner."

C. *Hilaskesthai* can at other times be used with a priest as subject. (1) In the LXX this is so. In Leviticus 4:20, 31, 35; 5:10, 13, 16, 18; 19:22, the priest shall make atonement (*exilasetai*) and the trespass/sin shall be forgiven them; in 16:16-17 to make atonement (*exilasetai*) for the uncleannesses and all the sins of Israel; in 16:18,20,24 the priest makes atonement (*exilasetai*) upon the altar; in 16:30,34, on the Day of Atonement the priest will make atonement (*exilasetai*) for you all to cleanse you all from all your sins, and you shall be cleansed. (2) In Hebrews 2:17 Christ as high priest *hilaskesthai* (makes atonement for) the sins of the people. Here the action covered seems to include two dimensions: both that of dealing with human deficiencies (expiation) and that of causing the divine disposition to shift from wrath to mercy (propitiation).

The Ark of the Covenant

(2) There is the question of whether *hilastērion* in Romans 3:25 should be taken as a noun or an adjective. In the first place, *hilastērion* could be an adjective agreeing with some noun that is understood (such as *dōrean* [=gift] or *thyma* [=sacrifice]). It was so used in antiquity. For example, Josephus, *Antiquities* 16.7.1+182, told how when King Herod tried to plunder David's tomb, two of his bodyguards were destroyed by a flame that met them as they entered. As a consequence, the frightened king built a *hilastērion mnēma* (=a propitiatory memorial) at the entrance. 4 Maccabees 18:22 says that the divine Providence saved Israel "by the blood of those pious ones, and their *hilastēriou thanatou* (=propitiatory death). *T. Levi* 3:5, in the Pseudepigrapha, speaks about "propitiatory sacrifices." In the LXX Exodus 25:17 one possible, but improbable, way of reading the text is: You shall make an *hilastērion epithema* (= an atoning lid).

In the second place, *hilastērion* could be taken as a noun meaning "the lid of the ark of the covenant." The LXX Exodus 25:17 is most likely to be translated: You shall make an *hilastērion* (=cover), a lid of pure gold; LXX Exodus 31:7 speaks about the *hilastērion* that is on the ark of the covenant; LXX Exodus 35:11-12 refers to the *hilastērion*, the lid of the ark; LXX Exodus 38:5-8 mentions the *hilastērion*, the lid of the ark, made of pure gold, with cherubs at either end; LXX Leviticus 16:13-15 refers to the *hilastērion* as the lid of the ark. In all of these passages the *hilastērion* is the lid or cover of the ark. This fits the Hebrew word it translates, *kaporeth* (= cover). It is an object that is distinct from both the altar of incense (Exod 30:1-10) and the altar of sacrifice (Exod 27:1).

The ark's lid served as the locus of the divine presence and revelation. The LXX Exodus 25:22 says God speaks above the *hilastērion* from between the two cherubim; LXX Leviticus 16:2 refers to the *hilastērion* on the ark where God appears in a cloud; LXX Numbers 7:89 says Moses heard the voice of the Lord speaking from the *hilastērion*. Thus, the verb (*hilaskesthai*) and the adjective (*hilastērion*) are related to the function of atonement while the noun (*hilastērion*) is associated with the function of divine presence and revelation. The choice, therefore, between taking *hilastērion* in Romans 3:25 as an adjective or a noun is critical for its meaning. It is the difference between Jesus' being understood as an atoning sacrifice and his being seen as a locus of divine presence and revelation (= an alternative way of speaking about "incarnation").

One way of arguing would run like this. In Romans 3:25 ("whom God put forward"—NRSV) it is God who offers the sacrifice! *Apocalypse of Abraham* 17:20 also contains the startling idea of a sacrifice offered *by* God *to* God. Since God has no need for self-appeasing, if *hilastērion* is taken as an adjective, the meaning would be "take away sin" rather than "appease God." But all of this is said in Romans in the context of the revelation of God's wrath (Rom 1:18-32). So the sacrifice that removes sin also averts God's wrath, a propitiatory meaning. This combination yields the following result: the expiation of sin effects propitiation (= atonement). A translation might run: "whom God set forth as an offering that removes sin and thereby averts divine wrath."

An alternate way of reading takes the following tack. In the LXX Pentateuch, the noun *hilastērion* is used of the lid of the ark (Lev 16). This is also its meaning in its only other use in the New Testament (Heb 9:5). For this cause, some advocate "mercy seat (or place of expiation?)" as the appropriate translation (see the note in NRSV). If so, then Paul would be saying that the ritual of

Leviticus 16 is fulfilled in Jesus' death. It is, however, usually assumed wrongly that this ritual of the Day of Atonement atoned for human sins. But throughout the LXX Pentateuch, *hilastērion* as a noun is not associated with the altars and their sacrifices. On the Day of Atonement, the high priest sprinkled blood on the *hilastērion*, the tabernacle, and the holy place, in order to purify them so that God's presence could dwell there. Its only connection with the rituals of atonement were when it, like the tabernacle and holy place, was purified so that God's presence could dwell there. The actual atonement for the people's sins in the LXX is found in the driving out into the wilderness of the scapegoat bearing the peoples' sins (Lev 16:20-28). Thus, *hilastērion*, correctly understood, is the locus of divine presence and revelation. If we accept this sense in Romans 3:25, Jesus' flesh would be the place where God's presence is known and revealed. His blood/death, manifesting his faithfulness, would have the same function as the sprinkling of blood on the lid of the ark in the Pentateuch: to purify his body so it would be a proper place for the divine presence to reside. A translation might run: Christ Jesus, whom God purposed as a locus of the divine presence and revelation through his faithfulness in his blood.

If *hilastērion* is taken as an adjective, then Romans 3:25 yields a view of Jesus' death as an atoning sacrifice. Elsewhere Paul spoke of Jesus' death in sacrificial terms but on close examination it is likely that these were not atoning sacrifices: Romans 8:3—sin offering? [a reading often proposed but rejected in this commentary]; 8:32— echo of the "sacrifice" of Isaac in Genesis 22:16 (but not an atoning offering); 1 Corinthians 5:7-8—sacrifice of the Passover lamb (not an atoning one); 11:25—covenant sacrifice (not an atoning one); 2 Corinthians 5:21—either a sin offering or a sacrifice of reparation? (an unlikely reading; the proper reading should take *hamartia* in the same way in both parts of v. 21= sin; hence nonsacrificially)[4]; Ephesians 5:2—peace offering or thank offering, not an atoning sacrifice.[5] In most of these passages, traditional material is being employed.

If *hilastērion* is taken as a noun, then Romans 3:25 yields a view of Jesus as the "mercy seat," the site of God's presence and divine revelation, and of his death as the purification of his flesh that made this possible. It is his being a locus of the divine presence, moreover, that was the reason for his resurrection from the dead (cf. Rom 8:11). This resurrection contributes to our justification (4:25), to the divine indwelling of believers, and our resurrection (8:11).

"Atoning sacrifice" or "Ark's lid"? Given the evenly divided evidence, it is difficult to make a compelling case for either position. The slight edge probably ought to go to the view that takes *hilastērion* as a noun and sees Jesus as a new locus of divine presence and revelation. There are, however, two arguments remains against this position. First, in the LXX when *hilastērion* is used for the lid of the ark, it almost always has the definite article, and in Hebrews 9:5 the article is present. Romans 3:25 does not have the definite article; however, in Exodus 25:17 the article is absent as well! The objection does not hold. Second, the use of an object (a lid) for a person (Christ) seems awkward to some. It is no more awkward, however, than comparison of Jesus to an animal used for sacrifice, another object. Furthermore, the immediate context in Romans—the emphasis on the revelation of God's righteousness (1:17; 3:21, 25b-26) in Christ—supports the proposed translation. Later, there will be a focus on Christ as a revelation of God's love (Rom 5:9). Finally, the probable absence of a sacrificial understanding of atonement elsewhere in the Pauline corpus argues for taking *hilastērion* to be an allusion to the lid of the ark. I propose then a tentative translation. "The righteousness of God has been disclosed . . . through the faithfulness of Jesus Christ, . . . through the redemption that is in Christ Jesus, whom God purposed to be a new locus of the divine presence through his faithfulness in his blood." If so, then Paul has used two images for the saving work of God in Christ: redemption (forgiveness) and new mercy seat (locus of the divine presence).

In Romans 3:25b and 26 there are two loosely parallel assertions about the purpose of the revelation of God's righteousness (= saving activity) in Christ. The first runs: "for a proof of His righteousness (= covenant faithfulness) because of the passing over of former sins" (v. 25b). The second reads: "for the proof of His righteousness (= faithfulness) in the present time, so He would be righteous (= faithful) and the One justifying (= saving) the one who lives out of the faithfulness of Jesus" (v. 26). The first of these statements wants to affirm divine faithfulness in the face of God's having passed over (= postponed punishment of, cf. Dionysius of Halicarnassus 7.37; Josephus, *Ant* 15.48) former sins. That is, God is faithful despite not always immediately vindicating the right and judging the wrong in the past.

Such a view would have been known to pagan and Jew alike. Plutarch, "On the Delays of Divine Vengeance," *Moralia* 549B,551E, said that far from allowing the slowness of judgment to destroy belief in divine providence, such delay must be understood as the granting of time for reform for those who have sinned in ignorance. Wisdom of Solomon 11:23 says to God: "But you are merciful to all . . . and you overlook people's sins, so that they may repent." At Qumran, 1QS 4.18-19 laments the existence of wickedness in the world, acknowledging that God has not and will not deal with it until the end times. Paul has already stated his perspective. In 2:4-5 he asked the disobedient Jew: "Or do you despise the riches of His kindness and forbearance and patience? Do you not realize that God's kindness is meant to lead you to repentance?" In spite of passing over former sins in forbearance, God is righteous (faithful).

The second member (v. 26) functions to guarantee that God is righteous (faithful) in the present time. As a result God justifies (saves) those who live out of the faithfulness of Jesus. If the passage began with the way God's righteousness is manifested in Jesus Christ, it closes with a purpose statement: the revelation of God's righteousness. It is to vindicate God's character and to rectify human life. Verses 21-26 have had a proclamatory character to them. They have asserted the divine remedy: God's righteousness (= covenant faithfulness made known in saving activity) is manifested in Jesus. Note that this passage is not about the inclusion of Gentiles along with Jews in the people of God. It is rather about the relation of both Gentile and Jew to their Creator, the Lord of history.

In 3:27-31 the implications of the manifestation of God's righteousness in Christ are dealt with. The form of the passage is that of the diatribe, a series of questions and answers.[6] (1) Paul's imaginary opponent asked: "Then what becomes of our boasting" (v. 27a)? That is, if justification is by God's grace and apart from law, can we boast about anything? Paul replied: "It is excluded" (v. 27b). (2) The dialogue partner again asked: "By what law (= principle)? By that of works" (v. 27cd)? To which Paul replied: "No, but by the law (= principle) of faith" (v. 27e). His reason was given: "For we hold that a person is justified by faith apart from works prescribed by the law (v. 28; remember 3:20, 21). Or is God the God of Jews only? Is He not the God of Gentiles also" (v. 29a)? (3) The interlocutor answered the question: "Yes, of Gentiles also" (v. 29b). Paul replied: "Since God is one . . . He will justify the circumcised on the ground of faith and the uncircumcised through that same faith" (v. 30; cf. Philo, *Special Laws* 1.52, where appeal to "one God" serves to promote acceptance of proselytes). The phrases "on the ground of faith" and "through faith" are a stylistic variation to avoid repetition. They mean the same thing.[7] (4) The questioner asked again: "Do we then overthrow the law by this faith" (v. 31a)? Paul responded strongly: "By no means! On the contrary, we uphold the law" (v. 31b). If salvation comes not through works of law but through faith, does that not undermine the Scriptures? This is the issue that is faced in Romans 4. Abraham is used as an example to prove Paul's gospel is in accord with the Scriptures of Israel. (In other contexts, Paul argued that Christians' love of the neighbor fulfills the law: Gal 5:14; Rom 13:8-10.) [Martin Luther on Faith and the Law]

Martin Luther on Faith and the Law

We reach the conclusion that faith alone justifies us and fulfills the law; and this because faith brings us the spirit gained by the merits of Christ. The spirit, in turn, gives us the happiness and freedom at which the law aims; and this shows that good works really proceed from faith. That is Paul's meaning in chapter 3 when, after having condemned the work of the law, he sounds as if he had meant to abrogate the law through faith, i.e., we fulfil it by faith.

Martin Luther, "Preface to Romans," in *Martin Luther: Selections from His Writings*, ed. John Dillenberger (New York: Anchor Books, 1961), 22.

Ancient teachers often used examples of notable figures from the past to make their case. For example, Epictetus appealed to Herakles (*Discourses* 2.16.44), Socrates (1.9.22), and Diogenes (2.22.58). The *Testaments of the Twelve Patriarchs* held up the twelve sons of Jacob as embodiments of a series of virtues to imitate and vices to avoid. Philo used Abraham (*On Abraham*), Joseph (*On Joseph*), and Moses (*Life of Moses*) to do the same thing. Philo used Abraham as the example of an ideal proselyte (*On Abraham* 219). It was appropriate that the apostle to the Gentiles use a similar technique. Like James 2:20-24, Hebrews 11, and *1 Clement* 10, Paul picked Abraham as his example.

Chapter four, with its focus on the role of the law, is launched by the continuation of the diatribe form. A fifth exchange is found in 4:1-2. (5) The Jewish questioner asked: "What then are we to say was gained by Abraham, our ancestor according to the flesh? For if Abraham was justified by works, he has something to boast about" (vv. 1-2a). To which Paul responded: "But not before God (v. 2b)! For what does the scripture say (v. 3a)? Abraham believed God, and it was reckoned to him as righteousness" (v. 3b; see Gen 15:6). Down through v. 12 Paul's first point is that Abraham's righteousness was a gift through faith.

In many Jewish circles Abraham was held up as a model of works-righteousness. First Maccabees 2:52 says: "Was not Abraham found faithful when tested, and it was reckoned to him as righteousness?" Sirach 44:19-21 says: "Abraham . . . kept the law of the Most High . . . and when he was tested he proved faithful. Therefore the Lord assured him with an oath that the nations would be blessed through his offspring." Jubilees 23:10 comments: "Abraham was perfect in all his deeds with the Lord, and well-pleasing in righteousness all the days of his life." These Jewish interpreters viewed Genesis 15:6 (Abraham was reckoned

---

1 Maccabees, James, and Paul on Abraham

ΑΩ A comparison of how three sources use Abraham reveals a lot about the standpoint of each.

(1) 1 Macc 2:52 offers a nonmessianic Jewish midrash on Gen 15 and 22. Two points comprise the argument. First, Abraham was found faithful when tested. This is a reference to the sacrifice of Isaac in Gen 22. Second, as a result, it was reckoned to him as righteousness. This is a reference to Gen 15. In this midrash, Gen 15 is read in light of Gen 22. The sequential order and connection of the plot are violated. The result is a position with which Paul is unhappy.

(2) Jas 2:21-23 presents a Christian-Jewish exegesis of the same texts. Here the order of events is respected in the two points that are made. First, the faith of Abraham mentioned in Gen 15 was active in Abraham's works and was completed by his works. Second, Gen 22 shows this to be the case. The sacrifice of Isaac demonstrated that Abraham's faith was completed by his works. So he was not justified by faith alone but also by his works. James wrote out of a context in which there was an attempt to separate the inner and outer person. It was claimed that one's inner faith is all that is needed. James assumed the wholeness of the human being's response to God. He, therefore, tried to hold inner belief and outer obedience together. Paul would not have disagreed but would have phrased it differently.

(3) Rom 4 focuses on Gen 15 and 17; it does not refer to ch. 22. Paul's two points are clear-cut. First, according to Gen 15, which comes before ch. 17, Abraham is justified through faith. Second, ch. 15, which speaks about his justification, comes before ch. 17, which talks about Abraham's circumcision. He was, therefore, justified through faith before he was ever circumcised. This shows Abraham was the father of Gentiles who have faith just as much as of Jews who have faith.

In these three sources one can see how basically the same material can be used by different authors in a variety of ways.

---

righteous) through the lens of Genesis 22 (the sacrifice of Isaac). As a result, Abraham's faith became his obedience to God. It was regarded as a work for which God owed Abraham a reward. Not so Paul, who would have regarded such a reading as legalism. For the apostle, Abraham's righteousness was a gift. "Now to one who works, wages are not reckoned as a gift but as something due. But to one who without works trusts Him who justifies the ungodly, such faith is reckoned as righteousness" (vv. 4-5). [1 Maccabees, James, and Paul on Abraham]

Paul understood Abraham's being reckoned righteous to mean that he was forgiven. In vv. 6-8, the apostle's argument follows the rabbinic practice of *gezerah shawah* (inference by analogy). According to this principle, when the same word occurs in two biblical passages, each can be used to illumine the other. The link between Genesis 15:6, referred to in v. 3b, and Psalm 32:1, cited in vv. 7-8, is the word "reckon." What does it mean to be reckoned righteous? David said it means not to have one's sin reckoned. In the parallelism of vv. 7-8, this is used synonymously with "iniquities are forgiven" and "sins are covered." For Abraham to be reckoned righteous was for him to have his iniquities forgiven, covered, not reckoned or counted. Granted, forgiveness of sin's guilt is only part of Paul's larger understanding of justification but it is an integral part. It is on that part that Paul focused here.

Abraham's being reckoned righteous in connection with his faith was, moreover, while he was as yet uncircumcised (= a Gentile). Paul asked, for whom is the blessing mentioned in Psalm 32:1? Is it only for Jews? Or is it also for Gentiles (v. 9)? At this point Paul uses yet another rabbinic rule of interpretation: *dabar halamed me 'inyano*: a passage is to be interpreted in its context.[8] Since Genesis 15:6 contains the word "reckon," it can be used to interpret Psalm 32:1. Since the circumcision of Abraham did not take place until Genesis 17, Abraham was, in religious terms, a Gentile when he was reckoned righteous (v. 10b). So he could be the father of all who believe without being circumcised, who have righteousness reckoned to them (v. 11b). This in no way excludes the Jew. Abraham was also the father of the circumcised who "follow the example of the faith that our ancestor Abraham had before he was circumcised" (v. 12). Paul has here made the pattern of Gentile righteousness by faith normative for Jewish righteousness rather than the reverse. A correct reading of Torah has shown this to be so!

From v. 13 to v. 25, Paul's argument focuses on the point that the promise to Abraham was from grace through faith. Verses 14-17a deal with the promise that rests on grace. Verses 17b-25 are concerned with the promise as appropriated by faith. We begin with Paul's thesis statement in v. 13. "The promise that he would inherit the world did not come to Abraham or to his descendants through the law but through the righteousness of faith" (v. 13). In this context, the promise to inherit the world refers not to taking possession of the land of Israel but to gaining life in the New World beyond the resurrection. Verses 14-17a focus on the foundation of grace underlying the promise to Abraham. The promise rests on grace. It is guaranteed to all Abraham's descendants, "not only to the adherents of the law but also to those who share the faith of Abraham" (v. 16). This assertion, of course, fulfills Scripture: "I

James and Paul on Abraham

AΩ Jas 2:18-24 poses a point-by-point counter-argument to Rom 3:27–4:25.

Issue posed: faith and works	Rom 3:27-28	Jas 2:18
Significance of claiming God is one	Rom 3:29-30	Jas 2:19
Appeal to Abraham as a test case	Rom 4:1-2	Jas 2:20-22
Citation of proof-text: Genesis 15:6	Rom 4:3	Jas 2:20-22
Interpretation of Genesis 15:6	Rom 4:4-21	Jas 2:23
Conclusion	Rom 4:22	Jas 2:24

Although their arguments move in different directions, the two authors seem to be following a traditional homiletic pattern. (Dunn)

James D. G. Dunn, *Romans 1–8* (WBC; Dallas: Word Books, 1988), 197.

God as the One Who Calls into Existence the Things that Do Not Exist

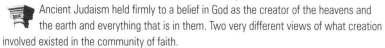

Ancient Judaism held firmly to a belief in God as the creator of the heavens and the earth and everything that is in them. Two very different views of what creation involved existed in the community of faith.

- The older view, reflecting ancient Near Eastern beliefs, saw creation as the activity of God that resulted in an ordered cosmos. Here God created from formless matter. Gen 1 presupposes a watery chaos out of which God brings order and life by means of His word. Gen 2 assumes an arid wasteland that God turns into a garden by his creative hands. This view is continued in Wis 11:17 where God is said to have created from formless matter.

- The second view, found from the 1st century BC on alongside the older perspective, holds that God creates out of nothing. 2 Macc 7:28 says that God did not make the heavens and earth out of things that existed. *Joseph and Aseneth* 12:2 asserts that God made the things that are from nonbeing. *2 Bar* 21:4 refers to God as the one who called that which did not yet exist and they obeyed. In 48:8 the same source claims that God, with a word, brings to life that which does not exist. *2 Enoch* 24:2 says that before anything existed at all, God created from the nonexistent. It is this latter view of creation that was assumed by Paul in Rom 4:17. His language, "calls things that have no existence into being," is very close to that of *2 Bar* 21:4. There God is the one who calls that which did not yet exist into being. In this view, creation is bringing into being that which formerly did not exist (= *creatio ex nihilo*). It is this God in whom Abraham and Christians put their trust.

---

have made you the father of many nations (= Gentiles)" (v. 17; Gen 17:5). [James and Paul on Abraham]

Verses 17b-25 emphasize that the promise is appropriated through faith. Abraham's faith is center stage in vv. 17b-22. Abraham's faith is described as his trust in the God who gives life to the dead and calls into existence the things that do not exist (cf. Philo, *Special Laws* 4.187). The meaning "trust" for Abraham's faith is made clear by its antonym. "No distrust made him waver concerning the promise of God, but he grew strong in his faith . . . being fully convinced that God was able to do what He had promised" (vv. 20-21). When we consider that in Romans 1:5 Paul spoke about the "obedience which is faith," it becomes clear that "faith" had a range of meanings for Paul. Perhaps it will help to sketch what Paul meant by faith. [God as the One Who Calls Into Existence the Things that Do Not Exist]

We may begin with a survey of how *pistos* (faithful), *pistis* (faith), and *pisteuein* (to believe/to have faith) were used in Paul's Bible. (1) In the LXX *pistos* (faithful) is used both of God (Deut 7:9—God is faithful . . . the Lord is righteous) and of humans (Tob 5:8—Tobias needs a trustworthy [*pistos*] man to accompany him on the journey). (2) In the LXX *pistis* (faith/faithfulness) is used both of God (1 Kgs 21:2—the faithfulness of God) and of humans (1 Kgs 26:23—The Lord will recompense each according to his righteousness and his faithfulness [*pistis*]). (3) In the LXX *pisteuein* (to believe/to have faith) is often used of humans' relation to God.

For example, Genesis 15:6—Abraham believed God (in context, he believed God's promise of an heir and a land: so, trust); Exodus 14:31—The people believed God (in context, after the water had destroyed Pharaoh and his hosts as God had promised: so, trust); Numbers 14:11—How long will this people not believe? (in context, not believe God's promise that He will give them the land: so, trust); Numbers 20:12—Moses and Aaron did not believe God (in context, they did not obey God's command that Moses speak to the rock that it give water: so, obey); Deuteronomy 9:23—Israel did not believe God (in context, God told them to go up and possess the land that He had promised to them but they disobeyed the word of the Lord and did not believe Him: so, obey); Tobit 14:4—Tobit tells his son and grandsons: I believe that [*hoti*] the prophetic words are true, so you act accordingly until God's promises are fulfilled: so, trust and obey); Psalm 77:22—Israel did not believe in (*en*) God and did not hope (*elpisan*) in His salvation; Wisdom of Solomon 1:2—God will be found of them that tempt Him not; He shows Himself unto those who do not distrust (*apistousin*) Him (so, trust); Sirach 35:24—The one who believes . . . the one who trusts (*pepoithōs*) the Lord (so, trust); Isaiah 43:10— that you may know and believe and understand that (*hoti*) I am He; Jeremiah 25:8—because you did not believe my words, I will send an enemy from the north (in context, Israel did not obey the prophetic words spoken to them and repent: so, obey).

In the LXX, the terms for faith are used in a covenant context to refer to appropriate behavior in that setting. Such behavior consists of faithfulness to the relation (whether God or humans). Faith is a synonym of righteousness (= covenant faithfulness). When used of humans' relation to God, it usually means either trust or obedience or both. Occasionally the verb can be used with *hoti* (that). When this happens, "to believe that" cannot be reduced to a mere intellectual assent but encompasses a conviction that involves trust and obedience.

There is one distinctive usage of the terms for faith in the LXX that merits attention. The conversion of sinful Gentiles to the one, true God is sometimes called faith. For example, Jonah 3:5—the people of Nineveh believed God, proclaimed a fast, put on sackcloth, and repented; Wisdom of Solomon 12:2—God corrects little by little those who are trespassing so they may be freed from wickedness and put their trust (believe/have faith) in the Lord; Judith 14:10—when the pagan general Achior saw all God had done, he believed firmly in God and was converted. Paul doubtless reflected this Jewish terminology of mission.

God's Promise to Abraham

In Genesis, God promises Abraham both a land and an heir. Abraham's challenge is to believe or trust in that promise. Although Abraham is not always able to do so, Genesis portrays God as always faithful to fulfill the promise.

James Jacques Joseph Tissot. 1836–1902. *God's Promise to Abraham.* Oil on canvas. The Jewish Museum. New York, NY. (Credit: The Jewish Museum, NY/Art Resource, NY)

How were the terms for faith used in Paul's letters? (1) *Pistos* (faithful) is used both of God (God is faithful—1 Cor 1:9; 2 Cor 1:18; 1 Thess 5:24) and of humans (a steward is to be found faithful—1 Cor 4:2). (2) *Pistis* (faith/faithfulness) is used of God (God's faithfulness—Rom 3:3), of Christ (Christ's faithfulness—Rom 3:22,25,26; Gal 2:16; Phil 3:9), and of humans. When using faith of humans Paul referred both to Abraham (Abraham's trust in God's promise of life—Rom 4:19-20) and to Christians. Both Jew and Gentile Christians have faith (Rom 3:22; 4:11; 10:4, 9-12). Faith was used both for saving faith (obedience—Rom 1:5; cf. 10:16 in context; 15:18; 16:19; 1 Thess 1:3; trust in God's promise of life—Rom 4:5) and for faith as a spiritual gift (Rom 12:3, 6;

1 Cor 12:9). In Romans 1:1–5:11 "faith" is persistently present. It is absent from 5:12–8:39. It appears again in Romans 9–16.

(3) *Pisteuein* (to believe/to entrust to) is used both of Abraham (he believed God/trusted in God's promise—Rom 4:17-18) and of Christians. (a) Christians believe in God (Rom 4:24—trust in God's promise of life). (b) They believe that God raised Christ (Rom 10:9). Behind Romans 10:8-9 are two pre-Pauline confessions: first, v. 8b (Jesus is Lord—cf. 1 Cor 12:3; Phil 2:11; 2 Cor 4:5; Acts 2:36; 19:5); second, v. 8b (God raised him from the dead—cf. Rom 4:24; 8:11; 1 Cor 15:3-5; 2 Cor 4:14; Gal 1:1; 1 Pet 1:21). The two confessions are joined because of the influence of the preceding OT quotation (Deut 30:14— "But the word is very near you; it is in your mouth and in your heart, so that you can do it"). Verse 8a reads: "But what does it say? The word is near you, on your lips and in your heart." The double confessional statement is, therefore, rhetorical and does not intend to distinguish between the effects of believing and confessing. Just exactly how Paul understood the meaning of believing the creedal statement "God has raised him from the dead" is indicated by two other passages in Paul. First, Romans 4:24 (those believing on the One who raised Jesus from the dead), in context, means to trust God's promise (i.e., that we will be raised). Second, 2 Corinthians 4:14 (the One raising the Lord Jesus), in context, means knowing that we will share Jesus' resurrection (= trust in the promise). This is also the meaning found in 1 Peter 1:21 (faith, hope, confidence are in God). Thus, to believe that God has raised Jesus meant for these early Christians a trust in God who is regarded as the One who will also raise us. (c) Christians believe in Christ (Rom 9:33; cf. Gal 2:16), meaning trusting Christ as the means of our sharing in God's promise. Faith in God and faith in Christ are not mutually exclusive concepts. Christ is the manifestation of God's righteousness. So faith in Christ is ultimately faith in God. The verb, to believe, can also be used in nontheological ways (e.g., Rom 3:2— the Jews were entrusted with the oracles of God; 6:8—Christians believe that). The verb occurs in Romans 5:12–8:39 only once and that in a nontheological way (Rom 6:8).

The bottom line of all this is that for Paul faith meant trust in, obedience to, and conviction that. How do these various pieces fit together into a coherent picture? What did Paul assume that enables all the data to make sense? In Romans the covenant with Abraham seems to underlie much of what Paul was doing. When God approached Abraham, according to Paul's Bible, He spoke both a promise and a demand. His promise was that Abraham's

Paul Tillich

descendants would be many (Gen 12:2; 15:4-5; 17:4-7) and that the land would be theirs (Gen 12:7; 13:17; 15:18; 17:8). His demand was that Abraham go from his father's house to a land God would show him (Gen 12:1). If Abraham responded positively to God's word, it would be because he believed it was true. That is, he trusted God's promise and obeyed God's demand because he was convinced that God was reliable, faithful, and true.

Paul closed his discussion of Abraham's faith with an application. "Now the words, 'it was reckoned to him,' were written not for his (Abraham's) sake alone, but for ours also" (vv. 23-24a; cf. 1 Cor 9:10). The story of Abraham's justification through faith (Gen 15:6) has a Christian application. It provides a pattern for Abraham's descendants. "It will be reckoned to us who believe in Him who raised Jesus our Lord from the dead" (v. 24). Christians, like Abraham, will be justified (= reckoned righteous) through their faith in the God "who gives life to the dead and calls into existence the things that do not exist" (v. 17b). That this is the God in whom Christians trust is spelled out in what is probably a pre-Pauline couplet in v. 25: who was handed over to death (*dia* =) because of our trespasses (LXX Isa 53:12) and was raised (*dia* =) for the sake of our justification (LXX Isa 53:11).

If Abraham's God gave life to the aged bodies of Abraham and Sarah, the Christians' God gave life to the dead Jesus. It is the same God. Just as Abraham responded to this God with trust and was justified, so Christians respond to God with faith and are reckoned righteous. This applies to Jew and Gentile alike. That justification comes through faith for both Jew and Gentile, moreover, does not overthrow the Scriptures of Israel. Rather, it upholds them, as the example of Abraham the Gentile's being justified through faith shows! Paul's use of Abraham as an example supported his stated principle about the divine remedy for the human condition.

CONNECTIONS

Justification as Forgiveness/Acceptance

One dimension of justification's meaning in Romans is seen in Romans 4. To be reckoned righteous is interpreted by Psalm 32:1-2 as having one's "iniquities . . . forgiven," one's "sins . . . covered" (Rom 4:7-8). This forgiveness is said to be "not by works" (Rom 4:5-6).

Paul Tillich's sermon "To Whom Much Is Forgiven," echoes the Pauline mind when he asserted:

> Forgiveness is unconditional or it is not forgiveness at all. Forgiveness has the character of "in spite of. . . ." God's forgiveness is unconditional. There is no condition in man which would make him worthy of forgiveness. If forgiveness were conditional, conditioned by man, no one could be accepted and no one could accept himself.[9]

In his sermon, "You are Accepted," Tillich spoke about the experience of grace as an overcoming of the sense of separation that humans know. The same Pauline note of "not by works" is present.

> Sometimes . . . it is as though a voice were saying: "You are accepted. *You are accepted*, accepted by that which is greater than you, and the name of which you do not know. Do not ask for the name now; perhaps you will find it later. Do not try to do anything now; perhaps later you will do much. Do not seek for anything; do not perform anything; do not intend anything. *Simply accept the fact that you are accepted!*" If that happens to us, we experience grace. After such an experience we may not be better than before, and we may not believe more than before. But everything is transformed. In that moment grace conquers sin, and reconciliation bridges the gulf of estrangement. And nothing is demanded of this experience, . . . nothing but *acceptance*.[10]

✳ *Faith*

Perhaps no issue in Pauline theology is more difficult for modern Christians than his understanding of faith. In order to peel away layers of misinterpretation, let us engage in a series of negations.

(1) For Paul, one is not saved by faith. God saves. We are saved by grace (= God's initiative). Faith is the human reception of salvation. So we are saved by grace and through faith. This is superbly summarized by the deutero-Pauline Ephesians 2:8-9.

(2) For Paul, faith is not a work (= something we do to cause God to respond favorably to us). Faith responds. It is not because of our faith that God justifies us but through our faith. Even justification by faith can be understood legalistically if faith is looked upon as the necessary precondition required for salvation.[11] Faith is not the condition of our justification. It is our acceptance of it or our experience of it.

(3) For Paul, faith is not believing doctrinal propositions. The object of faith is a person: either God (Rom 4:24; 1 Thess 1:8) or Christ (Rom 10:14; Gal 2:16). Note the earlier exegesis of Romans 10:8-10 in this commentary. This is the only passage where Paul seems to have equated saving faith with belief in a certain proposition. In the exegetical section of the commentary it has been shown that "believing that God has raised him from the dead" (10:14) is synonymous with "believing in Him who raised Jesus from the dead" (4:24). This means that faith is a religious/relational term rather than an intellectual one. Luther's words are to the point.

> There are two ways of believing. One way is to believe *about* God....
> This . . . is knowledge or observation rather than faith. The other
> way is to believe in God, as I do when I . . . put my trust in Him,
> surrender myself to Him and make bold to deal with Him.[12]

Out of a faith-relationship with God in Christ may come intellectual conviction and clarity. Belief, in the modern intellectual sense, arises out of faith, in the Pauline relational sense. "A person thus both 'has faith' (in something or other) and has 'a faith' (a belief system by which his or her life is ordered)."[13] From a Pauline perspective, the latter arises out of the former.

(4) For Paul, faith is not a subjective feeling or attitude that is acceptable to God when our actions are not. The difference between works and faith is not that one (works) is action and the other (faith) is feeling or attitude. In Paul, works can be a feeling or attitude as well as actions. Likewise, faith involves action as well as feelings and attitudes. At this point Paul and James are one. The difference between faith and works lies in whether one's feelings/attitudes/actions are done to gain God's approval (= works) or whether they are done in response to God's prior initiative (= faith). Anything that seizes the initiative from God in the relationship is works.

(5) For Paul, faith is not a one-time event. It is both an act that begins the Christian life (Rom 10:9) and an orientation by which the Christian life continues (Gal 2:20). A Christian believes in Christ and then goes on believing. This means that the Christian

life does not begin with faith and then passes on to something else like love or knowledge or works. The Christian life, for Paul, begins and ends with our faithful response to God in Christ. (Our faith may deepen, but it is never displaced by something else.)

(6) For Paul, faith is not a partial response to God. It is not a response of action only or attitude only. It involves the whole person. It is not a response of trust only or of obedience only. It is both together. Faith is one's total response to the total relation with God. An analogy might be a human love relationship. To enter such a relationship, one must trust the other party. Once in the relationship, the other party gives verbal and nonverbal signals about what pleases or displeases him or her. Following the other person's guidance (= obedience) is necessary if the relation is to continue and flourish. Just so in our relations with God. Faith is "the acceptance not only of the offer of grace, but also of the obligation of grace."[14]

(7) Faith is not only my decision to follow Jesus. It is God's gift (Phil 1:29). Just as one cannot merely decide to fall in love with another person because the time seems right or because the person meets all the specifications, so one cannot merely decide to have faith. For a love relation to exist, something has to happen. An event has to take place that enables one to enter the relationship. Just so, for a relation with God to exist a happening has to take place. There must be an event that enables one to respond to God in Christ. The event is the grace nature of the relationship. The enabled response is the faith dimension. In his *On Grace and Free Will*, XXIX, Augustine put it this way:

> Now if faith is simply of free will, and is not given by God, why do we pray for those who will not believe, that they may believe? This it would be absolutely useless to do, unless we believe, with perfect propriety, that Almighty God is able to turn to belief wills that are perverse and opposed to faith.

NOTES

[1] E.g., Sam K. Williams, *Jesus' Death as Saving Event: The Background and Origin of a Concept* (Atlanta: Scholars Press, 1975).

[2] Douglas A. Campbell, *The Rhetoric of Righteousness in Romans 3:21-26* (Sheffield: JSOT, 1992).

[3] A point made by Luke T. Johnson, *Reading Romans* (Macon GA: Smyth & Helwys, 2001) 55.

[4] N. T. Wright, "On Becoming the Righteousness of God: 2 Corinthians 5:21," in *Pauline Theology, Vol.2: 1 & 2 Corinthians*, ed. D. M. Hay (Minneapolis: Fortress, 1993), 200-208.

[5] Bradley H. McLean, "The Absence of an Atoning Sacrifice in Paul's Soteriology," *NTS* 38 (1992): 542-45.

[6] I am following Stanley Kent Stowers, *The Diatribe and Paul's Letter to the Romans* (Atlanta: Scholars Press, 1981), 164-65.

[7] Jan Lambrecht and Richard W. Thompson, *Justification by Faith: The Implications of Romans 3:27-31* (Wilmington: Michael Glazier, 1989), 40.

[8] Richard Longenecker, *Biblical Exegesis in the Apostolic Period* (Grand Rapids: Eerdmans, 1975), 118.

[9] Paul Tillich, *The New Being* (NY: Charles Scribner's, 1955), 8.

[10] Paul Tillich, *The Shaking of the Foundations* (NY: Charles Scribner's, 1948), 162.

[11] Anders Nygren, *Commentary on Romans* (Philadelphia: Muhlenberg Press, 1949), 67-71.

[12] Martin Luther, *A Brief Explanation of the Ten Commandments, the Creed, and the Lord's Prayer* (Hugh Thompson Kerr, *A Compend of Luther's Theology* [Philadelphia: Westminster, 1943], 33).

[13] B. C. Birch and L. L. Rasmussen, *Bible and Ethics in the Christian Life* (Minneapolis: Augsburg, 1976), 88.

[14] William Barclay, *The Mind of St. Paul* (NY: Harper & Brothers, 1958), 152.

THE GROUND
OF FUTURE HOPE

5:1-11

The argument of Romans 1:18–4:25 began with an indictment of humanity generally for its universal sinfulness. It then moved to a proclamation of the divine remedy: God's righteousness manifested in Jesus Christ. Such a claim raised questions about the law and its place in such a scheme. Paul insisted that the divine remedy he proposed upheld the law, as the example of Abraham shows. The apostle's argument then moves to the point of being able to speak about the future hope of believers. This hope is grounded in salvation history and in the readers' present experience.

In order to read Romans this way, it is necessary to confront the most difficult problem having to do with the surface structure of the letter. Where is the break in Paul's argument? Does the break come between chapters 5 and 6? Does it come between chapter 4 and 5? Or does it come between 5:11 and 5:12? This commentary espouses the last option, for the following reasons.

COMMENTARY

(1) The vocabulary of Romans 5:1-11 has greater affinities with chapters 1–4 than with chapters 5–8. For example, *dikaiōthentes* ("being justified," 5:1,9) is found in 2:13; 3:4; 4:2-5, 20, 25. In the rest of the letter, the verb "justified" is found only in 6:7; 8:30-33. The verb *kauchōmetha* ("we boast," 5:3, 11) is found in 2:17, 23; 3:27; 4:2. Elsewhere it appears only in 15:17. The noun *orgē* ("wrath," 5:9) appears in 1:18; 2:5, 8; 3:5; 4:15. Elsewhere it occurs only at 9:22; 12:19; 13:4, 5, but in a rather different sense. The phrase *tēn charin tautēn* ("this grace," 5:2) refers to 3:24. The phrase *ep' elpidi tēs doksēs* ("in the hope of glory," 5:2) recalls 3:23. The phrase *synistēsin de tēn heautou agapēn* ("proves his love," 5:8) corresponds to 3:5. The phrase *en tō haimati autou* ("by his blood," 5:9) corresponds to 3:25 and is found nowhere else in the letter.

(2) The thought of 5:1-11 goes better with chapters 1–4. Romans 1:17–5:11 is dominated by the ideas of righteousness and faith, while chapters 6–8 emphasize the ideas of life and salvation.

(3) The connection of 5:1-11 with chapters 1–4 is symbolized by the link word joining 4:25 ("justification") with 5:1 ("justified"). Romans 5:1-11 also continues the first person style of 4:24-25. "We" and "us" are in the forefront. Romans 5:12 shifts to the third person.

Others argue against dividing 5:1-11 from 5:12-21, noting that the themes of Romans 5:1-11 are repeated and elaborated upon in chapter 8. For example, hope/glory (5:2; 8:24-25, 18, 21); sufferings (5:3; 8:17, 18, 35-37); endurance (5:4; 8:25); Spirit (5:5; 8:9, 14-17, 23); God's love in Christ's death (5:8; 8:31-32); justified/saved (5:9; 8:30). Nils Dahl noted these and other similarities. He correctly saw that chapter 8 contains a fuller development of the themes that are briefly stated in 5:1-11. The close parallelism between 5:1-11 and chapter 8, he said, points to an inclusion. If so, then the break comes between 4:25 and 5:1. Romans 5–8 form a coherent whole held together by the inclusion.[1]

Although the evidence does show a remarkable correspondence between 5:1-11 and chapter 8, Dahl's inference cannot be sustained. Rather than creating an inclusion, the points of correspondence signal parallelism instead. F. J. Leenhardt has contended that Romans 1–8 falls into two corresponding panels.[2] His suggestion, with modifications, is persuasive. Both 1:18–5:11 and 5:12–8:39 run loosely from the sinfulness of humans, through the divine remedy, to the role of the law, to the future hope that is grounded in present experience and in salvation history.

The argument for a parallelism between 1:18-32 and 5:12-21 is as strong as the correspondences between 5:1-11 and chapter 8. For example, one can point to a corresponding use of the theme of Adam's sin in both passages. Romans 1:18-32 is generally thought to be a type of midrash on a number of OT traditions, among which are Genesis 1–3, Psalm 106, Deuteronomy 4:15-18, and Wisdom of Solomon 12–13. Several recent attempts have been made to say that Adam figures in at Romans 1:23. Others deny it, saying that though Genesis 1 does seem to be reflected, this does not prove an Adamic reference. N. Hydahl has shown, however, that Romans 1:23 differs from Deuteronomy 4:15-18 in vocabulary, order of creatures named, and the fact that Deuteronomy does not mention "man." In all these respects, however, Romans 1:23 resembles a part of the creation story in Genesis 1:20-31.[3] Out of this recent discussion, one thing seems certain. Romans 1:18-32 echoes the creation and sin of Adam in Genesis 1–3 and the ruin introduced by that sin. It is entirely legitimate to say that Romans 1:18-32 is built upon the theme of Adam's sin and its consequences. This, of course, is what Romans 5:12-21 is about. Even if the reference to Adam's sin in 1:18-32 is denied, however, 1:18–3:20 focuses on universal sinfulness just as Romans 5:12-21 does. Romans 1:18-32 and 5:12-21 are then parallel, though not identical, structures of thought. The two sections correspond to one another in much the same way that 5:1-11 and chapter 8 do. If we take these two sets of correspondences as fixed points, it is not at all difficult to agree with Leenhardt that Romans 1–8 falls into two parallel structures of thought, and that the division between them comes at 5:11 and 5:12.[4] The thought of Romans 1–8 is not to be conceived of as a single logical line moving directly towards a single conclusion. Rather there is a line of thought that is repeated, the second journey through the issues giving elaboration to the argument at many points. The parallelism is not synonymous but rather is complementary. This means that any interpretation of Romans 5:1-11 must set it in the context of 1:18–5:11. Any interpretation of Romans 5:12-21 must set that passage in the context of 5:12–8:39. If 5:12-21 picks up again the theme of human sinfulness originally addressed in 1:18–3:20, 5:1-11 offers an eschatological dimension that has so far been lacking in the argument of 1:18–4:25.

The argument falls into an ABB'A' pattern along these lines:

A—(vv. 1-4): Justified,
    through our Lord Jesus Christ,
    boast,
    future hope,
    not only, but
  B—(v. 5): God's love (known in experience)
  B'—(vv. 6-8): God's love (known from salvation history)
A'—(vv. 9-11): Justified
    future hope,
    not only, but
    boast,
    through our Lord Jesus Christ

Verse 1 picks up the thought of chapter 4: "Therefore, since we are justified by faith, we have peace with God through our Lord Jesus Christ." [Peace with God] The NRSV rightly translates "we have peace" (indicative) rather than "let us have peace" (subjunctive).

Peace with God

AΩ In Paul's Bible, the LXX, *eirēnē* translates the Hebrew *shalom*. It is used is two basic ways: of the present and of the future.

• Peace refers, in the present, to life in all its intended wholeness and harmony (e.g., bodily health [Ps 38:3] long life [Gen 15:15]; prosperity [Ps 37:11]; harmonious relationships in the family [Gen 13:8] and nation [2 Sam 17:3]). The source of this peace is God (Judg 6:24; Isa 45:7) who overcomes the forces of disharmony (Job 25:2).

• Peace refers, in the future, to both deliverance from exile (Isa 52:7; 55:12; 57:19; Ezek 34:25-30) and a final peace as God's gift in the coming age (Ezek 34:25-28; Isa 2:2-4; 65:25).

• In the Pauline corpus, peace results from justification (Rom 5:1). It is a synonym of the salvation that Christ brings (Eph 2:14-17). For Paul, then, the expression "peace with God" continues both the OT emphasis on a harmonious relationship and its focus on final peace as God's gift in the coming age.

Pablo Picasso. 1881–1973. *Vive la Paix.* 1954. Pen and Ink Drawing. Musee d'Art et d'Histoire. St. Denis, France. (Credit: /Scala/Art Resource, NY/©2002 Estate of Pablo Picasso/ARS, NY)

The context demands a statement rather than an exhortation. We have peace because we have been justified (cf. Isa 32:17—"the effect of righteousness will be peace"). Peace here is understood as it was in Paul's Bible, the LXX. It refers to the condition that exists when the covenant relation between God and humans is whole and right (18:23; Lev 26:6; Num 25:12). That Paul's words would have been at least partially understood even by someone with no knowledge of the LXX is evidenced by *Cynic Epistles.* Ps-Crates 8 reads: "We live in total peace, freed from every evil by Diogenes of Sinope." Another way of expressing the benefits of justification through Christ is in terms of "access to this grace in which we stand" (v. 2a). The image is that of a subject's access to the royal audience chamber (cf. Xenophon, *Cyropaedia* 7.5.45). [Access to God] Access for Christians is to the presence of God, the heavenly king (Eph 2:18; 3:12; Lev 16:17; Heb 10:19-22). Peace, access, and boasting (RSV, rejoicing) result from believers' justification.

Access to God

Oriental monarchs restricted access into their presence. Usually in the court there was a functionary whose task was to bring visitors into the royal chamber, vouching for their good intentions. It is likely this background against which Paul writes in Rom 5:2.

- The term *access* is used in the NT only at Rom 5:2; Eph 2:18; 3:12; and 1 Pet 3:18. In all cases it refers to humans' access to the presence of God, the heavenly king.
- Rom 5:2, Eph 3:12, and 1 Pet 3:18 all think of Jesus as the mediator who enables human access into the presence of God.
- Eph 2:18 links access to the presence of God to the Holy Spirit.
- For Paul, justification results in a harmonious relationship between humans and God (peace) that enables human entry into the presence of God (access).

This boasting (so correctly NRSV; RSV—rejoicing) is twofold. On the one hand, Christians boast "in our hope of sharing the glory of God" (v. 2b). On the other hand, believers boast (rejoice) both in our sufferings (v. 3a) and in our life in God (v. 11). The one is a future hope (our hope of glory); the other is a present experience (our suffering and our life in God). The unit, 5:1-11, is organized around these two occasions of boasting and their bases. The believers' boasting in our hope of sharing the glory of God (v. 2b; cf. 8:30) is based on the one hand on God's acts in Christ's death (vv. 6-10) and on the other on the character developed through suffering that is confirmed by the gift of the Spirit in believers' hearts (v. 5). The boasting in suffering (v. 3a) is based on the benefits accruing to those who suffer (vv. 3b-4). The boasting about our life in God is based on the reconciliation received through Christ (v. 11b).

Paul's Bible contrasted two types of boasting: self-boasting and boasting in God. The former was viewed negatively and regarded as a characteristic of the foolish and ungodly (Ps 52:1; 74:4) who attempted to be self-sufficient over-against God. Psalm 49:6 and Jeremiah 9:23, for example, equate boasting about one's wealth with trusting in it. The latter, boasting in God, was viewed positively (Jer 9:24). It was regarded as the equivalent of trusting in God (Ps 5:11-12) and could be used synonymously for rejoicing in God (1 Chr 16:28-31). Paul shared this perspective about boasting. Boasting in one's self, a negative, he saw as an attempt at self-reliance over-against God (Phil 3:7-10; Rom 3:27; 4:1-2), a trust in the flesh (Phil 3:3). Faith implies an end to all self-boasting (Gal 6:13). True boasting is in Christ (Phil 3:3; Gal 6:14) and God (Rom 5:11). This boasting is the equivalent of trusting and rejoicing in God. In Romans 5:1-11, therefore, for Paul to boast in God or in his hope for the future or in his sufferings was an expression of trust in the God whose saving activity Christians had experienced.

We begin with his boasting in sufferings. Paul made use of a traditional view of suffering in vv. 3-5. In antiquity one view of suffering held that such hard times functioned as divine education. There were two very different versions of this view.[5] On the one hand, some people held that suffering was God's way of disciplining children who had gotten off track. It was God's correction of human misdirection. Just as the parent disciplines a child, so God disciplines those who are children. For example, LXX Proverbs 3:11-12 reads: "My son, do not despise the Lord's discipline (*paideias*, education) or be weary of His reproof, for the Lord reproves him whom He loves, as a father the son in whom he delights." The purpose of such discipline is the correction/refinement/purification/growth of the one who suffers. For example, Judith 8:27 says: "The Lord scourges those who draw near to him, in order to admonish them"; Sirach 18:13 says: "The Lord rebukes and trains (*paideuon*, educates) and teaches them, and turns them back, as a shepherd his flock"; 2 Maccabees 6:12 reads: "these calamities were designed to discipline (*pros paideian*, for the education of) our people"; *Psalms of Solomon* 10:1-2 reads: "Happy is the one whom the Lord remembers with rebuking and protects from the evil way with a whip that he may be cleansed from sin that it may not increase. The one who prepares his back for the whips shall be purified, for the Lord is good to those who endure discipline"; in 16:11 there is the petition: "If I sin, discipline me that I may return." A variation on this view is found in Plato. In his *Republic* 380a-b, Plato argued that suffering can only be seen as sent by Zeus if the chastisement has some beneficial effect on those who suffer. Presupposed in this view is usually the view that the sufferer has strayed from the right path either consciously or unconsciously, knowingly or unwittingly. The pain is the discipline necessary to correct this misdirection.

Another view of suffering as divine education saw it as conditioning or training for virtue. The Roman Stoic philosopher Seneca used the image of parental discipline. In *On Providence* 2.5-6, he wrote: "Toward good men God has the mind of a father . . . and he says, 'Let them be harassed by toil, by suffering, by losses, in order that they may gather true strength.' Who has struggled constantly with his ills becomes hardened through suffering, and yields to no misfortune. . . . Do you wonder if that God, who most dearly loves the good, who wishes them to become supremely good and virtuous, allots to them a fortune that will make them struggle?"

The philosopher Epictetus, in his *Discourses*, used the image of "athletic training" instead of that of parental discipline. In 1.xxiv. 1-3, he said: "When a difficulty befalls, remember that God, like a physical trainer, has matched you with a rugged young man. What for? some one says. So that you may become an Olympic victor; but that cannot be done without sweat. To my way of thinking no one has got a finer difficulty than the one which you have got, if only you are willing to make use of it as an athlete makes use of a young man to wrestle with." In 4 Maccabees one finds a Jewish appropriation of this view. One of the martyrs, on the point of death, says: "We, vile tyrant, suffer all this for our training in divine virtue" (10:10). Another, struggling for breath, says: "A glorious favor you bestow on us, tyrant, though all unwillingly, enabling us as you are to manifest our constancy toward the Law by yet more noble suffering" (11:12). Yet another, amidst horrible tortures, says: "How sacred and seemly is the agony to which so many of my brothers and I have been summoned as to a contest in sufferings for piety's sake, and yet have not been vanquished. . . . Our reason remains undefeated" (11:20, 27). The narrator summed up: "On that day virtue was the umpire and the test to which they were put was a test of endurance" (17:12). Because of their endurance, "they now stand beside the divine throne and live the life of the age of blessing" (17:18). In some circles of the Greco-Roman world suffering was considered an educational kind of struggle that results in increased strength. Suffering in this view is not so much correction of misdirection as conditioning that builds one up for greater virtue.

Paul knew and used both of these views of suffering as educational. First Corinthians 11:17-34 is a discussion of the proper observance of the Lord's Supper. In vv. 29-32, the apostle said that improper observance results in judgment. Evidence of this is

Suffering

Reflecting some of the attitudinal changes coming out of the revolution of 1910, Jose Clemente Orozco began to paint murals in the 1930s that addressed the plight of the indigenous Mexican people. His art style reflects influences from both the Spanish as well as the ancient Mexican cultures. In this mural, Orozco graphically shows the heartfelt obedience and poverty of the Franciscan monks as they enter into the suffering and endurance of the Mexican people.

Jose Clemente Orozco. 1886–1949. *Franciscan Monk*. Mural. Escuela Nacional Preparatoria San Ildefonso. Mexico City, Mexico. (Credit: Schalkwijk/Art Resource, NY/©SOMAAP, Mexico City)

found in the fact that many of the Corinthians had been weak and ill and some had died (v. 30). The train of thought concludes with a statement about the purpose of judgment. "But when we are judged by the Lord, we are being chastened so that we may not be condemned along with the world" (v. 32). Here the suffering experienced by the Corinthian Christians because of their misdirection involving the Eucharist is designed to effect repentance. It is disciplinary. At this point Paul seemed to reflect the concept of suffering as divine correction of human misdirection.

In Romans 5:3-5 Paul reflected the other stream of thought. "We boast (rejoice) in our sufferings" (v. 3a). These sufferings (*thlipsesin*) certainly include the distress caused by outward circumstances (cf. 2 Cor 1:4, 8; 2:4; 6:4; 7:4; 8:2; Phil 1:17; 4:14; 1 Thess 1:6; 3:3) and possibly the tribulations of the last days (cf. 1 Cor 7:28; 2 Cor 4:17). Why do sufferings offer a ground for boasting? Sufferings, rightly responded to, produce benefits (cf. *Pss Sol* 10:1-2; 1 QH 9.24-25). The basis offered for this is a tradition that he and the Roman disciples held in common. Note the "knowing that" in v. 3b, and the parallels in thought with James 1:2-4 (where "we know" is also used) and 1 Peter 1:6-7. This is a common early Christian tradition that Paul held in common with other authors.

> . . . knowing that
> suffering produces endurance,
> and endurance produces character,
> and character produces hope. (vv. 3b-4)

Paul here used the rhetorical form "climax" (cf. Rom 8:29-30; 2 Pet 1:5-7; Jas 1:2-4; Wis 6:17-19). Augustine pointed out the trope (*Christian Doctrine* 4.7.11-13) and commented: "Therefore let us acknowledge that the canonical writers are not only wise but eloquent also, with an eloquence suited to a character and position like theirs" (4.7.21).[6]

The suffering experienced between conversion and consummation is not meaningless. It rather educates and strengthens the believer. Here suffering is the arena in which the Christian develops spiritual muscles. The reason for the positive attitude toward suffering is the benefits that accrue to the sufferers. The discussion of benefits accruing from suffering in the present leads back to the notion of hope. How does character produce hope? "There is a pattern of growth in the here and now, however imperfect, that indicates that we are changing. Believers, then, become assured that the process that God has begun He will complete (1 Cor 1:8; Phil 1:6)."[7] [Hope]

The focus of the unit is on Christians' boasting (rejoicing) in their future hope of God's glory (v. 2b). The basis for this boasting is found in v. 5, where the focus is on the Spirit, and in vv. 6-10, where the focus is on God's acts in Jesus' death. The two amount to an argument from experience and from salvation history. In v. 5 the evidence of experience is mentioned. "Hope does not disappoint us, because God's love (8:39; 2 Cor 13:13) has been poured into our hearts through the Holy Spirit that has been given to us" (15:30; cf. 2 Cor 1:22; 5:5 [Eph 1:13-14]). God's love here is "not simply something believed in on the basis of the gospel or the testimony of the cross, . . . but God's love itself . . . experienced in rich measure."[8]

In vv. 6-10 the evidence from salvation history is expounded. These vv. break into two parallel parts: vv. 6-9 and v. 10. The former speaks in terms of justification; the latter reconciliation. Both use a rabbinic interpretative principle called *kal wahomer* (light and heavy). It is essentially an argument from the minor to the major, reflected by the English "how much more." A rabbinic example is found in the Mishnah. In *m. Aboth* 1:5, Jose b. Jonathan of Jerusalem said: "Let thy house be opened wide and let the needy be members of thy household; and talk not much with womankind. They said this of a man's own wife: how much more of his fellow's wife!" It is this way of arguing that Paul used here.

Verses 6-9 form the first part. In vv. 6-8 the focus is on Christ's death. "For while we were still weak (*asthenōn*), at the right time Christ died for the ungodly (*asebōn*)" (v. 6). This runs counter to human predisposition. "Rarely will anyone die for a righteous person—though perhaps for a good person someone might actually dare to die" (v. 7). Ancient advice encouraged granting benefits only to the deserving. For example, the Jewish Sirach 12:1-7 says: "If you do good, know to whom you do it. . . . Give to the godly man, but do not help the sinner." The Roman Seneca, *De Beneficiis* 4.27.5, said that people should only grant benefits to those worthy to receive them. Of course, sometimes one might die for a friend. Earlier Aristotle, *Ethics* 9.8,1169a, had said: "To a noble man there applies the true saying that he does all things for the sake of his friends . . . and, if need be, he gives his life for them." The

Hope

The Pauline corpus frequently mentions hope.

- Christians have a hope (1 Thess 1:3 [Eph 1:18; 4:4; Col 1:5, 23; 2 Thess 2:16]) that is shared by the Creation (Rom 8:20). This is a hope pagans do not share (1 Thess 4:13).
- What is the hope? It is a hope for sharing the glory of God (Rom 5:2; [Col 1:27]); for the redemption of our bodies (Rom 8:24); for righteousness (Gal 5:5); for life after death (1 Thess 4:13); for salvation (1 Thess 5:8); for eternal life (Titus 1:2; 3:7); for the parousia (Titus 2:13). The hope, then, is for ultimate salvation.
- What enables it? The Scriptures encourage hope (Rom 15:4). Character produces it (Rom 5:4). The Holy Spirit confirms it (Rom 5:4-5).
- What fruit does it produce? It produces rejoicing (Rom 12:12) and boldness (2 Cor 3:12).

Christ Among Sinners

In this work, Bosch effectively communicates the utter "sinfulness" and alienation surrounding Christ, the Redeemer. Characteristic of Bosch, he is unrelenting in focusing upon the mask-like fiendishness of grotesque humankind, reduced to the point of virtual caricature. By contrast, the peaceful countenance of Christ, even while carrying the CROSS of his own demise, makes his way through a sea of broken humanity.

Hieronymus Bosch. 1450–1516. *Ecce Homo* or *Christ Carrying the Cross.* Oil on panel. Museum voor Schone Kunsten. Ghent, Belgium. (Credit: Scala/Art Resource, NY)

pre-Christian *Life of Philonides* (P. Herc 1044) says of the Epicurean philosopher: "For the most beloved of his relatives or friends he would readily risk his neck."[9] But Paul said Christ died for the ungodly (v. 6) and that "God proves His love for us in that while we still were sinners (*hamartōlōn*) Christ died for us" (v. 8; cf. 1 John 4:10; John 3:16). Divine behavior runs counter to cultural expectations! If God has done the unthinkable in Christ's death, how much more, then, "now that we have been justified by his blood, will we be saved through him from the wrath of God" (v. 9). The reference is, of course, to the Last Judgment (cf. 2:5,16; 1 Thess 1:9-10). On the basis of what God has done in and through Christ in the present, Christians can have a hope for their future. [Pauline Eschatology]

Pauline Eschatology

The ancient Jewish belief in two ages carried over into Paul's thought. The Actual (= what is) was conceptualized as a present evil age (Gal 1:4; 1 Cor 2:6-8) ruled over by Satan (2 Cor 4:4) and the elemental spirits (Gal 4:3; 1 Cor 2:8). It was, therefore, at odds with God (1 Cor 15:24-28; Rom 8:37-39). This present evil age, however, is passing away (1 Cor 7:31). The Ideal (= what ought to be) was thought of as a new creation or age (Gal 6:14; 2 Cor 5:17). Since the essence of the Ideal was God's rule over creation, the new creation was often called the kingdom of God (1 Thess 2:10-12; 1 Cor 15:20-28; 2 Cor 4:17; Rom 5:2, 21). Sin would there be abolished and suffering and death would be no more. Since Paul believed Christ had risen from the dead as the beginning of the general resurrection, his scheme of the two ages was a bit different from that of non-Christian Jews. Paul thought of an overlap of the ages (1 Cor 10:11; 2 Cor 5:16). The new had broken in with Jesus' resurrection but the old had not yet come to an end. Indeed, the old age would not come to an end until the parousia of Jesus. This means that in Paul's thought there was both a NOW (the new age has broken in) and a NOT YET (the old has not yet come to an end). This combination, NOW . . . NOT YET, gives to Christian life between Jesus' resurrection and his parousia a distinctive character.

In Paul's time (and ours) the challenge was to avoid a loss both of the NOW dimension of Christian existence and the NOT YET dimension. If one affirms the NOW and loses sight of the NOT YET, one has an over-realized eschatology. For example, if one maintains that because one has been converted or experienced the Holy Spirit one does not sin or get sick, that is claiming something for the NOW that belongs only to the future kingdom of God. The NOT YET has been lost. If one affirms the NOT YET and loses sight of the NOW, one has an under-realized eschatology. For example, one might say that because sin and suffering are not to be overcome ultimately until the parousia, one should not expect to experience God's power in victory over sin in this life or to expect miracles that heal and/or relieve suffering for some in this age. In this case the NOW has been lost. Holding the two, the NOW and the NOT YET, together constitutes the challenge for Paul and for us. Paul affirmed both "we have been saved" (the NOW) and "we will be saved" (the NOT YET).

The second part of the basis for boasting in the future hope comes in v. 10. "If while we were enemies (*echthroi*), we were reconciled to God through the death of His son, much more surely, having been reconciled, will we be saved by his life." One dies for friends, not enemies. In Mediterranean antiquity enemies were those one tried to destroy. Hatred of enemies even had a certain nobility about it (Plutarch, "On Envy and Hate," *Moralia* 536E-538E). Yet while we were enemies Christ died for us. This death reconciled us to God. Paul spoke about reconciliation in this text, in Romans 11:15, and 2 Corinthians 5:11-21 (cf. Eph 2:16; Col 1:20, 22). Paul's teaching about reconciliation stands out when viewed against the background of his context. Non-Christian Judaism generally spoke of God's being reconciled to humans. For example, 2 Maccabees 8:29 is a prayer, asking for divine reconciliation with God's servants (cf. also 5:20; 7:32-33); Philo, *Moses* 2.166; *On Joseph* 11.18; and Josephus, *JW* 5.415; *Antiquities* 7.153, referred to God's being reconciled to Israel or to David when they pray. The first-century Greek novel by Chariton, *Chareas and Callirhoe*, reflects the same mindset. In a narrative whose plot unfolds under the supervision of the goddess Aphrodite, the heroine in the midst of her trials petitions the goddess: "Be reconciled to me" (3.8.9). Then near the end of the novel, after the resolution of the problems, Callirhoe again speaks to the goddess in a prayer: "Now you are reconciled with me" (8.4.10). In Paul's milieu, then, God was reconciled to humanity, not humanity to God. In Paul, however, humans are reconciled to God (Rom 5:10; 2 Cor 5:18-20). This comes about through the death of Jesus (Rom 5:10). It is a gift that humans receive (Rom 5:11). Reconciliation is but a different metaphor to describe the same reality as justification (Rom 5:9-10). The parallelism of the two parts makes this clear:

(a) reconciled through the death of Jesus
(b) through the death of Jesus we shall be saved
(c) we shall be saved

If we have been reconciled in the here and now in spite of our being God's enemies, "much more surely, having been reconciled, will we be saved (= on Judgment Day) by his life (= his risen life; cf. 4:25)" (v. 10b). Again, the believers' future hope rests on God's actions within history in Christ's death.

Having spoken of the believers' future hope based on God's acts in Christ's death and in the gift of the Holy Spirit to us, the apostle concluded with a renewed focus on the present. "But much more than that, we even boast (rejoice) in God through our Lord Jesus Christ, through whom we have now received reconciliation" (v. 11). Boasting of human achievement is excluded by the revelation of God's righteousness (3:27). If believers are to boast, it must be in God who has manifested righteousness (= saving activity) in Christ.

CONNECTIONS

Some feminist theologians contend that suffering can never be redemptive, only abusive.[10] The Christian theology of atonement based on the suffering of Christ, they say, encourages martyrdom and victimization rather than healing.

> What is new is that many . . . are recognizing the role of christology in particular in justifying and perpetuating abuse. It is no coincidence that already scores of Christian feminists see the problem and

are naming it as a particularly . . . Christian problem clearly illustrated by the doctrine of the atonement.[11]

It makes God a tyrant, a divine sadist, who must be hated because He is responsible for so much suffering. They propose a Christianity without atonement.

> Jesus' death was tragic, but it neither had to happen nor was a part of a divine plan of salvation. . . . His dying is a testimony to the powers of oppression. It is neither salvific nor essential. . . . Just as the suffering of those who went before him and those who came after him has done, his suffering compels us not to despair but to remember him and all others who suffer and to seek erotic power by our own action.[12]

Christianity, they say, is about justice and liberation. Jesus did not choose the cross; he lived a life in opposition to injustice. His death was an unjust act, done by humans. It is a tragedy, revealing God's grief. To be a Christian means to keep faith with those who have heard and lived God's call for justice and liberation; who challenge injustice; and who refuse to be victims.

> Salvation in our time must be the task of all human beings working in concert with the loving power of God as a present and future activity. It is not what one individual did two thousand years ago that is critical but what we, with God, do now.[13]

This new model abolishes the theology of atonement and substitutes in its place a theology of justice for all, accomplished by human effort.

Such a revisioning of Christianity is both reductionist and naive. It is reductionistic because it focuses only on humans' relations to others of our own kind. It does not see that the essential or root problem is humans' relation to God. It is naive because it assumes both a view of humans as basically good victims of evil structures and the notion that wrong relationships may be rectified without the costly, but necessary, pain and suffering on the part of both wronged and wrongdoer. Paul, by contrast, was a realist about human evil. He saw us as we are: not victims but guilty sinners. He was also a theist. He knew sin is against God before it is against any human or our environment. As a result, he knew that only a theology of atonement can offer a remedy for what ails us.

No passage in Romans offers a better window into one dimension of Paul's understanding of the death of Jesus than Rom 5:1-11.

Jesus' death, Paul said, is a revelation of God's love (v. 8). First, it is important to see that it is God's love that is revealed.

> There is a way of presenting the gospel which comes perilously near to blasphemy, a way in which Paul's gospel especially is wrongly presented. Sometimes the gospel is presented as if there was a contrast between a stern and angry God and a gentle and loving Christ, as if there was a contrast between a God who was the judge of the souls of men, a contrast between a God who wished to condemn and a Christ who wished to save.[14]

In Paul's view, however, any love that is shown in the death of Jesus is God's love.

> Second, it is important to recognize that the death of Jesus is a revelation of who God is eternally. Sometimes the gospel is presented in such a way that it sounds as if Jesus Christ had done something to change the attitude of God, as if He had changed God's wrath to love, as if He had persuaded God's uplifted hand not to strike the contemplated blow.[15]

For Paul, God is eternally loving. The cross does not change the deity's mind but rather proves who God has been all along.

For Paul in Romans 5:1-11, Jesus' death was a revelation of God's love to the unlovely. In these vv. the apostle painted a picture of those to whom God's love is shown. Four brush strokes yield the following result. "While we were still weak" (v. 6a) Christ died. "Christ died for the ungodly" (v. 6b). "While we still were sinners Christ died for us" (v. 8b). "While we were enemies" (v. 10) the death of Christ reconciled us to God. This is anything but an appealing picture. It is human nature to step on the weak, to disdain those who fail to take us as seriously as we take ourselves, to scorn the failures, and to attempt to destroy our enemies.

> A Sunday school teacher was once telling the story of the Prodigal Son to a class in a slum mission. . . . She told the story of the son's rebellion, of his terrible fate in the far country, of his resolution to come home. And she went on, "What do you think his father would do to him when he got home?" From that class . . . back came the immediate answer: "Bash him!" That is the natural answer; that is what anyone would expect; but that is the wrong answer.[16]

Why? God is not like humans. God's love is shown to the unlovely.

In this text Jesus' death is depicted as the revelation of God's love to the unlovely for our salvation. This salvation comes in two installments. On the one hand, there is a present dimension to it. Two parallel statements in vv. 9 and 10 use two different terms for present salvation. "We have been justified" (v. 9) and "we were reconciled" (v. 10) are differing images, describing the same new relationship to God. On the other hand, salvation also has a future aspect to it. "We will be saved through him from the wrath of God" (v. 9) and "we will be saved by his life" (v. 10) attest believers' vindication at the Last Judgment and our sharing of Christ's victory over death. In between believers' having been saved and their hope of being saved lies their present experience. "We . . . boast in God through our Lord Jesus Christ" (v. 11). Christians can boast in God in the present while we wait for our ultimate vindication because "God's love has been poured into our hearts through the Holy Spirit that has been given to us" (v. 5).

Considering the three traditional views of the atonement, this reading of Romans 5:1-11 may sound like Paul was siding with Abelard (= the cross is a revelation of God's love designed to melt the hard human heart and evoke a human response of love toward God; cf. John Wesley's translation of Paul Gerhardt's "Jesus, Thy Boundless Love to Me") against Anselm (= the cross is satisfaction offered to God's offended honor; cf. William R. Featherstone's "My Jesus, I Love Thee"—"and purchased my pardon on Calvary's tree"; Philip P. Bliss's "I Will Sing of My Redeemer"—"In his boundless love and mercy, He the ransom freely gave") and the early fathers and Reformers (= the cross is Christ's victory over evil powers; cf. Luther's "A Mighty Fortress Is Our God").

Paul an Abelardian on the atonement? This is doubtful on two grounds. First, the Pauline letters contain multiple views of Jesus' death. Colossians 2:15 talks about Jesus' death as a victory over the evil powers. Romans 3:25 thinks of Jesus' blood as the purification of his flesh so he could be a new place of God's presence and revelation. Romans 5:18 and Philippians 2:8 understand Jesus' death an his obedience to God, a supreme act of righteousness (= covenant faithfulness). So the apostle would not have been playing off one view of atonement against another. Each of his several explanations is a partial attempt to give expression to what God did in Jesus' death. New Testament diversity is, then, complementary not contradictory. Second, to say the cross is a revelation of God's love is empty or meaningless unless something happened in the cross that made it love. If so, then the Abelardian view of atonement is hollow unless it is combined with one or more of the other views. For Paul in Romans, the cross could be said to be loving because in Jesus' faithfulness unto death the righteousness of

God is revealed. That is, the saving activity of God that forgives guilt (4:7-8), delivers from sin's bondage (6:7), and enables human faithfulness to God (5:19) is revealed in the cross. What God does for us in the cross is something that we cannot do for ourselves. That is truly loving. This is the love that God shows to us in Jesus' death.

NOTES

[1] N. A. Dahl, "Two Notes on Romans 5," *Studia Theologica* 5 (1951–1952): 37-48.

[2] Franz J. Leenhardt, *The Epistle to the Romans* (NY: World Publishing Co., 1961), 24-25.

[3] N. Hydahl, "A Reminiscence of the OT at Romans 1:23," *NTS* 2 (1956): 285-88.

[4] This division is also argued by Charles D. Myers, Jr., "The Place of Romans 5:1-11 within the Argument of the Epistle," Unpublished PhD dissertation, Princeton Theological Seminary, 1985, and A. Feuillet, "La Citation d'Habacuc 2:4 et les huit premiers Chapitres de l'Epitre aux Romains," *NTS* 6 (1959): 52-80.

[5] Charles H. Talbert, *Learning Through Suffering: The Educational Value of Suffering in the New Testament and in Its Milieu* (Collegeville, MN: Liturgical Press, 1991), 9-23.

[6] *NPNF* 1st series.

[7] Thomas R. Schreiner, *Romans.* (*ECNT*; Grand Rapids: Baker Books, 1998), 256.

[8] James D. G. Dunn, *Romans 1–8* (WBC; Dallas: Word Books, 1988), 252.

[9] Adolf Deissmann, *Light from the Ancient East* (NY: Harper & Brothers, 1922), 118.

[10] E.g., Joanne Carlson Brown and Rebecca Parker, "For God So Loved the World?" in *Christianity, Patriarchy, and Abuse: A Feminist Critique*, ed. Joanne Brown and Carole B. Bohn (NY: Pilgrim Press, 1989), 3-28.

[11] Beverly Harrison and Carter Heyward, "Pain and Pleasure: Avoiding the Confusions of Christian Tradition in Feminist Theology," in *Christianity, Patriarchy and Abuse*, ed. J. C. Brown and C. R. Bohn (NY: Pilgrim, 1989), 153.

[12] Rita N. Brock, *Journeys by Heart: A Christology of Erotic Power* (NY: Crossroad, 1988), 93, 98.

[13] Sallie McFague, *Models of God* (Philadelphia: Fortress, 1987), 54.

[14] William Barclay, *The Mind of Paul* (NY: Harper & Brothers, 1958), 40.

[15] Ibid., 40.

[16] Ibid., 78.

THE HUMAN CONDITION
AND ITS ANTIDOTE

5:12-21

With Romans 5:1-11 Paul's argument reached a conclusion of sorts. In 1:18–5:11 he moved from a description of the human condition to the divine remedy to the role of the law in God's scheme to the future hope of believers. What has still to be said can only go back to offer further explanations. This is what happens in 5:12–8:39. In a complementary fashion, the apostle moved once again from the human condition to the divine remedy to the role of the law to future salvation.[1] Early Christian authors often argued this way, as is evidenced by a statement from Athanasius.

> And do not be surprised if we frequently repeat the same words on the same subject. For since we are speaking of the counsel of God, therefore, we expound the same sense in more than one form, lest we should seem to be leaving anything out, and incur the charge of inadequate treatment; for it is better to submit to the blame of repetition than to leave out anything that ought to be set down. (*On the Incarnation of the Word* 20)

The roots of this reasoning are in ancient Greco-Roman rhetoric. The *Rhetorica ad Herennium* 4.42.54, puts it this way: "We shall not repeat the same thing precisely—for that, to be sure, would weary the hearer and not elaborate the idea—but with changes." The practice is that of repetition with variation.

If the focus in 1:18–5:11 was on freedom from the guilt of sin and the condemnation that guilt entails, the focus of 5:12–8:39 deals with freedom from the power of sin.[2] In the first segment of 5:12–8:39, Paul presented Christ as an antitype of Adam. Romans 5:12-21, thereby, presents not only a complementary statement of the human condition but also something of the divine remedy.

Many scholars have despaired of finding the organization of the unit. John Knox was typical.[3] The sense of the whole is clear, he thought. By the sin of Adam death and sin and condemnation came upon all humans; by the righteousness of Jesus Christ all humans can become righteous, be restored to a right relation to God, and hope for life. The section, however, is awkwardly constructed, said Knox, and is marked by no little repetition and confusion.

Formal considerations, however, enable one to see the passage as organized in what is essentially an ABB'A' pattern, with a diatribe insertion:

A—*hōsper di' henos* ("just as . . . through one"), *kai houtos* ("and so") v. 12

    B—*ouch hōs* ("not like") + "free gift"

        ei gar tō tou henos paraptōmati ("for if the trespass of the one") + death

        pollō mallon ("much more") + free gift, the one Jesus Christ, abounded v. 15

    B'—*ouch hōs* ("not like") + free gift v. 16

        ei gar tō tou henos paraptōmati ("for if the trespass of the one") + death v. 17 *pollō mallon* ("much more") + abundance, free gift, the one Jesus Christ v. 17

A'—*hōs di' henos* ("just as through one"), *houtōs kai* ("so also") v. 18

    hōsper . . . dia . . . henos ("just as by . . . one"), *houtōs kai* ("so also") v. 19 *hōsper* ("just as"), *houtōs kai* ("so also") v. 21

The reader is given a hint of the organization of the unit by the concentric plan of v. 12 which begins the section: A—sin, B—death, B'—death, A'—sin.

The only section of the unit not accounted for in this pattern is vv. 13-14. They utilize a diatribe form.

Verse 13a is a Pauline statement: "Sin was indeed in the world before the law."

Verse 13b is an objection to the preceding proposition: "But sin is not reckoned when there is no law."

Verse 14 is Paul's response: "Yet death exercised dominion from Adam to Moses."[4]

Recognition of Paul's use of both an ABB'A' pattern and a diatribe section allows one to follow his thought reasonably well. To that task we now turn.

COMMENTARY

Verse 12 begins with "therefore." This is best taken as a particle of transition, indicating only a loose connection between what has gone before and what will follow.

The rest of the verse is clear except for one expression (*eph' hō*, NRSV "because"). The first part of the sentence says that sin came into the world through one man, and that death came through sin. Paul is thinking here of the early chapters of Genesis (e.g., Gen 2:16-17; 3:3; 3:22-24).

Jewish writers differed on whose was the responsibility for sin and death entering human history. (1) Wisdom of Solomon 2:24 says it was through the envy of the devil that death entered the world (cf. 2 Cor 11:3). (2) *Jubilees* 3:17-32 lays the blame equally on the serpent, the woman, and Adam. (3) Sirach 25:24 claims that it was from a woman that sin had its beginning and that because of her we all die. A similar perspective is found in the *Life of Adam and Eve* 3. There Eve says to Adam that she is the reason God is angry with Adam (cf. 1 Tim 2:8-15). In 10:4 Adam attributes the loss of Paradise to Eve's actions. (4) In 4 Ezra 3:7 we hear that Adam transgressed and death resulted for him and his descendants; 3:21 says that Adam transgressed and was overcome, as were all descended from him; 4:30 speaks about the evil seed in Adam's heart that has produced much ungodliness; 7:48 [118] reads: "O Adam, what have you done? For though it was you who sinned, the fall was not yours alone, but ours also who are your descendants." That Adam was the origin of sin and death in human history is found again in *2 Baruch*. *Second Baruch* 23:4 says that when Adam sinned, death was decreed against those who were to be born from him; 54:15 reads: "For though Adam first sinned and brought untimely

The Fall

The corruption of God's good creation is depicted as due to the original couple's eating of forbidden fruit. Their act is called "the Fall" (i.e., into sin and death).

Hugo van der Goes. *The Fall. Adam and Eve Tempted by the Snake.* Left wing from the diptych of *The Fall and the Redemption.* c. 1470. Oil on Oakwood. Kunsthistorisches Museum, Vienna, Austria. (Credit: Erich Lessing/Art Resource, NY)

death upon all men, yet each one of those born from him has either prepared for his own soul (its) future torment or chosen for himself the glories that are to be"; 54:19 continues: "Thus Adam was responsible for himself only: each one of us is his own Adam." (5) R. Judah, a Tanna (= active before AD 200), interprets Deuteronomy 32:32 to be addressed to Israel and to mean: "You are sons of Adam who brought death upon you and upon all his descendants coming after him until the end of all generations" (*Sifre Deut*, sec 323 [138b]). These Jewish sources agree that the first sin was the cause of death's entrance into human affairs. They disagree about whose was the primary responsibility. In Romans 5 Paul placed the responsibility upon the first man, Adam. "Sin came into the world through one man, and death through sin."

The second part of the sentence is more difficult. The NRSV reads: "so death spread to all, (*eph' hō,* because, NRSV) all have sinned." The phrase *eph' hō* has been the source of much controversy. The four leading possibilities for translation are: "in whom," "because," "with the result that," and "from which it follows."[5] The first is the position of Augustine. It holds that all people sinned in the person of Adam. The second is the stance of Chrysostom. It maintains that all people sinned because of Adam. It is this interpretive tradition that is followed by the NRSV, NIV, TEV, JB, NAS. The strong support for such a translation is due to the fact that *eph' hō* is used only two other times in the NT. There, in 2 Corinthians 5:4 and Philippians 3:12, it seems to mean "because." The third suggestion fits well with the Greek Orthodox reading of 5:12.[6] "Death spread to all people, with the result that all sinned." As a result of Adam's sin, death (= alienation from God) entered the world and engulfed everyone. Hence everyone enters this world alienated from God. Since everyone enters the world in a state of death, everyone sins. This position holds that death not only is the result of sin but also that it is the cause of sin. The fourth possibility, which is dependent on some Greek fathers, would read, "wherefore, from which it follows." Diodorus Siculus 19.98 used the expression this way, and it makes sense in the context of Romans 5.[7] When Paul said "death spread to all," one should then read: "from which it follows that all have sinned." This reading assumes that death only follows sin. It is this translation that is preferred in this commentary, even though the third option is very attractive. Paul would then have reiterated his position in v. 13a: "sin was indeed in the world before the law." His opponent responded: "But sin is not reckoned when there is no law" (v. 13b). To which Paul made a telling reply: "Yet death exercised dominion

Typology

When Paul spoke of Adam as being a "type" of the one who was to come, what did he mean? What is typological writing? Typological writing is the method used by ancient Christian Jewish people that described a person, event, or thing in the New Testament in terms borrowed from the Old Testament description of its prototypical counterpart. Several examples clarify the matter. First, consider the case of the description of John the Baptist in the gospels. Mal 4:5 gave expression to the Jewish expectation that Elijah would return before the coming of the Messiah. Matthew and Mark describe John in terms borrowed from the description of his prototype in the Old Testament (e.g., Mark 1:6; Matt 3:4—clothed with camel's hair, with a leather belt around his waist: cf. 2 Kgs 1:8; Mark 9:11-13 has Jesus say Elijah has come; cf. Matt 17:10-13, which makes it explicit that John is Elijah). By describing John in terms used for Elijah, the evangelists were saying something about the nature of John. He is Elijah who has returned. Second, 1 Cor 10:6 speaks of the Israelites' passing through the sea and eating the manna/drinking the water from the rock as types (NRSV—examples) of the later Christians' baptism and Lord's Supper. Paul used the correspondences to say something about the early Christian observances. They, like Israel's prototypical events, are no automatic guarantee of spiritual security. So, third, when Paul spoke of the two Adams (1 Cor 15:45), he was writing typologically. Given the correspondences between the first Adam and the last (Christ), the typology shows the similarities and differences between the two originators of human community and life. In Rom 5:12-21, although Paul used the language "type," the relation between Adam and Christ focuses more on differences and so would best be described as "antitype" (cf. the use of antitype in 1 Pet 3:21 where the contrast is between the water that destroyed in Noah's time and the water that saves in Christians' time). Typological writing, then, aims to say something about the nature of an event, person, or thing by describing the New Testament phenomenon in terms taken from its Old Testament counterpart. Either similarities (type) or differences (antitype) can be accentuated.

from Adam to Moses." (v. 14). If so, then it follows that sin must have been present also. After all, death is a result of sin (Rom 1:32; 6:16, 21, 23; 7:5, 10, 13; 8:2).[Typology]

What did Paul mean when he spoke about "death"? Sometimes the apostle referred to bodily decease (Rom 5:10; 6:3; 1 Cor 11:26); sometimes he referred to a limited, precarious existence full of suffering (1 Cor 15:31; 2 Cor 6:9); at other times he implied separation from God at the same time that one is physically alive (Rom 7:9-10). These various meanings reflect dimensions of a conceptual whole. That whole can be discerned from Paul's Bible. There humans are characterized by four basic relationships: with God, with others of our own kind, with the natural world, and with oneself. Life is understood as the wholeness of these four basic relationships. Death is viewed as the disruption or loss of this wholeness. The reality is detailed in the story of Genesis 3. As a result of their sin, the man and the woman found these four basic relationships disturbed. They hid themselves from the presence of the Lord God (3:8). The relation with God was harmed. They saw that they were naked (3:10-11a), and they tried to shift the blame for their actions to others (3:11b-12,13). The relations with others of their own kind were disrupted. Because of their sin the woman was promised pain in childbearing (3:16), and a curse was put upon the ground so that it did not yield its fruit easily to the man (3:17-19). The relation with the physical world was affected.

The man said to the Lord that he was afraid, was ashamed, and so withdrew (3:10). The relation with the self was distorted. And to top it all off, there was physical death. They were separated from the tree of life (3:22-24). All of this comes under "death" in Paul's Bible. It was this conceptual whole upon which he drew. The context should indicate which aspect of the whole is being emphasized. Here in Romans 5:12 all of these dimensions of the concept seem implied. Death, understood in its totality, entered human history as the result of the first man's sin. Since death is the result of sin, it follows that since death reigned from Adam to Moses all humans were involved in sinning (cf. Gen 6:5). This is Paul's brief but incisive description of the human condition. ["Easter Hymn" by Henry Vaughan]

> **"Easter Hymn"**
> **by Henry Vaughan**
>
> Death and darkness get you packing,
> Nothing now to man is lacking;
> All your triumphs now are ended,
> And what Adam marred is mended;
> Graves are beds now for the weary,
> Death a nap, to wake more merry;
> Youth now, full of pious duty,
> Seeks in thee for perfect beauty;
> The weak and aged, tired with length
> Of days, from thee look for new strength;
> And infants with thy pangs contest
> As pleasant, as if with the breast.
>
> Then, unto Him, who thus hath thrown
> Even to contempt thy kingdom down,
> And by His blood did us advance
> Unto His own inheritance,
> To Him be glory, power, praise,
> From this, unto the last of days!

Beginning with v. 15 Paul presented Christ as the antitype of Adam. This means Paul saw both similarities and dissimilarities between the two. Adam and Christ are alike in the sense that each is the first in his respective setting. Adam was the first human in the first creation. Christ, by virtue of his resurrection, was the first in the new creation (cf. 1 Cor 15:45-50). In this sense Adam is a type of Christ. They are different, however, in their actions and effects. Adam sinned and enabled death to enter the world. Christ was righteous (= faithful to God) and brought life into the world (cf. 1 Cor 15:21-22). In this sense Christ is the antitype of Adam. In all of this Paul employed the ancient rhetorical device called *synkrisis*. This is a comparison/contrast of two figures designed to magnify the praise of one and the blame of the other. The thrust of what follows shows that the disaster of Adam is countered by the success of Christ. Note the contrasts that follow.

There are two small units in vv. 15-17: v. 15 and vv. 16-17. The first reads:

But the free gift is not like the trespass.
For if many died through the one man's trespass,
   much more surely have the grace of God and the free gift in the
   grace of the one man, Jesus Christ, abounded for the many.

A contrast begins the unit. Whereas Adam's sin brought death, the grace of God in Christ has brought the free gift for the many. The second unit reads:

> And the free gift is not like the effect of the one man's sin.
> For the judgment following one trespass brought condemnation,
> but the free gift following many trespasses brings justification.
> If, because of one man's trespass, death exercised dominion
> through that one, much more surely will those who receive the
> abundance of grace and the free gift of righteousness exercise
> dominion in life through the one man, Jesus Christ.

Again there is a contrast. Although the effect of Adam's sin was condemnation and death, the effect of Jesus Christ is justification and life.

The thought of vv. 18-21 is controlled by the recurrence of the expressions *hōs* or *hōsper dia henos* (just as through the one) and *kai houtos* (so also). The expressions recur three times. The first is found in v. 18:

> Just as one man's trespass led to condemnation for all,
> so one man's act of righteousness leads to justification and life for
> all (cf. MT Isa 53:11; also 1QIsa a).

The second comes in v. 19:

> Just as by the one man's disobedience the many were made
> sinners, so by the one man's obedience the many will be made
> righteous.

The parallelism of vv. 18 and 19 indicates Jesus' act of righteousness was his obedience. This is what Paul meant by the faith(fulness) of Christ. The third occurrence is found in v. 21:

> Just as sin exercised dominion in death,
> so grace might also exercise dominion through justification
> leading to eternal life through Jesus Christ our Lord.

The recurrence of these three parallel statements is broken by v. 20, which lacks the terminology but contains the contrast:

> Law came in, with the result that the trespass multiplied (cf.
> 3:20); but where sin increased, grace abounded all the more.

Christ's Decent into Limbo

In the depictions of Christ descending into Limbo or Hell, Christ is most often shown rescuing Adam and Eve from their original Fall.

Martin Schongauer. 1435–1491. *Christ's Descent into Limbo*. Oil on wood. Musee Unterlinden. Colmar, France. (Credit: Erich Lessing/Art Resource, NY)

Throughout the section the contrast between Adam and Christ is dominant. Adam, by his sin, brought death, condemnation, and sin to all. Christ, by his obedience, brought justification and life. In v. 18 Christ's act of righteousness leads to justification "for all." "All" does not always mean "every single individual" (8:32; 12:17-18; 14:2; 16:19). Here in v. 19 Christ's obedience causes "the many" to be made righteous. Apparently "all" and "many" are interchangeable. Is this a statement of universalism? Hardly! Verse 17 says those who exercise dominion in life are those "who receive . . . grace." Elsewhere in Romans Paul was explicit. Righteousness is for "all who believe" (3:22; 3:28; 4:24; 10:4, 9). Elsewhere the Pauline letters teach an outcome to human history that is other than universalism (Rom 2:12; 2 Thess 1:8-9). Christ is presented here again (remember 3:21-26) as the divine remedy for the human condition.

Implicit in this passage are Paul's views of Christ's saving work and of what salvation means for humans. In the first place, Christ's salvific activity is described as "one's man's act of righteousness" (v. 18) and "one man's obedience" (v. 19). How are these two expressions to be understood? The focus on Christ's obedience echoes Philippians 2:6-11. In this early Christian hymn the first part ends with the statement: "he . . . became obedient to the point of death" (v. 8). Christ's obedience is his obedience unto death. This is very much the same thing as his act of righteousness (= faithfulness to God). Indeed, the entire discussion of the "faith of Christ" is relevant here. Jesus' faithfulness is his faithfulness unto death, even death on a cross. Romans 6:10 indicates how Paul understood that death. "The death he died, he died to sin, once for all." In other words, Jesus died rather than sin. It is this act of righteousness that enabled Jesus' salvific work. In his faithfulness to God, Jesus became the locus of God's righteousness (= saving activity), as Romans 3:22 makes clear. Jesus became a place where the divine presence abides because of his faithfulness in his blood (Rom 3:25). Jesus' righteousness is his obedience unto death. This is what Paul meant by the faith of Christ. It is this faithfulness that enabled Jesus' salvific role. "One man's act of righteousness (= faithfulness) leads to justification and life for all" (v. 18).

In this unit one can also ascertain Paul's understanding of salvation. In v. 17 the apostle mentioned "the free gift of righteousness"; in v. 18 Paul spoke about "justification"; in v. 19 he said "many will be made righteous." If being "reckoned righteous" in 4:3, 6-8 means having one's iniquities forgiven and one's sins covered, in Romans 5:17, 19 another shade of meaning comes to the fore. Justification here does not mean to be acquitted or to be made moral. It means rather to be given a free gift of righteousness (= covenant faithfulness) and to be made righteous (= faithful to God). This is the language of divine enablement. God gives divine righteousness (= faithfulness) to the believer to enable that one to be faithful to God (cf. Phil 3:9; LXX Ps 71:1-2 [=72:1-2]; *Ep Arist* 280). Insofar as this happens, the person has been made righteous (= not acquitted or made moral but enabled to be faithful to the relation with God). Justification here, then, means more than forgiveness. It means divine enablement to be righteous (= faithful to God). "Righteous" in Romans 5, then, is neither a legal nor a moral term but rather a relational one.[Limitations of the Law]

Limitations of the Law

At the same time that Paul could say that the Law was good (7:13,16), holy (7:12), righteous (7:12), and spiritual (7:14), he could also speak about its limitations.

- Through the Law comes a knowledge of sin (Rom 3:20; 7:7).
- The Law increases the trespass (Rom 4:15; 5:13, 20; 7:5; 7:8, 9; 7:13; Gal 3:19).
- The Law is used by sin (Rom 7:5; 7:11; 7:13; 1 Cor 15:56).
- The Law is weak because of the flesh (Rom 8:3).
- The Law makes a promise that it cannot keep (Rom 7:10).

It is clear that Paul believed that the Law could identify sin but could not prevent it. It is a prescription but not a power. Indeed the Law actually incites sin. (Johnson) For Paul, the Law was a good thing but a good thing with severe limitations.

Luke Timothy Johnson, *Reading Romans* (NY: Crossroad, 1997), 110-11.

How is the faithfulness of Christ related to being justified—that is, being given a gift of righteousness from God? In his letters Paul expressed himself in multiple ways, but we will note two to illustrate his thinking. First, the apostle could speak about the living Christ indwelling the believer and then living through the believer with the same faithfulness to God that he manifested in the days of his flesh. Galatians 2:19-20 puts it plainly. "I have been crucified with Christ; and it is no longer I who live, but it is Christ who lives in me. And the life that I now live in the flesh I live by the faithfulness of the Son of God." The image of indwelling is one way of speaking about divine enablement. Second, Paul could also speak about being clothed with Christ. To put on something or someone meant in antiquity that one took over that thing's or person's qualities, energies, and abilities. Galatians 3:27 puts it well. "As many of you as were baptized into Christ have clothed yourselves with Christ." This is the equivalent of LXX Baruch 5:2 where the readers are exhorted to cast about themselves a garment of righteousness from God. To be clothed with God's righteousness means to experience the salvation that comes from God. This is the equivalent of "being justified." The Christians can receive a righteousness from God or be made righteous because of Christ's own faithfulness. Because he was faithful, he enables those whom he indwells or clothes to be righteous (= faithful). This enablement is called here "justification" (v. 18).

We have now seen two aspects of Paul's understanding of justification: forgiveness of one's guilt and enablement of one's faithfulness to God. It is no accident that the first comes in Romans 1:18–5:11 where the focus is on forgiveness of guilt and that the second comes in 5:12–8:39 where the concern is with breaking the power of sin.

In Romans 5:12-21 Paul did not spell out how the act of the one affects the situation of the many. He definitely said Adam's sin caused all to sin (v. 19), all to be condemned (v. 18), and all to die (vv. 15b, 17). At the same time, he said "all sinned" (v. 12b). This was in part the cause of death spreading to all (v. 12). Paul, then, did not answer the question about "how" that later interpreters have attempted. He did not side with Pelagius who claimed Adam influenced humanity by giving us a bad example. He did not stand with Augustine who argued that Adam influenced humanity by propagation, not imitation. Nor did he join existentialist theologians who have explained the "how" by saying that humans are created finite and free, which combination leads to anxiety, which results in sin. The fact is that Paul did not answer our question of "how." He merely affirmed that Adam's sin affects us all adversely and left it to us to explain "how" that could be. His concern was with Adam's antitype, Christ, whose obedience results in our justification and life.

It might help one's understanding of Romans 5:12-21 if at this point we provide a sketch of ancient Judaism's understandings of the origins of evil and set Paul in this context.[8] Ancient Judaism's speculations about the origins of evil encompassed existential, historical, and metaphysical theories. (1) Existentially, evil was believed to have arisen from the evil *yetzer* (impulse) (Gen 6:5; 8:21; 2 Esdr 3:21-22; 4:30; widespread in the rabbinic literature[9]). (2) Historically, evil was believed to have originated as described in Genesis 3 (Adam and Eve). Sometimes blame was placed on Adam's shoulders (2 Esdr 7:118; *2 Bar* 54:15); sometimes it was leveled at Eve (Sir 25:24; 4 Macc 18:8). Occasionally Eve's sin was understood as sexual seduction (*Ap Abr* 23; *2 Enoch* 31:6). (3) Metaphysically, evil's origin was believed to lie either with the watchers of Genesis 6 (*1 Enoch* 6–11; 85–90) or with Satan (*Wis* 2:23) or with the evil spirits that struggle in the hearts of humans (1 QS 3:17-21; 3:21-24; 4:15-17,23).

Paul's views on the matter also required these three dimensions. (1) Existentially, sin originates in human perversion of divine revelation by Gentile idolatry (Rom 1:18-32) and Jewish disobedience (Rom 2:17-29). (2) Historically, Genesis 3 furnishes an explanation for the presence of evil, whether through Adam's act (Rom 5:12-21) or Eve's deception (2 Cor 11:3). (3) Metaphysically, evil originates with Satan and the evil spirits (2 Cor 11:3; 4:4; 2:11; 1 Cor 7:5). It is significant that Paul did not use the notion of the evil *yetzer* (impulse), although it is reflected in James 1:13-14, the Shepherd of Hermas ("Mandate" 12), and Justin Martyr (*1 Apology* 10). Nor did he mention the Watchers, although they are referred to in Jude 6–7 and 2 Peter 1:4; 2:4.

By describing the sweep of human history in terms of two figures, Adam and Christ, Paul has omitted any reference to the Mosaic Law. In vv. 20-21, the apostle finally spoke about the Law's function in history. God gave it to increase sin! Instead of restraining the reign of sin, the Law actually promoted its rule (cf. 7:5, 7-11). It is rather grace abounding that provides a cure! These two assertions about Law and grace are the springboards for Paul's arguments that follow.

CONNECTIONS

Original Sin/ Inherited Sin

For Paul, sin has more than an act I commit. It is also an orientation to life. Indeed sin involves my being before it involves my doing. Furthermore, sin is more than that for which I am responsible. I am born into a world of sin before I contribute my share to it. There is an accumulated web of sin involving all human life that has grown, like the proverbial snowball, through the centuries. This accumulation affects the corporate life of humans and the history of humans. Historical and corporate fallenness then affect individuals born into this web. No one born into such fallenness stands in a neutral position with the possibility of deciding whether to choose to sin or not to sin. One stands in a sinful place and chooses to participate in it. It is not necessary, but it is inevitable! How is this accumulated fallenness to be explained? How is the human's inevitable participation in fallenness to be understood?

Several traditional answers have been offered. The first sees the sin of Adam being passed on to his descendants by propagation (Augustine). Basing such an interpretation on Psalm 51:5 and Romans 5:12-21, this reading speaks about hereditary sin. Sin is a disease inherited from one's ancestors and ultimately from the first man. Exegesis does not support such a reading. Psalm 51 means that I am the sinful son of a sinful mother. It does not mean that conception as such is tainted with sin. Rom 5:12-21 provides no assistance to such an interpretation either.

The second traditional answer views Adam's sin as affecting his descendants by means of Adam's example. He provided us an example to sin (Pelagius). Such a reading assumes that humans born into the world stand in a neutral position with the ability to choose good or evil. Only a bad example leads us astray. This runs directly counter to Paul's belief that humans are prisoners to sin.

The third traditional answer regards Adam as a representative of the human race. As such he was a pioneer who opened the way for others to follow in his steps. He committed the rest of us to a certain type of action. We are born into a history already going in a certain direction. We stand in that stream and choose to participate in it. Some such reading is closer to Paul than the other two. Since this answer seems so strange to modern individualistic westerners, as illustration may be of assistance.

The Body of Abel

Silhouetted by the mountain in the background, Adam expresses a sense of resigned bewilderment at the ghastly event before him. The body of his youngest son is being clutched by Eve as Cain, the older son, is being condemned to the outer reaches of creation. The Fall has 'propagated' into the next generation. Exactly how Adam's sin spread to future generations is a subject of perennial theological debate.

William Blake. 1757–1827. *The Body of Abel Found by Adam and Eve*. 1826. Tate Gallery. London, England. (Credit: Tate Gallery, London/Art Resource, NY)

If country A's leader declares war on country B, his country participates in his act. All of its citizens are, by his decision, at war with country B. Moreover, if children are born in country A after the declaration of war and while the war continues, they are also at war with country B. The participation of country A's citizens in their leader's declaration of war is first of all *official*. Even if some citizens would themselves not have chosen to go to war, still they are officially at war with country B. Usually the citizens' participation becomes *personal* as well. They agree with their leader and consider themselves identified with his declaration. They are then personally, as well as officially, at war. *We* are at war, they can say in the fullest sense of the word. The citizens, then, both went to war "in" their leader's action and by their own decision.

Since Paul also believed in spiritual evil, one would need to add to the third reading this extra dimension. When a human is born into the web of fallenness, its direction is determined not only by Adam but also by the devil/the god of this world. Just as there is evil that cannot be accounted for by what I have done, so there is evil that cannot be accounted for by the accumulated bundle derived from human history. Of course, in Romans 5:12-21 Paul was not dealing with spiritual evil but only the link between past human evil and that of individuals born into the world. In trying to explain how we are linked with our past history, it is far easier to eliminate wrong answers than to give an adequate one.

Perhaps one must ultimately rest content with Paul's own tactic: to affirm that fallenness is a fact, that "the orientation adopted by those who first committed sin seems now a fixture in human nature,"[10] without being able to explain exactly how it is so.

NOTES

[1] F. J. Leenhardt, *The Epistle to the Romans* (NY: World, 1961), 139.

[2] John Murray, *The Epistle to the Romans* (NICNT; Grand Rapids: Eerdmans, 1959), 1.274.

[3] John Knox, "Romans," in *The Interpreter's Bible* (Nashville: Abingdon, 1954), 9.465.

[4] S. Lyonnet, "Le sens de *eph' hō* en Rom 5:12 et l'exegese des Peres grecs," *Biblica* 36 (1955): 436-56.

[5] J. A. Fitzmyer, *Romans* (AB; NY: Doubleday, 1993), 413-16, gives an extended list of possibilities. He prefers "with the result that."

[6] John Meyendorff, *Byzantine Theology: Historical Trends and Doctrinal Themes* (2d ed.; NY: Fordham Press, 1983), 143-46. Among Protestant exegetes, this position is advocated by Thomas Schreiner, *Romans* (*ECNT*; Grand Rapids: Baker, 1998), 275-76.

[7] Lyonnet, *Biblica* 36 (1955): 452.

[8] Norman Powell Williams, *The Ideas of the Fall and of Original Sin* (London: Longmans, Green & Co., 1927).

[9] B. W. Bacon, "The Yecer Hara: A Study in the Jewish Doctrine of Sin," in *Biblical and Semitic Studies* (NY: Scribner's, 1901), 93-156.

[10] Stephen Westerholm, *Preface to the Study of Paul* (Grand Rapids: Eerdmans, 1997), 75.

IN CHRIST THE POWER
OF SIN IS BROKEN

6:1–7:6

Romans 5:12–8:39 offers a complementary treatment of themes encountered first in 1:18–5:11. The movement of thought is once again from the human condition to the divine remedy to the role of the law to ultimate salvation. In 6:1–7:6 the focus is again on the divine remedy for sin. Whereas 3:21–4:25 emphasizes God's righteousness at work to deal with the guilt of sin, 6:1–7:6 stresses divine liberation from the power of sin. Just as the covenant with Abraham lies behind Paul's argument in the first division (1–4), so the New Covenant lies behind this second division (5:12–8:39). This section is divided into three parts: 6:1-14, 6:15-23, and 7:1-6. In the first Paul focused on baptism into Christ as an experience of death to sin; in the second, he spoke about conversion as the change of masters; and in the third, the apostle used the example of a woman's being set free from her marriage bond by the death of her husband to speak about freedom from the law, an instrument of sin. In all three illustrations Paul contended that something happens when one is converted to Christ that brings an old state of life to an end and opens the possibilities for a new state of being. In the first two he affirmed that the experience of grace destroys the power of sin; in the third that it liberates from the law, which fact also contributes to one's freedom from sin's power.

The structure of the section revolves around two questions from Paul's opponent (6:1 and 6:15) and the Pauline answers to them. An outline enables one to see the logic of the argument.

Query (6:1)—"Should we continue to sin in order that grace may abound?"
    Answer (6:2-14)—No! Those who have died to sin cannot go on living in sin.
Query (6:15)—"Should we sin because we are not under law but under grace?"
    Answer One (6:16-23)—No! Rather we do not sin because we are under grace.

How so? Living under grace involves a change of masters: from sin to righteousness.

Answer Two (7:1-6)—No! Rather we do not sin, in part, because we are not under the law. How so? It is the law that arouses sinful passions.

Reading the section in terms of this outline enables understanding.

COMMENTARY

The section is launched by an opponent's query that has grown out of Paul's statement in 5:20-21. At the end of the previous thought unit, 5:12-21, Paul had said: "where sin increased, grace abounded all the more" (v. 20b). This leads to the provocative question of 6:1: "What then are we to say? Should we continue in sin in order that grace may abound?" The query is not surprising. Paul has already alluded to such charges made against himself in 3:8. "And why not say (as some people slander us by saying that we say), 'Let us do evil so that good may come'?" Some obviously believed that Paul's doctrine of grace led to lawlessness. Indeed, Paul repeatedly had such charges leveled against him in the ancient church. The extreme Jewish Christians, the Ebionites, for example, repudiated Paul, maintaining that he was an apostate from the law (Irenaeus, *Against Heresies* 1.26.2; 3.15.1). That this was an early phenomenon is confirmed by the evidence of Acts 21:20-21. Paul, of course, wanted to disavow the alleged libertine consequences of his gospel of God's righteousness in Christ. So in 6:2 he responded: "By no means! How can we who died to sin go on living in it?"

Died to sin? In what sense have Christians died to sin? How has this happened? What follows in vv. 3-14 are two units: vv. 3-11, which offer an explanation of v. 2, and vv. 12-14, which deal with its implications.

The first unit, vv. 3-11 consists of a tradition (vv. 3-5) and its exposition (vv. 6-11). "Do you not know" (v. 3) signals material Paul and the Romans had in common (cf. 11:2; 1 Cor 3:16; 6:2-3). One can hear the early kerygma in the background (1 Cor 15:3-5—Christ died, he was buried, he was raised, he appeared).

All of us who have been baptized into Christ have been baptized into his death. Therefore we have been buried with him by baptism into death (vv. 3-4a), so that, just as Christ was raised from the dead . . .

we too might walk in newness of life (v. 4b).[For if we have been united to the likeness of his death (cf. Phil 3:10), we shall also be united to the likeness of his resurrection (cf. Phil 3:21) (v. 5).][1]

The material within brackets is designed to show that "with him" in v. 5 is not in the Greek text. Christians' union is with the likeness or form of Jesus' death and with the likeness or form of his resurrection. The tradition only speaks of Christ's death and that of believers as similar, not identical. The similarity is in their rejection of sin.

The Pauline teaching would have been intelligible to citizens of the Mediterranean world, at least in part. In certain pagan cults entry was by means of washings understood as an initiate's regeneration (Tertullian, *De Baptismo* 5).[2] In an ancient Roman novel by Apuleius called *Metamorphoses*, in chapter 11 Lucius described his initiation into the cult of Isis as "like a voluntary death," which made one "new-born," and his service of the deity as "liberty." While the Pauline teaching has formal similarities that would have enabled Mediterranean peoples to have some initial openness to the faith, the distinctive Christian teaching about baptism as a death to sin would require a type of instruction mentioned in 6:17.

The Pauline teaching would also have been understandable to non-Christian Jewish auditors who knew what it meant to appropriate for their own experience the events of the exodus. In the Passover ritual the Jew appropriated to himself/herself the history of his/her people. Each Jewish participant in the seder had been in bondage in Egypt and had been delivered therefrom. In *m. Pesahim* 10:5 it is said: "In every generation a man must so regard himself as if he came forth himself out of Egypt."[3] The Passover Haggadah reinforces the same theme.

> In every generation each one of us should regard himself as though he himself had gone forth from Egypt, as it is said (Exod 13:8): "And thou shalt shew thy son in that day, saying, This is done because of that which the Lord did unto ME when I came forth out of Egypt." Not our ancestors alone did God redeem then, but he did US redeem with them as it is said (Deut 6:23): "And he brought US out from thence that he might bring US in to give US the land which he sware unto our fathers.[4]

The individual Israelite realized in his/her own experience the external facts of history. It was this appropriation of by participation in the events that made one a part of the community. By analogy, Jesus' followers became a part of the Christian community by participation in the defining events of their community's history: Jesus' death, burial, and resurrection.

The exposition comes in two parts. Verses 6-7, the first part, constitute an exposition of vv. 3-4a, which refer to death and burial:

> We know that our old self was crucified with him so that the body of sin might be destroyed, and we might no longer be enslaved to sin. For whoever has died is freed (*dedikaiōtai,* justified) from (*apo*) sin.

The "we know" here implies that what follows is an obvious deduction from the previous argument. The "old self" is the self that was "in Adam." The "body of sin" is the total personality, in its visible aspect, that is characterized by sin. Tertullian put it this way: "We maintain . . . that what has been abolished in Christ is not *carnem peccati,* 'sinful flesh,' but *peccatum carnis,* 'sin in the flesh'—not the material thing but its condition; not the substance but its flaw."[5] The "old self" and the "body of sin" are virtual synonyms. They are enslaved to sin (= not free). Being crucified with Christ (cf. Gal 2:20) is sharing his death to sin. This experience results in our liberation from sin's power. In this context, having been justified refers to our having been set free from the bondage that has enslaved us (cf. 6:18, 22). "People are not just guilty, they are enslaved, and they need to escape."[6] Thus, in chapter 4 justification meant "forgiveness" and in 5:12-21 "being made righteous/faithful," but in this context it means "deliverance from bondage" or "being set free from the power of sin."[7] It is synonymous with being "set free from sin" in 6:18, 22. All three meanings of justification are, of course, present in Paul's Bible. They make up a total conceptual whole, parts of which are accented in different contexts.

> Grace does not simply involve forgiveness of sins; it also involves a transfer of lordship, so that believers are no longer under the tyranny of sin. [R]ighteousness is more than forensic in Paul. Those who are in a right relation to God have also been dramatically changed; they have been made righteous.[8]

In chapter 6 the emphasis is on our deliverance from the power of sin! Older Protestant commentaries often contended that Romans 1–4 deal with justification understood as acquittal from the guilt of sin while Romans 5–8 deal with sanctification viewed as deliverance from sinning. That Romans 1–4 focuses on sin pardoned and Romans 5:12–8:39 on sin subdued is correct. It is erroneous, however, to assign the first of these two aspects of the divine remedy to justification and the second to sanctification.

Justification in Paul encompasses not only forgiveness (Rom 4:6-8) but also deliverance (Rom 6:7) and empowerment for righteous living (Rom 5:19). Likewise, sanctification in Paul's letters is often used as a synonym for conversion (e.g., 1 Cor 1:2—"sanctified" is used in synonymous parallelism with "called to be saints"; 6:11—conversion is described with three synonymous terms: washed, sanctified, justified; 2 Thess 2:13—God chose the readers to be saved through sanctification by the Spirit). If justification here emphasizes the being set free from sin, sanctification focuses on the being set free for God.

Verses 8-9, the second part of the exposition of vv. 3-5, offer an explanation of vv. 4b-5, which focus on resurrection and new life.

If we have died with Christ, we believe that we will also live with him (cf. 2 Tim 2:11-12).

We know that Christ, being raised from the dead, will never die again; death no longer has dominion over him.

If Christians share Christ's death, they will share his resurrection. [Resurrection and Resuscitation] That event is future, however. In the present, we walk in newness of life. There is no over-realized eschatology here, rather there is an eschatological reservation. (Contrast Col 3:1 ["you have been raised with Christ"] and Eph 2:5-6 ["made us alive together with Christ, . . . raised us up with him and seated us with him in the heavenly places"] where the texts can be read [wrongly] as if an eschatological reservation is absent.)

The explanation (vv. 3-11) of Paul's answer (v. 2) to the charge of libertinism (v. 1) concludes with a general summary (v. 10) and an exhortation (v. 11). The summary reads:

The death he died, he died to sin, once for all;
but the life he lives, he lives to God.

What is the death Christ died and which Christians share? It is a death to sin! If Christ's death was a death to sin, so also is that of the Christians who identify with him. Paul gave a bit more light on the subject in Galatians 2:19b-20:

I have been crucified with Christ;
and it is no longer I who live, but it is Christ who lives in me.
And the life I now live in the flesh I live by the faithfulness of the Son of God.

Resurrection and Resuscitation

Two sets of data must be set alongside one another. On the one hand, Rom 6:9 says that "Christ being raised from the dead will never die again." On the other hand, the gospels tell stories of Jesus' raising people from the dead: the twelve-year-old daughter of Jairus (Mark 5:21-24, 35-43); the widow's son at Nain (Luke 7:11-17); and Lazarus (John 11). How would early Christians have understood the difference between what happened to Jesus and what happened to the other three? The accounts of Jesus' raising the three individuals in the gospels must be understood as stories of resuscitations. They are not stories of resurrections. Why? Because in these three cases the person who was raised would eventually die again of something else. The corpses had been reanimated or resuscitated but they had not experienced the ultimate victory over death. In the case of Jesus, however, the early Christians believed that he had experienced the ultimate victory over death. He would, therefore, never die again. They regarded Jesus' being raised as a resurrection, not a resuscitation. Ancient Jews mostly thought in terms of one resurrection: the general resurrection when everyone would be raised. Many Christian Jews, like Paul,

Peter Paul Rubens. 1577–1640. *Resurrection of Lazarus.* c. 1600. Oil on wood. Louvre. Paris, France. (Credit: Erich Lessing/Art Resource, NY)

believed that the general resurrection had begun with Jesus' resurrection and that the rest would be raised soon completing the process (1 Cor 15:20, 23). Hence Paul could speak of Jesus' resurrection as "the first fruits of those who have fallen asleep" (1 Cor 15:20).

The same thing is referred to in Romans 5:18b: "one man's act of righteousness leads to justification and life for all." Christ's death on the cross was his death to sin. It was his act of righteousness (= faithfulness to God). It was his obedience unto death (Phil 2:8). This is what Paul spoke about elsewhere as the faithfulness of Christ (Rom 3:22, 25, 26) "in his blood" (3:25). As Christ died to sin, so the persons who are converted to Christ, baptized into Christ, die to sin.

What does death to sin mean for Christ and for Christians when one is sinless and the others are sinful? The best assistance in understanding this issue comes from 4 Maccabees 16:24-25. There, in the context of a mother's exhorting her seven sons to remain faithful to God in spite of martyrdom, we read:

With these words the mother of the seven exhorted each one and persuaded them to die rather than transgress the commandment of

God, and they knew full well themselves that those who die for the sake of God live unto God, as do Abraham and Isaac and Jacob and all the patriarchs.

For Jesus to die to sin was for him to die rather than sin. For Christians to die with Christ to sin means for them to identify with Jesus' bringing to an end all the ties and relationships to the values of Adam's world because of his (Jesus') commitment to God. This identification does not mean merely that Jesus models an act for us to repeat. Nor does it mean that when Jesus died to sin at the cross we were in him and so died to sin at that time. Rather, Jesus is the pioneer/leader who has opened the way for others to follow.[9] The experience is ours but it is ours only because he has made it possible. For Christians, to be crucified with Christ means the sinful Ego or the old self dies. Another way to express the experiential reality is that found in *T. Gad* 5:7: repentance destroys disobedience. Origen, in his *Commentary on the Epistle to the Romans*, also put it this way:

> Just as living for God means living according to God's will, so living for sin means living according to sin's will. . . .To live to sin, therefore, means to obey the desires of sin. . . . To die to sin is the opposite of this; it means refusing to obey the desires of sin. . . . If someone dies to sin, it is through repentance that he dies.[10]

For Christians, to be crucified with Christ means the sinful Ego or self dies (cf. Gal 2:19—died to the law; Col 2:20—died to elemental spirits; Ign *Magn* 5:2—died to the world). In this light Paul's question in response to his opponent makes sense: "How can we who died to sin go on living in it" (v. 2)? Grace does not lead to sin because those who have experienced grace have died to sin.

The section, 6:1-14, closes with a unit devoted to the implications of Paul's answer in v. 2. Verses 12-14 are cast in the imperative mode. "Therefore," since you have died to sin,

Do not let sin exercise dominion in your mortal bodies,
    to make you obey their passions.
No longer present your members to sin as instruments of wickedness, but
    present . . . your members to God as instruments of righteousness.
For sin will have no dominion over you
    since you are not under law but under grace.

The power of sin is broken by our dying with Christ to sin, but the freedom we gain thereby is a freedom to choose to whom we present our members as instruments. The implication is that prior to our dying with Christ to sin we had no freedom to choose whom we would serve. The only freedom we had was a freedom to sin. After dying with Christ to sin, our freedom from sin is not automatic but must be chosen. With the power of sin broken, we have the freedom to make a choice for righteousness. "Your members" refers not just to one's body parts but to the various facets of one's personality or self. Do not, said Paul, give the various parts of your selves to sin so that they are instruments of wickedness. Rather present the various parts of your selfhood to God as instruments of righteousness. This is possible, he said, because sin will have no dominion over those who have died with Christ and live under grace. Being dead to sin and alive to God means that one obeys God in the concrete decisions of everyday existence. Romans 6:1-14 says that grace does not have libertine consequences because those who have been baptized into Christ cannot act as if they were still in Adam.

Although baptism is not the focus of Paul's argument in 6:1-14, it is integral to his argument. The argument deals with the victory over sin's power that prevents libertine consequences from flowing from Paul's gospel. The argument assumes something about baptism in the Pauline churches, however. It would be a help, then, if we considered briefly how baptism was understood in the Pauline letters. From the undisputed letters one needs to consider Romans 6:1-11, Galatians 3:26-28, and 1 Corinthians 1:11-17, 6:11, and 12:13. From the deutero-Pauline letters one must note at least Colossians 2:12-13, Ephesians 4:4-6, and 1 Timothy 6:12-13. Since the information about baptism is essentially the same in both groups of letters, they may be considered together in this instance. (1) Romans 6:1-11 makes several points. What is being said is a common tradition (v. 3—"Do you not know?"). The verbal form, "have been baptized" is passive voice. Baptism is, therefore, something that happens to the person being baptized. The context makes it unavoidable that the actor is God (cf. vv. 4-5). Baptism here is synonymous with conversion. This conversion involves a death to sin and a rising to a newness of life, with a hope of future resurrection. (2) Galatians 3:26-28 also uses a passive, "as many of you as were baptized" (v. 27). Baptism into Christ is a shortened form of baptism into the name of Christ (cf. 1 Cor 1:13; 6:11). Being baptized is effective because of the initiates' faith (v. 26— "with faith"; v. 27—"have clothed yourselves with Christ").

Baptism is into the church, a community where social status is relativized (v. 28). (3) First Corinthians 1:11-17 again uses a passive, "were you baptized?" Baptism was into the name of Christ. Implied in this act was the belief that one then belonged to the one in whose name one was baptized. (4) First Corinthians 6:11 again uses the passive ("you were washed"). Again baptism is in the name of Jesus. Here it is associated with the Spirit, God's presence and power. (5) First Corinthians 12:13 once again uses the passive ("we were all baptized"). Baptism is the entrance into the body of Christ, the church. Baptism is associated with the Spirit. It is associated with the relativizing of social status. (6) Colossians 2:1-13 again uses the passive ("were buried," "were raised"). It also associates the act with believers' faith ("through faith"). (7) Ephesians 4:4-6 focuses on the bases for Christian unity. Baptism is among them. Since there is one baptism, let us maintain unity as believers. (8) First Timothy 6:12-13 associates baptism with believers' making "the good confession in the presence of many witnesses." This is in response to God's calling of them.

Having surveyed the various texts, what can be said by way of summary about baptism in the Pauline churches? Baptism was an initiation rite connected with Christian conversion. Three actors were involved in the rite: the church which used it as an occasion to preach the death, burial, and resurrection of Christ; the person being baptized (faith; making confession; joining the church in its act of proclamation by submitting to the rite); and God (the passives and the association with the gift of the Spirit). The effects of the baptismal rite were various: attachment to Christ; reception of the Spirit; death to sin/being washed/putting off-putting on; involvement in the church where social status was relativized. Out of this total picture as it can be reconstructed from the Pauline letters, the apostle focused on the aspect of dying to sin/rising to a new lifestyle in Romans 6:1-11. He did this in order to answer the query of his opponent: does the gospel of God's grace lead to libertine consequences? Paul's response was: No! Why? Because to experience God's grace is to die to sin.[11]

Romans 6:15-23 and 7:1-6 are attempts to deal with the implications of 6:14b: "you are not under law but under grace." Verses. 15-23 of chapter 6 explain "under grace"; vv. 1-6 of chapter 7 explain "not under law." Paul's opponent again raised a question: "What then? Should we sin because we are not under law but under grace" (v. 15a)? This is a variant of the question asked in 6:1. Both are concerned with the potential libertine consequences of life under grace. In 6:1-14 Paul eliminated the libertine option by arguing that Christians died with Christ to sin in baptism. In 6:16–7:6 he would argue that libertine behavior is impossible for Christians for two reasons. First, in 6:15b-23 he contended it is impossible to embrace lawlessness because we have changed owners: from sin to righteousness. Second, he argued in 7:1-6 that we do not sin, in part, because we are not under the law, which arouses our sinful passions. So when the opponent asked in v. 14, "Are we to sin because we are not under law but under grace?" v. 15b replies: "By no means!"

The first part of the reason comes in v. 16: "Do you not know that if you present yourselves to anyone as obedient slaves, you are slaves of the one you obey, either of sin . . . or of obedience?" The issue, then, is whose slaves Christians are. Paul believed no one is ever free from a master. No one can stand in a neutral position and choose whether or not to belong to a master. One is under the authority of either sin or God. So the choice with which humans are faced is not whether or not to give up our freedom and submit to God. It is rather whether or not we should serve sin or God. It is either the one or the other! There is no third option. To think freedom is attained by jettisoning obedience to God is to opt for sin as one's lord. Verses 17-18 constitute a Pauline thanksgiving that leaves no doubt to whom his readers belong:

> But thanks be to God that you, having once been slaves of sin,
>   have become obedient from the heart to the form of teaching
>   to which you were entrusted,
> and that you, having been set free from sin,
>   have become slaves of righteousness.

The Roman Christians had transferred their allegiance from sin to righteousness. The language, "once a slave, I am now free," was used for conversion in antiquity by pagans as well as Christians (e.g., Lucian, *Nigrinus* 1-5). The thanksgiving implies that early Christians, in connection with their conversion, were taught certain standard things (cf. 1 Thess 4:1; 2 Thess 3:6; Heb 5:12-14; 1 John 2:24, 27). It was not so much that the tradition was delivered to them. Rather they were delivered to the tradition. That is, they came under its authority (= slaves of righteousness).[Tradition]

When Paul spoke of "the form (*typos*) of teaching to which you have been entrusted," what did he mean? *Typos* seems to have been used here of an impression or imprint stamped on the soul or mind of a person. For example, Plato, *Republic* 377B, said the critical time for teaching is when a child is young, "for it is above all then

Tradition

The Pauline letters assume that their readers had been instructed in and knew a general tradition that was supposed to govern their lives (e.g., Rom 6:17; 15:14; 16:17; 1 Cor 1:5; 11:2; Phil 4:9; Col 2:7; 1 Thess 4:2; 2 Thess 2:15). This tradition included

- information about Jesus' death, burial, resurrection, and appearances (1 Cor 15:3-5),
- information about Jesus' last supper (1 Cor 11:23-25),
- information about eschatology (1 Thess 5:1-2),
- information about ethical living (1 Thess 4:1-2; 2 Thess 3:6),
- information about certain sayings of Jesus (1 Cor 7:10-11; 9:14).

The Pauline churches were not alone in this matter.

- Heb 5:12-14 shows that the church to which this homily was addressed had been instructed in the tradition. Heb 6:1-2 makes explicit what that instruction was: repentance from dead works and faith toward God; instructions about baptisms, laying on of hands, resurrection from the dead, and eternal judgment.
- 1 John 2:7; 3:11; 2 John 5 demonstrate that this stream of early Christianity assumed instruction in a basic tradition. This tradition consisted of information both about christology (1 John 2:20-24) and ethics (1 John 3:11; 2 John 5).

---

that it is molded, and whatever impression (*typos*) one wants to be stamped on each child is received." Philo had a couple of references that reinforce the idea. In *Special Laws* 1.5+30, he said Moses repeatedly taught the devotees of piety about the sole sovereignty of God. Thereby, "he stamped upon their minds, as with a seal, deep imprints (*typoi*) of holiness, so that no . . . smoothing in the course of years should ever blur their distinctiveness." In *Special Laws* 4.18+107, Philo said: "The pupil after receiving from the teacher . . . wisdom prolongs the process of learning . . . , till by using memory . . . , he stamps a firm impression (*typos*) of them on his soul." So the teaching to which Paul's readers had been committed was that which had left a deep imprint upon their inner persons.[12] This may very well be yet another way of saying that in the new covenant the law is written on their hearts (Jer 31:31-34).

The explanation that follows comes in two parts: v. 19 and vv. 20-23. In each case the outcome of one's allegiance is made clear. Part one reads:

For just as you once presented your members as slaves to impurity and to greater and greater iniquity, so now present your members as slaves to righteousness for sanctification (v. 19).

The "members" referred to are the various facets of one's personality. When they are slaves of righteousness the outcome is sanctification (*hagiasmon*). Sanctification is a gift, a status conferred by God that is already possessed (1 Cor 6:11). Christians can, therefore, be called saints (*hagioi*). It is also a goal to be reached, involving human effort (2 Cor 7:1; 1 Thess 4:3; [1 Tim 2:21]). Its basic idea is separation for God's use. It is an alternate image, alongside justification, reconciliation, adoption, redemption, and others to describe the nature of Christian conversion and growth. Here Paul called for moral effort. The effort is enabled by God, but humans do it.

Part two (vv. 20-23) of the explanation gives a variation on the same theme that is found in v. 19. Note the comparison between the two slaveries:

> When you were slaves to sin, you were free in regard to righteousness. . . .
> The end of those things is death (v. 21).
> But now that you have been freed from sin and enslaved to God,
> The advantage you get is sanctification. The end is eternal life.
> For the wages (1 Esdr 4:56; 1 Macc 3:28; Luke 3:14; 1 Cor 9:7) of sin is death, but the free gift of God is eternal life in Christ Jesus our Lord.

Sanctification in v. 22 can be taken as if it is a later stage than being set free from sin's power. The more likely reading, however, is to take it as the other side of the coin. One side is being set free from sin; the other side is being set free for God. If the second option is taken, then sanctification is an alternate image for Christian conversion. If sanctification is the fruit of slavery to God in this life, beyond this age there is the ultimate outcome, eternal life (= life

---

Eternal Life

AΩ The expression "eternal life" is used regularly by early Christians as a description of salvation, of life in the age to come. It is used

- for the future life of blessedness beyond the resurrection and the Last Judgment (e.g., Matt 19:16, 29; Mark 10:30; Acts 13:46-48; 1 Tim 1:16; 6:12; Titus 1:2; 3:7; 1 John 2:25)
- as opposed to a destiny characterized as eternal punishment (Matt 25:46), or the wrath of God (John 3:36), or corruption (Gal 6:8), or eternal judgment (Heb 6:2), or eternal fire (Jude 7)
- which, because of the early Christians' inaugurated eschatology, could be experienced in the here and now as a foretaste of what is to come (John 3:15,16; 1 John 3:15; 5:13)
- which, whether future or present, is mediated through Jesus (John 6:54; 6:68; 10:28; 17:2).

Edward Hicks. 1780–1849. *The Peaceable Kingdom*. c. 1844–1845. (Credit: Art Resource, NY)

beyond the resurrection; cf. Gal 6:8; 1 Tim 1:16; 6:12; Titus 1:2; 3:7; Matt 19:16; John 3:16; Acts 13:46-48; 1 John 1:2; 2 Macc 7:9-36; 4 Macc 15:3). This benefit comes "in Christ." Pauline soteriology is tied to Christ. [Eternal Life]

"In Christ" is a recurring expression in the Pauline letters. Where does it come from? The expression seems to have been part of the common Christian vocabulary in the first century. "In Christ" or its equivalent is found in John 6:56; 15:4 (abide in me); in Acts 4:2 (in Jesus); in 1 Peter 3:16; 5:10; 5:14 (in Christ); and Revelation 14:13 (in the Lord). This would seem to argue that Paul was using a conventional phrase. What does it mean in Paul's letters? Paul assumed that it is impossible for anyone to live in the world as an isolated individual. All humans belong to some corporate entity. For Paul, there were only two possibilities. Either one lives "in Adam" or "in Christ" (cf. 1 Cor 15:22—"for as all die in Adam, so all will be made alive in Christ"; Rom 5:12-21). The corporate solidarity referred to by "in Adam" is humanity identified with Adam in his sin and ruled over by death. It is into this corporate solidarity that all humans are born. We are born "into Adam" and live "in Adam." The corporate solidarity referred to by the phrase "in Christ" is humanity identified with Christ in his righteousness. Just as Israel in the OT can refer to both an individual, Jacob (Gen 32:28), and to a people (2 Sam 19:41), so in Paul's letters Christ can have an individual (Rom 5:17) and a corporate (1 Cor 12:12-13) meaning. To belong to the solidarity "Christ" requires God's grace and a human response of faith. So in Paul, humans are born into Adam (the corporate solidarity) and identify with Adam (the individual). Likewise, for Paul humans can identify with Christ (the individual) and live in Christ (the corporate entity). For Paul, to be "in Christ" means that one is identified with the individual Christ and is a part of the corporate Christ. Both individuals (Phil 1:1; 4:21; 1 Thess 5:12) and churches (1 Thess 1:1; Gal 1:22) can be said to be "in Christ." Here in Romans 6:23, God's gift of eternal life is "in Christ," understood in its twofold meaning.

Whereas 6:15-23 deals with what life under grace (6:14b) was like, 7:1-6 focuses on what it means for Christians to be "not under law" (6:14b). The argument in 7:1-6 is difficult. This difficulty is resolved if one recognizes that Paul's analogy requires the reader (= a Christian) to identify with both the husband and the wife.[13] An outline of its components also helps one to read properly:

The principle (v. 1)
Illustration of the principle (vv. 2-3)

Application of the principle (v. 4)

Implication of the principle's application (vv. 5-6).

Let us read in these terms.

What is the principle (v. 1)? Jewish auditors or Gentile God-fearers knew that the law (= Jewish law) was binding only while one was alive. Death cancels the law's rule (later rabbinic writings express the view that is assumed here—*b. Sabb* 30a; *b. Nid* 61b; *b. Pesah* 51b; *j. Kelim* 9:3). An illustration is given (vv. 2-3). Take the case of a married woman. If her husband dies, she is no longer bound by the law to her husband and is free to marry another. Death has canceled the law's hold on her (cf. 1 Cor 7:39; *m. Qidd* 1:1—"she acquires her freedom by a bill of divorce or by the death of her husband"). How does this apply to Christians (v. 4)? A death has taken place that releases Christians from the law (cf. Gal 2:19— "I died to the law," so the reader identifies with the husband of v. 1) so they can be legally united with another partner, namely, the risen Christ (here the reader identifies with the wife). What are the implications of all this (vv. 5-6)? The two conditions are contrasted. On the one hand, there is the life in the flesh. On the other hand, there is the life of the spirit. As a result of the death, Christians are transferred from life in the flesh to the life of the spirit. What did Paul mean by these two contrasted conditions?

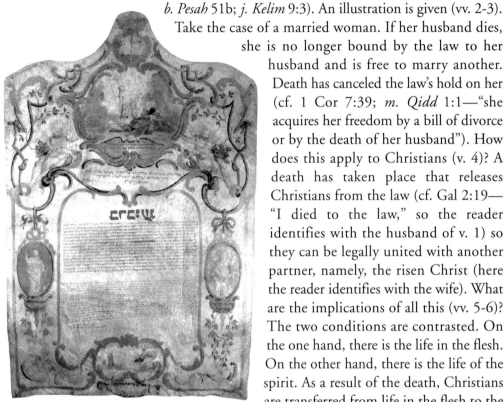

Ketubbah

Paul uses marriage as a metaphor for being under the law, drawing on Jewish traditions regarding marital contracts. An example of such a contract is shown in the Mishnah tractate *Ketubbah*, an illustrated frontispiece of which is shown here.

Ketubbah. Watercolor on parchment. Ancona. 1781. Legacy of the Danzig Jewish Community. The Jewish Museum. New York, NY. (Credit: The Jewish Museum, NY/Art Resource, NY)

Paul used "flesh" (*sarx*) in basically two ways in his letters. Sometimes "flesh" referred to the realm of the physical and finite. So humans are physical, have bodies, and are finite—they die. When Paul used "flesh" in this way, there was no negative connotation to the term. God has created us physical and finite, as flesh, and that is good. So it is possible to live "in the flesh" and live "by faith" (Gal 2:20—"the life I now live in the flesh I live by faith"). At other times, however, Paul used "flesh" with a negative connotation. A number of passages reflect this usage: for example, Galatians 5:16-17 (the works of the flesh); Galatians 5:24 ("Those who belong to Christ Jesus have crucified the flesh with its passions and desires"); Romans 8:12-13 ("we are debtors, not to the flesh, to live according to the flesh—for if you live according to the flesh, you will die"); Romans 13:14 ("make no provision for the flesh, to gratify its desires"). What kinds of evils are associated with the "flesh" when it has this negative connotation? The list of the works of the flesh in Galatians 5:16-17 enable an answer. There is, of course, behavior that can be classed as sensuality. "Fornication," "impurity," "licentiousness," drunkenness," carousing," clearly belong to sensuality. Sensuality refers to an excessive or illegitimate satisfaction of a legitimate appetite. So thirst is a normal appetite but drunkenness is an excessive satisfaction of a normal physical appetite. Also, sexual desire is a normal human appetite, but fornication is an illegitimate satisfaction of a normal appetite. Paul clearly understood some works of the flesh to be in the realm of sensuality. But not all. "Enmities," "strife," "jealousy," "anger," "quarrels," "dissensions," "factions," "envy" belong to another dimension. These are what we would call psychological maladies: antisocial attitudes and behavior. Moreover, "idolatry" and "sorcery" involve false religion. Indeed, legalistic religion is understood by Galatians 3:3 as a work of the flesh. How can these different types of evil be understood as "works of the flesh"? Living according to the flesh was understood by Paul to be an orientation to life in which humans who are flesh (= physical and finite) turn back onto the realm of flesh and absolutize it. The creation is worshiped and served instead of the Creator. This amounts to giving a relative good an absolute value. In doing so, the relative good is perverted. So when humans who are flesh turn back onto the created world and absolutize a physical appetite, the result is sensuality. When humans absolutize their own egos, status, and power drives, the result is antisocial attitudes and behavior. When humans turn back onto the created order and absolutize their own moral and spiritual power, the result is false religion. For Paul, to live according to the flesh was an orientation to life that is characterized by idolatry. When humans make the physical and finite order an absolute value, they are living in the flesh or according to the flesh. In Romans 7:5 the apostle said that "while we were living in the flesh (= an orientation that absolutizes the physical and finite order), our sinful passions, aroused by the law, were at work in our members to bear fruit for death."

By contrast Christians' new life is in the Spirit (v. 6). Again, the apostle could use "spirit" (*pneuma*) in two very different ways. On the one hand, Paul sometimes used "spirit" of human beings. Indeed there are times when "spirit" means the whole person and can take the place of the personal pronoun: 2 Corinthians 7:13 (for Titus's spirit to be at rest is for Titus himself to be at rest); Romans 8:16 (when the Spirit bears witness with our spirit that we are children of God, the Spirit is bearing witness to us); Galatians 6:18 (for the grace of our Lord Jesus to be with your spirit is for his grace to be with you). On the other hand, most references to "spirit" should be capitalized because they refer to God. "Spirit" is used of God's presence and power active in the world. For Paul, the whole of the Christian life is lived in relation to the Spirit. This can be seen most easily if we note how the past, present, and future dimensions of salvation are related to the Spirit. (1) Past—the Spirit validates the preached word (1 Thess 1:5-6); the Spirit enables the confession, "Jesus is Lord" (1 Cor 12:3); the Spirit is given at baptism (1 Cor 12:13); the Spirit sets one free from sin and death (Rom 8:2). (2) Present—the Spirit has role in piety (prayer—Rom 8:26-27; understanding Scripture—2 Cor 3:12-15; assurance—2 Cor 1:22; joy—Rom 14:17), in ethics (Rom 8:4; Gal 5:22-23, 25), and in the church's unity (1 Cor 3:16) and edification (1 Cor 12–14; Rom 12:6-8). (3) Future—"If the Spirit of Him who raised Jesus from the dead dwells in you, He who raised Christ from the dead will give life to your mortal bodies also through His Spirit that dwells in you." One can conclude that for Paul there was no dimension of the Christian life that is lived apart from the activity of God's spirit. Indeed, the alternative to life in the flesh is life in the Spirit. Life in the Spirit is an orientation in which God, rather than that which God created, is one's ultimate concern. Moreover, God's active presence and power are one's resource to accomplish the divine will (Phil 2:12-13). When Christians have a relation with the risen Christ and life is lived out of the Spirit, fruit is borne for God (cf. Gal 5:22-23).

The language of Romans 7:6, the "old written code," and "in the new life of the Spirit," is similar to that in 2 Corinthians 3:6. The context of the Corinthians passage treats the new covenant as a replacement of the old. Likewise here in Romans 7:6 it is the new covenant's contrast with the old Mosaic one that is in view. For Paul, the coming of the Spirit meant the end of the time of the law. Whereas Romans 1–4 focuses primarily on the covenant with Abraham, chapters 6–8 play the new covenant off against the Mosaic one.

The point of 7:1-6 has been to emphasize the Christians' freedom from the law that is made possible by a death. To speak of this freedom in this context is important because the law, in the realm of the flesh, is a tool of sin. It is the means by which sin is able to get to us and to induce us to follow sin's promptings (1 Cor 15:56; 2 Cor 3:6, 7, 9). When, therefore, Paul's opponent in 6:15 raised the question about the libertine implications of life under grace and not under law, the apostle's answer was twofold. First, life under grace does not have libertine consequences because we have shifted masters: from sin to righteousness (6:15-23). Second, life not under law does not yield libertine consequences in part because freedom from the law takes away one of sin's instruments.

Law vs. Grace

This woodcut captures the early Lutheran emphasis on the dichotomy of law and grace. The central Tree of Life is withered on the left side, where sin and death rule and where law-burdened people are doomed to judgment. On the right side, the Tree of Life is filled with leaves and grace abounds. The empty tomb signifies the triumph over sin and death made possible by Christ's resurrection.

Lucas Cranach the Younger. 1510–1537. *Law vs. Grace*. c. 1530. Woodcut. Wittenberg, Germany. (Credit: Northwestern University)

Twice, the opponent has raised the question of the libertine implications of Paul's gospel of God's grace (6:1; 6:15). Twice the apostle has turned the charge aside. Christians cannot continue in sin because they have died to sin (6:2-14). Christians will not persist in sin because they are no longer slaves of sin but are now slaves of God and righteousness (6:16-23) and because they are set free from one of sin's instruments, the law (7:1-6). The divine remedy for the human condition as it is expounded in 6:1–7:6 is presented as deliverance from the power of sin. This includes being discharged from the law, which has been a tool of sin (7:1-6). It is this last claim that is the catalyst for the next section of Paul's argument.

CONNECTIONS

Does justification through faith produce libertine behavior? The interlocutor's questions about the possible libertine implications of Paul's teaching on grace are not limited to Paul's time. Calvin said he had to deal with the same charges:

> Some impious persons . . . accuse us, in the first place of destroying good works, and seducing men from the pursuit of them, when we say that they are not justified by works, nor saved through their own

merit; and secondly of making too easy a road to righteousness, when we teach that it consists in the gratuitous remission of sins, to which they have naturally too strong a propensity.[14]

Nor is the concern without some basis, given human nature. Consider what Voltaire allegedly said: "God will forgive, that is His 'business.'"[15] W. H. Auden said: "I like committing crimes. God likes forgiving them. Really the world is admirably arranged."[16] Grounds for concern still exist. But is a works righteousness the right way to address the issue? Paul did not think so!

The Issue of Human Freewill

In Romans 6 Paul raised the question of the meaning of human freedom. His ancient interpreters gave two very different readings of Romans 6. On the one hand, Pelagius read Paul in a way that regarded sin as purely voluntary and individual. All have the power not to sin, he claimed. If I ought, I can. This clearly cannot be what Paul was saying. On the other hand, Augustine maintained that human freedom is not freedom from restraint but freedom from evil. So the one who is most truly free is the one who cannot do wrong (*Enchiridion* 105). Augustine used four expressions to clarify the human position with reference to sin. (1) Adam before the Fall was able not to sin (*posse non peccare*). (2) After the Fall, Adam and his descendants (we are included) are not able not to sin (*non posse non peccare*). (3) After conversion to Christ we are once again able not to sin (*posse non peccare*). (4) After the parousia, Christians will not be able to sin (*non posse peccare*). Augustine's second and third positions describe what Paul was saying in Romans 6. Before dying with Christ to sin or before becoming a slave of righteousness, humans "in Adam" find ourselves not able not to sin. Even our good deeds are tainted by our idolatries and immoralities and rationalizations. "Ironically, sin, once committed, does not aid one to become one's *own* master, but rather proceeds to become one's master; sin reigns as a lord in the fallen creature" (cf. Rom 6:6; 6:12; 6:17; 6:19-20).[17] After dying with Christ and changing masters, Christians are in a position where there is once again the possibility not to sin. This does not mean that we live beyond sinful acts. "Sin remains, but in the Christian it does not reign. The Christian is no longer in bondage."[18] This means that because of a new master and our freedom from sin as a master we can choose not to allow sin to exercise dominion in our mortal bodies. We can choose to present our members as slaves of righteousness. In other words, the dying to sin and the change of masters effects a changed situation. In the new situation one has to choose and struggle not to sin. But the freedom to choose is there. Formerly it was not. Formerly our only freedom was freedom to sin.

This view of Christian freedom is very different from that of contemporary American culture. The view of the self that underlies contemporary culture is that humans are autonomous individuals whose purpose in living is to maximize personal freedom. Freedom is understood in this context as freedom of self-determination, freedom from restraint. The casting off of all restraint is maximum freedom. For Paul freedom is freedom from evil. Maximum freedom is the casting off of all evil and utter submission to the One who is good. Paul believed that one is either a slave of evil or of God. Luther, in his *Bondage of the Will*, said: "in things which pertain unto salvation or damnation he [humankind] has no 'Free-will,' but is a captive, slave, and servant, either to the will of God, or to the will of Satan."[19] For Paul, there are no other options. Christian freedom, for him, was liberation from sin and slavery to God/Christ/righteousness. It was the freedom not to sin! It was also life lived in hope of a time when one will not be able to sin. As the Anglican *Book of Common Prayer* puts it: "whose service is perfect freedom."[20]

Baptism

There are multiple views of baptism in the New Testament writings. For example, Matthew 28:19-20 regards Christian baptism as (1) something done by the church (2) in obedience to the command of the risen Christ, (3) in the name of the Father, Son, and Holy Spirit, (4) after a person has been evangelized, (5) which has no explicit connection with the gift of the Spirit. Paul viewed Christian baptism as (1) a rite done by the church (2) as a part of its proclamation of the life, death, and resurrection of Christ, (3) in the name of our Lord Jesus Christ, (4) usually because the Spirit had fallen on a person after hearing the gospel (Gal 3:2; 1 Cor 2:2-5; 1 Thess 1:5; cf. the pattern in Acts 10:44-48's case of Cornelius); (5) as part of an individual's conversion enabled by God. Our task here is to speak to the relevance of the Pauline perspective for today.

Paul was explicitly concerned about children's spiritual well being and their parents' role in ensuring that (1 Cor 7:12-16), but he did not connect this issue with baptism. Second Timothy 1:5 and 3:15

I Baptize Thee

African-American artist William Johnson reflects something of the influence of folk art in his style as well as his immersion into the European avant-garde scene. The abstracted relationship of shapes takes on a rhythm appropriately suggesting the immensity of baptism in the African-American community. The woman to be baptized is interlocked with the minister and an attendant—this group, in turn, is framed by the outlying congregation. The pastor's seeking hand, looming large above the head of the communicant, embodies subliminal associations with the hand of God as a passive cloud drifts by.

William H. Johnson. 1901–1970. *I Baptize Thee*. c. 1940. Smithsonian American Art Museum. Washington, DC.
(Credit: Smithsonian American Art Museum/Art Resource, NY)

show how a Paulinist late in the first century viewed positively Christian nurture within the family. First Timothy 6:12 shows how that same Paulinist assumed an adult confession (in connection with baptism) of the nurtured child when the child became of age.

Paul assumed that those baptized (converted) experience not only the forgiveness of their sins but also deliverance from the power of sin. As Augustus Toplady (1740–1778) in his hymn "Rock of Ages" put it: "Be of sin the double cure, Save from wrath and make me pure." The same sentiment is heard in Charles Wesley's "O for a Thousand Tongues to Sing," one stanza of which ends with these words: "He breaks the power of canceled sin, He sets the prisoner free." A baptism that is not this inclusive in its effects is not Pauline baptism.

Paul's theology of baptism rules out any understanding of the rite as exclusively something the baptized individual does (e.g., "promises the baptized person makes to God"). Baptism is not the time one promises to be good for the rest of one's life. This moralizing view of the rite is alien to Paul. It is rather a time when the church preaches Christ's death, burial, and resurrection in dramatic form. It is a time when the person being baptized is enabled by God to die to sin and rise to a new life. It is a time when the baptized is allowed to participate for the first time corporately in the church's proclamation of the gospel. If the church is constituted by the proclamation of the Word, entrance into the church is facilitated by one's participation in that proclamation.

Paul's practice involved the baptized person in both individuation (= becoming an individual) and participation in community. Much church life today is polarized into two camps: one wants to emphasize community and the other stresses individualism. The issue, in extreme form, becomes "the herd" versus "the autonomous individual." Neither is a Pauline position. The early English Baptists' emphasis upon believer's baptism reflected two movements. First, for an adult to be baptized meant his/her individuation, a standing over against the collective of the state church and becoming an individual. Second, since baptism meant entry into the church, it meant becoming involved in a community of individuated Christians. What this says is that the early Baptists recognized that before one can be a member of a community (as opposed to a herd or collective) one must become an individual by conscious decision. Such autonomy, however, is not a stopping place but a stage on a journey into community. Community (as opposed to collectivism) is only possible, however, if there are individuated people who compose it. Paul's theology of baptism undergirded this early English Baptist stance. If we, like the early English Baptists, are to recapture a Pauline perspective on baptism, it will be by our reclaiming both individuation and community, not only the one or the other.

Justification Viewed Holistically

A forensic interpretation of Paul's doctrine of justification is a reductionist reading of the apostle's teaching. This way of interpreting the matter often sets justification as a judicial act over against regeneration or the new life in Christ. This has led people to think that salvation is a legal transaction in which they might be delivered from the penalty of sin—be declared just—whether they were ever made righteous or not. Paul's doctrine of justification is something more radical than that.[21]

In Romans Paul reflected at least three dimensions of what it means to be justified. In Romans 4:3-8 being reckoned righteous clearly means being forgiven. If someone says to a human being afflicted with sin as Paul saw it, "Your sins are forgiven; your guilt is taken away," would that be good news? Yes and No! Yes, it is good news in that a sinful human needs forgiveness of sin and guilt. No, it is not good news because although one's past sins are absolved by forgiveness, what will help the sinner with the problem of sin in the present? From Paul's perspective, the sinner sins because he/she is in bondage to sin. Forgiveness does not take care of bondage! It is at this point that Paul's understanding of justification as deliverance from bondage (Rom 6:7) comes into play. God has not only forgiven our guilt but has also freed us from our bondage (= addiction) to evil. Now we have the freedom not to sin. Is that good news to the sinner? Yes and No! Yes, it is good news in that the self is now free from bondage to sin/evil in the present. No, it is still news that is deficient. What if the sinner is now free but impotent to do good? What is there that God has done or is doing that will enable the person who is forgiven and delivered to be faithful to God now and in the future? It is at this point that Paul's understanding of justification as being made righteous (Rom 5:19) comes into play. By virtue of his righteousness (faithfulness to God unto death) in the days of his flesh, Christ Jesus, now risen from the dead, can live in and through believers, giving them his righteousness (faithfulness to God). Christ lives in and through believers with the same faithfulness to God that he manifested in the days of his flesh (Gal 2:20). It is this power that enables Christians to be faithful as well as forgiven and free. Now this is good news! The gospel is that God through Christ has done for us all that we could not do for ourselves. God has forgiven us, freed us; and is faithful through us. Since we are justified in all three senses of the word, we have peace with God (= a whole and harmonious relationship).

Dying to Sin:
What Does That Mean and How Is That Possible?

If sin is understood as idolatry, what does dying to sin mean? It means dying to idolatry. Whatever in the created order is a functional deity in one's life must be given up and replaced with the Lordship of the Creator. How does this happen? Sometimes the best way to think about death to sin/idolatry is to reflect on the matter in terms of one's life of prayer.

The conscious dimension of death to idolatry can be taken care of through verbal prayer. The prayer of surrender lays before God all of our idols (cf. Judson W. Van DeVenter's "I Surrender All"). One may pray: "Here is my will; will through my will today; here are my thoughts; think through my thoughts today; here are my emotions; feel through my emotions today." Such a prayer ensures that in those areas idols do not stand in God's place. One form of such a prayer of surrender is that which uses the image of a house (= the self). One invites the risen Lord into the house, into all of the rooms, even the secret room which contains the throne on which we sit, and gives the Lord the right of redecoration of each room and the right to sit on the throne instead of ourselves. In such a prayer, idols are banished and the ultimate idol is cast down. This process is a conscious dying to sin/idolatry.

> **Centering Prayer**
>
> "With regard to our psychological experience of Centering Prayer, we have to be careful not to project our own judgment on God. God responds to each of us where we are and takes into account what we are capable of doing. Everyone of good will who offers prayer of any kind is certainly going to be heard. We do not have to wait until we have reached deep interior silence in order to pray. We must pray as we can and hope for the mercy of God."
>
> —Thomas Keating

Once one has prayed through all the areas of life that are consciously out of Christ's control and allowed him to take control of every area, then one must confront his/her unconscious idolatries. Centering prayer[22] is an effective tool in this matter. [Centering Prayer] In centering prayer one is attentive to the God who dwells within the self and tries in this form of prayer to become centered entirely upon Him. To facilitate this centeredness one may choose a word such as Jesus, Lord, God, to repeat when one's attention strays. Quietly focusing on the God who has come to dwell within, one speaks the name: Jesus. When one tries to be centered, various distractions will intrude. I will itch; I will think about all of the chores that must be done; I will think about what we will have for dinner. When that happens, one repeats the word, Jesus, and returns to the focus on the One who dwells within. If one is able to move beyond the level of such distractions, then often what manifests itself is a tremendous burst of creativity. I suddenly can solve the problem about which I had been puzzling for so long; I can work out the details of the task which lies before me when I stop praying. When this happens, one repeats the word, Jesus, and returns to the focus on the One who dwells within. If one is able to move beyond the dimension of creativity, one often begins to feels the presence of God: warmth, love, electricity flowing through the body. When this happens, repeat the word, Jesus, and return to the focus on the One who dwells within. If one can move beyond all of these distractions, then one can be focused on the Lord. This type of prayer is helpful in dissolving various idolatries: the idolatries of minor duties, the idolatries of creative energies, the idolatry of the felt presence of God. None of these is allowed to become more important to us than being centered upon the Lord. None is allowed to remain an idol.

When verbal prayer and contemplative prayer work together in this way, one finds progress in the process of dying, like Christ, to sin/idolatry. Gradually nothing remains as an ultimate concern except the One who now dwells within the self.

NOTES

[1] The material in brackets [. . .] is the author's translation. It is based on the argument of Florence M. Gillman, *A Study of Romans 6:5a: United to a Death Like Christ's* (San Francisco: Mellen Research University Press, 1992).

[2] *ANF* 3. 671.

[3] Herbert Danby, ed., *The Mishnah* (London: Oxford University Press, 1938), 151.

[4] Cited in W. D. Davies, *Paul and Rabbinic Judaism* (London: SPCK, 1955), 103.

[5] Tertullian, *On the Flesh of Christ* 15 (*ANF* 3.535).

[6] E. P. Sanders, *Paul* (NY: Oxford University Press, 1991), 79.

[7] Douglas J. Moo, *The Epistle to the Romans* (Grand Rapids: Eerdmans, 1996), 377.

[8] Thomas R. Schreiner, *Romans* (Grand Rapids: Baker, 1998), 298-99, 319.

[9] Eduard Schweizer, *Lordship and Discipleship* (Naperville IL: Allenson, 1960), 1.

[10] Gerald Bray, *Romans: Ancient Christian Commentary on Scripture, NT VI* (Downers Grove: IVP, 1998), 153.

[11] Helpful studies of early Christian baptism include G. R. Beasley-Murray, *Baptism in the New Testament* (Grand Rapids: Eerdmans, 1962) and Rudolf Schnackenburg, *Baptism in the Theology of St. Paul* (NY: Herder & Herder, 1964).

[12] Robert A. J. Gagnon, "Heart of Wax and a Teaching that Stamps: *Typos didachēs* (Rom 6:17b) Once More," *JBL* 112 (1993): 667-87.

[13] Keith Augustus Burton, "The Argumentative Coherency of Romans 7:1-6," *SBLSP 2000* (Atlanta: Society of Biblical Literature, 2000), 452-64.

[14] John Calvin, *Institutes of the Christian Religion* III.xvi.1 (Hugh Thomson Kerr, *A Compend of the Institutes of the Christian Religion by John Calvin* [Philadelphia: Presbyterian Board of Christian Education, 1939], 115).

[15] Moo, *Romans*, 355.

[16] W. H. Auden, *For the Time Being* (London: Faber & Faber, 1958), 116.

[17] Ben Witherington III, *Paul's Narrative Thought World* (Louisville: Westminster/John Knox, 1994), 290.

[18] Witherington, *Paul's Narrative Thought World*, 28.

[19] Kerr, *A Compend of Luther's Theology*, 88.

[20] *The Book of Common Prayer* (NY: Church Pension Fund, 1945), 17.

[21] W. T. Conner, "Is Paul's Doctrine of Justification Forensic?" *RevExp* 40 (1943): 48-54. Conner aligns himself with James Denney (*Expositor's Greek Testament*, II.575) who contends that justification is a regenerative transaction. Justification regenerates; nothing else does.

[22] M. Basil Pennington, *Centering Prayer* (Garden City NY: Image Books, 1982).

THE ROLE OF THE LAW
AND THE DIVINE REMEDY

7:7–8:17

In Romans 5:12–8:39 Paul retraced the basic train of thought covered earlier in 1:18–5:11. In both 1:18–5:11 and 5:12–8:39 the apostle's argument moves from the human condition to the divine remedy to the role of the law to ultimate salvation. In 7:7–8:2 the focus is once again on the role of the law. The discussion of this topic was provoked by 7:1-6 where Paul has argued that the law is a tool of sin in the life of a person living in the flesh (v. 5). If this is so, then it raises serious questions about the law. Paul's rhetorical opponent puts two questions to him: one in 7:7, the other in 7:13. The first asks: is the law sin? The second queries: did the law bring death? Paul's argument in 7:7–8:2 is largely shaped as answers to these two questions.

Any reading of this section of Romans must start with the structure of the argument. Simply put, 7:7–8:2 falls into three smaller units, each organized in a symmetrical fashion. Recognition of this fact solves some, but not all of the interpretive problems of the passage. The organization of 7:7-12 is as follows:

A diatribe introduction (7:7)
    The opponent's query: What then should we say? That the law is sin? (v. 7a)
    The Pauline answer: By no means! The law makes sin known. (v. 7b)
An elaboration of Paul's statement in v. 7b (vv. 8-11)
    A—Sin, seizing opportunity in the commandment, produced in me all kinds of covetousness (v. 8a)
      B—Apart from the law, sin lies dead (v. 8b).
      I was once alive apart from the law (v. 9a)
        B'—When the commandment came, sin revived (v. 9b)
        I died (v. 10a)
    A'—Sin, seizing opportunity in the commandment, deceived me and through it killed me (v. 11)
Conclusion: The law/commandment is holy, just, and good (v. 12).
Implied: it is sin that is evil, not the law. Let us read vv. 7-12 in these terms.

COMMENTARY

Paul's conversation partner posed a question that must be asked in light of v. 5. In 7:5 Paul had said that "while we were living in the flesh, our sinful passions, aroused by the law, were at work in our members to bear fruit for death." If so, "What then should we say? That the law is sin?" To which the apostle replied: "By no means! Yet, if it had not been for the law, I would not have known sin. I would not have known what it is to covet if the law had not said, 'You shall not covet.'" The law is not sin; rather by the law comes a knowledge of sin (cf. 3:20b). This information is given in the form of a confession by an "I."

Who is the "I" in v. 7? The options are basically three. First, does the "I" signal that this is an autobiographical section in which Paul was speaking about himself (cf. 1 Cor 9 where the "I" is self-referential)? If so, was he speaking of his pre-Christian (Augustine, *Propositions* and *Confessions*) or Christian experience (so Augustine, *On Marriage and Concupiscence* 28-32; *Retractions* 2.1.1, where he changed his mind; Luther, *Lectures on Romans* [Scholia on 7:7]; Calvin, *Romans*[1])? Or, second, does the "I" serve a rhetorical function and reflect Paul's identification with someone else: Adam, humanity from Adam to Moses, Israel, a Jewish child at age twelve, humanity in general (cf. 1 Cor 13 where the "I" includes all Christians, of which Paul is a part)?[2] Third, does the "I" function as a fictive "I" and contain no personal reference at all?

Although the first option seems the most natural one to a beginning reader, it seems less so when one realizes that ancient Judaism did not always use the "I" in an autobiographical fashion. For example, 1 QS X-XI uses "I" to refer to humankind as flesh rather than to some particular individual. Likewise, the philosophers used a rhetorical "I." Epictetus, for example, used the "I" form for the speech of a would-be philosopher (3.22.10). This ancient rhetorical device was called *prosōpopoiia* (= making a mask). We would call it "taking on a character" or "playing a part."[3] This rhetorical device was one of the elementary exercises closely related to learning prose and poetic composition. It was also used for training in letter writing (Theon 2.1125.22). Such a speech-in-character could be of a known person or of one invented who represented a type of character (e.g., such as a husband, a general, a farmer). The device was often used for emotional effect. Quintilian (6.1.25-26), for example, said: "The bare facts are no doubt moving in themselves: but when we pretend that the persons concerned themselves are speaking, the personal note adds to the emotional effect." It could be used with or without identifying the imaginary speaker

(Quintilian 9.2.37). It could begin with the character starting to speak about himself in the first person. Traditionally, its contents referred to present misery, past happiness, and wretched future prospects. It was expected that such characterizations fit the persons described (cf. Origen's critique of Celsus in *Against Celsus* 1.43; 1.49; 2.1, for lack of a fit; Aristophanes' critique of Euripides in *Acharnians* 393ff. for the same problem). As early as Origen, Romans 7:7-25 was understood in terms of *prosōpopoiia*. Elsewhere, Paul often uses the first person in this way in an inclusive sense (e.g., 1 Cor 6:15; 13:1-3; 14:11, 14-15; Rom 3:7). Each option, autobiographical or speech-in-character, has its strengths. Modern scholars prefer the latter option. It is this approach with which we begin.

If Paul here is using the "I" as a speech-in-character in 7:7-25, who is being represented? Keep in mind that ancient Mediterranean people assessed themselves in terms of stereotypes derived above all from family history.[4] As often was the case, the speaker is not identified by name. In terms of what family history, then, is the "I" speaking? It is difficult to avoid hearing echoes of the experience of the original couple in the garden. When vv. 8 and 9 speak first about the "I" as being alive apart from the law, second of the commandment's coming, and third of sin's using it as an opportunity to seduce the self, and fourth of its resulting in death, how can one avoid hearing echoes of the first man and woman (Gen 2:7; 2:16; 3:1-5; 3:22-24)? Moreover, when v. 11 says "sin . . . deceived me and through it killed me," how can one avoid thinking of Genesis 3:13 ("The serpent deceived me, and I ate.")? That Paul knew and used this story is evidenced by 2 Corinthians 11:3 ("I am afraid that as the serpent deceived Eve . . . your thoughts will be led astray"; cf. 1 Tim 2:14). The major complaint against such a reading is that the commandment against covetousness (v. 7) comes from the Decalogue (Exod 20; Deut 6) and not Genesis 2–3. A careful reading of the serpent's use of the prohibition against eating the fruit of the tree of the knowledge of good and evil alleviates some of the difficulty. Genesis 3:5 has the serpent say to Eve: "God knows that when you eat of it your eyes will be opened, and you will be like God, knowing good and evil." This transposes the temptation into one of covetousness. The woman covets being like God. The tree was to be desired to make one wise, like God (3:6). That this is a central motif in the story is evident from the Lord's words in 3:22. "See, the man has become like one of us, knowing good and evil." That it was so regarded in Paul's time is seen in the *Apocalypse of Moses* 19:3 where Eve attributes her failure to "desire, the root and beginning of every sin" (cf. the echo in James 1:15). Of course, ultimately such desire/covetousness is idolatry (Rom 1:29; Col 3:5; Eph 5:5).

It is also difficult not to hear something of the experience of ancient Israel. Before Sinai, Israel may have been sinful, but it was not conscious transgression (cf. 5:14). When the Law was given at Sinai the trespass multiplied (cf. 5:20). It may be possible to say that the experience of Israel with the law recapitulates the experience of Adam. Indeed, if the experience of a Jewish lad before the age of accountability is changed by his acceptance of the yoke of the law at age twelve (cf. *m. 'Abot* 5:24), this may also be but a recapitulation of the national experience, which is a recapitulation of the Adamic experience.

If vv. 7-12 are in any sense autobiographical (i.e., typical "I"), Paul here was speaking as one who is "in Adam" (remember 5:12-21). If he referred here to a Jewish lad at the age of accountability, or to Israel, or humanity as a whole, he was referring to one or more as people "in Adam." As such, vv. 7-12 clearly refer to pre-Christian experience.[5] "There is not a syllable in Romans 7:7-25 about life in Christ, and . . . Paul himself has signaled to his readers in both 7:6 and 8:1-2 that the rest of chapter 7 is to be understood as the antithesis to chapter 8 and not in simple continuity with

---

📖 Struggle between Good and Evil Prior to Conversion and After

• Before one becomes a Christian there is a struggle in the self between good and evil. In this commentary Rom 7:7-25 is interpreted in this light. This passage reflects the bondage to sin characteristic of those apart from Christ.

• After one becomes a Christian there is also a struggle in the self between good and evil. The difference is that in this struggle the power of sin has been broken and divine enablement assists the believer in the struggle. It is this struggle that is reflected, for example, in *Journal of a Soul: The Autobiography of Pope John XXIII*. A typical youthful confession runs: "The good Jesus sees that I have no other desire than to serve him. . . . And yet I still fall, and so frequently!" (22, cf. 38, 138) As a seminarian in Rome we hear: "I foresee more backslidings, alas! but they will be against my will, O Jesus, against my will"(147). In the year of his ordination as a priest we hear: "Today I have been looking back over my progress this month to see how my spiritual life is faring. . . . I have made progress, to be sure, but very little. In fact I am still a sinner, and very slow to reform"(152). While a papal representative in Bulgaria, he said: "In twenty five years of priesthood what innumerable failings and deficiencies! My spiritual organism still feels healthy and robust, thanks to God, but what weaknesses!" (212, note the detailed list of "deficiences") When a papal representative in Turkey and Greece, past mid-life, he said: "I have now formed the habit of constant union with God 'in thought, word and deed', of bearing in mind the twofold prayer: 'thy kingdom come, thy will be done', and of seeing everything in relation to these two ideals. But how unsatisfactory are my daily actions and my religious practices!" (227) As pope he said: "I am very far from attaining this holiness in fact, although my desire and will to succeed in this are whole-hearted and determined"(303). The difference in tone between these struggles and that in Rom 7 is striking. The difference is due to the fact that in the one case (Rom 7) the self is in bondage to sin and is free only to sin; in the other case the self is free to choose but does so only imperfectly.

Journal of a Soul: The Autobiography of Pope John XXIII (NY: Image Books Doubleday, 1980).

it."[6] Arguments for understanding this text as a description of an unregenerate person include the following. (1) Romans 7:7-24 is an answer to the question raised by 7:5. In 7:5 what is described is life "in the flesh." This connection of the self with the flesh is echoed in vv. 14 ("I am of the flesh"), 18, and 25b. (2) The "I" struggles on its own without divine help (7:25b). There is no reference to the Holy Spirit. (3) The "I" is under the power of sin ("sold into slavery under sin"). This is in contrast to the regenerate person's "having been set free from sin" (6:18,22). (4) The "I" is prisoner of the rule of sin (v. 23). The regenerate person, however, has been freed from sin (6:22). (5) The "I" struggles with the need to obey the Mosaic Law (vv. 22, 25). The Christian is free from the old written code (7:6). (6) What is described here is not the Christians' struggle with sin but the absolute defeat of the self by sin's power in the unregenerate state. Such arguments are compelling. [Struggle between Good and Evil Prior to Conversion and After]

The difference between the unregenerate and regenerate states can be seen in the contrast of the following chart:[7]

7:14 One is sold under sin.	8:2 The Christian is liberated from sin.
7:17 Sin lives within one.	8:9 The Spirit lives within one.
7:18 Flesh and "I" are equated.	8:9 You are no longer in the flesh.
7:23 The "other law" is at war.	8:6 The mind of the Spirit is peace.

These vv. (7-12) fall into an ABB'A' pattern. In A and A' Paul reflected an insight found elsewhere in antiquity. From the pagan world, we may cite Livy 34.4, who said that limitations are precisely what makes desire wild. Also Ovid, *Amores* 3.4.17, put it this way: "We ever strive for what is forbidden, and ever covet what is denied." In 2.19.3, he said: "What one may not do pricks more keenly on." In his *Metamorphoses* 3.566, Ovid stated: "The more one is warned, the more one is provoked to contrary tendencies." From the Jewish milieu, the *Life of Adam and Eve* 19, depicts the serpent as seeking to seduce Eve precisely by holding back the promised fruit. "I have changed my mind," he says, "and will not allow you to eat." The same viewpoint is implicit in 4 Maccabees 1:33-34. Paul's argument is an adaptation of the general mindset. A, v. 8a, says that "sin, seizing an opportunity in the commandment, produced in me all kinds of covetousness." A', v. 11 makes a nearly identical statement. "Sin, seizing an opportunity in the commandment, deceived me and through it killed me." Both say that it was not the law or commandment that was evil. It was rather sin that used the commandment as an opportunity.

B, vv. 8b-9a, makes two related assertions: first, apart from the law, sin lies dead, and second, "I" was once alive apart from the law. B', vv. 9b-10a, also makes two related points: first, when the commandment came, sin revived, and second, "I" died. The picture that emerges from this small unit personifies sin. It then portrays sin's sleeping in the self, sin's being awakened by the noise of the commandment, and sin's then taking control of the self in which it resides. The law itself is not evil. Indeed, it promised life (v. 10; cf. Lev 18:5, used by Gal 3:12; Deut 4:1; 6:24; Rom 10:5). It is merely the occasion for evil to take over the self. With such an argument, Paul rejected the opponent's inference, made on the basis of the Pauline statement in 7:5, that the law is sin. Not so, the apostle responded. His conclusion to this unit is that the law is holy, just, and good (v. 12; cf. 7:16; [1 Tim 1:8]). Sin merely uses the good law for bad ends.

This brings us to the second of the smaller units in 7:7–8:2. The organization of 7:13-20 is likewise helpful in reading. It looks like this:

A diatribe introduction (7:13)
> The opponent's question: Did that which is good, then, bring death to me?
> The Pauline answer: By no means! It was sin that was responsible.

An elaboration of Paul's statement in v. 13b (vv. 14-20)
> A—We know that. . . . I am of flesh, sold into slavery under sin (v. 14)
>> B—I cannot determine what I do (v. 15a).
>>> For I do not do what I want, but I do the very thing I hate (v. 15b)
>>> C—If I do what I do not want (v. 16) It is no longer I that do it, but sin that dwells within me (v. 17)
> A'—I know that good does not dwells within me, that is, in my flesh (v. 18a)[8]
>> B'—I can will what is right, but I cannot do it (v. 18b)
>>> For I do not do the good I want, but the evil I do not want is what I do (v. 19)
>>> C'—If I do what I do not want,it is no longer I that do it, but sin that dwells within me (v. 20).

Let us read vv. 13-20 along these lines.

Like the previous small unit, vv. 7-12, this unit also begins with an opponent's query and a Pauline response. This question, like that of v. 7, is evoked by Paul's statement in 7:5. "While we were living in the flesh, our sinful passions, aroused by the law, were at work in our members to bear fruit for death." The opponent asked: "Did what is good, then, bring death to me" (v. 13a)? To which the apostle responded: "By no means! It was sin, working death in me through what is good, in order that sin might be shown to be sin, and through the commandment might become sinful beyond measure" (v. 13b). Sin, not the law, is responsible for death's entry into the world (remember 5:12).

The claim in v. 13b is elaborated in what follows (vv. 14-20). The material is arranged in an ABCA'B'C' pattern. A, v. 14, says "I" am of the flesh, sold into slavery under sin. Flesh here does not refer to humanity "in Adam" as physical and finite but to humanity's being idolatrous. To be of the flesh means to live according to the flesh. It means that one's orientation to life absolutizes the physical and finite order, worshipping and serving the creature/creation instead of the Creator. This orientation to life, once chosen, is not something from which one can extricate himself/herself. Once in the orientation, one is a prisoner, a slave of sin. Sin here is not something the self does or does not do but is a power that does its work in the self when it hears the law. "The self is a P.O.W. made to work against its will, like a captured slave."[9] ["Holy Sonnet XIX" by John Donne]

> ### 📖 "Holy Sonnet XIX" by John Donne
>
> Oh, to vex me, contraries meet in one:
> Inconstancy unnaturally hath begot
> A constant habit, that when I would not
> I change in vows, and in devotion.
> As humorous is my contrition
> As my profane love, and as soon forgot:
> As riddingly distempered, cold and hot,
> As praying, as mute; as infinite, as none.
> I durst not view heaven yesterday; and today
> In prayers, and flattering speeches, I court God:
> Tomorrow I quake with true fear of his rod.
> So my devout fits come and go away
> Like a fantastic ague: save that here
> Those are my best days, when I shake with feare.

This description of the "I" clearly indicates that the "I" is in a pre-Christian existence. Romans 6:15-23 described the two slaveries: that to sin and that to righteousness. The slavery to sin is what is described in 7:14-20. If so, then the "I" probably remains the self "in Adam." "Adam is not the *subject* of the conflict in Rom 7:7ff. but rather its *model*."[10] A', v. 18a, makes a similar claim. "I know that good does not dwell within me, that is, in my flesh." The orientation according to the flesh is one in which the self presents its members as slaves to impurity and greater and greater iniquity (6:19b).

B, v. 15a, is a lament. It may be translated either "I cannot determine what I do" or "I do not understand what I do." Verse 15b explains. "For I do not do what I want, but I do the very thing I hate." B', vv. 18b-19, makes a similar complaint. "I can will what is

Addiction

Addictions in their many varied forms are extreme examples of the human being becoming "slaves of the flesh." In the 19th century, absinthe was the addictive drink of choice by many in Parisian society. Many artists have explored the devastating effects of this liquor upon the addicts. One such devastation can be seen in the this work by Edgar Degas where the pathetic inebriated woman is stewing in her stupor—so self-neglected that she barely casts a shadow. This pale green liquor was made from wormwood and was later outlawed.

Edgar Degas. 1834–1917. *At the Café.* Musee d'Orsay. Paris, France. (Credit: Giraudon/Art Resource, NY)

right, but I cannot do it. For I do not do the good I want, but the evil I do not want is what I do." Here a battle is portrayed between the ego of the flesh dominated by sin and the spiritual law of God. The ego finds itself on both sides and is torn by the division. Paul is articulating an experience common to Jew and Gentile alike.

The pagan world was divided about optimistic and pessimistic anthropologies. Xenophon's Socrates supports the optimistic.

"I think that all men have a choice between various courses, and choose and follow the one which they think conduces most to their advantage" (*Memorabilia* 3.9.4). Many differed. Plato cite the pessimistic opinion that people act against their better insight as the view of "many": "while knowing what is best, refuse to perform it" (*Protagoras* 352D). From the pagan world the pessimistic statements often spoke about the struggle between reason and passion. For example, Euripides, *Medea* 1077-79, read: "I am overcome of evil. Passion overmasters sober thoughts." Ovid's *Metamorphoses* 7.19 has Medea say: "Oh, if I could, I should be more like myself! But against my own wishes, some strange influence weighs heavily upon me, and desire sways me one way, reason another." In 7.21 she continues: "I see the better and approve; the lower I follow." Diodorus Siculus 1.71.3, said: "Oftentimes people who know they are about to commit a sin nevertheless do base acts when overpowered by passion." Seneca, *Hippolytus* 177, had Phaedra say: "I know what you say is true but passion forces me to take the worser path. With full knowledge my soul moves to the abyss and vainly seeks the backward way in quest of counsels of shame." Epictetus 2.26.1, put it thusly: "Since the person who is in error does not wish to err but to be right, it is clear that he is not doing what he wishes." Dio Chrysostom, *Discourses* 36.23 and 69.8, asserted that humans are so wicked that there is no possibility that laws will make them live properly. This is a pessimistic anthropology. Did all pagans feel this way? Hardly. Did many? Most likely.

In the Scriptures of Israel different strata reflect varying degrees of anthropological optimism or pessimism. The prophets normally held an optimistic view of evil. Evil was a problem that could be corrected by proper discipline (the exile). The theologians who put Genesis together after the exile held a more realistic view. The Noah stories tell how good and evil are intertwined even in the righteous so that the two cannot be separated within history. The apocalyptic sections of Daniel manifest a pessimism about evil. Evil is a mystery so deep-seated and radical that only God can resolve it and that at the last day. A similar pessimistic judgment is heard in certain post-biblical Jewish sources. At Qumran, 1 QS 11.9-10, using the "I" form, says: "I belong to evil humankind to the assembly of wicked flesh; my failings, my transgressions, my sins. . . . with the depravities of my heart, belong to . . . those who walk in darkness. For to man (does not belong) his path, nor to a human being the steadying of his step."[11] The Jewish apocalypse, 4 Ezra 3:19-22, 25-26, speaks to the same point. This apocalypse uses the concept of the evil yetzer to deal with the moral impotence of

The Caprices

This print is one of eighty included in the series *Los Caprichos* (*The Caprices*), which in its entirety was desribed in 1799 by the Spanish newspaper *Diario de Madrid* as a critique of "human errors and vices."

Francisco de Goya y Lucienter. 1746–1828. *The Sleep of Reason Produces Monsters.* Etching and Aquatint. Victoria and Albert Museum. London, England. (Credit: Victoria & Albert Museum/Art Resource, NY)

Israel. God gave the Law to Israel (v. 19). He did not, however, take away their evil heart (v. 20). So just like Adam, who was burdened with an evil heart, they transgressed (v. 21). In their hearts there were both the law and the evil root (v. 22). The latter prevented obedience to the former. Jerusalem, after David, also had the evil heart and transgressed (v. 26). Unlike Paul who spoke of "sin" personified, 4 Ezra uses the concept of the evil yetzer (= impulse). Both, using different conceptual tools, talk about the moral impotence of Israel. Israel cannot obey the law because of the evil in their hearts. This is a pessimistic anthropology (cf. 4 Ezra 9:36-37). Did all Jews feel this way? Hardly. Did some? Definitely. But even in the pessimistic stream of thought in the Jewish Scriptures and in post-biblical Judaism there is still the assumption that some few will be able to be obedient out of their own resources.

In Romans 7, therefore, Paul described a conflict between will and performance. It is one known to humans generally. Paul was, therefore, using a standard *topos* of the ancient world—the conflict between what is the right thing to do and the moral incapacity to do it. The pagans may have described it as a tension between reason and passion and the Jew as a split in the human will or as the dominance of an evil impulse, but the battle is recognized by all. For Paul, as with 4 Ezra, it was the conflict within those who live "in Adam."

C, vv. 16-17, draws a conclusion from the experience. "If I do what I do not want, I agree that the law is good. But in fact it is no longer I that do it, but sin that dwells within me." C', v. 20, draws the same conclusion. "Now if I do what I do not want, it is no longer I that do it, but sin that dwells in me." Again sin is personified and is treated like a demon dwelling within the self. Sin's having control of the will, the self cannot do what it wants. But if the self wants to do what the law commands, then the law is good, not evil. The second unit, like the first, describes realities that belong to the pre-Christian period: the flesh (cf. 7:5), the power of sin (6:2, 6, 11, 12-14). The "I" who utters these laments is the self "in Adam."

The third little unit does not begin with a query by an opponent. It summarizes and then looks beyond the argument of the first two little units. Like the previous unit, Romans 7:21–8:2 also largely falls into an ABCΛ'B'C' pattern. This segment of the text looks like this:

A statement of the problem: When I want to do what is good, evil lies close at hand (v. 21)

An elaboration of the issue:

    A—I delight in the law of God in my inmost self (v. 22)

      B—In my members is another law making me captive to the law of sin (v. 23)

        C—Who will deliver me from this body of death? Thanks be to God through Jesus Christ our Lord (v. 25a)

    A'—With my mind I am a slave to the law of God (v. 25b)

      B'—With my flesh I am a slave to the law of sin (v. 25c)

        C'—There is no condemnation for those in Christ (8:1). For the law of the Spirit has set me free from the law of sin and death (8:2).

Recognition of this pattern removes the need to rearrange vv. as some scholars want to do (e.g., 7:25a + 8:2 + 8:1 + 8:3) and/or excise vv. as later glosses (e.g., 7:25b; 8:1). Given the repetitive pattern, the order is a logical one.

Paul opens the third unit with a statement of the problem. "So I find it to be a law (= a principle; cf. 3:27) that when I want to do what is good, evil lies close at hand." The ABCA'B'C' pattern that follows both expounds it and responds to it. A, v. 22, explains: "For I delight in the law of God (= law of Moses) in my inmost self." A', v. 25b), echoes the thought: "So then, with my mind I am a slave to the law of God" (= law of Moses). Part of the self adheres to God's demands. Paul's addressees must be either Jewish Christians or Gentile Christians who had come out of the synagogue where they were God-fearers. Otherwise, there would not be this devotion to the Jewish law. B, v. 23, then gives the other side. "I see in my members (= facets of my personality) another law (= demand) at war with the law (= demand) of my mind, making me captive to the law of sin (= rule of sin) that dwells in my members." B', v. 25c, echoes the thought. "With my flesh (= my orientation in which the physical, finite order is absolutized) I am a slave to the law (= rule) of sin." Taking A, A', B, and B' together, the picture is complete. The self is split and the will is pulled in two directions. The self is divided between the law and sin.

C and C' look beyond the dilemma. In C, vv. 24-25a, the "I" cries out: "Wretched man that I am! Who will rescue me from this body of death (= personality characterized by death in all its meanings)?" A thanksgiving answers the cry: "Thanks be to God through Jesus Christ our Lord!" C', 8:1-2, provides a parallel encouragement. In 8:1-2 Paul responded to the "I" caught in a divided will and impotent in the face of sin. The apostle said: "There is therefore now no condemnation for those who are in Christ Jesus. For the law (= the rule) of the Spirit of life (= the Holy Spirit who gives life) has set you free from the law (= rule) of sin and death." Paul offered God's acts through Jesus Christ and the gift of the Spirit as the solution to the divided, impotent will of the person living "in Adam."

The two objections raised in 7:7 and 13 are likely Jewish objections Paul had encountered in his missionazry work. In answering these two Jewish objections, Paul appealed to the experience of Jews and God-fearers with and under the law. In each case, he argued that it is sin rather than the law that is the evil. The law, while good, is nevertheless weak and impotent in the face of sin. Rather than dealing with sin, it merely awakens sin and sets it in motion to subdue the self. Something other than the law is required to deal with sin. That something else is God's acts in Jesus Christ and through the Holy Spirit. These acts are salvific because they are able to overcome the power of sin and set persons free from the rule of sin and death.

If the "I" in 7:7-25 has been the self "in Adam," is this self intended to be a Gentile self or a Jewish self? Paul was writing to Gentile congregations in Rome. But if the "I" is a Gentile self, it is a Gentile self that has become identified with the synagogue (= a God-fearer). Otherwise how can the impotent self talk about the Jewish law's involvement in its life (v. 22—"I delight in the law of God in my inmost self")? The law must be the Jewish law because the entire section is a response to 7:5, which is focused on the role of the Jewish law. One possibility, then, is that the "I" is Gentile God-fearers who love the law but who cannot carry out its demands as long as they are "in Adam." But the interlocutors in 7:7, 13 (as in 6:1; 6:15), as well as the addressees in 7:1, appear to have a Jewish personna. The argument in 7:7-25 would make little sense if it appealed only to Gentile experience. How could an appeal to Gentile experience answer the questions put by a Jewish questioner? The context seems to demand that, in addition to Gentile God-fearers, the impotent self "in Adam" be Jewish as well.

This entire section, if it depicts Jewish existence apart from Christ as morally impotent to any degree, poses significant questions. Research since World War II has tended to reject an autobiographical reading of Romans 7. This is largely because Paul's statements about his pre-Christian existence elsewhere in his letters do not reflect this moral struggle. So, in Philippians 3:6, he said: "as to righteousness under the law, blameless." In Galatians 1:14 he said: "I advanced in Judaism beyond many among my people of the same age, for I was far more zealous for the traditions of my ancestors." Neither of these statements seems to reflect a moral struggle within Paul between sin and the law. Hence, scholars have tended to dismiss an autobiographical reading of Romans 7. This struggle, it is argued, does not describe Paul in his pre-Christian days as he describes them elsewhere. Luke Johnson speaks for the consensus: "Before his experience of the risen Lord, . . . Paul considered that perfection in the law was not only possible but that he had accomplished it."[12] This assumes that the pre-Christian Paul had an optimistic anthropology, at least as regards himself.

Eliminating an autobiographical reading does not remove the basic problem, however. Did any Jew have the experience described in Romans 7:7–8:2? If Romans 7 talks about pre-Christian experience and if it does so at any level in Jewish terms, then Paul was saying that Jewish experience with the law apart from Christ involves moral impotence. This seems to be Paul's point here. In Romans 3:9b he said that "we have already charged that all, both Jews and Greeks, are under the power of sin." If Paul equated the behavior of 1:18–2:29 with being "under the power of sin," then he saw such behavior as a demonstration of the phenomenon dealt with in 7:7-25. If this is not an accurate description of Paul's pre-Christian experience, is it an accurate depiction of any non-Christian Jewish experience?

Many modern scholars deny that ancient Judaism thought this way. Instead, it is claimed, Jews believed the law could be obeyed if one wanted to do so (= an optimistic anthropology). Many streams of Middle Judaism did in fact assume that humans have free will. For example, Sirach 15:14-15 says God created humans and left them in the power of their own inclination. "If you will, you can keep the commandments, and to act faithfully is a matter of your

Paul on the Road to Damascus

In this painting by Pieter Brueghel the Younger, one is hard put to discern any explicit event surrounding this journey to Damascus. Rather, Saul is depicted as if part of a hunting party—not an isolated, distinct image. It appears that they may be in the process of apprehending someone, perhaps associated with "the Way" (Acts 9:1-12). Though Saul is indistinctly shown as part of a group—hunters in search of the hunted—his status will soon change along his journey to Damascus as his conversion is imminent. In a sense, the hunter will become the hunted.

Pieter Brueghel the Younger. 1564–1636. *Saint Paul on the Road to Damascus before His Conversion.* Musee de Beaux-Arts. Lille, France.
(Credit: Réunion des Musées Nationaux/Art Resource, NY)

own choice." *Psalms of Solomon* 9:4 puts it this way: "Our works (are) in the choosing and power of our souls, to do right and wrong in the works of our hands, and in your righteousness you oversee human beings." The *Mishnah* assumes human free will. *m. 'Abot* 3:16 makes this clear: "All is foreseen, but freedom of choice is given." The roots are deep in the Scriptures of Israel (cf. Deut 30:15-20). Much of Middle Judaism believed that on the basis of free will humans had not only the capacity always to choose good instead of evil, they had also the power always to do good.[13] Moreover, a number of them claimed to be blameless in this regard. A late Talmudic tradition illustrates the spirit. In *b. Sukka* 45b, one rabbi, confident in his righteousness, said: "If the saved numbered only a hundred, I and my son are among them; and if only two, they are I and my son." If so, would Paul's auditors in Rome have understood his section that assumes moral impotence on the part of humans, including Jewish persons, "in Adam"?

There are two problems here. On the one hand, Paul did not recognize free will in the area of soteriology.[14] One is either a slave of sin or of righteousness. One never stands in a neutral position belonging to neither. So the optimistic anthropological presuppositions of certain streams of Middle Jewish thought and the Pauline pattern of messianic Jewish religion with its pessimistic anthropology differ drastically. Would Jewish auditors have made any sense of Paul's argument that denied free will and presupposed human bondage to sin? Or was Paul in Romans talking only to Gentile readers who were God-fearers? On the other hand, if Paul included Jewish experience apart from Christ in 7:7-25, would any Jewish auditor have been able to recognize himself/herself in his description of moral impotence? This issue is normally dealt with in terms of the claim that Paul's analysis was done as a Christian looking back on pre-Christian existence. It is the way a person converted to Christ sees human life apart from Christ. So, it is claimed, in Romans 7 Paul looked back as a new convert does to his pre-Christian existence to find inner conflict that perhaps was not as clear to him at that time.[15] "To what extent Paul was conscious of this conflict and his failure at the time of that conflict is difficult to ascertain."[16] This in no way solves the dilemma! Paul's conversion could have relativized the absoluteness of the Torah and replaced it with Christ. But that the Damascus encounter would have caused him to see conflict in the self where there was none before is beyond belief.

> [I]f Paul had been a completely "happy" Jew before he met Christ, his Christian hindsight of his "unhappy" Jewish past in Rom 7:7-25 would be false and inauthentic, because his statements would lack any foothold in his own experience. . . . It is unlikely that Paul could have written Rom 1:18–2:29 without any knowledge of a Jewish awareness of sin and boasting. When he indicts the Jews for transgressing the law and for boasting in spite of their trespasses, he must have experienced this tension within his own Jewish life.[17]

Is Paul's Christian description of non-Christian experience, Gentile and/or Jewish, accurate? If Paul did not see it that way prior to Christ and if other Jews did not see it this way apart from Christ, in what sense can such a Christian analysis of Jewish experience with the law make any sense?

It seems better to reconsider the entire issue. Two points need to be made. First, we know from Qumran materials and from 4 Ezra that some Jews in Mediterranean antiquity had the experience of moral impotence (= a pessimistic anthropology).[18] However it was expressed, this impotence in obeying the law was believed to be because of the presence of evil in the human heart. Paul in Romans 7 fit into this stream of Middle Judaism. Romans 2:17-24 also seems to assume such moral impotence on the part of the Jew apart from Christ (cf. 3:9b). The Jew knows God's will and does not do it. If Paul wrote in these terms to the Roman Christians, he must have believed that they too would share his convictions. Otherwise no communication would have taken place.[19] Failure to take account of this stream of Middle Judaism with a pessimistic anthropology is due in large part to modern scholarly selectivity in the choice of sources to examine: rabbinic texts and others that share the rabbinic slant on things. To describe the Hellenistic Judaism of Paul's time on the basis of such sources is to build on sand.[20] Since Paul's writings offer us "the only witness to a world of everyday Hellenistic Judaism now vanished,"[21] the apostle must be regarded as "our best witness to the issues that affected first-century Jews."[22]

Second, we know that it was possible for at least some ancient Jews to possess both a deep sense of personal sin and the conviction that they were righteous. Qumran is a prime example. The Qumranites combined a self-righteous attitude vis-á-vis outsiders and Israel at large together with a profound recognition of personal and collective sinfulness vis-á-vis God.[23] This dual conviction in certain circles of Middle Judaism was sometimes expressed with an "I" style: for example, a sense of sin expressed with an "I" style (Pss 32:3-5; 38; 51; 1 QH IV.18-19; IX.21-22; XVII.13-15); a conviction of righteousness expressed in an "I" style (Ps 17:1-5; Ps 26; 1 QH VI; VIII.18; X; XV). The same persons would pray both ways. Even in the later rabbinic material this duality is found.

> When someone is debating about the definition of a commandment, he naturally talks as it religion is under his control. But when, in prayer, he feels himself before his God, he is impressed by his own worthlessness and recognizes his reliance on God's grace.[24]

It was possible, therefore, for at least some ancient Jews to feel both blameless and guilty. If so, then Paul's statements of his blamelessness during his pre-Christian days do not rule out a sense of personal sin on his part.[25] We know that Paul was aware of past failings. Galatians 1:10, for example, has Paul ask: "Am I now seeking human approval, or God's approval? Or am I trying to please people? If I were still pleasing people, I would not be a servant of Christ." This assumes a common conviction voiced by Epictetus, *Encheiridion* 23: "If it should ever happen to you that you turn to externals with a view to pleasing someone, rest assured that you have lost your plan of life." It implies, moreover, that Paul at some time in the past had attempted to please people. So he was aware of past transgressions.[26] It is simply that Paul's contexts in Philippians and Galatians did not require him to speak about his personal sins or consciousness of them. Only in Romans 7 does the context demand such. He was, of course, speaking primarily about the law's not being evil. He merely used his comments about Jewish experience with the law apart from Christ as a component in his argument. But they are there! If he was identifying with his compatriots by birth in Romans 7, as he did in Romans 9:3, Paul had to have been saying that this was also his experience. Otherwise the argument makes no sense. What is true of every person must also be true of him. In sum: "Romans 7:7-25 is not primarily autobiographical; but it seems most unlikely that Paul had no personal experience of the dilemma he there describes in the first person."[27]

Luther as a Monk

"Though I lived as a monk without reproach, I felt I was a sinner before God."

Martin Luther as a Monk. 1521.

That such a dual consciousness is a human reality and is not limited only to certain streams of ancient Jewish experience, we see from Luther's comments about himself. In his *Preface to Latin Writings* of 1545, Luther wrote: "Though I lived as a monk without reproach, I felt I was a sinner before God."[28] That Luther's experience reflects the same duality as that of certain streams of ancient Judaism indicates why the Reformers were often more correct in their reading of Romans than many modern revisionists.[29] It seems legitimate to conclude that when Paul wrote about Judaism (including God-fearing Gentiles) apart from Christ as characterized by a moral and spiritual impotence, he would have been understood by his Gentile Christian and Jewish Christian auditors. The only way out of this impotence, according to Paul, is God's activity in Christ and through the Spirit. Paul's soteriology, then, builds on his pessimistic anthropology, a view he shared with others in Middle Judaism. Where Paul deviated from even the most pessimistic Jews was in his conviction that no one was able to be faithful/righteous without God's enablement. Only in rare instances does one find Jewish evidence of belief that God enables Gentile conversion and/or His people's faithfulness.

Sola gratia (by grace alone) was characteristic of other early Christian streams besides Paul. Acts 11:20, confirmed by Galatians 2:11-14, indicates a pre-Pauline Gentile church at Antioch that was law-free. Galatians 2:15-16, if addressed to Peter in the context of 2:11-14, indicates that Paul and Peter were in agreement on soteriology. This confirms the claim of Acts 15:7-11 that Peter supported the soteriology of Paul. The Johannine circle, whose origins are obscure but undoubtedly ancient, not only knows a law-free gospel but shares the radical *sola gratia* of Paul (cf. John 15:16). So *sola gratia* was not limited to Paul among Christian messiaists. Can it be found outside of Christian Judaism? Yes, but not widely. First, the new covenant of MT Jeremiah 31:31-34/LXX Jeremiah 38:31-34 begins and continues on the basis of grace. Second, the *Apocalypse of Abraham,* written between AD 70 and the early second century with no direct relation to the New Testament writings, tells of the Gentile Abraham's reasoning from the world to God (chs. 1–7). Then God reveals Himself to Abraham (chs. 8–9) and sends the angel Iaoel (= a variant of Yahweh), in whom God's name dwells (10:8), to assist him (ch. 10). Abraham is told he has been chosen by God (14:2) and needs to offer a sacrifice to God (9:8; 10:16). The sacrificial animals are provided by God (12:6). Instructions for the sacrifice are given by the angel (12:8-9). Abraham is then carried up into God's presence (ch. 16). The angel kneels down and worships (17:2) and tells Abraham to do the same (17:4-5). This involves reciting the song the angel taught him (17:7-21). In the midst of the song (17:20), Abraham says: "(accept) also the sacrifice which you yourself made to yourself through me." The similarity with Paul is striking! Did such a view exist as early as Paul? Since the view apparently arose independent of Christian influences, there is no reason it could not have existed early. Third, the eschatological inclusion of the Gentiles will be an act of sheer grace (Isa 2:1-4; Tob 14:6-7). *Sola gratia,* then, was one of a number of competing soteriologies outside of as well as within Christian messianic Judaism. It was with this stream of ancient Jewish soteriology that Paul was allied.

How do we explain this rule of the Spirit of life in Christ Jesus? Romans 8:3-17 offers Paul's answer. This section picks up the thread of 7:6b (the new life of the Spirit), just as 7:7-25 did of 7:5 (sinful passions, aroused by the law, were at work in our members to bear fruit for death). One way of viewing the organization of 8:1-17 is to see vv. 1-2 as Paul's thesis, vv. 3-4 as the basis for the thesis, vv. 5-11 as the explanation of v. 4b, and vv. 12-17 as a statement of the implication of vv. 5-11. In other words, vv. 3-17 are a continuation of the argument of 7:7–8:2. An outline would look like this:

Paul's thesis (vv. 1-2): The rule of the Spirit has set Christians free from the rule of sin.

The basis for the thesis (vv. 3-4): God's acts in the Son and in the Spirit

An explanation of the Two Ways: life according to the flesh and life according to the Spirit (vv. 5-13)

Implications drawn from the explanation in vv. 5-13 (vv. 14-17)

Let us read Romans 8:3-17 in these terms.

Paul concluded his argument in 7:7–8:2 with a little unit, 7:21–8:2, which looked beyond the bondage to sin's power. Verse 25a sang: "Thanks be to God through Jesus Christ our Lord!" This was echoed in 8:2 in the statement: "For the law (= rule) of the Spirit of life in Christ Jesus has set you free from the law (= rule) of sin and death (cf. 7:23)." How can this be?

Verses 3-4 provide the basis for this new found freedom. "God has done what the law (= Jewish law), weakened by the flesh, could not do." God has done two things. First, God has sent the Son (cf. Gal 4:4-5; John 3:17; 1 John 4:9) "in the likeness of sinful flesh, and to deal with sin." This involved condemning sin in the flesh. Second, God gave the Spirit so that those who walk according to the Spirit can have the just requirement of the law fulfilled in them. More attention to detail is required.

When Paul said that God sent the Son, the sending statement conveys a sense of divine "invasion from outside."[30] With the statement, "in the likeness of sinful flesh," he was not making a docetic claim. To say "likeness of" does not mean that Christ was not truly human. The expression conveys Christ's full participation in the human condition, with one exception. The apostle was not saying that Christ was a sinner when he spoke of "sinful flesh." Rather Christ participated in our physical and finite existence, but he did not sin (2 Cor 5:21; cf. Heb 2:14; 4:15). Augustine put it this way:

> What does sinful flesh have? Death and sin. What does the likeness of sinful flesh have? Death without sin. If it had sin it would be sinful flesh; if it did not have death it would not be in the likeness of sinful flesh. As such he came.[31]

Why did Christ come amongst us? Paul said it was *peri hamartias* ("to deal with sin," NRSV; "to be a sin offering," NIV). There are two competing possibilities for interpretation. Since the expression frequently refers to the sin-offering in the LXX (Lev 5:8; 6:25, 30; 7:7; 9:7, 10, 22; 10:17, 19; 14:13, 19; 16:25; Num 29:11) and is so used in Hebrews 10:6, 8 and 13:11, many translate with the NIV, "to be a sin offering." Since, however, the expression in many places in the NT has a judicial meaning (John 8:46—"Which of you convicts me of sin?"; 16:8—the Holy Spirit will "convict the world of sin"; Acts 23:6—Paul said, "I am on trial concerning the hope of the resurrection"; cf. Acts 24:21; 25:9, 20; Jude 15), some translate with the NRSV, "to deal with sin." It is the latter possibility that this commentary follows because of the context. Chapters 5–8 are participationist in their soteriology. Christ then was sent by God to deal with sin in the flesh, condemning sin in his flesh. This must surely be interpreted in terms of Christ's obedience unto death (Phil 2:6-11), his faithfulness (Rom 3:22, 25, 26), his righteous act (5:18), his death to sin (6:10). By dying rather than sinning, Christ condemned sin and carried out the sentence against it. He broke its power in the realm of the flesh (= both his own flesh in particular and the physical and finite order in general).

The purpose and outcome of God's acts in Christ and the Spirit are "that the just requirement (*dikaiōma*) of the law might be fulfilled in us, who walk not according to the flesh but according to the Spirit" (v. 4). This fulfills the prophetic expectation that God's people's obedience would be due to the Spirit (Ezek 11:19-20; 36:26-27). What is the "just requirement of the law"? Is it the command not to covet (7:7), the command to love (cf. Rom 13:8-10; Gal 5:14), or all the moral norms of the law? In the context of Romans, it must surely be God's desire for righteousness (= faithfulness) on the part of people in covenant with Him. This faithfulness is fulfilled (= it is God's doing) in those who walk "according to the Spirit" (cf. Gal 5:16, 22-23). In this life style God is not only one's ultimate concern, but God is also the one who enables disciples "both to will and to work for His good pleasure" (Phil 2:13). If life according to the flesh is characterized by sinful passions at work in our members (7:5), life according to the Spirit is depicted in terms of faithfulness to the relationship with God (= righteousness—cf. 5:19; 6:19).

Romans 8:5-13 provides an explanation of life according to the flesh and life according to the Spirit (cf. 1QS 3.13-4.26). It must be remembered that flesh and Spirit in this context designate not two parts of human nature (e.g., lower and higher selves) but two ways of living (i.e., two orientations to life). On the one hand, living according to the flesh (= an orientation to life in which absolutizing some part of the physical, finite order is the defining characteristic) involves having one's mind set on the things of the flesh (= things that reflect the idolatry of this lifestyle; v. 5). The mind set on the flesh is hostile to God (v. 7a). It cannot submit to God's law (v. 7b; cf. 7:18, 23). The fact is that those in the flesh (= involved in this orientation) cannot please God (v. 8). The outcome of this orientation is death (v. 6a; cf. 6:23a; 7:5).

On the other hand, living according to the Spirit (= an orientation in which God is one's ultimate concern and one's enabling power) involves setting one's mind on the Spirit (v. 6b). Its outcome is life and peace (v. 6c; cf. 6:23b; 5:1). Paul's readers were believers. They, then, were not in the flesh but were in the Spirit (v. 9a). Why? They were "in the Spirit" because "the Spirit of God dwells in you" (v. 9b; also v. 11; in contrast to sin's dwelling in the self—7:18,20,23; cf. Jas 4:5). Since the Spirit is given by the risen Christ (cf. Eph 4:10-13; Acts 2:33; John 20:22), it can be called "the Spirit of Christ" (v. 9c; cf. Gal 4:6; Phil 1:19). Since the Spirit makes Christ present, Paul could speak of Christ being in believers (v. 10a; cf. Gal 2:19-20). Spirit of God, Spirit of Christ, and Christ (cf. 1 Cor 15:45) are used interchangeably in this context to speak of the indwelling presence of God that enables believers to live faithfully in their relation to God. If the outcome of a life according to the flesh is death (v. 10—"the body is dead because of

---

The Faith of Christ
and the Resurrection of Christ

In Romans Paul spoke about the resurrection of Christ being related to his faith(fulness). In 1:17 one should read: "The Righteous One (= Christ) shall live (= be resurrected) out of his faith(fulness)."

The apostle also spoke about Christ's being raised as due to God's activity. In 6:4 he said, "Christ was raised from the dead by the glory of the Father." In 8:11 he referred to "the Spirit of Him who raised Jesus from the dead." What is the link that enables one to see the complementary nature of the two statements?

Rom 3:25 says God purposed Christ Jesus "as an *hilastērion* (= place of dwelling for the divine presence) by his blood through his faithfulness." In this imagery, the blood of Christ's faithfulness unto death functions as the purification of his flesh/humanity so as to make it an acceptable dwelling for the divine presence. The presence of the Spirit/glory of God was then lifegiving—raising Jesus from the dead. So Christ "lived" out of his faith(fulness). The entire event was purposed by God (Rom 3:25).

William Blake. 1757–1827. *The Resurrection: The Angel Rolling Away the Stone from the Sepulchre.* Victoria & Albert Museum. London, England. (Credit: Victoria & Albert Museum/Art Resource, NY)

sin"; cf 6:23; 7:24), the outcome of the way of righteousness enabled by the Spirit is life (v. 10b; cf. 6:23). In 8:11 this is stated clearly: "If the Spirit of Him who raised Jesus from the dead dwells in you, He who raised Christ from the dead will give life to your mortal bodies also through His Spirit which dwells in you" (cf. Ezek 37:14—"I will put my Spirit within you, and you shall live"; *m. Sota* 9:15—"the Holy Spirit leads to the resurrection of the dead"; cf. Polycarp, *To the Philippians* 2). [The Faith of Christ and the Resurrection of Christ] The two orientations to life are laid out together with their ultimate outcomes in vv. 5-11. An exhortation ends this unit's argument. "So then, brothers and sisters, we are debtors, not to the flesh, to live according to the flesh" (v. 12). Implied is the call to live by the Spirit (cf. Gal 5:16, 25).

The implications of the argument in vv. 5-13 are set forth in 8:14-17. "All who are led by the Spirit of God are children of God" (v. 14). [Adoption] The evidence of this new status in God's family is the believers' prayer. "When we cry, 'Abba! Father!' it is that very Spirit bearing witness with our spirit that we are children of God" (v. 16; cf. Gal 4:6—crying, "Abba! Father!"). God is addressed as "Father" in Cleanthes' "Hymn to Zeus."[32] Adysseus and Herakles call God "Father" in Epictetus 3.24.13-16 (cf. 26.30-33). God is also occasionally addressed as Father in ancient Jewish prayers (Ps 89:26; Sirach 23:1,4; 51:10; Wis 14:4; 3 Macc 6:3,8; 4 Q372, 1:16; 4 Q460, 5:6; Blessing 4 of the *Eighteen Benedictions* from the Cairo Genizah—"Favor us with your knowledge, our Father"; Blessing 6—"Forgive us, our Father"; in the *Ahabah Rabbah*—"our Father, our King"; in the *Qaddish*—"Father who is in heaven"; in the third section of the Grace after festive meals—"Our God, our Father, tend and nourish us"). Jesus was depicted as teaching his disciples so to address God (Luke 11:1-4; Matt 6:9-13). Such teaching seems to have come out of Jesus' understanding of who God was. [Son of God / Sons of God] God was his Father, he was God's Son (Luke 10:21-22//Matt 11:25-27; Mark 13:32; 14:36; John 11:41-42; 12:27-28). The "Abba" reflects the Aramaic tradition from the earliest Palestinian Christians (cf. 1 Cor 16:22, Maranatha = "Our Lord, come," for another Aramaic tradition brought over into the Greek speaking church of Paul's

Adoption

AΩ One way that the Pauline tradition understood the connection of Jesus and his followers with God was in terms of the concept of adoption. The term (*huiothesia*) does not appear in Paul's Bible, the LXX. It is, however, found widely in inscriptions and literature of the Greco-Roman world. If Christians are God's children, they are so by adoption.

• God destined us for adoption (Eph 1:5).
• God sent the Son that we might receive adoption as children (Gal 4:4-5; Eph 1:5).
• Adoption as God's children comes in two stages. Stage one involves believers' present. In this time where the ages overlap, believers have received a Spirit of adoption (Rom 8:15). The Spirit is a foretaste of the fullness of one's status as God's child. Stage two involves believers' future. We wait for our adoption, the redemption of our bodies (Rom 8:23). This, of course refers to the future resurrection from the dead.

Son of God/Sons of God

AΩ In the Scriptures of Israel, Paul's Bible, son(s) of God is used in a variety of ways.

- A reference to heavenly beings (Job 1:6; 2:1; Pss 29:1; 82:6; Wis 5:5). This usage continued in postbiblical writings (*1 Enoch* 6:2; 13:8).
- A reference to Israel/Israelites (Deut 14:1; 32:5-6; Isa 43:6-7; Jer 2:27; Hos 1:10; Sir 36:12; Wis 9:7; 4 Ezra 5:28). Such usage continued in postbiblical Judaism (*m. 'Abot* 3:15).
- A reference to the individual righteous person (Wis 2–5)
- A reference to the king (2 Sam 7:14; Ps 2:7). 4 QFlor 10–14 cites Ps 2:7 and gives it a messianic interpretation. This likely indicates that by the beginning of our era, Son of God was beginning to be used as a title for the Messiah. 4Q246, col II, line 1, also uses Son of God in a way that seems to be a reference to the Messiah.

In the Pauline corpus, son(s) of God is used in similar ways.
- A reference to Israel/the Jews (Rom 9:4)
- A reference to Christian believers (Rom 8:15; Gal 4:5-7; Eph 1:5)
- A reference to Christ (Rom 1:4; 8:3; Gal 4:4, 6)

The meaning in both the Scriptures of Israel and in Paul has to do with a type of relationship between God and the one(s) so designated. It is a relation of intimacy and of assumed obedience to the divine will and purpose.

---

time). The "Father" represents the Greek translation of the original Aramaic form of address. When Pauline Christians prayed "Abba! Father!" they did so because they believed that they were children of God who had received a Spirit of adoption. If so, then like children they were "heirs of God and joint heirs with Christ." Children inherit. Christ had inherited the life of the New Age by virtue of his resurrection. He was the first born (8:29), but Christians, as members of the larger family of God, will share his resurrection (6:5; Phil 3:21). Paul's argument is already moving towards a focus on ultimate salvation, the topic to be treated in Romans 8:18-39. [Heirs/Inheritance]

CONNECTIONS

Impotence of the Law

In Romans 7:5 Paul said that the law aroused one's sinful passions. In 7:8 he said that "sin, seizing an opportunity in the commandment, produced in me all kinds of covetousness." In 7:11 the apostle said: "sin, seizing an opportunity in the commandment, deceived me and through it killed me." In all three of these vv., the law is seen as a catalyst for sin. How can this be understood?

Luke Johnson has put it this way: "the law can *identify* sin but cannot *prevent* it."[33] The law "is a prescription but not power."[34]

Heirs/Inheritance

If Christians are understood as God's children, then one way salvation can be viewed is as an inheritance which the children as heirs inherit.

- As God's unique Son, Christ is heir to all things (Heb 1:2)
- Christians are understood as joint heirs with Christ (Rom 8:17)
- In Christ they have received an inheritance (Eph 1:11)
- They are those who have an eternal inheritance (Heb 9:15; 1 Pet 1:4) among the saints (Acts 20:32; Eph 1:18), in the kingdom of Christ and of God (Eph 5:5), which will be their reward (Col 3:24)
- What will they inherit? The world, understood not as the land but as the New Age beyond the resurrection (Rom 4:13-14); eternal life (Titus 3:5; 1 Pet 3:7); salvation (Heb 1:14); the promise (Heb 6:17); the kingdom (Jas 2:5).

The rule reveals sin to be what it is, because even when the rule is kept, the relationship can be distorted. I can, for example, avoid 'coveting' everything on the list provided by the Torah, but that list cannot relieve the itch of the craving disease. I can still covet, let us say, God's favor and seek to possess it, precisely by being able to claim not to *covet* the things on God's list.[35]

A. M. Hunter cited a young American girl's negative estimate of the Ten Commandments: "They . . . just put ideas into your head."[36] "It is characteristic of human nature that as soon as a thing is forbidden it becomes desirable."[37] When the law says, "Thou shalt not" (= a command externally imposed), the human will apart from Christ (= a human will bent on its self-assertion) says, "I will." Augustine, *Confessions* 2.6, bemoaned the connection between the prohibition and desire. The former provokes the latter. Such is the power of sin and its abuse of the law.

Law, understood as a prescription/God's will, does not transform human life. Why? Paul believed two things that explain why. First, he saw sin as an idolatrous orientation by which one is held prisoner. Second, he believed faithfulness to God/human righteousness is not possible, even for one delivered from the power of sin, without God's enabling power. Law cannot break the sinful orientation; it is rather used and abused by the sinful orientation. Law cannot enable one's faithfulness to God. It rather provokes the sinful orientation to resist its guidance.

Moral and Spiritual Power

Romans 7:7–8:17 deals with the two conditions of human life: moral and spiritual impotence on the one hand and moral and spiritual power on the other. Paul saw the former as due to sin that dwells in the self, as an enemy occupies a conquered country. He thought the latter is due to the Spirit that dwells in the self.

The second-century Christian apologist, Athenagoras, in his *A Plea for the Christians*, addressed to the emperors Marcus Aurelius and Commodus, dealt with the same issue. In chapter XI he contrasted the pagan philosophers and simple Christians. Of the philosophers, he asked:

who of them have so purged their souls as, instead of hating their enemies, to love them; and instead of speaking ill of those who have reviled them . . . to bless them; and to pray for those who plot against their lives? On the contrary, they . . . are ever bent on working some ill.

Such people, Athenagoras believed, are morally impotent, whatever their ideals. They may have high ideals but are unable to implement them. Paul would say that this is so because of sin that dwells in them. Of the simple Christians, however, Athenagoras had a higher opinion.

> But among us you will find uneducated persons, and artisans, and old women, who, if they are unable in words to prove the benefit of our doctrine, yet by their deeds exhibit the benefit arising from their persuasion of its truth: they do not rehearse speeches, but exhibit good works; when struck, they do not strike again; . . . they give to those who ask of them, and love their neighbors as themselves.[38]

Here is a manifestation of moral and spiritual power. From Paul's perspective, this arises from the Spirit that dwells in the believers.

Augustine, in his *On the Spirit and the Letter* 19, said: "Law was given that grace might be sought, grace was given that the law might be fulfilled." For Paul, the law's demands make our sin obvious because we are unable to do what is asked of us. If we are ever able to do what is asked of us by God, it is only because God's initiative (= grace, Spirit) enables it. In his *Confessions*, Book 10, Augustine summed it up well in his prayer to God: "Give what you demand, and demand what you will."

The Sources of Moral and Spiritual Power

Paul believed the problem of human bondage is dealt with by Christ's condemning sin in the flesh. When one person defeats sin's power, as Christ did, that power is broken. Sin has been condemned in the flesh. Paul also believed the problem of human moral and spiritual impotence is dealt with by the indwelling presence of God/Spirit/Christ. In the new covenant, God enables his children's faithfulness to Himself.

Romans 8:14 says that those led by the Spirit are the children of God. That is, those who live out of the indwelling presence of God/Spirit/Christ are God's children. Assuming that God's presence is available to all Christians, how can believers live out of that presence? In the history of Christian spirituality a helpful image

Henri Nouwen on the Indwelling Presence of Christ

Our faith in Jesus is not our belief that Jesus, the Son of God, lived long ago, performed great miracles, presented wise teachings, died for us on the cross, and rose from the grave. It first of all means that we fully accept the truth that Jesus lives within us and fulfills his divine ministry in and through us. This spiritual knowledge of the Christ living in us is what allows us to affirm fully the mystery of the incarnation, death, and resurrection as historic events. It is the Christ in us who reveals to us the Christ in history.

Henri Nouwen, *Bread for the Journey* (San Francisco: HarperCollins, 1997), entry for October 6.

---

comes to mind: emptying and filling. One empties the self of things that clutter the self and prevent God's access to the whole of the self; then one prays for God to fill the space freed up for Him. Once again, the experience of prayer makes Paul's reflections concrete. [Henri Nouwen on the Indwelling Presence of Christ]

This process of emptying can be done in terms of three lists. First, make a list of all those people you need to forgive. Start from your childhood and come down to the present. Include parents, siblings, spouse, children, pastor and all intimates who have hurt you during your lifetime. Pray through that list until everyone has been released to Jesus. It may be that God has to be included in your list. Anger at God is as real as anger at one's human intimates. If so, release Him. Why is this prayer necessary? It is because anger and grudges take up space in the self that only God needs to fill. Second, make a list of all those things starting from childhood for which you need to be forgiven. It will likely include sins against those closest to you. Pray through that list until Jesus takes every one. Why do this? It is because guilt takes up space in the self that only God needs to fill. Praying through this list, as through the first, empties the self of clutter. Third, make a list of all the areas of your life over which Jesus does not have absolute control. Pray through that list until every one is open to him and subject to redecorating rights by him. Why do this? It is because idols/closed areas (= those areas not surrendered to Jesus) take up space in the self that ought to be available for God. When the self has, through prayer, been emptied of anger, guilt, and idols, then ask God to fill the space made available with Himself. When asked, God does it! When the presence of God/Spirit/Christ is given this kind of space in the self, it is possible for Christians to be led by the Spirit (8:14).

Prayers that make space for God sometimes occur in one extended session of prayer. Most often, they take place over an extended period of time (weeks or even months). Sometimes they are done alone, in solitude. Often they are done with a trusted spiritual friend who prays alongside, as a helper. Sometimes such prayers are done with pictures: for example, angers/grudges are pictured as burdens on one's back that are cast in a deep well; guilts are pictured as wounds in one's body that are healed by the Lord's touch; unsurrendered areas of life are pictured as rooms shut off to God that are made available to Him when the key is provided. In other instances, no pictures are used; prayers are entirely conceptual. In all cases, it is not the how that matters but the fact that space is made for one's Creator so He can be one's Enabler. Moral and spiritual power is not a commodity separate from God's presence) God's presence is moral and spiritual power. If dying to sin breaks sin's power, making space for God's presence enables "being led by the Spirit."

NOTES

[1] John Calvin, *Epistle of Paul the Apostle to the Romans*, trans. John Owen (Edinburgh: Constable, 1849), 259, 261, 270.

[2] Gerd Theissen, *Psychological Aspects of Pauline Theology* (Minneapolis: Fortress, 1987), 190-201, 234-43, offers a detailed critique of Kümmel and strong support for a "typical I."

[3] Stanley K. Stowers, "Romans 7:7-25 as a Speech-in-Character (*prosopopoiia*)," in *Paul and His Hellenistic Context*, ed. Troels Engberg-Pedersen (Minneapolis: Fortress, 1995), 180-202.

[4] Bruce J. Malina and Jerome H. Neyrey, *Portraits of Paul: An Archaeology of Ancient Personality* (Louisville: Westminster John Knox, 1996).

[5] Jan Lambrecht, *The Wretched "I" and Its Liberation* (Louvain: Peeters, 1992).

[6] Paul W. Meyer, "The Worm at the Core of the Apple: Exegetical Reflections on Romans 7," in *The Conversation Continues: Studies in Paul and John*, ed. R. T. Fortna and B. R. Gaventa (Nashville: Abingdon, 1990), 68.

[7] Theissen, *Psychological Aspects of Pauline Theology*, 183.

[8] The NRSV's "I know that nothing good dwells within me" is less accurate than the revised TEV's "good does not live in me." Cf. Leander E. Keck, "The Absent Good: The Significance of Rom 7:18a," in *Text und Geschichte*, ed. S. Maser and E. Schlarb (Marburg: N. G. Elwart, 1999), 66-75.

[9] Keck, "The Absent Good," 70.

[10] Theissen, *Psychological Aspects of Pauline Theology*, 203.

[11] Florentino Garcia Martinez, *The Dead Sea Scrolls Translated* (2d ed; Grand Rapids: Eerdmans, 1996), 18.

[12] Luke T. Johnson, *Reading Romans* (NY: Crossroad, 1997), 109.

[13] Timo Laato, *Paul and Judaism: An Anthropological Approach* (Atlanta: Scholars, 1995), 73.

[14] Ibid., 75.

[15] Douglas J. Moo, *The Epistle to the Romans* (Grand Rapids: Eerdmans, 1996), 450.

[16] Ibid., 456.

[17] J. Christiaan Beker, *The Triumph of God: The Essence of Paul's Thought* (Minneapolis: Fortress, 1990), 108.

[18] Timo Eskola, *Theodicy and Predestination in Pauline Soteriology* (Tübingen: Mohr Siebeck, 1998), 283, contends that the Dead Sea Scrolls and 4 Ezra describe the human plight almost in the manner of Paul.

[19] Dan Sperber and Deirdre Wilson, *Relevance: Communication and Cognition* (Cambridge: Harvard University Press, 1986), argue that communicators will attempt to produce a text that will be maximally relevant to their audience. This requires the use of information shared with an audience as a springboard for introducing new information.

[20] Timo Laato, *Paul and Judaism*, 8-9.

[21] Alan F. Segal, *Paul the Convert* (New Haven: Yale University Press, 1990), xiii.

[22] Ibid., xvi.

[23] Susanne Lehne, *The New Covenant in Hebrews* (Sheffield: JSOT Press, 1990), 44.

[24] E. P. Sanders, *Paul and Palestinian Judaism* (Philadelphia: Fortress, 1977), 224.

[25] Robert H. Gundry, "The Moral Frustration of Paul Before His Conversion," in *Pauline Studies: Essays Presented to F. F. Bruce on His 70th Birthday*, ed. D.A. Hagner and M. J. Harris (Grand Rapids: Eerdmans, 1980), 228-45, argues that Phil 3:6 deals with the outer manifestation of Paul's Jewishness while Rom 7:14-25 speaks of his inward disposition. If so, the advancement in Judaism does not contradict an inward struggle with sin.

[26] If so, then the deuteropauline 1 Tim 1:12-14, which shows Paul aware of his pre-Christian sinfulness, may be an accurate reflection of the Paul's experience instead of a later distortion of it.

[27] Stephen Westerholm, *Preface to the Study of Paul* (Grand Rapids: Eerdmans, 1997), 87. Note 32 continues: "Philippians 3:6 does not rule out such a reading of Paul. The text is not in any case a claim to sinless perfection, but only to a serious attempt to observe the law, including its prescribed rites of atonement for shortcomings. . . . The argument calls for evidence of Paul's erstwhile devotion to the law; it need not exclude an experience of moral struggle such as that attested in Romans 7."

[28] J. A. Fitzmyer, *Romans* (AB; NY: Doubleday, 1993), 261.

[29] E.g., Krister Stendahl, "The Apostle Paul and the Introspective Conscience of the West," *HTR* 56 (1963): 199-215. For a criticism of Stendahl's argument, see John M. Espy, "Paul's Robust Conscience Re-examined," *NTS* 31 (1985): 161-88. It seems to me that the appeal of Stendahl's essay lies not in the strength of its argument so much as in its close fit with the cultural *Zeitgeist* of our time.

[30] Brendan Byrne, *Romans.* (Sacra Pagina; Collegeville: Liturgical Press, 1996), 236.

[31] Augustine, *Sermons for Easter Season*, Homily 233.3 (cited in Gerald Bray, *Romans* [IVP, 1998], 204).

[32] Line 33. ET in Hans-Josef Klauck, *The Religious Context of Early Christianity* (Edinburgh: T.&T. Clark, 2000), 351-52.

[33] Luke T. Johnson, *Reading Romans* (NY: Crossroad, 1997), 110.

[34] Ibid., 111.

[35] Ibid., 114.

[36] A. M. Hunter, *Interpreting Paul's Gospel* (Philadelphia: Westminster Press, 1954), 69, n.1.

[37] William Barclay, *The Mind of St. Paul* (NY: Harper & Brothers, 1958), 185.

[38] *ANF*, 2: 134.

THE FUTURE HOPE

8:18-39

Paul's thought in Romans 5:12–8:39 has to this point moved from the human condition to the divine remedy to the role of the law. Now the apostle reaches the conclusion to this cycle of argument. As in 5:1-11, the focus of 8:18-39 is on the future hope grounded in salvation history and the Christians' present experience. This final stage of Paul's argument in the cycle that runs from 5:12–8:39 is composed of two sections: 8:18-27 and 8:28-39.

A reading of Romans 8:18-27 requires a grasp of how the material is organized. The structure of the argument in Romans 8:18-27 looks something like this:

A thesis statement (v. 18): A contrast between present suffering and future glory
An explanation (vv. 19-25): The solidarity of nonhuman and human worlds in both present suffering and future glory
Assistance for Christians in their present sufferings (vv. 23, 26-27)
The Spirit as a guarantee of the future hope (v. 23)
The Spirit as intercessor for Christians in their present weakness (vv. 26-27)

Let us read this section in these terms.

COMMENTARY

The thesis statement for 8:18-27 comes in v. 18. "I consider that the sufferings of this present time are not worth comparing with the glory about to be revealed to us" (cf. 2 Cor 4:16-17; Col 3:4). Paul would be speaking about present sufferings and future glory. The latter is far greater. (Remember this type of comparison in 5:15, 20). His categories reflect his Jewish affinities. *Second Baruch* 15:8 reads: "For this world is to them a struggle and an effort with much trouble. And that accordingly which will come, a crown with great glory." This contrast is explained in vv. 19-25. In these vv. the focus is on the solidarity of humans and their world in both the present and the future. Paul could no more think of persons apart from their environment than he could conceive of them apart from their bodies. If so, then sin and salvation affect not only the bodies of humans but also their environment. These vv. can be split into two smaller units, each with the same components but in reverse order. In vv. 19-22 we hear about the creation (= the non-angelic, non-human created order).

> A—The creation *waits* for the revealing of the children of God (v. 19).
>   B—It waits *in hope* (v. 20)
>   C—It waits for its salvation (v. 21)
>   D—While it waits, it *groans* (v. 22; cf. Mark 13:8). In vv. 23-25 Paul concentrates on Christians.
>   D'—We *groan* while we wait (v. 23; cf. Isa 13:6-8)
>   C'—We wait for our salvation (v. 23)
>   B'—*In hope* we were saved (v. 24)
> A'—We *wait* for it with patience (v. 25)

The creation (= nonhuman creation, as in Wis 2:6; 16:24; 19:6) waits for salvation because it "was subjected to futility, not of its own will but by the will of the one who subjected it, in hope" (v. 20). This reflects first the belief that human sin had bad effects on the natural world (Gen 3:17-19). 4 Ezra 7:11 has God put it this way: "For I made the world for their sake, and when Adam transgressed my statutes, what had been made was judged." As a result of human sin the material world is subjected to futility—that is, to decay, and to pain. It reflects second the belief that the physical world can look forward to a future salvation. The reversal of Adam's fall was assumed to require the reversal of the curse on the ground (Gen 3:17-18). Numerous texts make reference to this conviction (Isa 65:17; 66:22; *1 Enoch* 45:4-5; 51:4-5; 72:1; 4 Ezra 7:30-31,75; *2 Bar* 29; 32:6; 44:12; 57:2; Rev 21:1; 2 Pet 3:13). If human sin affects the physical world negatively, then salvation from human sin will affect it positively. The ultimate destiny of the physical world is not annihilation but transformation. Chrysostom summed it up in these words:

> Paul means by this that the creation became corruptible. Why and for what reason? Because of you, O man! . . . The creation suffered badly because of you, and it became corruptible, but it has not been irreparably damaged. For it will become incorruptible once again for your sake. This is the meaning of in *hope*.[1]

Resurrection of the Flesh

In this fresco by Signorelli, the dead are in the process of being resurrected. Bones are coming together to form skeletons and skeletons are beginning to put on a "new" flesh. These resurrected bodies seem to be at home in the spiritual flesh as a calm interchange is shared by the new bodies with casual and convivial conversation occurring between the various members. There is no sense of shame or lust in these new bodies—made whole in their resurrection from the dead.

Luca Signorelli. 1441–1523. *Resurrection of the Flesh*. Fresco. Duomo. Orvieto, Italy. (Credit: Scala/Art Resource, NY)

In between the fall and future salvation the creation groans "in labor pains" (v. 22; Mark 13:8b).

Likewise, Christians are groaning inwardly while we wait for our salvation (v. 23; cf. 2 Cor 5:4). This is described as "adoption" (omitted by P[46], D, F, G, and 614), the "redemption of our bodies (cf. 7:24—this body of death)." First Corinthians 15:54 speaks about the matter thusly: "When this perishable body puts on imperishability, and this mortal body puts on immortality." The whole person will be redeemed just as will the physical world. Of course, what Christians have already experienced can be called being "saved" (v. 24). Nevertheless, Paul also said we will be saved (5:9-10). This is our hope. There are a number of other expressions used in the Pauline letters for future salvation: for example, saved from wrath (1 Thess 1:10; Rom 5:9); being with Christ (1 Thess 4:17; Phil 1:23); inheriting the kingdom of God (1 Cor 6:10); being given eternal life (Rom 2:7); being transformed into the image of Christ (2 Cor 3:18; Rom 8:19). The multiple images refer to the one reality in the future just as multiple images like justification, sanctification, reconciliation, redemption, and salvation refer to the one reality in the present. Paul's vision here includes a picture of humans as wholes together with their physical environment totally freed from sin and sin's effects. In the meantime, we wait for our future salvation with patience (v. 25), a patience made possible by the activity of the Spirit.

There are two ways that the Spirit assists us in the present time as we wait amidst our sufferings. The first, specified in v. 23, is that we have "the first fruits of the Spirit." The expression refers to a first stage in God's gift to us. It is sometimes used in the sense of "earnest money," or a guarantee of what is to come (1 Cor 15:20-23). As such it is a synonym for *arrabōn* (2 Cor 1:22—"giving us His Spirit in our hearts as a first installment" [*arrabōn*] ; 5:5— "God, who has given us the Spirit as a guarantee" [*arrabōn*]). This term means both a down payment and a pledge to pay the rest in the future. So Paul saw the Spirit's presence in Christians' lives as a first installment by which God guarantees that the full payment will certainly come. This gift of the Spirit, then, functions as an assurance or guarantee that the future hope is real and certain. Christians can hope for the future salvation because of their present experience.

The second way that the Spirit assists Christians in our present weakness is found in vv. 26-27. These verses are arranged in a concentric pattern.[2]

A—The Spirit helps us
  B—in our weakness.
  B'—we do not know what to pray for;
A'—The Spirit intercedes for us.

The Spirit's intercession is "with sighs too deep for words" (v. 26), "according to the will of God" (v. 27). [Prayer in the Pauline Corpus] (1) Ancient Judaism knew of human intercessors: Noah (*Jub* 9:3-6; 10:3); Abraham (Gen 18:23-33; 20:7); Isaac (Gen 25:21); Jacob (*T. Reub* 1:7; 4:4; *T. Gad* 5:9; *T. Benj* 3:6; 10:1); Moses (Exod 8:8-13; 32:11-14; Lev 27:5; Num 14:13-20; Deut 9:25-29; Jub 1:19-22); Samuel (1 Sam 7:5, 8-9; 12:19; Jer 15:1);

Prayer in the Pauline Corpus

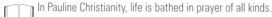

In Pauline Christianity, life is bathed in prayer of all kinds.

- It is striking that Paul speaks about the Holy Spirit's praying to assist us (Rom 8:26-27) and the risen Christ's praying for us (Rom 8:34).
- The apostle himself engages in prayers of thanksgiving (all of his letters except Galatians begin with thanksgiving, e.g., Rom 1:8).
- He also engages in prayers of intercession for his readers (e.g., Rom 1:10; 15:5-6, 13; 2 Cor 13:7; Phil 1:9-11; 1 Thess 3:12-13; 5:23-24; 2 Thess 1:11-12; 2:16-17; 3:16; Col 1:9-10; Phlm 6; [Eph 1:17-23; 3:14-21]; [1 Tim 2:1]; [2 Tim 1:16-18]).
- Paul requests and assumes the prayers of his readers for himself (Rom 15:30; 2 Cor 1:11; Phil 1:19; Phlm 22; Col 4:2-4; 2 Thess 3:1-3; [Eph 6:19-20]).
- Paul prays for Israel's salvation (Rom 10:1).
- Christian believers pray for one another (2 Cor 9:14).
- Paul prays for his own needs (2 Cor 12:7-9).
- Christians pray for their own needs (Phil 4:6).
- Christians pray in tongues (1 Cor 14:14, 18) and pray for the power to interpret tongues (1 Cor 14:13), thereby praying both with the spirit and with the mind (1 Cor 14:15).
- Paul exhorts his Christian readers to "pray without ceasing" (1 Thess 5:17), "persevere in prayer" (Rom 12:12), and to "devote themselves to prayer" (Col 4:2), as he himself had done (Col 1:9).

Illustration by Barclay Burns

---

priests (Lev 16:21-22; Num 6:23-27; 2 Macc 3:1,16-17, 31-33); kings
(2 Sam 12:16; 1 Kgs 8; 2 Chr 6; 2 Kgs 19:4; 2 Chr 10:18-19; Jer 26:19); prophets (1 Kgs 18:22-40; Isa 37:4; Jer 27:18; *Lives of Prophets*, Elijah 21:4-5, 7, 9; Isa 1:2-3, 8; Jer 2:3; Ezek 3:10; Dan 4:4,12); Enoch (*1 Enoch* 83:10; 84:106); holy men (*2 Bar* 85:1-2); Judith (Jdt 8:31; 9:2-14; 11:17; 12:8); Judas Maccabeas (1 Macc 4:30-33; 7:41-42; 2 Macc 11:6; 12:36; 15:22-24); Maccabean martyrs (2 Macc 7:37-38; 4 Macc 6:28-29). Indeed, 4 Ezra 7:36-41 [106-111] offers an extended list of human intercessors in Israel.

(2) Ancient Jews also believed there were heavenly intercessors: angels (Zech 1:12; *1 Enoch* 9—where archangels intercede on behalf of the suffering, crying, praying for creation; 39:5; 40:6; 47:2; 99:3; 104:1; *T Levi* 3:5; 5:5-6—angels make intercession for the pious; *T. Dan* 6:2; *T. Adam* 2:1-12); upright persons in the afterlife (2 Macc 15:12-16—Jeremiah, after death, prays much for the people and the holy city, as does the martyred priest, Onias; *1 Enoch* 13:4,6; 14:4—Enoch is asked to pray for the fallen angels. He is called their intercessor (15:2; 16:3). *Second Enoch* 7:4-5 says Enoch is the intercessor who is forever in God's presence. *Second Enoch* 53:1-2 has Enoch exhort his readers not to say that he, after

departing this earth, will stand in front of God and pray for them, keeping them from sin. This obviously is countering a popular belief that the saint did in fact intercede for them after his death. The point is that no prayer offered by another may amend an evil life or negate God's judgment (cf. Ps-Philo, *Bib.Ant.* 33:4-5; 4 Ezra 7:105). *Apocalypse of Zephaniah* 11:1-6—Abraham, Isaac, Jacob, and a multitude of the righteous pray for the souls of those in torment; *3 Enoch* 44:7—the souls of Abraham, Isaac, and Jacob pray for Israel; *Testament of Isaac* 1:3 and *Testament of Jacob* 1:3; 7:11—the patriarchs make heavenly intercession for sinners. *Exodus Rabbah* 25:26 on 12:2—the patriarchs have been interceding for Israel from the moment of their deaths until the destruction of the first temple; Isaiah intercedes in heaven—*Lives of the Prophets* 1:2-3,8; *b. Sotah* 13b—Moses is forever standing and ministering before the Lord (cf. *3 Enoch* 15B:2-5). An inscription of King Antiochus I of Commagne (1st century BC) reflects pagan belief. It says that after death the king expected to be transported to the heavenly thrones of Zeus where he would be able to intercede with all the gods on behalf of his successors.[3] Some scholars want to see Paul's reference to the Spirit's intercession as an extension of that of angelic beings in Judaism. The evidence seems to support this connection.

In ancient Judaism and early Christianity, "spirit," and "angel" were often used interchangeably (Jewish—1 QM 13:10-11; *Jub* 1:25; 15:31-32; *2 Enoch* 16:7; *T. Abr* 4:18; 9:1-3; Christian—Heb 1:14; Rev 1:4b; 4:5; Origen, *Against Celsus* 8.64). In one Jewish source, for example, Holy Spirit and archangel seem to be used as synonyms. In the *Testament of Abraham* 4:15, the Holy Spirit puts into Isaac's mind the thought of death; in 7:22, Michael, an archangel, puts into Abraham's mind the thought of death. In some circles of early Christianity, moreover, the Holy Spirit was thought of as an angel. The *Shepherd of Hermas*, "Mandate," 11:9, says regarding a true prophet, "the angel of the prophetic spirit rests on him and fills the man, and the man, being filled with the Holy Spirit, speaks to the congregation as the Lord wills." The *Ascension of Isaiah* 7:23 refers to the angel of the Holy Spirit: 9:35 says, "I saw the Lord and the second angel" (= the angel of the Holy Spirit who had spoken in Isaiah and in the other righteous); 10:4 speaks of the Lord and the angel of the Spirit; and 11:4 mentions the angel of the Spirit. The closest thing to what is found in Romans 8:26-27 is found in the *Testament of Abraham*. There it is time for Abraham to die. So God sends the angel Michael to bring Abraham's soul. In the narrative two things stand out. First, the

📖 Prayer with Groanings Too Deep for Words

The 8th-century East Syrian writer Symeon said:

> Prayer in which the body does not toil by means of the heart, and the heart by means of the mind, together with the intellect and the intelligence, *all gathered together in deep-felt groaning*, but where prayer is just allowed to float across the heart, such prayer, you should realize, is just a miscarriage, for while you are praying, your mind is drawing you away to some other business that you are going to see to after praying. In such a case you have not yet managed to pray in a unified manner.

This ancient sentiment has it modern counterparts. *US News & World Report* (27 September, 1999, 50-57), published an article on Pope John Paul II. In it we find this description of the Pope's prayer life.

> Moreover, he is a mystic who would find it virtually impossible to describe his deepest religious experiences. Those who have heard him *groaning in prayer* in his private chapel know that there is a dimension of Karl Wojtyla's life in which God is his sole interlocutor, in a conversation literally beyond words.

Gian Lorenzo Bernini. 1598–1680. *The Ecstasy of Saint Teresa.* Cornaro Chapel. Saint Maria della Vittoria. Rome, Italy. (Credit: Scala/Art Resource, NY)

Is this what Paul was referring to in Rom 8? Paul Tillich spoke about the experience in his sermon, "The Paradox of Prayer."

> Just because every prayer is humanly impossible, just because it brings deeper levels of our being before God than the level of consciousness, something happens in it that cannot be expressed in words. Words, created *by* and used *in* our conscious life, are not the essence of prayer. The essence of prayer is the act of God who is working in us and raises our whole being to Himself. The way in which this happens is called by Paul "sighing." . . . Only in terms of *wordless sighs* can we approach God, and even these sighs are His work in us.

This, he said, accounts for the surprising picture of God interceding for us before Himself.

Sebastian Brock, "The Prayer of the Heart in Syriac Tradition," in *Forms of Devotion*, ed. E. Ferguson (New York: Garland, 1999), 135.

Paul Tillich, *The New Being* (New York: Charles Scribner's, 1955), 137-38.

---

angel is called "the spirit" (3:5; 4:18; 9:3; 15:6,9). Second, he carries Abraham's requests/prayers to God (9). That is, he intercedes on Abraham's behalf. In a context where some early Christians thought of the Holy Spirit as an angel, it would be an easy move to seeing the Holy Spirit as an intercessor. In any case,

Romans 8:26-27 is the only NT writing explicitly to speak this way about the interceding Spirit.

The Spirit's intercession is effective, moreover, because of the affinities between "God who searches the heart" (1 Sam 16:7; 1 Kgs 8:39; 1 Chr 28:9; 1 Cor 4:5; Acts 15:8; Rev 2:23) and the Spirit (v. 27; cf. 1 Cor 2:10-11). "The Spirit's groanings are not spoken, because they do not need to be, since God knows the Spirit's intention without its being expressed."[4]

The Spirit compensates for Christians' inability to discern God's will clearly in the many things for which we pray. The language, literally translated, is: "we do not know what we should pray for according to the divine will (*katho dei*)." Origen commented on the matter thusly:

> Just as a sick man does not ask the doctor for things which will restore him to health but rather for things which his disease longs for, so likewise we, as long as we are languishing in the weakness of this life, will from time to time ask God for things which are not good for us. This is why the Spirit has to help us.[5]

So Paul here saw the Spirit's activity not in the heights of spiritual rapture but in the depths of human inability to discern and cope.[6]

In the third century the church father Origen, in his *De oratione* 2, suggested that the language "with groans that are wordless" refers to a kind of private praying in tongues (1 Cor 14:2, 18-19). [Prayer with Groanings Too Deep for Words] Since it is difficult to find other known phenomenon in the early church apart from this practice that even remotely resembles what is described in Romans 8:26-27 as an everyday event among believers, some modern scholars follow Origen's lead.[7] Paul's language, however, is "wordless groans." This does not sound like *glōssolalia*, even the private type, which involves words that someone could hear and interpret. The only plausible alternative is the Christian experience of deep, wordless yearning directed towards God when one senses the presence of the Spirit in one's heart. The sighs, then, would be the groaning associated with the birthpangs of the Coming Age. [Dark Night of the Soul] Regardless of how the form of the prayer is understood, its essence is "the divine in us appealing to the God above us."[8] (Cf. Castor's statement, cited by Plutarch [*Moralia* 266C-E]: "The Spirit within entreats and supplicates the gods without.")

The Spirit, then, assists Christians between their conversion and their taking possession of their future hope. This comes in two ways: the presence of the Spirit in the present, functioning as a guarantee that the future is certainly coming (v. 23), and the inter-

Dark Night of the Soul
The depths of the human inability to discern and cope and its dependency upon the Spirit's activity is meticulously described and analyzed in this work by the Spanish mystic, St. John of the Cross. The Christian experience of deep, wordless yearning directed toward God is part of the journey of the dark night of the Soul.

Chapter VII (#5)
Let it suffice here to have described these imperfections, among the many to be found in the lives of those that are in this first state of beginners, so that it may be seen how greatly they need God to set them in the state of proficients. This He does by bringing them into the dark night whereof we now speak; wherein He weans them from the breasts of these sweetnesses and pleasures, gives them pure aridities and inward darkness, takes from them all these irrelevances and puerilities, and by very different means causes them to win the virtues. For, however assiduously the beginner practises the mortification in himself of all these actions and passions of his, he can never completely succeed—very far from it—until God shall work it in him passively by means of the purgation of the said night. Of this I would fain speak in some way that may be profitable; may God, then, be pleased to give me His Divine light, because this is very needful in a night that is so dark and a matter that is so difficult to describe and to expound.
The line, then, is: In a dark night.

Chapter XI (#4)
This going forth is understood of the subjection to its sensual part which the soul suffered when it sought God through operations so weak, so limited and so defective as are those of this lower part; for at every step it stumbled into numerous imperfections and ignorances, as we have noted above in writing of the seven capital sins. From all these it is freed when this night quenches within it all pleasures, whether from above or from below, and makes all meditation darkness to it, and grants it other innumerable blessings in the acquirement of the virtues, as we shall now show. For it will be a matter of great pleasure and great consolation, to one that journeys on this road, to see how that which seems to the soul so severe and adverse, and so contrary to spiritual pleasure, works in it so many blessings. These, as we say, are gained when the soul goes forth, as regards its affection and operation, by means of this night, from all created things, and when it journeys to eternal things, which is great happiness and good fortune:[78] first, because of the great blessing which is in the quenching of the desire and affection with respect to all things; secondly, because they are very few that endure and persevere in entering by this strait gate and by the narrow way which leads to life, as says Our Saviour.[79] The strait gate is this night of sense, and the soul detaches itself from sense and strips itself thereof that it may enter by this gate, and establishes itself in faith, which is a stranger to all sense, so that afterwards it may journey by the narrow way, which is the other night—that of the spirit—and this the soul afterwards enters in order in journey to God in pure faith, which is the means whereby the soul is united to God. By this road, since it is so narrow, dark and terrible (though there is no comparison between this night of sense and that other, in its darkness and trials, as we shall say later), they are far fewer that journey, but its benefits are far greater without comparison than those of this present night. Of these benefits we shall now begin to say something, with such brevity as is possible, in order that we may pass to the other night.

Chapter XII (#1)
FROM what has been said we shall be able to see how this dark night of loving fire, as it purges in the darkness, so also in the darkness enkindles the soul. We shall likewise be able to see that, even as spirits are purged in the next life with dark material fire, so in this life they are purged and cleansed with the dark spiritual fire of love.

Translated and edited by E. Allison Peers. www.catholicfirst.com

cession of the Spirit to enlist God's aid in their present journey (vv. 26-27). At this point, the first section of 8:18-39 is at an end.

The second section consists of Romans 8:28-39, which falls into three parts:

(1) A thesis (v. 28): God's acts work for our good.
(2) An explanation (vv. 29-30): God's acts for our ultimate salvation run from before the creation through human history into the New Age beyond the resurrection.
(3) The implications of God's acts (vv. 31-39): The assurance of believers

Let us examine each in turn.

Verse 28 is Paul's thesis. He began with "we know," indicating that what follows may be traditional material. Literally translated, the sentence may be laid out as follows:

With those loving God (cf. 1 Cor 2:9; 8:3; Exod 20:6; 1 Kgs 3:3; Sir 2:15-16), [. . .] cooperate(s) for good,
With those being called according to God's purpose.

The first line speaks of the human dimension of the relationship; the third line of the divine. The difficulty is with the center line whose subject is omitted here. What is the subject of the verb? An answer is made more difficult by a textual variant. On the one hand, P[46], A, B, 81 and others include *ho theos* (God). If this is accurate, then the middle part of v. 28 reads: "God cooperates in all things for good." On the other hand, Sinaiticus, C, D, F, G and others omit "God." If this is accurate, then the middle line may be translated: "all things cooperate for good." It may, however, also be translated "He causes all things to cooperate for good." Some scholars, moreover, resisting the notion that "things" work together for good, opt for carrying over "the Spirit" from the previous unit. In this case the translation would read: "the Spirit works in all things for good."

If the translation is "all things" work together for good, it meshes well with pagan belief. In antiquity skeptics challenged God's control of events. In particular, God's ability to bring good results out of bad circumstances was questioned. Philosophers often wrote in response in defense of God's providence (e.g., Seneca, *On Providence*; Epictetus, *Discourse* 1.16; Plutarch, *On the Delays of Divine Vengeance*). Their sentiments were well expressed by Plato, *Republic* 10.12 + 612e-613a. He said:

Shall we not agree that all that comes from the gods turns out for the best for him who is dear to the gods? This, then, we must conclude about the just man, that whether he is beset by penury or sickness or any other supposed evil, for him these things will in the end prove good, whether in life or in death. (cf. *Apology* 41c-d)

A similar position was taken by Seneca in *Epistle* 74:20. In the *Hermetica* 9.4 the focus is on the godfearing person: "for all things are good to such a person, even things that others find evil." It was a widespread philosophical conviction that all things, even bad circumstances, worked out for the best if one was dear to the gods. A similar point of view is found in ancient Judaism (Gen 50:20; Eccl 8:12; Sir 39:27). This is how a number of translations have taken the sentence (e.g., KJV; NRSV; NAB).

Interpreters of Romans 8:28 often resist the notion of "things" working together and attempt to find a way to have the theologically necessary "God" as subject of the sentence. Rabbi Akiba's words signal the way a rabbinic mind would think. "All that the Almighty does, He does for good" (*b. Ber* 60b). If the textual variant *ho theos* is accepted, then God is clearly the subject (so RSV; JB; NIV; NASV; TEV). The uncertainty about this variant leads others to derive the subject from the verb: "He cooperates in all things." After all, the word God occurs in the initial clause ("to those loving God"). The problem with deriving God from the verb is that "works together" does not usually take a direct object. But since the "He" is ambiguous, some pick up "the Spirit" from the context as the referent in "He" (NEB). The instinct that the subject needs to be "God" is so strong among Christian interpreters that it is likely that the textual variant that reads *ho theos* is an early insertion to clarify what the text must be saying. Since vv. 26-27 go with the previous section, however, it is unlikely that "the Spirit" should be taken as the subject of the sentence.

Is there another option? If the textual variant *ho theos* (God) is rejected, then is "all things" the subject of the verb? The term is *panta* and means "all something" but not necessarily "all things." In Paul's letters *ta panta* can mean "all things" (2 Cor 4:15; Phil 3:8; [Col 3:8]) or "all these things" (Rom 8:32). The extent and content of "all things" are decided by the context. The material that follows in vv. 29-30 speaks of God's acts: God foreknew, predestined, called, justified, glorified. This material speaking of God's acts is introduced by *hoti* ("for" or "because"). So the statement in v. 28 is true "because of" God's acts described in vv. 29-30. The logical inference is that *panta* in v. 28 ought to be translated "all God's acts" or "all God's activity." This is linguistically a possible reading since one use of *panta* is of someone's deeds or works, whether it be a human subject (e.g., LXX 4 Kgdms 24:5—"and the rest of the acts of Joakim and all [*panta*] that he did, are not these written in the book of . . . ") or God (e.g., LXX Ps 32:4—" all [*panta*] His works are with faithfulness"; Mark 14:36). I propose, then, that v. 28 be translated: "All God's acts cooperate for good with those who love Him, with those who are called according to His purpose."

"Good" can mean relative goods in this world and time (e.g., Gen 50:20; Sir 39:24-27; Did 3:10; R. Akiba [*b. Ber* 60b]—"Let a man always accustom himself to say, 'All that the Almighty does, He does for good'."). It can also refer to God's act of salvation (Exod 18:9—"good" here refers to the exodus). In Israel's Scriptures "good" was often associated with eschatological glory (Isa 32:42; 52:7; Jer 8:15). In the context of Romans 8, it must surely refer to ultimate salvation (= being conformed to the image of His Son—v. 29). So all God's acts contribute to the ultimate salvation of those who love Him. This is Paul's thesis statement. It is explained in the verses that follow. [William Willimon on God in Conversation with Creation]

Verses 29-30 are symmetrically arranged in a stairstep parallelism or climax (remember 5:3-4). This could be because Paul is here including a piece of oral tradition.

William Willimon on God in Conversation with Creation

One of the great contributions of Judaism is the belief that God not only speaks, but that God listens. Yahweh is in conversation with creation. Yahweh answers our cries of pain. Jesus is the supreme communicative event of this dialogue. In his story is our hope, a confidence that, in spite of our suffering, "in everything God works for the good, with those who love him" (Rom 8:28) and that even on our lonely crosses of pain, "we are more than conquerors through him who loved us" (Rom 8:37).

William Willimon, *Sighing for Eden* (Nashville: Abingdon Press, 1985), 175-76.

> Whom He foreknew, He also predestined,
> whom He predestined, these He also called,
> and whom He called, these He also justified,
> and whom He justified, these He also glorified.

The verbs point to a series of God's acts that begin before the world was ever made, continue through human history, and come to consummation in the New Age beyond the resurrection.

The two verbs that speak of precreation activity are "foreknew" and "predestine." Although the terms do not, of necessity, contain within them the notion of precreation activity, the context demands it (cf. Eph 1:4-5; 1 Pet 1:20). These are terms used by ancient Jews (foreknew—1 QH 1:7-8; CD 2:8; cf. Jer 1:5—"Before I formed you in the womb I knew you"; predestine—1 QS

3:15-16; 11:10-11,17-20). The terms are virtually interchangeable. Perhaps if a distinction can be drawn, it would be that "foreknew" places the emphasis upon "choice" (cf. Amos 3:2), while "predestine" emphasizes the "purpose" of the choice. Paul was very clear about the purpose of God's act of predestination. It is that we be "conformed to the image of His Son, in order that he might be the firstborn within a large family" (v. 29b; cf. 1 Cor 15:49; 2 Cor 3:18; Phil 3:21). This is a reference to future glory. Note that here predestination involves a destination that God had in mind for certain humans before creation. Only some ("those whom") have been predestined! Note also that there is no reference to any rejection of anyone as a counterpart of divine election. Paul did not speak about a double-edged predestination. Origen put it this way: "In Scripture, words like *foreknew* and *predestined* do not apply equally to both good and evil. For the careful student of the Bible will realize that these words are used only of the good. . . . When God speaks of evil people, He says that He *never knew* them."[9] The emphasis here is on the fact that from before the creation of the world God has been at work for our good/ultimate salvation.

The verbs that speak of God's activity within history are "called" and "justified." These are also terms used by ancient Jews (e.g., "called"—Hos 11:1, "Out of Egypt I have called my son"; 1 QM 3:2; 4:10-11; "justified"—Isa 53:11, "By his knowledge shall the righteous one, my servant, justify many"). Here again the terms are virtually interchangeable. If there is any difference in emphasis it is perhaps that "calling" focuses on the divine choice while "justification" emphasizes what is necessary for the choice to be effective. The point here is that God's acts for our good/ultimate salvation, which began in the period even before the world was created have continued into and throughout human history.

The final verb is "glorified." From the context, it seems that "glorified" must refer to the ultimate future. In v. 18, for example, Paul has spoken of "the glory about to be revealed to us" as the future hope. In v. 17, he said: "if, in fact, we suffer with him so that we may also be glorified with him." Again, the reference is to the ultimate future (cf. 1 Thess 2:12). The difficulty is that "glorified" in v. 30 is an aorist tense just like all the other verbs previously mentioned. How can it be that an aorist tense is used for a future event? Perhaps this is best explained as analogous to the prophetic perfect in biblical Hebrew. In that construction the future action of God is regarded as so certain that it is spoken of as a completed action. So Paul, certain of ultimate salvation, could speak of God's climactic act of glorification as though it were already completed. God's acts for our salvation that began even before the world was created and have continued through human history will continue into the New World. All these acts bring to completion our ultimate salvation. Whether they be precreation, in history, or in the ultimate future, they all cooperate with those who love God for our ultimate salvation. If Paul's focus on the Christians' experience of the Holy Spirit in the previous section based our hope on present experience, his argument in this section grounds Christians' assurance in salvation history. Just as in Romans 5:1-11, this dual argument is designed to undergird the Christians' hope.

Verses 31-39 move to an explicit focus on Christian assurance. There are two smaller units making up the passage: vv. 31-34 and vv. 35-39. Verses 31-34, the first unit, focus on the Last Judgment. They are arranged as follows:

A transitional question (v. 31a): What are the implications of verses 28-30?

A rhetorical question (v. 31b): If God is for us, who is against us? The implied answer is, No One! (cf. Ps 56:9, 11) The evidence supporting the implied answer (v. 32): If God gave His own Son for us (cf. Gen 22), then He will give us everything else as well.

A rhetorical question (v. 33a): Who will bring any charge against God's chosen? The implied answer is, No One! The evidence supporting the implied answer (vv. 33b): It is God who justifies (cf. Isa 50:8).

A rhetorical question (v. 34a): Who is the one who condemns? The implied answer is, Not Christ! The evidence supporting the implied answer (v. 34b): It is Christ who died, was raised, and now intercedes for us.

Let us read in this way.

Since Paul has said that all God's acts cooperate for the benefit of our ultimate salvation, what are we to say (v. 31a)? What inferences can be drawn? Assumed here is that the Last Judgment will be like a law court with accusers, defenders, and a judge. How will believers fare in that context given God's acts for us? The first rhetorical query raises the question whether God will bring a charge against us. Will the Creator be our accuser? In the OT God

Sacrifice

In this depiction of Abraham's sacrifice of Isaac, Mantegna overtly depicts the ram in the thicket as an alternative sacrifice. In this interpretation, Mantegna leaves no room for speculation as to the whereabouts of the ram. Here, it takes on vestiges of the lamb of God ritually positioned upon a pedestal with the hand of God breaking though the clouds above.

Andrea Mantegna. 1431–1506. *The Sacrifice of Abraham (Isaac)*. Monochrome painting. c. 1490. Kunsthistorisches Museum. Vienna, Austria. (Credit: Erich Lessing/Art Resource, NY)

on occasion says He is against someone: either the nations (Nineveh—Nah 2:13; 3:5; Babylon—Jer 50:31, 51:25; Egypt—Ezek 29:3; 30:22; Tyre and Sidon—Ezek 26:3; 28:22) or Israel (Ezek 5:8; 15:7; 21:3; Lev 26:17). Will this be the case at the Last Judgment when Christians appear before God? The implied answer is, No. Why?

Verse 32, which may be a traditional formula, answers: "He who did not withhold His own Son, but gave him up for all of us, will He not with him also give us everything else?" God who cared enough about the relationship with us to sacrifice Jesus for us will not be against us. Many interpreters hear an echo of Abraham's binding of Isaac (Gen 22:1-8) in v. 32. The story of Isaac's binding and near sacrifice by his father Abraham was widely cited in ancient Judaism (e.g., Sir 44:20—when tested, Abraham was found faithful; 1 Macc 2:52—when tested, he was found faithful; Wis 10:5—he showed faithfulness to God over compassion for a child; 4 Macc 16:18-20—he was an example of those enduring hardships for God; Philo, *Abraham* 167-207—he demonstrated his obedience to God; Ps-Philo, *Bib.Ant.* 18:5—on account of Isaac's blood God chose the people; *Jub* 17:15–18:19—Abraham showed he was faithful and a lover of the Lord; *m. 'Abot* 5:3—Abraham stood steadfast to show how great was his love for God). In the last two sources cited, Abraham's act is seen as a demonstration of his love for God. This is the emphasis that fits Paul's argument in Romans 8:32. In the Pauline allusion, however, it is God who acts in the role of Abraham. If Abraham was willing to give up his own son to demonstrate his love for God, God is willing to give up Jesus for us all. This is the ultimate sacrifice that a parent can make: to sacrifice a child. Yet God also gave up a child to show love for us (cf. Rom 5:8).

The objection to this way of reading v. 32 is the claim that pre-Christian Jewish teaching about the binding of Isaac did not see Isaac as the prototype of the Messiah and did not mention that Isaac was sacrificed on behalf of Israel or anyone else.[10] In response, one can say first that no Messianic connection is required by the context. Second, the primary emphasis is on demonstration of love for the other, not atoning sacrifice. Third, there is at least one early source. Ps-Philo, *Bib.Ant.* 18:5, said that it was on account of Isaac's blood that God chose Israel (cf. Rom 3:25). Finally, all Paul was saying is that God, like Abraham, in the sacrifice of Jesus has demonstrated the greatest love to us. Given that fact, can there be any doubt that God will not be our accuser at the Judgment?

The second rhetorical question again raises the possibility that there might be someone, God or Christ, who might bring a charge against believers at the Last Judgment. "Who will bring any charge against God's elect" (v. 33a)? Paul's response says that it cannot be God. Why? "It is God who justifies" (= final vindication and acquittal—v. 33b). There may very well be here an echo of Isaiah 50:8-9.

Who will contend with me? . . .

It is the Lord God who helps me; who will declare me guilty?

The third rhetorical question focuses on the judge at the Last Day. "Who is to condemn?" The implied answer is that it cannot be Christ. Why? "It is Christ Jesus, who died, yes, who was raised, who is at the right hand of God, who indeed intercedes for us" (v. 34). Christ is not our judge. He is our advocate. That Christ is at God's right hand (Ps 110:1; Acts 2:33; 5:31; Col 3:1; Eph 1:20) means he is in the spot of honor in relation to God. The right hand was the place where one stood when he/she came to intercede (cf. 1 Kgs 2:19 where Bathsheba is on Solomon's right hand when she comes to intercede for Adonijah). From that appropriate place of honor, he intercedes for us (cf. Heb 7:25; 9:24; 1 John 2:1; see also Matt 10:32-33; Luke 12:8-9; Acts 7:55-56[11]). That he prays for us means he is for us. That he is at God's right hand means his prayers cannot but be effective. Moreover, it was widespread belief that one's righteousness undergirds the efficacy of one's intercession (e.g., Ps 34:15; Prov 15:29; 2 Macc 3:1-33; *Ep Arist* 192; Josephus, *Ant* 1.99; *2 Bar* 85:1-2; Jas 5:16; John 9:31). Jesus is, in Romans, the Righteous One (1:17; 5:18). Since God is the justifying judge and Christ is our advocate, then there can be nothing to fear at the Last Judgment. Nothing on the divine side stands in the way of our being glorified. All God's acts cooperate for our ultimate salvation.

The second small unit making up Romans 8:31-39 consists of vv. 35-39. These verses focus on the circumstances of human existence. This little unit is organized as a question and answer sequence. There are two questions (v. 35a; v. 35b) and two answers (v. 37; vv. 38-39). The first question is answered last; the second question is answered first.

A—First question (v. 35a): Who will separate us from the love of Christ?

B—Second question (v. 35b): Will hardship, or distress, etc?

B'—Answer to second question (v. 37): No, in all these things we are conquerors.

A'—Answer to first question (vv. 38-39): Neither death, nor life, etc., will separate us.

Let us read in this way.

The basic issue in vv. 35-39 is whether or not there is anything external to the relationship that can separate believers from the covenant love of Christ/God in Christ. The focus is on tragedy and fate, external threatening factors. Question one (v. 35a) asks: "Who will separate us from the love of Christ?" The answer reveals that the concern is with fate. Verses 38-39 reply: "Neither death, not life, nor angels, nor rulers, nor things present, nor things to come, nor powers, nor height, nor depth, nor anything else in all creation will be able to separate us from the love of God in Christ Jesus our Lord." The astral world view is assumed here. The heavens are peopled with spiritual powers which impact the lives of humans on earth. Humans live their lives within the web of fate created by the rule of these spiritual powers. Paul's concern was whether or not these powers under which all live can separate believers from God's love. His reply was, No.

Question two (v. 35b) asks: "Will hardship, or distress, or perse-cution, or famine, or nakedness, or peril, or sword" (be able to separate us)? The question indicates that here Paul was focused on historical tragedies. The quotation from Psalm 44:23 in v. 36 indi-cates that these tribulations Christians encounter are what have always characterized God's people. Can historical tragedies any more than universal fate separate believers from Christ's love? Paul's answer was: "No, in all these things we are more than conquerors through him who loved us." Neither historical tragedies that snatch some people out of life in an untimely manner nor heavenly powers to which all humans are subject can separate believers from God's/Christ's love. Not only are all God's acts cooperating for our ultimate salvation (vv. 28-30), the personnel at the Last Judgment are stacked in our favor (vv. 31-34), and the covenant love of God/Christ is something from which we can not be separated by life's circumstances (vv. 35-39). Can there be any greater ground on which Christian assurance about the ultimate future can rest?

CONNECTIONS

Predestination

Predestination is a perennial problem for Christians who take Scripture seriously. Paul teaches it. Two very different approaches to defining it have been tried: the logical and the experiential approaches. On the one hand, there have been a series of logical approaches to the understanding of predestination in the history of Protestantism. John Calvin accepted the concept of double predes-tination.[12] God decreed, he said, which individuals would be saved and which would be damned.[13] Eternal life is foreordained for some and eternal damnation for others. Every person is predestined either to life or to death. When God grants mercy, it because such is His good pleasure; when He hardens others, there is no other cause than His will. The function of the doctrine was the exclusion of any concept of merit on the one hand and the affirmation that our destiny is entirely in the hands of God on the other. Of Paul, Calvin said: "By saying that they were elected before the creation of the world, he precludes every consideration of merit."[14] Both Martin Luther and the Thirty Nine Articles of Anglicanism affirmed a single predestination. There is only a predestination to life. Rom 8:29b,c shows Luther and the Anglican articles closer to Paul than Calvin. Calvinistic orthodoxy developed two theories about predestination. One group advocated supralapsarianism. This position held that before the creation of the world God had decreed who would be saved and who would be damned. Then God created humans and permitted the Fall as a means by which the decree could be carried out. The other group contended for infralapsarianism. This position maintained that before the creation of the world God foresaw that humans would fall. God permitted, having made the decree. These two positions have to do with the order of the divine purposes. Which comes first, predestination or foreknowledge?

Arminians affirmed that the idea of predestination has reference only to God's plan for the world. It means no more than that God has declared that whoever accepts Christ will be saved and whoever does not will be excluded. Every individual is able to make a free decision to be or not to be a Christian. Predestination describes a general situation, the outcome of which is determined by each individual's decisions. Romans 8:29 certainly describes a general destination God has intended for humans: to be like Christ. That all individuals have a free decision to make is less obvious for two reasons. First the phrase is not "that which He predestined" but rather "those whom He predestined." Paul is not saying that God established a precreation destination for all but for "those," as opposed to "all." Second, Paul regarded faith as a gift of God (Phil 1:29). One is not free to have faith or not to have faith as one wills. The problem with all these approaches is that when an attempt is made to reconcile divine sovereignty and human freedom logically, inevitably one side devours the other. Either divine sovereignty swallows human freedom or human freedom devours divine sovereignty. The tension between them is lost.

On the other hand, there has been an experiential approach to the understanding of predestination. John Knox is a twentieth-century representative of this position. He has insisted that all of Romans 8 is written from the standpoint of Christian religious experience.

Martin Luther's 95 Theses

Gustav Koeing. *Martin Luther Posting the 95 Theses on the Scholsskirche Door in Wittenberg.* Engraving.
(Credit: Foto Marburg/Art Resource, NY)

Now one who has received the grace of God finds himself ascribing the whole process of his salvation to God's action; he himself has had nothing to do with it whatever. Even his faith appears to be God's gift.[15]

Knox's contention is that some doctrine of predestination is a required rationalization of this experience, just as some doctrine of freedom is a required rationalization of the sense of responsibility we feel.

C. J. Vaughn was a nineteenth-century expressor of the same approach. He said that all who are saved can only ascribe their salvation to God's doing.

Human merit must be excluded: and this can only be by tracing back the work far beyond the obedience which evidences, or even the faith which appropriates, salvation; even to an act of spontaneous favour on the part of that God who foresees and foreordains from eternity all his works.[16]

This approach sees doctrines as conceptualizations of experiential realities. The only way to reconcile the two affirmations, divine sovereignty and human freedom, is to go back to the experience out of which they come. When that is done, both must be affirmed because both are needed to explain the complexity of human experience. Neither affirmation can be allowed to swallow the other. Note that this explanation of Paul's teaching about predestination preserves Calvin's view of the function of the teaching (to exclude all merit) but without the problems created by Calvin's too logical mind.

A way of refining Knox's interpretation of predestination in Paul is derived from reflections on the nature of religious language. Among the many types of religious language, the two most basic are confessional and defensive language. Religious language derives directly or indirectly from believers' ongoing relationship with God/Christ. An analogy would be how language arises out of a marriage relationship. Because husband and wife have an ongoing relationship with each other, each is able to speak about the other person (he/she is . . .), about himself/herself (I have been . . .), and about the nature of the relationship (it is . . .). To say, for example, she is the most interesting person I have ever known; I have been changed by this relationship; and it is a relation characterized by mutual respect, is to speak confessionally. It is analogous to Paul's saying: Jesus is Lord; I have been justified; this relation is by grace through faith. Such language is confessional language enabled by an ongoing relationship about which one speaks. When Paul speaks this way, he emphasizes the priority of grace, God's initiative.

Sometimes when problems arise against which one needs to protect the community, defensive language emerges. It starts from the same ongoing relationship and the experiential realities known there and formulates religious language in a defensive way. If one wants, for example, to protect the divine initiative in the relationship with humans, one might say: We have been predestined. That is to claim that any relation that we have with God/Christ is due to divine initiative. Why? Because before we were even created, God/Christ took the initiative to have the relationship with us. Once again, Calvin's desire to formulate a doctrine of predestination in order to rule out any claim of human merit is preserved. Predestination says that God's relation with us is rooted in eternal love for us. God loved us before we had an opportunity to perform satisfactorily. The relationship depends upon God's initiative, not ours.

That the initiative is with God does not rule out our active response to the divine initiative. From Paul's point of view, however, even our response to God's initiative (faith) is enabled by God. Nevertheless, it is our response. How can this be? Consider an analogy. When, in pursuit of a love relationship, one finds the possibilities failing in spite of their apparent appropriateness, it becomes clear that one cannot merely choose to love someone. When, in the same pursuit, one falls in love with the other, one becomes aware that this was an event that went beyond human choice. It was something that happened. This is analogous to grace. If, however, one is asked about the happening: You mean you had no choice in the matter whatsoever? One responds: Of course, I did. It happened and I chose it. This is an analogy of how grace and faith work in the divine-human relationship. The relationship happens: but within the context of its happening, we choose it.

Predestination, then, is defensive language aimed to exclude any human claim to have merited a relationship with God. It is a doctrine by believers for believers. It is uttered by believers after the fact. It speaks only about the believers' awareness that this relation with God/Christ does not depend upon us but upon God's initiative. Our performance or lack of it had nothing to do with God's initiative toward us or love for us. The relation is a matter of sheer grace on God's part. As such, the doctrine of predestination functions also as an assurance for believers. The relationship ultimately depends upon God. "Predestination therefore has meaning only for believers and is not a concept for general speculation."[17]

Life After Death

Romans 8 with its focus on future salvation inevitably raises the question of life after death. Why believe in life after death? In Paul's theology, as in all good theology, the starting point is the relationship between God and humans in the here and now. So Romans 8 begins (v. 1—"There is . . . no condemnation for those who are in Christ Jesus") and ends (8:39—Nothing "in all creation will be able to separate us from the love of God in Christ Jesus") with Paul's technical expression for that relationship: in Christ. In 8:28-39 the apostle speaks first of the importance which that relationship has for God and second of the implications of that fact.

First, the relationship with humans is important for God! When saying this, it is important to make clear what is not being implied. Paul did not think God needs humans as an emotionally dependent parent needs the child in an unhealthy way. What is being said is that considering both the time involved and the sacrifice made on God's part to insure the relationship with us, it must be important to God.

On the one hand, consider the time involved. In vv. 28-30 Paul probably quoted a tradition from the church before him. This tradition makes two points. Verse 28 contends: God is working for our ultimate salvation. Verses 29-30 view God's work in three stages. Before the creation God was at work (foreknew, predestined); throughout human history God has been at work (called, justified); into the New Age beyond the resurrection God's work continues (glorified). Anything someone spends that much time on must be very important.

On the other hand, consider the sacrifice made by God. In v. 32 Paul was quoting what is probably another tradition from the church before him. In this tradition the image is that of Abraham's sacrifice of Isaac as a demonstration of the importance the relation with God had for him. The image in v. 32 is reversed, however, so that it is God who sacrifices a son. This demonstrates how important the relation with us is to God. Anything someone makes that kind of sacrifice for has to be desperately important to him/her. So Paul affirmed that considering the time involved and the sacrifice made on God's part for the relation with us, the relationship with us must be extremely important.

Second, what are the implications of this fact? The question and answer sequence in vv. 35-39 make this clear. The question in v. 35b and its answer in v. 37 look at death as a historical tragedy which takes some in an untimely way. Together they assert that the

One who loves us will not allow us to be separated by such a tragedy. The question in v. 35a and its answer in vv. 38-39 view death as a fate to which we all are subject. Together they assert that the One who loves us will not allow such a fate to override the security of the relationship. Neither death as a historical tragedy nor death as a fate will be able to break the relationship. Nothing external to the relationship will be allowed to destroy it.

In sum, Paul's position may be stated thusly. If the relation with me means enough that God will spend so much time and make so great a sacrifice for it, then I cannot believe that God will allow an enemy (death) to destroy that relation in any permanent way. That is one reason to believe in life after death.

The Security of the Believer

In Romans 8:31-34 Paul contended that neither God nor Christ would act in any way at the judgment that would separate Christians from their Lord. In 8:35-39 Paul said that neither the astral powers nor historical circumstances could separate us from the love of God in Christ in this life and beyond. In a final rhetorical flourish, the apostle said: "nor anything else in all creation" will be able to separate us from God's love. The question often asked about such an affirmation is this. Are even responsible decisions of Christians themselves included in "anything else in creation"? If so, then the statement functions as evidence for the eternal security of believers; if not, then the question of the final perseverance of the saints is left open, at least insofar as this passage is concerned.

A good example of the Calvinist argument is Judith M. Gundry Volf's *Paul and Perseverance: Staying in and Falling Away.*[18] She has argued basically from the faithfulness of God (e.g., Phil 1:6; 1 Cor 1:8-9; 1 Thess 5:23-24; Rom 5:9-10). Paul taught the perseverance of Christians unto ultimate salvation because of who God is. If Christians persevere, it is because God preserves them unto the end. At the same time, however, those possessing faith manifest a certain behavioral orientation as a witness that they are indeed being preserved and persevering.

A clear example of the Arminian argument is I. Howard Marshall's *Kept by the Power of God: A Study of Perseverance and Falling Away.*[19] He has contended that Paul does indeed base assurance of ultimate salvation on the faithfulness of God to fulfill the divine promises. Nevertheless, various exhortations are addressed to believers that imply that they also have their part to play in the attainment of their final salvation (1 Cor 6:9-11; 8:7-13; 9:27;

10:1-12; Gal 5:19-21). Divine protection does not rule out the need for human vigilance. Human action for good ultimately is ascribed by Paul to God (Phil 2:12-13). Divine working, however, does not mean automatic progress. Perseverance is not automatic. The possibility of falling away exists. Ben Witherington III has summarized this viewpoint. Paul did not include in the list in 8:35-39 the individual himself/herself, who may indeed commit apostasy. Hence all of Paul's warnings and urgings about faithfulness and perseverance. "Paul believes that one is eternally secure only when one is securely in eternity."[20]

Both sides of the debate over the perseverance of the believer agree on certain things. (1) Both take a relational view of the Christian life. Neither side is willing to allow a transactional view of conversion. Such a transactional view assumes wrongly that when the right formula is pronounced (e.g., I believe Jesus is Son of God and that he died for my sins), a legal transaction takes place in heaven. It is recorded in heaven that such and such a one is hereby awarded a "fire insurance policy" that is good no matter what he/she does for the rest of his/her life. This transactional view of conversion as a legal fiction assumes an automatic preservation of anyone so converted. Once saved, always saved! Neither a mature Calvinist nor a mature Arminian position would accept such a distortion. Both camps would assume that the Christian life begins, continues, and is consummated with a personal relationship between God in Christ and the believer. (2) Both sides would agree that there is certain habitual behavior that puts one outside the kingdom of God (e.g., 1 Cor 6:9-11; Gal 5:19-21; 6:8).

The issue between the two camps is whether or not the one who is engaged in behavior that puts one outside the kingdom ever had faith. The Calvinist camp, on the one hand, would argue that such people were never really saved/living in faith. Their slogan runs: those who falter before they finish had a flaw in their faith from the first. Anyone with true faith would persevere because God preserves such unto the end. The Arminian camp, on the other hand, would contend that such people were once living in faith but are doing so no longer. Their slogan runs: having started with the spirit, they are now ending with the flesh (Gal 3:3); they have fallen away from grace (Gal 5:4). God preserves unto the end only those who persevere.

The argument about the perseverance of the saints is similar to that about predestination. In both cases we are dealing with the matter of divine grace and human freedom. In both cases we are dealing with a paradox. Remember: paradoxes cannot be resolved logically. When this is tried, either grace swallows free will or free will devours grace. When this happens, half of what the apostle affirms is lost. Paradoxes must be resolved experientially. Go back to the experience out of which the affirmations came and see if that experiential reality is so complex that it demands both affirmations in order to describe the fullness of what has been experienced. I suggest that when this is done, the believer finds that two things must be confessed at the same time. (1) God is faithful. (2) We are responsible. One cannot release the one and affirm only the other. Both are part of the relational reality that we call primary religious experience or having a relationship with God in Christ. When Paul made statements about God's faithfulness, he was voicing one dimension of the experience. When he confessed human responsibility in and for the relationship, he was voicing the other dimension. Both types of confessions are set side by side in the Pauline letters with no attempt to resolve the paradox logically. So when we speak either of the preservation of the saints or of the perseverance of the saints, two things must be included. First, if we are faithful, it is because God is working in us. This is God's preservation of believers. Second, God "does not work *in* us *without* us."[21] This is the believers' perseverance in the relationship with God. If Paul's speech about predestination was defensive language, his remarks about the security of believers were confessional language. In both cases paradox is unavoidable because of the complexity of relational reality.

NOTES

[1]Chrysostom, *Homilies on Romans* 14 (cited in Gerald Bray, *Romans* [Downer's Grove IL: InterVarsity, 1998], 224).

[2]Thomas Schreiner, *Romans* (*ECNT*; Grand Rapids: Eerdmans, 1998), 443.

[3]David M. Hay, *Glory at the Right Hand* (Nashville: Abingdon, 1973), 131.

[4]C. E. B. Cranfield, *A Critical and Exegetical Commentary on the Epistle to the Romans* (ICC; Edinburgh: T. & T. Clark, 1975), 1.423-24.

[5]Origen, *Commentary of the Epistle to the Romans* (cited in Bray, *Romans*, 229).

[6]James D. G. Dunn, *Romans 1-8* (WBC; Dallas: Word Books, 1988), 479.

[7]Gordon D. Fee, *God's Empowering Presence: The Holy Spirit in the Letters of Paul* (Peabody MA: Hendrickson, 1994), 575-86.

[8]C. H. Dodd, *The Epistle of Paul to the Romans* (New York: Harper & Brothers, 1932), 136.

[9]Origen, *Commentary of the Epistle to the Romans* (cited in Bray, *Romans*, 234-35).

[10]Joseph A. Fitzmyer, *Romans* (AB; NY: Doubleday, 1993), 531-32.

[11]David Crump, *Jesus the Intercessor: Prayer and Christology in Luke-Acts* (Grand Rapids: Baker Books, 1999), sees these passages as also belonging to the heavenly intercession of Jesus.

[12]Sebastian Brock, "The Prayer of the Heart in Syriac Tradition," in *Forms of Devotion*, ed. E. Ferguson (New York: Garland, 1999), 135.

[13]John Calvin, *Institutes* III.xxi-xxii.

[14]John Calvin, *Institutes* III.xxii.2.

[15]John Calvin, *Institutes* III.xxii.2.

[16]*The Interpreter's Bible* (New York: Abingdon, 1954), 9.526-27

[17]C. J. Vaughn, *St. Paul's Epistle to the Romans* (London: Macmillan, 1885), 163.

[18]John Dillenberger and Claude Welch, *Protestant Christianity* (New York: Charles Scribner's Sons, 1954), 34.

[19](Louisville: Westminster/John Knox, 1990).

[20](Minneapolis: Bethany Fellowship, 1969).

[21]Ben Witherington III, *Paul's Narrative Thought World* (Louisville: Westminster/John Knox, 1994), 232.

THE PROBLEM OF ISRAEL'S UNBELIEF AND GOD'S FAITHFULNESS

9–11

COMMENTARY

Romans 9–11 forms a distinct unit in the letter between chapters 1–8 and 12:1–15:13. This section of Romans is neither peripheral nor central, rather it is integral to Paul's argument. On the one hand, it is linked with chapters 1–8 by their mutual contention that God has consigned all to disobedience in order to have mercy upon all (3:19-20, 23-24; 11:32). On the other hand, it has the same goal as 14:1–15:13, to subvert Gentile pride and boasting.

The difficulties associated with the understanding of these three chapters require special assistance for the reader. Three aids will, therefore, be offered prior to the commentary proper: (1) a history of interpretation of this unit, (2) an outline that enables one to see the train of thought running throughout the chapters, and (3) a warning about proper procedure in one's reading.

Any reading of the material must follow some attention to the various ways that these chapters have been interpreted in Christian history. A glance at the early Fathers, at the Humanists and Reformers, at Dispensationalists, and at post-Holocaust interpreters gives perspective in reading.

(1) Patristic evidence—The early Fathers struggled with Romans 9 in terms of human freedom and divine predestination. It was their aim to preserve human freedom and responsibility. In the East, Chrysostom, in his sixteenth homily on Romans, argued that God's choice of Jacob over Esau was based on God's foreknowledge of what kind of person each of the twins would be, choosing the one God knew would be good and rejecting the bad one. In the West, in his *Commentary on Paul's Epistles*, Ambrosiaster gave prominence to divine foreknowledge. God, he said, has mercy on those whom God

knows will be converted, calling the ones who will obey but not calling the ones who will not obey.

Although the early Augustine reflected the previous train of thought, by the time he wrote *To Simplician* his stance had changed. Then he contended that one cannot say it was because of foreknowledge that Jacob would be good and Esau bad that God called and did not call. Were this so, it would mean that God's choice would be based on works, even if they had not yet been performed. The election of God, however, cannot be based on works but depends entirely on divine grace.

Romans 11 presented another problem. What would be the destiny of the unbelieving Jews? "All Israel" was normally not taken to mean everyone in ethnic Israel but "those who believe" (e.g., Theodoret of Cyr, *Interpretation of the Letter to the Romans*). Most Fathers were silent on how this would take place. Theodoret of Cyr, however, argued:

> After the Gentiles accepted the gospel, the Jews would believe, when the great Elijah would come to them and bring them the doctrine of faith. The Lord himself said as much: "Elijah will come and will restore all things."[1]

(2) The Sixteenth Century—The reading of Romans 9–11 by the early Greek Fathers continued into the sixteenth century, as did that of Augustine. In the sixteenth century the focus was still primarily on predestination or election. All believed that Romans 9–11, particularly 9:6-13, 17-18, 21, provided the foundation for a doctrine of predestination, understood as God's election of certain persons to salvation. The battle revolved around whether the ground of divine election was the divine will alone or whether election followed foreseen merit.

Luther and Calvin, following Augustine, held the certainty of election depended upon its grounding in the divine will alone. The basis of election was not God's foreknowledge of human worthiness, for no person was worthy. Melancthon from the Lutheran side and Bullinger from the Reformed followed Erasmus in expressing strong reservations about ascribing election in Romans 9:6-29 to the will of God alone. Erasmus, in his *Annotations on Romans* (1516) argued that God's elective choice occurred *post praevisa merita* (following foreseen merit).

Regarding reprobation, Erasmus, following Origen, contended that the individual, not God, was responsible for sin. God's hardening of Esau and Pharoah was a reaction to their unbelief. Luther concurred with Augustine that God's rejection of Esau, no less than

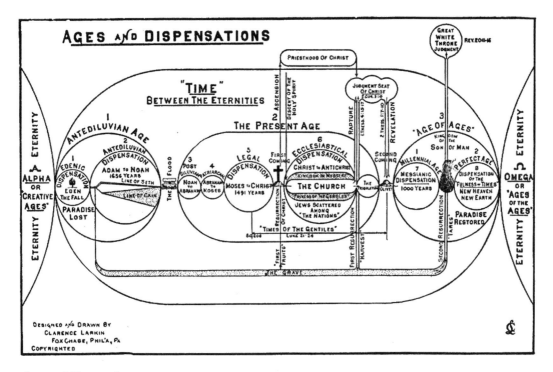

Ages and Dispensations

Chart by Clarence Larkin. c. 1914–1919.

his blessing of Jacob, had no human occasion. For the most part, Luther thought reprobation was God's withholding of mercy from some rather than condemning them by decree. Calvin and Zwingli were alike in their claim that both election and rejection are the work of God's free will and decree.

Erasmus believed that God foreknew that all Israel would ultimately believe in Christ (11:26) and elected them, confirming their faith. Luther could not determine if God conducted Gentile election individually and Jewish election corporately because he did not think Paul could decide either. Calvin thought in terms of two elections. The corporate election of the nation of Israel was to earthly blessing, while the individual election of spiritual Israel was to salvation. Hence, "all Israel" in 11:26 refers not to the Jewish race but to all the people of God, both Jew and Gentile (= the church).

(3) Dispensationalism—Dispensationalism originated in mid-nineteenth-century Britain among an interdenominational group of pre-millenial pastors led by John Nelson Darby. It was popularized by Cyrus Scofield's Reference Bible which appeared in 1909.[2]

In such a system, one usually believes there are a number of dispensations (= principles on the basis of which God governs

Sealing of the Elect

This painting indicates the tribes of Israel as under the blessing of Christ as indicated by the cross looms above them, carried aloft by an angel. Many interpreters of Romans 9–11 have believed that at the return of Jesus, many Jews will accept him as the messiah.

Juan Gerson. *The Sealing of the Elect of the Tribes of Israel.* Oil on canvas. c. 1560. Franciscan Monastery. Tecamachalco, Puebla, Mexico.
(Credit: Gilles Mermet/Art Resource, NY)

groups of people). For example, (1) Innocence (in Eden), (2) Conscience (until the Flood), (3) Human government (until Abraham), (4) Promise (until Moses), (5) Law (Jews only, until Christ), (6) Grace (until the Parousia), (7) Millennial kingdom (post-Parousia). According to this scheme, the past twenty-one centuries have been the Church Age or the Time of the Gentiles, which extends from the resurrection of Jesus to the Parousia. During this time, believing Gentiles live in the dispensation of God's governance by grace, Jews remain under the dispensation of law, and unbelieving Gentiles live under the dispensation of human governance. Dispensations, then, are not simply successive aeons of time but are different ways God governs groups of people. Believers, unbelieving Gentiles, and unbelieving Jews may, then, be in different but simultaneous dispensations.

The agenda of Dispensationalism is to prove that the church and Israel comprise two distinct peoples of God distinguished by two different principles of governance. The church is God's heavenly people created to share God's glory in heaven. Ethnic Israel is God's earthly people with whom all the covenants were made and to whom the promises were given. These promises will be fulfilled literally for ethnic Israel here on this earth in the future. There is here no supercessionism. The church does not replace Israel. There is rather a complementary, as opposed to a relacement, relationship between Israel and the church.

The Advent of Christ will take place in two stages. In the first, his church will be secretly removed to heaven. It is not the subject of prophecy. In the second, the rapture of the church will be followed by a period of unparalleled tribulation for the Jews. Then the Parousia of Christ will occur as God's final intervention. Secular history will come to an end. Israel will then recognize the Lord as her Messiah and become the kingdom of God on earth. During this time she will convert the rest of humankind. The Son of David will rule the earth from a restored Zion for a literal 1,000 years. During this time, the prophecies made to ethnic Israel will be fulfilled.

As regards a reading of Romans 9–11, Dispensationalism sees Paul's vision of salvation history in the following terms. God chose ethnic Israel and gave her promises. God offered Israel the Kingdom but, she refused her Messiah. Then God included Gentile believers in Christ. This was but an interruption of God's dealings with Israel. After this interruption is past, God will again resume His dealings with ethnic Israel. At the Parousia, Israel will believe in her Messiah and will share in the Messianic Kingdom on earth. At this time, the prophecies made to Israel will be literally fulfilled on earth.

(4) Post-Holocaust interpreters—The traditional reading of Pauline interpreters has been (and continues to be) that Paul envisioned only one way to salvation: through Jesus Christ. So when the apostle said in Romans 11:26 that all Israel will be saved, he was speaking of the result of Israel's faith in Christ. This judgment is made by both supporters[3] and detractors[4] of Paul.

After the Holocaust, however, a number of Christian scholars have come to espouse a two-covenant view: that is, there is one way of salvation for Gentiles, another for Jews. Gentiles will be saved through Christ; the Jews will be saved without him. Exactly how God will accomplish Israel's salvation remains a mystery, but it does not depend on any acceptance of Jesus as Messiah. Krister Stendahl,[5] Lloyd Gaston,[6] and John Gager[7] are representative of this view.

A view that fits neither into the one nor the other of the two positions just outlined is that of Franz Mussner.[8] He has maintained that the salvation of all Israel will be apart from conversion to the gospel. The Parousia of Christ saves all Israel without a preceding conversion of the Jews to the gospel. God saves Israel through a special path, but it likewise rests on the principle of grace. At the same time, it is through Jesus that the Jews will be saved.

Given the diversity of interpretations of Romans 9–11 in the history of Christian thought, it is not surprising that the general reader experiences dismay when faced with Paul's argument. It is a help if the train of thought can be traced in Romans 9–11. To that we turn now. Moreover, it is necessary to see the logic of the argument in Romans 9–11 as a whole before proceeding with the parts. An outline assists the reader in this task. Following the train of thought is assured neither by the chapter divisions nor by the rhetorical questions nor by the Old Testament quotations that are interspersed through the chapters. The logic of Paul's argument often cuts across these markers, though sometimes reflecting one or more of them. What follows reflects the reading of this commentary.

The three chapters begin with an oath (9:1-5) and end with a hymn (11:33-36). In between, the material falls into an ABA' pattern: A (9:6-29); B (9:30–10:21); A' (11:1-32). In outline form, it looks like this.

Paul's Oath (9:1-5)—Paul swears that he would choose to be damned if it could mean the salvation of Israel, his kinspeople according to the flesh.

  A (9:6-29)—Unbelief by a part of Israel and belief by some of the Gentiles shows, not that God's promises have failed, but that they have been fulfilled. Why?
    1. The promise was made only to the elect/the called (9:6b-13)
      a. Intra-Jewish argument number one over the legitimacy of God's behavior (9:14-18) dismisses objections to God's election
      b. Intra-Jewish argument number two over the legitimacy of God's behavior (9:19-21) dismisses objections to God's election
    2. The promise included Gentiles as well as Jews (9:22-29)
      a. The affirmation of the principle (9:22-24)
      b. The scriptural support of the principle (9:25-29)
        (1) in support of the inclusion of Gentiles (9:25-26)
        (2) in support of the inclusion of a remnant from Israel (9:27-29)
  B (9:30–10:21)—What are we to make of the exclusion of some from Israel? Viewed from the perspective of human responsibility, Israel resisted God.
    1. Israel pursued righteousness in the wrong way (9:30–10:4)
    2. Why?
      a. Not because the news about God's way was inaccessible or too hard (10:5-13),
      b. Nor because Israel had not heard or understood (10:14-15; 10:17-20) but because Israel has been disobedient and contrary (10:16; 10:21).
  A' (11:1-32)—God has not rejected the people. Why? Because Israel's rejection is both partial and temporary.

1. Israel's unbelief is partial. There is a remnant that has rightly obtained righteousness (11:1-10). The evidence includes:
   a. Paul's situation is evidence of a believing remnant (9:1b)
   b. The current situation is analogous to the time of Elijah when there was a remnant chosen by grace (11:2-6)
   c. Scripture testifies that the elect obtained what they sought but the rest were hardened (11:7-10)
2. Israel's unbelief is only temporary (11:11-32)
   a. Two statements of principle (11:11-12; 11:13-15): Jewish unbelief led to the inclusion of the Gentiles; Gentile belief will lead to the inclusion of the Jews; Jewish belief will lead to even greater blessings.
   b. Illustration of the principle: the olive tree (11:16-24)
   c. Explanation of the mystery (11:25-32)
   d. Hymn in Praise of God's Transcendent Wisdom/Plan of Salvation (11:33-36)

As noted earlier, it will be an aid to our understanding of Romans 9–11 if we heed a warning and receive some guidance. C. E. B. Cranfield has warned that:

> It is of utmost importance to take these three chapters together as a whole, and not to come to conclusions about Paul's argument before one has heard it to the end; for chapter 9 will certainly be understood in an altogether un-Pauline sense, if it is understood in isolation from its sequel in chapters 10 and 11.[9]

Steven Fraade, moreover, has contended that rabbinic homilies should be read backwards to analyze properly their structures and grasp their intentions.[10] Since Paul reflected rabbinic ways of arguing elsewhere and since chapters 9–11 have a homiletic tone to them, it may very well be that the clue to the apostle's intention is to be found at the end, rather than the beginning, of this unit. Fraade's guidance reinforces Cranfield's warning. In what follows, the reading offered will constantly be aware of the ending of Paul's argument as it attempts to grasp the beginning of it. With these three aids to reading in place, it is time to begin with the interpretation of 9:1-29 proper.

Romans 9:1-29 consists of two components: vv. 1-5, an oath by Paul, and vv. 6-29, "A" in the concentric pattern. We look first at the oath. Paul's oath in vv. 1-5 grew out of his personal anguish over his kinspeople's failure to believe the gospel. His "kindred according to the flesh" (v. 3) possess seven God-given prerogatives (vv. 4-5a): the sonship (Exod 4:22), the glory (Exod 34:30;

1 Kgs 8:11); the covenants (Gen 15:18; 26:3-5; Exod 24:7-8; 2 Sam 23:5; Wis 18:22; Sir 44:12); the law (Exod 20:1-17); the worship (Exod 25–31); the promises (Gen 12:2; 26:3-5; 28:13-14; Deut 18:18-19; 2 Sam 7:11-16); and the patriarchs (Exod 3:13; 13:5). An eighth blessing follows as well (v. 5): "from them, according to the flesh, comes the Messiah" (Rom 1:3; Matt 1:1-17; Luke 3:23-38). The point is that the Israelites have been specially privileged by God. How, then, could they not believe in the Messiah? This unbelief caused Paul to assume a role like that of Moses (Exod 32:32) and say: "I could wish that I myself were accursed and cut off from Christ for the sake of my own people" (v. 3). The apostle was willing, he said, to be damned if his people could be saved. In this he did not lie (v. 1; cf. 2 Cor 11:31; Gal 1:20; 1 Tim 2:7). Of course, if his people who disbelieve needed to be saved, they were, in Paul's opinion, lost as long as they persisted in unbelief (cf. 10:1).

The one debatable issue in vv. 1-5 comes in v. 5b. How does one read the words after "the Christ according to the flesh"? They run: *ho ōn epi pantōn theos eulogētos eis tous aiōnas, amēn* (the one being over all God blessed into the age amen). Two options distill the essence of the possibilities. Either the words refer to Christ or they refer to God. If they refer to God, then one would translate: "from them comes the Messiah. The One being over all, God, be blessed into the age, Amen" (Nestle-Aland 26 ; REB; RSV; TEV; NAB). If they refer to Christ, then one's rendering would be: "from them comes the Messiah, the one being over all, God, blessed into the age, Amen" (UBS 1; NIV; NRSV; NJB; NASV). The linguistic arguments favor the latter option. The natural antecedent of "the one being" is Christ because doxologies are virtually always attached to a preceding word (cf. Rom 1:25; 2 Cor 11:31; Gal 1:5; Eph 3:21; Phil 4:20; 1 Tim 1:17, 4:18; Heb 13:21; 1 Pet 4:11; 2 Pet 3:18). Moreover, if this were an independent doxology to God, then the word *eulogētos* would be expected to occur first (e.g., LXX Gen 9:26; 14:20; 24:27, 31; Exod 18:10; Ruth 4:14; 1 Sam 25:32; 2 Sam 6:21; 18:28; 1 Kgs 1:48; 8:15, 56, etc.; Luke 1:68; 2 Cor 1:3; Eph 1:3; 1 Pet 1:3; one possible exception = LXX Ps 67:19 [68:19], which reads: "The Lord, the God be blessed"). The major obstacle to a reference to Christ is theological. Would Paul call Jesus "God"? Those favoring the reading of Christ as God contend that it would not be out of step with Paul's thought. The apostle applied LXX passages intended for Yahweh to Christ (e.g., Rom 10:13; Phil 2:10-11), invokes Christ in prayer (Rom 10:12-14; 1 Cor 16:22), refers to Christ and the Father together

(Rom 1:7b; 8:35, 39; 2 Cor 13:13), and spoke of Christ as "in the form of God" (Phil 2:6). Also noted is that in the Deuteropauline Titus 2:13 Christ is likely referred to as God. Probably v. 5 should be translated as in the NRSV, with God refer-

ring to Christ. If so, then Paul would not have been referring to Christ as God in an exhaustive sense. What was intended is the claim that Christ shares the divine nature with the Father (cf. John 1:1-2,18; 20:28).[11]

Romans 9:6-29, "A" in the pattern, is held together by an inclusion: vv. 7b-8a and vv. 24-29 (only some from Israel have been chosen). [Israel in Paul's Letters] It deals with the issue expressed in the question implied in v. 6a: If many Jews have not believed in Christ and if

Israel in Paul's Letters

AΩ When Paul referred to Israel, he did so with two different meanings implied.

- Most of the time Israel refers to ethnic Israel (Rom 9:6a, 27, 31; 10:19, 21; 11:2, 7, 11, 25; 1 Cor 10:18; 2 Cor 3:7, 13; Phil 3:5).
- Sometimes Israel refers to spiritual Israel + either those from among ethnic Israel who have believed the gospel (Rom 9:6b; 11:26; references to the remnant belong here—Rom 9:27; 11:5); + or believers from the Gentiles as well (Gal 6:16).

many Gentiles have believed, does this mean that God's promises to Abraham and his descendants have failed? Paul's answer was NO. His reasons were two. First, for God's promises to Abraham and his descendants to be fulfilled does not require every Israelite to believe in Jesus, because God's promises were not made to Abraham's physical descendants but to those to whom, in God's mercy, the promise applied (vv. 6b-16). In pursuing this argument Paul appealed to God's choice of Isaac instead of Ishmael (Gen 21:12) and to God's call of Jacob instead of Esau (Gen 25:23). "So it depends not on human will or exertion, but on God who shows mercy" (v. 16). Augustine observed:

> No one could say that Jacob had conciliated God by meritorious works before he was born. . . . Nor had Isaac conciliated God by any previous meritorious works so that his birth should have been promised. . . . Good works do not produce grace, but are produced by grace. (*To Simplician on Various Questions* 1.2.3)[12]

Promise and calling, rather than ethnic belonging, mark the pattern of divine action.

In so arguing Paul captured the spirit of Genesis. This narrative emphasizes the reversal of the law of primogeniture (= the first born son carries on the family line). Over and over Genesis tells how through some twist of destiny a younger son was chosen to carry on the line. God preferred the sacrifice of Abel, the younger, over that of Cain, the elder (4:5). God preferred Isaac over Ishmael and Jacob over Esau. Again, God preserved the seed of Abraham through Joseph (45:4-7; 49:4) rather than through Reuben, the legitimate heir. At the end of his life, Jacob blessed Ephraim, the

Isaac Blesses Jacob

Reversal of the law of primogeniture. Here, old and bleary of vision, Isaac is in the midst of giving his blessing to Jacob, the younger son. At the guidance of his mother, the younger son deceived his father into thinking that the person before him was Esau, the eldest son. With the figures large and imposing on the foreground plane, the dramatic lighting highlights this sacred moment of blessing as the father, Isaac, is seeking to verify the correct identity of his son. Notice Isaac's stroking of Jacob's hair, looking for clues that would suggest the more hairy Esau.

Domenico Fetti. 1589–1624. *Isaac Blesses Jacob.* Accademia, Venice, Italy. (Credit: Alinari/Art Resource, NY)

second born, rather than the first born Manasseh, despite the protests of their father, Joseph (48:17-22). The motif in Genesis makes clear that all depends on God's merciful choice, not on human behavior, structures, or preferences. Implied in Paul's argument is that all that would be necessary for God's promise to Abraham and his descendants to be fulfilled would be that some

Jews believed in Christ. "Provided *some* Jews find seats in the pews of the church, God's promise is not called in question by the conspicuous absence of their compatriots."[13] This was Paul's first reason.

The second reason that Paul offered in support of his claim that Jewish unbelief and Gentile belief do not undermine God's faithfulness to his promise to Abraham is that Gentiles as well as Jews are called by a merciful God (9:22-24). God has called "not from the Jews only but also from the Gentiles" (v. 24). Of course, the promise to Abraham included the Gentiles. Genesis 12:3 says that all the families of the earth will be blessed by Abraham; 18:18 asserts that all the nations of the earth shall bless themselves by Abraham; 22:18 repeats that by Abraham's descendants all the nations of the earth will bless themselves. Paul did not quote these passages but he assumed them. It may at first sight be surprising that Paul did not quote these Genesis passages that are so directly relevant. Instead he quoted from Hosea. Verse 25 cites Hosea 2:25 and v. 26 quotes Hosea 2:1. The reason is Paul's use of the key word "call." In v. 24 he affirmed that God has "called" Jews and Gentiles. Now he cited Scripture that uses the key term to bolster his claim that Gentiles are called. Hosea 2:25 says: "Those who were not my people, I will *call* my people, and her who was not beloved I will *call* beloved" (9:25). Hosea 2:1 says: "they shall be *called* children of the living God" (9:26). Gentile inclusion in God's people, then, does not make void God's promise; it fulfills it.

Scripture is used in the same way to bolster Paul's claim that God has called some Jews as well. In 9:27 he cited Isaiah 10:22: "only a remnant of them (the children of Israel) will be saved." [Remnant]

Remnant

AΩ In the Old Testament, remnant refers to a small segment of a community that survives a crisis. For example:
- Noah and his family were a remnant that survived the flood (Sir 44:17).
- Joseph enabled a remnant from his family to survive the famine (Gen 45:7).
- Survivors of war are called a remnant (2 Kgs 19:30-31).
- Those who return from exile are a remnant (Isa 10:22).

In the Dead Sea Scrolls, the Qumran Covenanters call themselves a remnant (e.g., 1 QH 6:7-8), meaning thereby that they are the faithful survivors among God's people.

The only explicit language in the New Testament that refers to the remnant theme is found in Rom 9:27 and 11:2-6.
- In Rom 11:5 the remnant is the faithful few of the Jews whom God has kept, chosen by grace (analogous to the 7,000 who had not bowed the knee to Baal in Elijah's time). In Rom 9:27 the remnant is the few, called by God from the Jews, who escape God's judgment. So in Romans the remnant is composed of Jews like Paul who have accepted the gospel. The church as a whole was never called remnant by Paul.
- In Romans the remnant is a temporary phenomenon, to be superseded when God's work is complete. It is a provisional measure, not a final eschatological reality. (Watts) When all Israel is saved, the remnant will disappear.

James W. Watts, "The Remnant Theme: A Survey of New Testament Research, 1921–1987," PRS 15 (1988): 109-29.

Abraham Representing Paradise

In Abraham, all the families of the earth shall be blessed (Gen 12:3).

Master Berthold Sacramentary. *Abraham Representing Paradise*. Page from a missal. Abbey of Weingarten, Germany. c. 1200–1232. M.710, f.123. The Pierpont Morgan Library. New York, NY. (Credit: The Pierpont Morgan Library/Art Resource, NY)

Verse 28 conflates Isaiah 10:23 and 28:22b. Verse 29 quotes Isaiah 1:9. The burden of these quotations is that the Scriptures testify that Israel would fare as Sodom and Gomorrah of old, except for a remnant. The assertion that Gentiles as well as Jews have been called by God was Paul's second reason why God's promises to Abraham have not failed but have been fulfilled.

Looking back from the conclusion of the argument to an earlier piece of it (9:14-18, 19-21) enables one to read the difficult prior piece better. Verses 14-18 are a first question raised about the legitimacy of God's choosing some and not others. Verses 19-21 are a second. In both of these little paragraphs Paul addressed ethnic Jewish complaints about God's not making ethnicity the criterion for inclusion in His saving purposes. It is critical for an accurate reading of these two little units that one remember that Jacob and Esau, mentioned earlier, represent believing and unbelieving Israelites! Likewise, it is crucial that one perceive that Pharaoh here illustrates God's dealing with unbelieving Israelites!

In both small units Paul dismissed the complaint with a wave of the hand. In the first, the apostle said that God is free to act in accord with mercy. That may be to choose some and not others; it may be to use even the hardened opponents for God's saving purposes. So Pharaoh's obstinancy was used by God in the deliverance of the Hebrew slaves from their bondage. If one is reading from the end of Romans 9–11, then one knows that those with hardened hearts (= unbelieving Jews) do not remain that way but are changed by God's mercy after they serve their purpose in the plan of salvation (11:12,14-15, 23-24, 26, 31-32). The word about Pharaoh, then, is not about predestination to damnation! It is about how a hardening can ultimately serve a wider, salvific purpose.

In the second instance, Paul said that human beings have no more right to argue with God about His purposes than a pot does to challenge the potter (cf. Isa 29:16; 45:9; Sir 33:13; Wis 15:7). A creature cannot really ask God to account for His ways. "The Creator as Creator has the right to proceed in a way totally unaccountable to human beings."[14] Paul in these two paragraphs was not so much attempting to argue the question of theodicy as simply rejecting it. Nor was Paul in these vv. arguing for double predestination, if one reads chapter 9 in light of chapter 11.

Romans 9:30–10:21, "B" in the pattern, shifts the focus from a consideration of Jewish unbelief from the point of view of God's promises (9:6-29) to a treatment of the issue from the perspective of human response. What then are we to say about Gentile attainment of righteousness and Jewish stumbling (9:30-31)? The argument follows a simple "what + why" sequence. In 9:30–10:4 Paul offered the "what": Israel pursued righteousness in the wrong way. In 10:5-21 he presented the "why": not because the news about God's way was inaccessible or too hard (10:5-13), nor because Israel had not heard or understood (19:14-15, 17-20), but because Israel has been disobedient and contrary (10:16, 21). Let us begin with the "what."

In 9:30–10:4 Paul stated that Israel did not attain righteousness (= faithfulness to the relation to God) because they went about it in the wrong way. "They have a zeal for God (Num 25:10-13; Sir 48:2; 1 Macc 2:19-26; 1 QS 4:4), but it is not enlightened" (10:2). Several statements clarify why the way was wrong. Israel strove "for the righteousness that is based on the law" (9:31). They sought righteousness "as if it were based on works" (9:32). "Seeking to establish their own (righteousness), they have not submitted to God's righteousness" (10:3). In 9:11-12 Paul had already indicated that being within God's salvific purposes does not depend on human effort: "not by works but by His call." The right way to a faithful relation to God (= righteousness) is "through faith (*ek pisteōs*)" (9:30), "on the basis of faith (*ek pisteōs*)" (9:32), through "believing" (10:4), through submission to "God's righteousness" (10:3). Christ is the faithful one in whom human faith is to be placed, but Israel has not done this. A quotation from a combination of Isaiah 28:16 and 8:14 in Romans 9:33 shows Israel's plight and the Gentiles' success (cf. 1 Pet 2:6-8; Matt 21:42; Luke 20:17; Eph 2:20). Christ has become a stumbling stone to Israel.

> See, I am laying in Zion a stone that will make people stumble,
> a rock that will make them fall (v. 33a).

Jewish Expectations about Gentiles in the Endtime

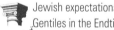 Jewish expectations about the destiny of Gentiles in the Endtimes varied greatly.

- Some believed that the Gentiles would be destroyed at the End (e.g., *Jub* 15:26; 22:20-22; the War Scroll from Qumran [1 QM]; *t. Sanh* 13.2—Rabbi Eliezer).
- Others believed that some Gentiles would share in the Age to Come
  - either because they had become proselytes in this Age (e.g., *2 Bar* 41:1-6; CD 14.4-5),
  - or they were righteous Gentiles who had kept the law without belonging to Israel as proselytes (e.g., Rom 2:1416; *t. Sanh* 13.2—Rabbi Joshua),
  - or because they would be among the Gentiles drawn to Israel's God in the Endtimes when God exalted Israel (e.g., Isa 2:2-4; Tob 14:5-7; *Pss Sol* 17:30-31).

But for the Gentiles who have faith, Christ is their hope: "And whoever believes in him (Christ) will not be put to shame" (9:33b). [Jewish Expectations about Gentiles in the Endtime]

What is at issue here? Throughout Romans 9–11 are several contrasts: between grace and works (11:5-6); between election/call and works (9:11); between a righteousness from God and their own righteousness (10:3); and between a righteousness through faith and a righteousness based on law (9:30-31). The first three of these are contrasts between God's initiative and enablement on the one hand and human initiative and enablement on the other. This should surely control how one reads the fourth. It is not a contrast between human faith and human works but rather between Christ (in whom trust is put) and law. Further, it is not law as a sign of ethnic superiority but law as a vehicle of human striving that absolutizes the human ability to be faithful to God. Shreiner has observed, "The Jews who had heard the gospel and rejected it focused on achieving instead of believing."[15] From Paul's point of view, the problem of unbelieving Israel was legalism/synergism. It was this attempt to gain righteousness by works that led to Israel's not believing in Christ.

That this is the wrong way to have a faithful relation to God is made clear in 10:4. "Christ is the *telos* (= end, so NRSV) of the law so that there may be righteousness for everyone who believes." The Greek term *telos* has been translated as either termination (NEB, TEV, Centenary, Moffatt, Phillips) or goal (Weymouth, NJB). In the history of Christian thought, this division goes back to the earliest Fathers. On the one hand, many have understood *telos* to mean that Christ is the fulfillment of the law. Athanasius, *Letter XIV*, referred to Romans 10:4. Immediately before quoting the verse, he stated that Christ came to earth not to abolish the law but to establish it (echoing Matt 5:17). Immediately after quoting 10:4, he cited Romans 3:31. In the context of Matthew 5:17 and Romans 3:31, Romans 10:4 could not be read other than as Christ's establishing/fulfilling the law. Erasmus in his *Annotations on Romans*, argued that Christ is the consummation and perfection, not the destruction, of the law. Many modern scholars have followed suit.[16] On the other hand, others have taken *telos* to mean termination. The Jewish scholar H. J. Schoeps contended that, for Paul, now that the Messiah has come, the Mosaic Law is no longer valid.[17] The German Lutheran Hans Conzelmann argued that, for Paul, since the death of Christ, the law has come to an end as a way of salvation, even though its moral demands are still in force.[18] Still others scholars see Christ both as the fulfillment of the law and as its termination. F.F. Bruce is typical.[19] He said Christ both embodies the righteousness prescribed by the law and terminates the law as a way of acquiring righteousness. Scholars are obviously divided. In support of termination, appeal is made to passages like Romans 7:6, Galatians 2:19; 3:25; 4:1-7; 2 Corinthians 3:7-11,13-14. In support of goal, attention is called to texts like Romans 3:31 and 13:10. How is the dilemma to be resolved?

If law in Romans 10:4 is understood to mean the Sinai covenant, just as promise is often used by Paul to mean the Abrahamic covenant, then progress can be made. When Paul thought about ways of relating to God, he thought in terms of covenants in the Jewish Scriptures. The covenant with Abraham was a paradigm for him of a relation to God based on God's promises/grace. The Mosaic covenant was a paradigm for him of a relation to God based on human performance/works (= law whose purpose was righteousness). When Paul said Christ was the end of the law, he meant that the Mosaic covenant of obligation and performance had been terminated by God's acts in Christ. The Sinai covenant is demoted from being the high point in salvation history to serving only an interim between Abraham and Christ (5:20). Christ is the fulfillment of the Abrahamic covenant. This covenant can be referred to by terms like "promise" and "faith." So in Romans 9:30–10:4 when Paul contrasted works and faith, he was contrasting a relation to God based on human performance (Mosaic covenant = law) and one based on God's promises/faith (Abrahamic covenant = grace).

When Paul in 10:3 contrasted a righteousness from God (cf. Phil 3:9) with Israel's own righteousness, he was implying a new covenant paradigm in which God accepts responsibility for enabling human faithfulness (cf. 7:6) over against a Mosaic covenantal paradigm in which humans can be faithful to God out of human resources (like gratitude for past acts of kindness). Again, Christ is the end of a Mosaic paradigm in which human abilities are assumed.

This did not mean for Paul that material in the Jewish Scriptures was no longer relevant for Christians. Quite the contrary, passed through the Christian sieve or filter (= Christ), the Scriptures became a part of the law of Christ. They functioned, however, not as a means of gaining righteousness (= faithfulness in the relation to God) but as "a way of going to the land that God would show and would make possible through the Spirit." For Paul, Christ was the end of paradigms of relating to God that were legalistic or synergistic and that depended on human moral resources to achieve faithfulness to God.

Why did Israel pursue righteousness (= faithfulness to God) in the wrong way? Romans 10:5-21 gives Paul's answer to this question in a "not-but" form. When Israel pursued righteousness wrongly, it was first of all not because the news about God's way was inaccessible or too hard (10:5-13). The righteousness that comes from the law may, of course, be too difficult. After all, it requires human performance (10:5; Lev 18:5). The righteousness that comes by faith, however, is not too difficult. In vv. 6-13 Paul used Deuteronomy 30:11-14 to make his case. Originally, this passage was used to contend that the law was accessible. Israel knew the law and could do it. It was not too hard and not too far off. It was used later by Baruch 3:29-30 and Philo (*Posterity of Cain* 84-85) to make the same point. Paul used it in vv. 6 (Deut 30:11) and 8 (Deut 30:14) to argue that the righteousness by faith is accessible

Believing and Confessing

The "Roman Road" is a method of evangelism in which one walks through five passages of Romans to demonstrate a person's need of salvation and how to obtain it. The Scriptures used in order are 3:23; 6:23; 5:8; 10:9-10; and 10:13. The fourth, 10:9-10, is often used in a way that makes faith seem mechanical. How should these verses be read?

- The language "confess" and "believe" is derived from the OT quotation in 10:8. Deut 30:14 says: "The word is near you, in your mouth and in your heart." Paul's interpretation runs: This quotation means "the word of faith which we are preaching."
- In Rom 10:9, *hoti* should probably be translated "that." If so, then it refers to the word of faith being preached. So the preaching asks that one confess with the mouth and believe with the heart. These are not separate acts; they are two parts of one act: the outer and the inner. Hence what is asked for is a response of the total self. This response is to Jesus as resurrected Lord. The result is righteousness and salvation. Again, these are not two separate matters but two ways of speaking about one reality: ultimate redemption.

Viewed in this way, Rom 10:9-10 fits into the overall Pauline way of understanding the human response to Jesus. It is a relational, not a mechanical or a magical, response, one involving the whole person, inner and outer. It is directed to the risen Jesus who rules from heaven (1 Cor 15:24-28) and in the human heart (Gal 2:19-20) as Lord. Since Paul nowhere else viewed salvation as a legal transaction, neither should this material be interpreted in that way. Since Paul elsewhere viewed salvation as not only a beginning (Eph 2:5, 8) and a consummation (Rom 5:9-10) but also as a process (1 Cor 1:18; 2 Cor 2:15), this text should not be read in a way that eliminates the totality of the apostle's understanding of salvation.

---

and possible. It is unnecessary to search for Christ because the word is near you, has been heard by you, and you are able to believe it. What is required as a response is possible. "If you confess with your lips that Jesus is Lord and believe in your heart that God raised him from the dead, you will be saved" (10:9). "For one believes with the heart and so is justified, and one confesses with the mouth and so is saved" (10:10). [Believing and Confessing]This is supported by Scripture: "No one who believes in him (Christ) will be put to shame" (10:11; quoting Isa 28:16). The emphasis is on "no one." The basis for God's promise follows: "For there is no distinction between Jew and Greek; the same Lord . . . is generous to all who call on him" (10:12). This too is supported from Scripture: "Everyone who calls on the name of the Lord (Christ) shall be saved" (10:13, quoting Joel 3:5). The bottom line: the gospel of Jesus is accessible (v. 8); what is expected in response is possible (vv. 9-10); its benefits are available to all, Jew and Gentile alike, who call on the Messiah (v. 12-13). If, therefore, Israel has pursued righteousness in a wrong way, it is not because news about God's way was inaccessible, too hard, or unavailable.

Romans 10:14-21 explains that Israel's pursuit for righteousness in the wrong way was, in the second place, not due to their failure to hear and understand God's way. Two small units present the case: vv. 14-16 and vv. 17-21. The first unit has two components: what is necessary in order to believe + a disobedient response. Verses 14-15 present what is necessary to believe in terms of four rhetorical questions, each with the implied answer: they cannot.

> How are they to call on one in whom they have not believed?
> How are they to believe in one of whom they have never heard?
> How are they to hear without someone to proclaim him?
> How are they to proclaim him unless they are sent? (Isa 52:17 offers support.)

This, however, has happened! Preachers have been sent; they have made proclamation; they have been heard. Now the hearers must call upon the Lord (Christ). Verse 16 presents the problematic response of Israel. Isaiah 53:1 asks: "Lord, who has believed our message?" Not all have obeyed the good news (v. 16a).

The second small unit (vv. 17-21) has the same two components as the first. Verse 17 tells what is necessary for faith to be born. "Faith comes from what is heard, and what is heard comes through the word about Christ." This has happened. The gospel has been proclaimed and has been heard. Verse 18 asks and then answers: "Have they not heard? Indeed they have." A quotation from Psalm 19:4 supports the assertion. Verse 19a asks: "Did Israel not under-stand?" Verse 21 answers: "All day long I have held out my hands to a disobedience and contrary people" (quoting Isa 65:2). Israel's disobedience is in contrast to Gentile inclusion (v. 20, quoting Isa 65:1), a fact that will be used to make Israel jealous (v. 19b, quoting Deut 32:21). Why has Israel sought righteousness the wrong way? It has not been due to any flaw in the gospel or to any deficiency in its presentation. Israel has not believed because she is a disobedient and contrary people (v. 21).

The line of Paul's argument in chapters 9–11 so far runs like this. Some Jews (a remnant) and some Gentiles have believed the gospel. Not all, however, have obeyed the message (10:16). Why has a large segment of ethnic Israel disbelieved Christ? Chapter 9 has said that Israel's misstep is within the plan of God based on election. Chapter 10 has said that Israel's disobedience actually rests not with God but with Israel herself. For Paul, divine sovereignty and human responsibility were complementary, not contradictory, real-ities. In wrestling with Israel's unbelief here, as in his dealings with predestination and perseverance in chapter 8, Paul's position affirmed the two (logically opposed) relational realities at the same time. In so doing, Paul shared a biblical perspective. For example, if one looks in Acts for explanations of the death of Jesus, the same polarity is present. Jesus was betrayed by a people who had always opposed God's servants (Acts 7:51-52); he was executed by lawless soldiers (2:23); the soldiers acted on behalf of two kings who opposed God (4:25-27). Yet, the predetermined plan of God was being accomplished (2:23; 4:26-28). This paradox can only be resolved if one goes back to the experiential roots of both assertions. Then one sees that both are true and at the same time. The paradox can never be resolved logically. To attempt to do so always results in one pole's swallowing the other. It is best to allow Paul's two assertions to stand side by side and to refuse to allow either to displace the other. "This tension between determinism and voluntarism, between divine initiative and human response, is finally truer to religious experience than is either one alone."[20]

Romans 11:1-32, "A'" in the pattern, falls into two parts that make two points. First, 11:1-10 deals with the question: "Has God rejected His people" (11:1a)? The answer is NO, because Israel's unbelief is partial. There is a remnant that has rightly obtained righteousness. The argument unfolds in three steps. Paul's situation was an initial evidence of a believing remnant. "I myself am an Israelite, a descendant of Abraham, a member of the tribe of Benjamin" (v. 1b). Paul was an example of Jews who had believed in Christ. The current situation, moreover, is analogous to the time of Elijah when there was a remnant chosen by grace (vv. 2-6). At the same time that this second evidence is offered, the apostle made it clear that any remnant then, as now, is due to grace. "But if it is by grace, it is no longer on the basis of works" (v. 6; remember 9:11-12; 10:3). Finally, Scripture confirms the division between the elect and the rest. "The elect obtained it, but the rest were hardened" (v. 7b), as a conflation of Deuteronomy 29:3, Isaiah 29:10, and as Psalm 69:23-24 shows in vv. 8-10. The bottom line is that God has not rejected His people, Israel, because Israel's unbelief is partial. An elect remnant has believed.

Second, Romans 11:11-32 deals with the question: "Have they stumbled so as to fall" (11:11a)? The question is a logical one given the quotation from Psalm 69:23-24 in v. 10: "let their eyes be darkened . . . and keep their backs *forever* bent." Does this scriptural "forever" mean Israel's stumbling results in her falling? Origen, in his *Commentary on the Epistle to Romans* observed: "Note that Paul distinguishes between stumbling and sinning on the one hand and falling on the other. For he envisages a cure for stumbling and sinning but not for falling."[21] Has Israel fallen? Paul's answer was NO, because Israel's unbelief is only temporary. The argument here unfolds in three stages.

The first stage involves two statements of principle (11:11-12; 11:13-15) that are roughly equivalent in meaning that set up a scheme of salvation history involving three periods. (1) Jewish unbelief led to the inclusion of the Gentiles (vv. 12, 15). (2) Gentile belief will lead to the inclusion of the Jews (vv. 12, 15). (3) Jewish belief will lead to even greater blessings (vv. 12, 15). Twice Paul spoke hopefully of the time of Jewish belief. First, "if their (unbelieving Jews') defeat means riches for Gentiles, how much more will their full inclusion mean" (v 12b)! Second, "if their rejection is the reconciliation of the world, what will their acceptance be but life from the dead" (v. 15)! The first seems to say that Jewish belief will lead to even greater blessings upon Gentiles than they have already derived from Jewish unbelief. The second describes that greater benefit as "life from the dead." Although some interpreters have taken this to be symbolic of an unprecedented success of the gospel in the world among Gentiles, it sounds more like the Jewish and early Christian belief that Israel's conversion would precipitate the coming of the End of the World. If so, then perhaps the first blessing, that upon the Gentiles, can be understood. There was a Jewish belief that Gentiles would not be allowed to repent when the Messiah came at the end of history. Rabbi Jose (a 2d-century rabbi) said: "In the time to come, idol worshippers will come and offer themselves as proselytes. But will such be accepted? Has it not been taught that in the days of the Messiah proselytes will not be received" (*b. Aboda Zarah* 3b)? If such a belief existed as early as Paul's time, it may be that he contradicted it with the claim that Israel's repentance, which will precipitate the End, will instead open up even greater opportunities for the conversion of Gentiles. Or perhaps, more likely, the preferable reading is that the greater blessing experienced by the Gentiles is simply the glory of the Age to Come.

A number of rabbinic traditions ascribed to the Tannaitic period spoke of the hope that Israel's repentance would usher in the Age to Come (*b. Sanh* 97b—Eliezer b. Hyrcanus, AD 90–120; *b. Sabb* 118b—Simeon b. Yohai, AD 140–160; *b. B Bat* 10a—R. Judah, AD 170–200; *Sifre Deut* 4 [79b], Tannaitic). That the notion was present at the end of the first century AD is evidenced by 4 Ezra 4:35-43's rejection of the idea. The *Testaments of the Twelve Patriarchs* know the tradition (*T. Sim* 6:2-7—"If you divest yourselves of . . . every hardness of heart . . . then the whole earth shall be at rest from trouble. and everything under heaven shall be free from war"; *T. Jud* 23:5; *T. Dan* 6:4—"the enemy is eager to trip up all who call on the Lord, because he knows that on the day in which Israel trusts, the enemy's kingdom will be brought to an end"; *T. Benj* 10:11—"If you therefore, my children, walk in holiness according to the commandments of the Lord, you shall dwell securely with me, and all Israel will be gathered unto the Lord."). Philo, *On Rewards and Punishments* 162-69, in his own way reflected this belief early in the first century. When Israel repents, he said, a miraculous change will occur. The scattered peoples will be allowed their freedom; they will rise up and hasten all to one place, guided by a vision known only to the saved; and the eschatological hopes will be fulfilled (e.g., the desert will become fertile). Acts 3:19-20 seems to reflect the tradition. "Repent therefore, and turn to God so that your sins may be wiped out, so that times of refreshing may come from the presence of the Lord and that He may send the Messiah appointed for you, that is, Jesus, who must remain in heaven until the time of the universal restoration that God announced long ago through His holy prophets." It also appears in the double tradition, Matthew 23:39//Luke 13:35b. The Lukan version runs: "I tell you, you will not see me until the time comes when you say, 'Blessed is the one who comes in the name of the Lord'." Matthew's version makes it explicit: "You will not see me again (= the parousia), until you say, 'Blessed is he who comes in the name of the Lord'." The Q tradition and Acts link the parousia to Israel's conversion to Christ. Depending on the translation of 2 Peter 3:11-12, the belief may appear yet again in a Christian source. "Since all these things are to be dissolved in this way, what sort of persons ought you to be in leading lives of holiness and godliness, waiting and *hastening* the coming of the day of God." *Second Clement* 12 also reflects the belief that when believers act in a certain way, then the Kingdom will appear. The belief manifests itself, then, in three forms: (1) when Israel acts properly/ethically, the End will come; (2) when the church acts properly/ethically, the End is hastened; and (3) when Israel believes in Christ, the End will come. Romans 11:15 appears to fit nicely into form (3) of the general belief. Paul and Q, then, would represent two very early Christian sources holding the conviction that Israel's conversion to Christ will lead to the parousia and the ultimate victory over death.

The second stage of Paul's contention that Israel's unbelief is only temporary comes in 11:16-24, the illustration of the olive tree (= an emblem of Israel—Jer 11:16; Hos 14:5-6). Verse 16 reflects Paul's assumption that Israel's origins in Abraham have to count for something. "If the part of the dough offered as first fruits (Abraham) is holy (= set apart for God), then the whole batch

Grafting and Planting Trees
Illustration based on a 16th-century manuscript printed by William Copland in London.

(Israel) is holy; and if the root (Abraham) is holy, then the branches (Israel) also are holy" (cf. 1 Cor 7:14). That in no way denies that "some of the branches were broken off" (= unbelieving Jews; v. 17a). Given the schema in salvation history previously described, however, one should not be surprised to hear Paul saying the purpose of Israel's unbelief was to benefit Gentiles. "You, a wild olive shoot, were grafted in their place to share the rich root of the olive tree" (v. 17b). Columella, a contemporary of Paul, knew a mode of grafting "a green slip taken from a wild olive tree" and putting it tightly into a hole made in an old olive tree (*De re rustica* 5.9.16). Gentiles came to share in the Abrahamic root as a result of Jewish unbelief. Since the Jewish root supports the Gentile branches, however, there should be no boasting on the part of the Gentiles (v. 18).

A diatribe form follows.[22] A Gentile will say: "Branches were broken off so that I might be grafted in" (v. 19). The implication is that Gentiles replace Jews. A sense of the historical situation in Rome enables one to appreciate this question and its implication. Remember, the earliest church in Rome had been a Jewish Christian one. The only Gentiles in it had come out of the synagogues. When Claudius expelled the Jews and Jewish Christians from the city in AD 49, the church then became exclusively Gentile.

It then included many who had not come out of the synagogues. These Gentiles would have held many of the common Roman prejudices about Jews in general. After Claudius's death when Jewish Christians returned to the city, they found themselves a minority in a predominantly Gentile church that had little sympathy with Judaism. One manifestation of this new situation was that Gentile Christians made claims to the effect that Gentile belief and Jewish unbelief meant that Gentiles had replaced Jews in God's salvific plan.

To which Paul responded: "They (the unbelieving Jews) were broken off because of their unbelief, but you stand only through faith. So do not be proud . . . For if God did not spare the natural branches, perhaps He will not spare you" (v. 20). If one's inclusion or exclusion depends on one's faith in Christ or lack thereof, then Gentiles cannot be arrogant and Jews cannot be robbed of hope. "Even those of Israel, if they do not persist in unbelief, will be grafted in, for God has the power to graft them in again" (v. 23). In fact, it would be easier to graft natural branches in again than it was to graft in wild ones (v. 24). The point: Gentile pride is out of place. Gentiles belong to Abraham's heirs only through faith. They remain grafted in only through faith. There is no special privilege for Gentiles. Likewise, Jews are excluded only because of lack of faith. They will not remain broken off branches if they do not persist in their unbelief. There is no special disadvantage in being Jewish; on the contrary, given their future faith it would be easy to graft them back in again. Here again there is the schema in salvation history encountered earlier: Jewish unbelief>Gentile belief>Jewish belief. The impact of this illustration using the olive tree is that in salvation history there is room neither for complacency (vv. 20-21) nor despair (v. 23). As Chrysostom observed: "None of these things is immutable, neither your good nor their evil" (*Homilies on Romans* 19).[23]

The third stage of Paul's argument that Jewish unbelief is not permanent comes in 11:25-32 in the form of an explanation of a mystery. In Jewish apocalyptic, "mystery" had the sense of something revealed about what will be in God's governance of His creation (e.g., Dan 2:19, 27-30; *1 Enoch* 103:2-4; *2 Bar* 81:4; *T. Levi* 2:10-11; 1 QS 4:18; 9:18). In Pauline and Deuteropauline writings "mystery" carries a similar meaning (e.g., Rom 16:25—the revelation of the mystery = to bring faith to the Gentiles; 1 Cor 15:51—we will not all die but we will all be changed at the parousia; Eph 1:9-10—to gather up all things in Christ; 6:19—the mystery of the gospel; Col 1:26-27—the mystery is Christ in you, the hope of glory; 2:2—Christ himself; 1 Tim 3:16—the mystery of our faith is Christ's incarnation and exaltation). Hence, when Paul said "I want you to understand this mystery," a reader would expect something about God's salvific plan. What it turns out to be is a repetition of the schema that recurred in various forms in chapter 11: a hardening of part of Israel> the full number of the Gentiles come in> all Israel will be saved (vv. 25-26).

Understanding the statement "and so all Israel will be saved" (11:26) involves the reader in three problems. The first concerns the two words translated in the NRSV by "and so" (*kai houtōs*). At least four options have been offered by scholars: (1) "In this way all Israel will be saved, namely, just as it is written, 'The redeemer will come from Zion.'"; (2) "As a consequence of events described in 11:11-25, all Israel will be saved"; (3) "In this manner, as described in vv. 11-25, all Israel will be saved"; (4) "And then, after the full number of Gentiles have come in, all Israel will be saved." Although the third has been the dominant view in modern times, recent evidence for the temporal use of *kai houtōs* (option 4) has made it the more probable.[24] The NEB rendering is to be preferred: "When that has happened" (referring to the full number of the Gentiles coming in) all Israel will be saved."

Second, what did Paul mean by "all Israel"? Four options have been proposed: (1) every Israelite/every living Jew; (2) the total of elect Jews who believe in Christ during the gospel era; (3) the church, that is, both the Jews and the Gentiles who follow Christ; (4) the corporate people of Israel in contrast to a remnant and in contrast to each individual Israelite. Given the context, it must mean ethnic Israel (option 4), with the rest (11:7) now joining the elect/remnant (11:5, 7). It is a corporate expression (e.g., *T. Benj* 10:11—"All Israel will be gathered to the Lord"). It does not, however, include every individual Israelite. When, for example, *m. Sanhedrin* 10:1-4 says, "All Israel will have a share in the world to come," this is said in the context of a lengthy list of individual Israelites who will not inherit the Age to Come. "All Israel" is the counterpart to "the full number of the Gentiles" (v. 25). The verse probably reflects the Jewish belief that before the final events of this age, the faithless Jews would be reunited with faithful Jews in preparation for the End. For example, 1 QSa 1:5-7 (= 1 Q28a) says that in the last days "all Israel" will join the sectarians of Qumran before the final war against the Gentiles. Paul's position, then, was that the Jewish people outside of Christ are temporarily wayward brethren destined to return to the house of their fathers.[25]

The third issue is when Paul thought these events would take place? Three options have been suggested. (1) Paul was envisaging here a steady flow of Jews into the church, by grace through faith, as a result of Israel's being made jealous by the inclusion of the Gentiles? Romans 11:13-14, taken alone, could be read in this way. After "the full number of the Gentiles has come in" (v. 25), however, sounds like the end of history (cf. Matt 24:14—"And this good news of the kingdom will be proclaimed throughout the world, as a testimony to all the nations; and then the end will come"). (2) A salvation event will occur in the events associated with the parousia. Verses 26-27 have been interpreted as a reference to the parousia, either of God or of Christ.

> Out of Zion will come the Deliverer;
> he will banish ungodliness from Jacob (Isa 59:20-21).
> And this is my covenant with them (Isa 59:21a)
> when I take away their sins (Isa 27:9).

If so, then all Israel is saved at the parousia. This, however, seems to fly in the face of other evidence in chapter 11. In 11:12 Paul said that the inclusion of unbelieving Israel would mean even more riches for believing Gentiles. In 11:15 he said that the acceptance of unbelieving Israel by God will result in "life from the dead." These two references point to an interval between all Israel's being saved and the End times. The former is the catalyst for the latter. If so, then the salvation of all Israel is not at the parousia but before it. In this case, the quotations in vv. 26-27 refer not to the parousia but to an earlier coming (e.g., if the coming of Jesus, then his first coming not his second). If so, then the covenant referred to (v. 27) would be the new covenant (Jer 31:31-34; Rom 7:6; 2 Cor 3:6), associated with Jesus' death (1 Cor 11:25; Luke 22:20) and with the forgiveness of sins (Matt 26:28).

(3) Salvation will occur in a future time, perhaps in a great event preceding the parousia. This conversion will result in the parousia. Two strands of evidence already presented in this section seem to render this the preferable option. First, 11:12, 15 point to an interval between Jewish inclusion and the End. Second, 11:15 echoes the belief that Israel's faithfulness would be a catalyst for the shift of the ages. If so, then Paul believed that after the full number of the Gentiles has come in, all Israel will be reunited. When this happens, the shift of the ages will take place.

How will all Israel be saved? Will the part of Israel that does not believe in Christ be saved by an act of God's mercy at the end of

Paul Preaches to the Jews

For Paul to fail to preach the gospel to unbelieving Jews would reflect Gentile pride and prejudice. "... do not boast over the branches. If you do boast, remember that it is not you that support the root, but the root that supports you" (Rom 11:18).

St. Paul Preaches in the Synagogue to the Jews. Byzantine. Mosaic. c. 1180. Duomo. Monreale, Italy. (Credit: Giraudon/Art Resource, NY)

history without accepting Jesus as Messiah? Or will unbelieving Israel be saved as the believing remnant and the Gentiles also are saved: by faith in the Christ? Again, context is determinative. Throughout Romans the apostle has been arguing that all are sinners and therefore that all are saved through the righteousness of God revealed in the faithfulness of Jesus and through their faith in Jesus. This way of salvation has been contrasted with another: righteousness through works of the law. Jewish legalism and synergism have been rejected repeatedly. Jewish ethnicity has been relativized over and over. The Mosaic covenant has been displaced by the Abrahamic and New Covenant. Given this weight of argument throughout the letter, how could the apostle have returned in chapter 11 to reinstate ethnicity, the Sinai covenant, and righteousness by some other means than Christ? It is inconceivable!

Hence, a right reading of the salvation of all Israel must be that, for Paul, all Israel is saved because all Israel comes to believe in Christ (11:23)—by whatever means. Christian preaching, Paul believed, has some effect (11:13-14). For Paul, to fail to preach the gospel to unbelieving Jews would reflect Gentile pride and prejudice (11:19); in modern terms, it would be antisemitic.[26] That Paul believed that the mass ingathering of unbelieving Jews to Christ at the end of history would be due solely to Christian preaching is unclear. Salvation history, as Paul saw it, is an extension of God's grace. Divine grace, as Paul observed it, is, moreover, full of surprises. Gentiles were elected to salvation when Jews were expecting to be special objects of God's favor. Jews will be grafted in again even though Gentiles may think they are superior to ethnic Israel. Saving grace seems to surprise its recipients! Perhaps, alongside Christian preaching God has some surprises yet in store for Gentiles and Jews about the way unbelieving Israel will be brought to faith in their Messiah. One thing is certain: God's mercy is for all, unbelieving Israel as well as Gentiles (11:30-32). (This does not contradict 1 Thessalonians 2:14-16, which does not claim that all Jews are forever excluded from salvation.)

Faced with such a mystery, Paul concluded with a hymn in praise of God's transcendent salvific plan (11:33-36; cf. Rev 4:11; 7:12; 15:3-4; 16:7). It is simply beyond our understanding. First come two exclamations in v. 33:

> O the depth of the riches and wisdom and knowledge of God!
> How unsearchable are his judgments and how inscrutable his ways!

Then come two rhetorical questions from Scripture that reinforce the previous point:

> Who has known the mind of the Lord? Or who has been His counselor? (Isa 40:13)
> (Implied answer: No one!)
> Who has given a gift to Him, to receive a gift in return? (Job 35:7; 41:11)
> (Implied answer: No one!)

Then comes a theological assertion of God's ultimate transcendence:

For from Him and through Him and to Him are all things.

Finally, a doxology concludes the hymn:

To Him be the glory forever. Amen.

Exactly how this hymn should be taken remains unclear. It must certainly be read as an expression of apostolic awe at God's transcendent salvific purpose. In so expressing himself, however, did Paul assume that he knew that transcendent purpose entirely and had set it out with certainty for others who do not know it? Or did the apostle stand in awe of God's transcendent purpose, of which he hoped he had grasped an inkling by projecting into the future a hope based on the way God had acted in the past? The issue is the level of certainty Paul felt about the concretes of his vision in 11:11-32. Either way, Paul's vision seems an appropriate inference from the observable surprising mercy of God manifest already in the history of salvation to date.

CONNECTIONS

Synergism in Sanctification?

It is not uncommon to hear Christians teachers say: Now that you have been saved by grace, you ought to do thus and so. Our acceptance of God's grace, we are told, obligates/commits us to living according to what may be called an ethic of gratitude. To Paul, this was synergism, the same synergism he rejected in ancient non-Christian Judaism. Why?

Paul believed not only that one enters into a relation with God by grace but that one continues in that relation by grace. If God enabled one's entry into the relationship, then God enables one's continuance in it. So it is a matter of grace from first to last. To speak in traditional terms: Paul did not believe justification is by grace and that sanctification is by works. Paul believed that justification (the beginning of the Christian life) is by grace and so is sanctification (the continuation of the Christian life). How so?

For the apostle, in the new covenant God takes responsibility for doing something inside the believer to enable the believer's faithfulness to the relationship. It is God who causes us "both to will and to work for His good pleasure" (Phil 2:13). It is not out of gratitude alone that the Christian lives but in submission to the leading and empowering of the God who indwells the believer. This is submitting to God's righteousness/faithfulness (Rom 10:3).

Jewish-Christian Relations

Any reading of Romans 9–11 in the period after the Holocaust must be sensitive to issues raised by a long history of Christian mistreatment of Jews.[27] One attempting a reading of these chapters in a way that is faithful to the text walks a razor's edge between making an apology to Jewish people because of past Christian culpability on the one hand and offering an apologetics for Christian positions that cannot be surrendered without a religious tradition's committing spiritual suicide on the other. Fortunately, there are two aids in the task: a proper view of Middle Judaism that answers many misconceptions and a Baptist distinctive that offers light at the end of the tunnel. Repentant of past Christian sins against Jewish people, we proceed.

Perhaps the most helpful thing that can be done before attempting a question and answer sequence is to describe as accurately as possible ancient Judaism of the period with which we are concerned. I speak of Middle Judaism, ancient Judaism of the period 300 BC to AD 200.[28] Formerly the model used to think about the relations of Jews and Christians was that of mother Judaism and daughter Christianity. Now it is recognized that the two groups must be seen as siblings springing from one mother.[29] "We need to speak of a twin birth of Christianity and rabbinic Judaism as two forms of Judaism, and not of a genealogy in which one—Judaism—is parent of the other—Christianity."[30] The church and the Rabbis arose more or less together "out of the old biblical religion of ancient Israel after the crises that attended the people of Israel in the first century."[31] In the first century the Pharisees and the Christian messianic Jews were only two of many Judaisms of their time. As a result of the great anti-Roman revolts of the late first and second centuries AD, most of the Middle Judaisms fell into oblivion, leaving these two survivors to become increasingly estranged and hostile, separating from one another. Each rewrote their common history after its own likeness and proclaimed itself the only legitimate heir of ancient Israel and her

Scriptures. Christian Judaism and Rabbinic Judaism matured into the two living religions that we know today. To say that one (Rabbinism) is a development from ancient Judaism while the other (Christianity) is a new religion is to rely unjustifiably on Rabbinism's revision of the common history. The answers given to the following questions must be heard in the context of this view of ancient Judaism.

First and foremost is the question: did Paul believe Jesus was the only way to salvation? Undoubtedly he did. He shared this belief with other early Christian messianic Jews (e.g., Matt 10:32-33; 28:18-20; Mark 8:38; Luke 12:8-9; John 14:6; Acts 4:11-12; Heb 9:26-28; 10:12-14; 1 Pet 2:4-8; 1 John 2:1-2; 2:23; Rev 5:2-10). Did this belief mean these Christian messianic Jews were anti-Judaic? Hardly. Rabbi Akiba in the early second century acclaimed Bar Cochba the Messiah and remained a faithful member of rabbinic Judaism (*j. Ta'anit* 68d).[32] Christian messianists such as Paul were Jews still. Did the relativizing of the Mosaic covenant mean they were anti-Judaic? No. Other Jews did not make Moses central to Jewish identity (e.g., *History of the Rechabites, 4 Bar, T. Abr, Ap Zeph*) and often looked to an alternate religious authority. Among the varieties of Middle Judaism, Paul's Christian messianic Judaism was but one more stream of ancient Judaism claiming to be the fulfillment of the promises made to ancient Israel. Such claims were no more anti-Judaic than were those of the Pharisees, Sadducees, or the Qumran covenanters.

Is Paul's claim that salvation comes exclusively through Christ and faith in him supercessionism? That is, was Paul replacing Judaism with Christianity? Two comments are in order. First, given the picture of ancient Judaism that must be assumed, Paul did not represent another religion. He was a Jew, a Christian messianic Jew but a Jew nevertheless. He was not arguing that Christianity is a new religion that replaces a decadent one, but that his Messianic Judaism represents true Judaism. His was an intra-Jewish struggle. To speak of this as supercessionism, therefore, makes no sense. Second, if the Christian messianic Jewish claim to be the true form of Judaism is supercessionist, then the Rabbinic claim to be the true form of Judaism must be as well. These are two siblings going different directions but each claiming to be the heir of ancient Israel's Scriptures and promises. What applies to one, applies to the other! If Paul's claim is supercessionistic, then Rabbinism's claim is also. Both survivors of the revolts came to see themselves as normative, not only the one.[33] Moreover, if rabbinic Judaism is not a direct descendant of the Pharisees but is only partially rooted in them,[34] then Christian messianic Judaism is the older brother (pre-AD 70) and rabbinism the younger (post-AD 70). If there is supercessionism, then it is the younger claiming to replace the elder as true Judaism. In the light of such data, arguments about supercessionism are not really helpful in the Jewish-Christian dialogue.

Can a religious group believe it is *the* religion and not be harmful to others? Several comments are in order. First, it is a fact that certain adherents of modern rabbinic Judaism, like ancient rabbinic Judaism, consider themselves as *the* religion. Orthodox rabbi Henry Siegman has written:

> As a believing Jew, I affirm that Judaism is the "truest" religion. That affirmation is part of what makes me a believing Jew, and I do not expect Christians to be offended by it. Conversely, I cannot be offended by parallel affirmations of faith made by Christians—or by Muslims, Hindus, or Buddhists, for that matter. To insist that Christians may not entertain such beliefs about their own faith is to cut the ground from under the Jewish position.[35]

Siegman has made the claim that rabbinic Judaism is *the* religion. Representatives of "Christian messianic Judaism" made and make the same claim for Christianity. The two sides make their claims in spite of the fact that they worship the same God, the God of Abraham, Isaac, and Jacob, of Moses and David (although they disagree at points about God's nature and name), and use some of the same scriptures (but often disagree on how to interpret the common parts). Do their claims to normativity endanger others?

There is certainly the potential for danger to others. For example, in ancient Judaism forced conversions of Gentiles was practiced. In Christian history in the West forced conversions of Jews was practiced. It is at this point that a Baptist contribution can be made. Baptists have stood for religious liberty, the freedom of conscience, and the separation of church and state. The intent of the last of these tenets has been to forswear the use of power in matters religious. In religious issues, Baptists have historically believed that persuasion must always be the only tool used. State power must never be employed for or against the conscience of any human being in the area of religion. If this rule is granted, then each religion's claim to normativity may be granted. Each religious community can maintain its theological integrity, even where this involves radical differences in its midrashim (= interpretations of scripture), and still agree on the necessity to guarantee all peoples their full civil liberties—including but not limited to, their religious freedom. If Christians (= a messianic form of Judaism) and

Jews (= rabbinic Judaism) today could agree on the principle of religious freedom, then there would be no danger for the one from the claims of the other.

The most sensitive issue in Jewish-Christian relations today is whether or not the church has a continuing mission to Israel. Types of answers from the Christian side include the following. (1) Krister Stendahl is representative of a number of scholars who hold that in Romans 9–11 Paul was taking essentially the same position as Franz Rosenzweig. There are two covenants. Israel and the church are to coexist in the plan of God with no proselytizing of the other on either side. Christian evangelism must be directed to the Gentiles.[36] (2) E. P. Sanders has rejected Stendahl's reading of Paul as inaccurate but indicates his disagreement with Paul and his personal agreement with Rosenzweig.[37] (3) Rosemary R. Ruether has asserted that the root of anti-Judaism is christology. She has affirmed that there is not one covenant, or even two, but actually many ways to the Father. There are as many ways as there are religions.[38] (4) A. Roy Eckhardt has said: "To keep the door of the church open is . . . an entirely opposite position from any program to seek out Jews for the purposes of conversion. . . . The closed door means antisemitism. But the missionary visitation to the Jews means the repudiation of God's election."[39] (4) H. Berkhof has argued that Paul said the duty of the church is to make Israel jealous (Rom 11:11, 14). This is a category different from both missions and ecumenical dialogue. It is not for Christians to convert Jews by our words but offer the demonstration of spirit and power.[40] (5) Karl Barth claimed that the church must first share with Israel through friendly dialogue the message it possesses. This is not missions because a mission is to those who worship a false God. The church must also secondly live authentically as a community of the God of Israel to attract Jews. Neither of these two approaches, however, will do more than convert a few individuals. The conversion of unbelieving Jews about which Paul spoke in Romans 11 will be the result of the Lord's return.[41] (6) Jacob Jocz has argued that for the church to reduce her high christology in order to accomodate the synagogue would spell dissolution for the church. The New Testament does not know two ways to salvation. If Christ is the one Messiah, then the church is obligated to preach the gospel to all humanity, including the Jews. But only a repenting church can be a missionary church. Furthermore, only individuals, not entire racial or ethnic groups, can experience salvation.[42] Does the Pauline text, as we have read it, offer some assistance in arbitrating among these options?

Paul told us that there was an early Christian mission to Israel associated with Peter (Gal 2:7-8). He also said he engaged in such an enterprise (1 Cor 9:20; cf. 2 Cor 3:15-16). In Romans 10:1 he wrote: "My heart's desire and prayer to God for them is that they may be saved." In 11:13-14 he stated: "Inasmuch then as I am an apostle to the Gentiles, I glorify my ministry in order to make my own people jealous, and thus to save some of them." That he attempted to do some of his evangelization in synagogues seems attested to by 2 Corinthians 11:24: "Five times I have received from the Jews the forty lashes minus one." This confirms the picture found in the later Acts of the Apostles to the effect that Paul approached the synagogue first on most occasions. These data prevent a reading of "making Israel jealous" solely in terms of Jesus' followers setting a good example so as to elicit a positive Jewish response to the gospel. There was some direct approach to the synagogue in early apostolic Christian messianic Judaism.

The issue of Christian evangelization of Jews is made more problematic by the fact that 75 percent of the world's fifteen million Jews no longer practice rabbinic Judaism. Most are secular Jews, some even atheists. Secular Jews are, moreover, assimilating into Gentile culture at such a rapid rate that the future existence of Judaism seems threatened. Given what happened in the holocaust and given the current threat due to assimilation, Christian evangelization efforts directed at Jewish people seem to many Jewish leaders as yet another form of genocide. Missiologists estimate that 130,000 to 150,000 Jews worldwide follow Jesus. About 5,000 Messianic Jews exist in Israel in about eighty congregations; about 110,000 in the United States in more than 100 congregations. These figures indicate that the possibility of Judaism's virtual disappearance in this century will not be due to conversions to a rival Christianity but to Jewish assimilation into the secular culture. Still, the sense of a threatened future makes the issue of a Christian mission to Israel a sensitive issue for Jewish religious leaders. It seems to threaten Jewish identity and survival. Consequently, some ask their Christian contemporaries to eschew evangelism directed to other religious traditions.

The problem is compounded by the fact that Christian identity is tied to the practice of evangelization of all peoples. The gospels portray Jesus as focusing his mission on Jews in Palestine prior to the resurrection (Matt 10:5-6; John 12:20-23); after the resurrection he is depicted as having a concern for the evangelization of Jews and Gentiles everywhere (Matt 28:19-20; Luke 24:45-47; Acts 1:8; John 21:10-11). The narrative of Acts sketches a

Christian messianic mission to Jews and Gentiles all over the Mediterranean world. The epistles in the New Testament assume such a mission. For Jesus and his earliest followers, evangelization of nonbelievers was integral to a Christian confession. For followers of Jesus, therefore, a request that they abstain from mission to non-believers is a demand for the sacrifice of something central to Christian identity. It would be the equivalent of rabbinic Judaism's being asked to sacrifice its ethnicity because it is off-putting to Gentiles. This is cannot be done because to do so would be to undermine the integrity of a given religious tradition. At this point, then, rabbinic Jews and Christians (= a form of messianic Judaism) will have to agree to disagree because neither has a choice in the matter. Again, the Baptist stance in favor of religious freedom with no power employed either for or against religious belief and practice must be our common defense. Such freedom will protect both Jewish ethnicity and Christian evangelization. The historical future of each form of religion will then rest on their powers of persuasion in the marketplace of ideas. Both sides have every right, however, to ask that displays of ethnicity and the practice of evangelization be done in ways that are the least offensive to the other sibling.

Nearly as sensitive as missionizing is the issue of the State of Israel (= the Land). Does the New Testament support Judaism's historic claim to the land? Some scholars say, Yes.[43] Some go so far as to contend that Christian failure to support the State of Israel is anti-Semitism.[44] Others are more cautious, saying that the New Testament is ambivalent about the land.[45] Still others contend that "Christians cannot and should not justify the existence of the present State of Israel on theological grounds. The argument must be made rather on moral, cultural, and political grounds."[46] Paul reinterpreted the land to mean the Age to Come (e.g., Rom 4:13; 8:17; Gal 3:14, 18, 29; 4:7). This eschatological reality is the inheritance promised to Abraham. Paul, therefore, would agree with the last mentioned modern stance. The State of Israel would not, in the apostle's mind, be connected to the promise of Israel's ultimate conversion. Modern Christians may, then, be supporters of the State of Israel for moral, cultural, and political reasons. They may also, for some of the same types of reasons, expect and insist on an even handed justice for all who live in Palestine.

NOTES

[1] Cited in Gerald Bray, *Romans* (Downers Grove IL: InterVarsity, 1998), 298.

[2] Vern Polythress, *Understanding Dispensationalists* (Grand Rapids: Zondervan, 1987); Larry V. Crutchfield, *Origins of Dispensationalism: the Darby Factor* (NY: University Press of America, 1992); Peter E. Prosser, *Dispensationalist Eschatology and Its Influence on American and British Religious Movements* (Lewiston: Edwin Mellen Press, 1999).

[3] Thomas R. Schreiner, *Romans* (Grand Rapids: Baker, 1998), 616, says: "Paul never envisioned a salvation for Israel apart from trusting in Jesus as Messiah." James D. G. Dunn, *Romans 9–16* (WBC; Dallas: Word, 1988), 282-83.

[4] Rosemary R. Ruether, *Faith and Fratricide: The Theological Roots of Anti-Semitism* (New York: Seabury, 1974); E. P. Sanders, *Paul and Palestinian Judaism* (Philadelphia: Fortress, 1977), 551, says: "Paul in fact explicitly denies that the Jewish covenant can be effective for salvation."

[5] Krister Stendahl, *Paul among Jews and Gentiles and Other Essays* (Philadelphia: Fortress, 1976). In his *Final Account: Paul's Letter to the Romans* (Minneapolis: Fortress, 1995), x, Stendahl denies that he proposes two ways to salvation. To try to outline the specifics of what Paul has in mind goes too far. It is a mystery (41).

[6] Lloyd Gaston, *Paul and the Torah* (Vancouver: University of British Columbia Press, 1987).

[7] John Gager, *The Origins of Anti-Semitism* (New York: Oxford University Press, 1983) and "Re-Inventing St. Paul: Was the Apostle to the Gentiles the Father of Christian Anti-Judaism?" in *A Multiform Heritage: Studies on Early Judaism and Christianity in Honor of Robert A. Kraft*, ed. B. G. Wright (Atlanta: Scholars, 1990), 49-63.

[8] Franz Mussner, *Tractate on the Jews: The Significance of Judaism for Christian Faith* (Philadelphia: Fortress, 1984).

[9] *A Critical and Exegetical Commentary on The Epistle to the Romans* (ICC; Edinburgh: T. & T. Clark, 1979), 2.447-48.

[10] Steven Fraade, "Sifre Deuteronomy 26 (ad Deut 3:32): How Conscious the Composition," *HUCA* 54 (1983): 301.

[11] Thomas R. Schreiner, *Romans*, 489.

[12] Cited in Gerald Bray, *Romans*, 252.

[13] Stephen Westerholm, *Preface to the Study of Paul* (Grand Rapids: Eerdmans, 1997), 103.

[14] Brendan Byrne, *Romans* (Collegeville: Liturgical Press, 1996), 298.

[15] Thomas R. Schreiner, *Romans*, 540.

[16] Robert Badenas, *Christ the End of the Law* (Sheffield: JSOT Press, 1985).

[17] H. J. Schoeps, *Paul: The Theology of the Apostle in the Light of Jewish Religious History* (Philadelphia: Westminster Press, 1961), 171.

[18] Hans Conzelmann, *An Outline of the Theology of the New Testament* (2d ed.; NY: Harper & Row, 1968), 224.

[19] F. F. Bruce, *The Letter of Paul to the Romans* (2d ed.; Grand Rapids: Eerdmans, 1985), 190.

[20] E. Elizabeth Johnson, "Romans 9–11: The Faithfulness and Impartiality of God," in *Pauline Theology, Volume III: Romans*, ed. D. M. Hay and E. E. Johnson (Minneapolis: Fortress, 1995), 246.

[21] Cited in Bray, *Romans*, 290.

[22] J. C. T. Havemann, "Cultivated Olive—Wild Olive: The Olive Tree Metaphor in Romans 11:16-24," *Neotestamentica* 31 (1997): 87-106.

[23] Cited in Bray, *Romans*, 295.

[24] Bruce Corley, "The Significance of Romans 9–11: A Study in Pauline Theology," (unpublished PhD dissertation, Southwestern Baptist Theological Seminary, 1975), 204-205; Peter W. van der Horst, "Only Then Will All Israel Be Saved: A Short Note on the Meaning of *kai houtos* in Romans 11:26," *JBL* 119 (2000): 523.

[25] Gregory Baum, *The Jews and the Gospel: A Re-examination of the New Testament* (London: Bloomsbury, 1961), 251.

[26] John Stott, *Romans: God's Good News for the World* (Downers Grove IL: InterVarsity, 1994), 305.

[27] In September, 2000, a large group of influential Jewish scholars and rabbis signed a theological statement calling on Jews to relinquish their fear and mistrust of Christianity and to acknowledge church efforts in the decades since the Holocaust to amend Christian teaching about Judaism. The statement, "Dabru Emet" (= speak truth), was signed by nearly 170 Jewish scholars and leaders from all four branches of Judaism. Perhaps the most significant item is the statement that "Nazism was not a Christian phenomenon." Nazism itself was not an inevitable outcome of Christianity. Had the Nazis succeeded in exterminating all Jews, Christians would have been the next targets.

[28] The name, Middle Judaism, comes from Gabriele Boccaccini's book *Middle Judaism: Jewish Thought 300 B.C.E. to 200 C.E.* (Minneapolis: Fortress, 1991).

[29] This is recognized not only by Boccaccini, a Christian, but also by Jewish scholars like Alan Segal in his *Rebecca's Children: Judaism and Christianity in the Roman World* (Cambridge: Harvard University Press, 1986) and *Paul the Convert* (New Haven: Yale University Press, 1990) and Daniel Boyarin, *Dying for God: Martyrdom and the Making of Christianity and Judaism* (Stanford: Stanford University Press, 1999).

[30] Boyarin, *Dying for God*, 2.

[31] Ibid., 3. Boyarin contends the not until the 4th century do we have independent Judaism and Christianity (6). Boccaccini holds that Christianity and Rabbinism became normative systems only from the 2d century AD. David Flusser, *Das Christentum: Eine jüdische Religion* (Munich: Kösel, 1990), argues that Christianity is a Jewish religion.

[32] A fact noted by Boyarin, *Dying for God*, 17, who says: "There is no reason, a priori, . . . why believing that Jesus was the Messiah would be considered as beyond the pale of rabbinic Judaism, any more than Rabbi Akiva's belief in Bar Kolchba as Messiah rendered him a heretic."

[33] Jon D. Levenson, *The Death and Resurrection of the Beloved Son* (New Haven: Yale University Press, 1993), see the two as rival midrashic systems, competing for their common biblical legacy. Both were supercessionistic.

[34] As Jacob Neusner and others have taught us to think.

[35] Henry Siegman, "Ten Years of Catholic-Jewish Relations: An Assessment," *Encounter Today* 11 (1976): 87-88.

[36] Krister Stendahl, *Paul among Jews and Gentiles* (Philadelphia: Fortress, 1976), 3-4.

[37] E. P. Sanders, "Paul's Attitude towards the Jewish People," *Union Seminary Quarterly Review* 33 (1978): 175-87.

[38] Rosemary R. Ruether, *Faith and Fratricide: The Theological Roots of Anti-Semitism* (New York: Seabury, 1974).

[39] A. Roy Eckhardt, *Elder and Younger Brothers: The Encounter of Jews and Christians* (New York: Charles Scribner's Sons, 1967), 157.

[40] H. Berkhof, "Israel as a Theological Problem in the Christian Church," *Journal of Ecumenical Studies* 6 (1969): 340.

[41] Karl Barth, *Church Dogmatics* (Edinburgh: T. & T. Clark, 1956, 1962), IV/1,671 and IV/3, 876-78.

[42] Jacob Jocz, *The Jewish People and Jesus Christ* (London: Eyre & Spottiswoode, 1961); *Christians and Jews* (London: SPCK, 1966); *The Jewish People and Jesus Christ after Auschwitz* (Grand Rapids: Baker, 1981).

[43] Walter Brueggemann, *The Land* (Philadelphia: Fortress, 1977).

[44] A. Roy Eckhardt, *Your People: The Meeting of Jews and Christians* (NY: Quadrangle, 1974), ch. 9.

[45] W. D. Davies, *The Gospel and the Land* (Berkeley: University of California Press, 1974).

[46] John T. Pawlikowski, *What Are They Saying about Christian-Jewish Relations?* (NY: Paulist, 1980), 110.

HOW SLAVES OF RIGHTEOUSNESS BEHAVE, PART ONE

12:1–13:14

In the unfolding argument of Romans, exhortation (12:1–15:13) now takes the place of theological teaching (1:16–11:36). "I appeal to you" (12:1) signals the shift in emphasis. The shift in emphasis, however, does not mean discontinuity in Paul's argument. In the theological section the apostle focused on the righteousness of God; in the parenetic section he will concentrate on what God's righteousness, of which believers are now instruments (6:11-23), looks like.

Romans 12:1–15:13 consists of two distinct sections: 12:1–13:14 and 14:1–15:13. The first deals with more general issues of Christian living; the latter is concerned with a particular issue that is agitating the Roman church. In this commentary these two sections of Paul's parenesis will be treated separately. This unit of commentary will focus on Romans 12:1–13:14; the next on Romans 14:1–15:13.

COMMENTARY

In both sections themes treated in Romans sound like teaching one encounters elsewhere in the Pauline corpus and/or elsewhere in the New Testament. For example,

- the renewing of the mind (Rom 12:1-2—Eph 4:23; cf. 1 Pet 1:14; 2:5)
- unity of the body of Christ + diversity of gifts (Rom 12:3-8—1 Cor 12:4-26; Eph 4:11-17; cf. 1 Pet 4:10)
- obedience to rulers + payment of taxes (Rom 13:1-7; cf. 1 Pet 2:13-17; Mark 12:13-17)
- love as the fulfillment of the law (Rom 13:8-10—Gal 5:13-15; Jas 2:8; Matt 22:34-40)
- spiritual wakefulness + day of the Lord (Rom 13:11-14—1 Thess 5:1-11; Mark 13:32-37)

• weak and strong + matter of food (Rom 14:15—1 Cor 8–10; Rev 2:14)

These parallels suggest that Paul was using traditional material in Romans 12–15. The tradition is, of course, adapted to the situation in Romans. That Paul would do this fits cultural expectations. Seneca wrote about the use of traditional ethical teaching:

> Assume that prescriptions have been handed down to us for the healing of the eyes; there is no need of my searching for others in addition; but for all that, these prescriptions must be adapted to the particular disease and to the particular stage of the disease.[1]

The Roman Stoic's directions about the use of traditional parenesis corresponds to the Pauline practice: use it and adapt it.

The organization and arrangement of Romans 12:1–13:14 has been a mystery to many. Commentators speak about the unsystematic character of this section, of not being able to find any principle of arrangement for the material. This is often coordinated with the claim that Paul here was not writing a treatise on ethics. While the latter is true, the former is not.

(1) Parenetic material in antiquity was sometimes arranged in terms of relationships in which humans live (e.g., Josephus, *Against Apion* 2.190-219—within the household [199-206]; within the community [207-208]; towards outsiders [209-213]; *Ps-Phocylides* 175-227—wife, father, sisters, infants, children, elderly, slaves). In Romans 12–13 one finds material that relates to life in the Christian community (12:3-13, 15-16), that concerns outsiders (12:18-21), and that provides guidance about the State (13:1-7).

(2) Parenetic material also oftentimes was linked by key words or phrases (e.g., Mark 9:42-50—v. 42 has "stumble" and "it would be better"; vv. 43-48 also have "stumble" and "it is better"; vv. 43-48 close with "fire"; v. 49 contains "fire"; v. 49 contains "salted"; v. 50a has "salt"; v. 50b has "salt"). In Romans 12–13 one finds such link words (e.g., "think" [*phronein*] in v. 3 and "zeal" [*spoudē*] in v. 8 link vv. 3-8 to vv. 9-21 in which one finds "zeal" [*spoudē*] in v. 11 and "thinking" [*phronountes*] in v. 16. Romans 12:1-2 has "the good" [*to agathon*], as do 12:9, 21 and 13:4. Romans 12:21 has "evil" [*kakon*], as do 13:4 and 13:10. Romans 13:7 has "due" [*opheilas*] and 13:8 "owe" [*opheilete*]. The material is thereby held together by link words as well as by relations in which humans are involved.

(3) Ancient parenetic material was, moreover, often arranged in concentric patterns (e.g., *Ps-Phocylides* 79-96—ABCDED'C'B'A';

9-21—ABCDEFE'D'C'B'A').[2] That 12:1–13:14 is framed by an introduction (12:1-2) and conclusion (13:11-14), both of which emphasize the genuinely eschatological existence of those exhorted, has long been recognized.[3] The pattern, however, can be developed further. The material, taken as a whole, looks in its arrangement like this:

A—12:1-2: Ethical implications of eschatological existence (behave, think)
  B—12:3-13: Genuine love
    C—12:14-21: Christian life and God's wrath (cf. 12:19)
    C'—13:1-7: Christian life and God's wrath (cf. 13:4)
  B'—13:8-10: Love one another
A'—13:11-14: Ethical implications of eschatological existence (think, behave).

In various ways Paul organized chapters 12 and 13 into a coherent whole. It is now time to examine each component.

Romans 12:1-2, "A," is the introduction to the entire parenetic part of the letter. It begins with: "I appeal to you therefore, brothers and sisters." The "therefore" links what follows to what has come before. "It is futile to give practical exhortation apart from the basis on which it rests or the spring from which compliance must flow."[4] In 1:16–11:36 Paul spoke about the righteousness of God that justifies sinners and fulfills the promises to Israel. On the basis of this activity of God, the apostle rested the ethical behavior of Christians. "Paul . . . does not know, and has also never approved, of a justification which does not introduce and lead to a life of righteousness."[5] Therefore, since God's righteousness has been revealed and Christians have received its benefits and are now slaves of God's righteousness, this is how they are to behave and think.

Such an expectation of right behavior on the part of God's people was, of course, characteristic of ancient Judaism generally. The Decalogue is a normative example ("I am the Lord your God who brought out of the land of Egypt, out of the house of slavery; you shall have no other gods before me," etc). Contrary to much modern opinion, it was also a part of some pagan devotion as well. Diodorus Siculus, speaking about the Great Mother of the gods, said:

Now the details of the initiatory rite are guarded . . . and are communicated to the initiates alone; but the fame has traveled wide of how these gods appear to mankind and bring unexpected aid to those initiates of theirs who call upon them in the midst of perils.

The claim is also made that men who have taken part in the mysteries become both more pious and more just and better in every respect than they were before.[6]

That this is not the sole exception is evidenced by Theophrastus, *On Piety*, extant in fragments attested by Porphyry (*De abstinentia*), who discussed the relationship between ethics and sacrifice (e.g., "One must go to the sacrifices having a soul pure from evils") and Porphyry, *De abstinentia*, who quoted an inscription at the entrance to the sanctuary at Epidauros: "Pure must one be when entering the temple. . . . But purity is thinking holy things." This is not to deny that in some pagan religion ethics were irrelevant, but not all pagan cultic religion was devoid of ethical concern. Certain pagans, as well as Jews, would then have heard Paul's call as a legitimate one. Receiving divine benefactions leads naturally to certain improved behavior.

The phrase with which Paul continued, "by the mercies of God," could modify either Paul's exhortation ("I appeal to you by the mercies of God," as the NRSV following UBS takes it. This is indicated by the comma that follows the phrase, separating it from the infinitive that follows. The phrase then has a causal meaning: I appeal to you because of the mercies of God) or the Romans' expected behavior ("by means of the mercies of God present your bodies as a sacrifice," as REB following Nestle takes it, as indicated by the absence of a comma between "mercies of God" and "present"—so instrumental: by means of God's mercies present your bodies as a sacrifice). For Paul, God's righteousness (= faithfulness) is communicated to humans through Christ/the Spirit who lives out his righteousness (= faithfulness) within and through believers.[7] In Romans 8:4 the apostle said that as a result of what God has done in Christ "the just requirement of the law might be fulfilled in us who walk . . . according to the Spirit." The law's demand for faithfulness in our relation to God is made possible because

Animal Sacrifice

An example of animal sacrifice is seen here in a representation of Mithras, for whom the blood of animals would be spilled in sacrifice. Roman worship of Mithras began sometime during the early Roman empire, perhaps during the late 1st century AD, and flourished from the 2d through the 4th centuries AD.

Mithras Immolating the Bull. Roman. Marble. c. 1000. Louvre. Paris, France.
(Credit: Erich Lessing/Art Resource, NY)

of the Spirit's indwelling believers. "For Paul the Christian story is a story . . . in which . . . the believer . . . (works) out what God has worked in."[8]

The "mercies of God," in Paul's thought, are experienced in believers' ongoing lives. For example, Philippians 2:1-2 consists of four bases and four injunctions. The injunctions are found in v. 2: (1) be of the same mind, (2) have the same love, (3) be in full accord, and (4) be of one mind. These are all calls for Christian unity. The bases come in an "if clause" that could be translated "since." The four bases are: since in your Christian experience with God (1) there is encouragement in Christ, (2) there is consolation from God's love, (3) there is a sharing in the Spirit, and (4) there is God's compassion and "mercies" (*oiktirmoi*). In Philippians 2:1-2, Christian behavior arises out of how God is relating to believers in their present experience (cf. Phil 2:12-13). One aspect of the divine relating is "mercies." Likewise in Romans 12:1, enabled by divine mercies, Christians are to present their bodies as a sacrifice to God. There is, then, in v. 1 both a remembrance of God's activity in the past as the basis of Paul's appeal (= therefore) and an enablement by God's activity in the present as the possibility of the readers' presentation of their bodies to God (= through the mercies of God).

Enabled by the mercies of God, Christians are to present their bodies (= selves) as a sacrifice—one that is living, holy, and pleasing to God—which is their rational (*logikēn*) worship (*latreian*). [A Living Sacrifice] Only such a structured sentence can capture Paul's point. How did Paul understand sacrifice and what did he mean by rational worship? In a reaction against the bloody sacrifices of animals, some Mediterranean peoples spoke about a sacrifice/worship of God that was appropriate to humans as beings endowed with reason.[9] (1) Some said it was speech offerings, like singing hymns to the deity (Epictetus 1.16, 20-21; 2.9.12—"I am *logikos* [rational] so I must praise God"; *Corpus Hermeticum* 1.31; 13.18— a *logikē thysia* (rational sacrifice) equals a speech offering, that is, hymns of thanksgiving and praise; cf. Pss 69:30-31 and 50:14, 23 where a song of thanksgiving replaces animal sacrifices; Heb 13:15—offer up a sacrifice of praise to God). (2) Others saw the rational, bloodless offering as prayer (Heliodorus, *Ethiopian* Story

---

A Living Sacrifice

John Stott asks: "What . . . is this living sacrifice, this rational, spiritual worship?" Then he answers in terms of where, what, and wherefore:

- It is not to be offered in the temple courts or in the church building, but rather in home life and in the marketplace.
- It is the presentation of our bodies to God.
- Then our feet will walk in His paths, our lips will speak the truth, . . . our hands will lift up those who have fallen, and perform many mundane tasks as well . . . ; our arms will embrace the lonely and unloved, our ears will listen to the cries of the distressed, and our eyes will look humbly and patiently towards God.

John Stott, *Romans: God's Good News for the World* (Downers Grove IL: InterVarsity Press, 1994), 321-22.

10.9—Ethiopian gymnosophists tell the king that they "wish it were possible to put an end to all animal sacrifice . . . and be satisfied with offerings of prayers and incense."; *T. Levi* 3.5-6—angels in heaven offer propitiatory sacrifices for the sins of ignorance of humans, which are rational, bloodless ones; cf. Ps 141:2—human prayer and lifting of hands replace incense and sacrifice). (3) Still others regarded right behavior as a substitute for animal sacrifice (Sir 35:1-3—keeping the law is a sacrifice; Tob 4:10-11—charity is an offering to God; 1 QS 9:5; 4QFlor 1:6—observance of the rules of the sect is a kind of spiritual sacrifice; Phil 4:18—gifts from the Philippians to Paul are an offering; Heb 12:28 together with 13:1-9, 16—sacrifice is right living). Of all the offerings, it was that of oneself as virtuous that was the most holy sacrifice (Philo, *Special Laws* 1.201—a person embodying the perfect virtues is the most holy sacrifice; 1.272—persons who bring completeness of virtue offer the most excellent sacrifice with hymns and thanksgiving, some with the reason alone; *Every Good Man* 75—Essenes showed themselves devoted servants of God "not by offering animal sacrifices but by resolving to sanctify their minds"; *Worse Is Wont* 20-21—"Genuine worship is that of a soul bringing simple reality as its only sacrifice"; Ps 51:17—a broken spirit and a contrite heart are the acceptable sacrifice; *2 Enoch* 45:3 [5]—pure hearts are the sacrifice God demands; Rom 15:15-16—Gentiles rightly related to God are an offering/sacrifice). Josephus, *Against Apion* 2.192, put it well: "Him must we worship by the practice of virtue; for that is the most saintly manner of worshiping God." That seems also to be the viewpoint of 1 Peter 2:5's "spiritual sacrifices." Porphyry (so Augustine, *City of God* 19.23) advocated spiritual worship that consisted of an individual's "inquiring into and imitating God's nature" so as to "make life itself a prayer to Him."

In light of this cultural trend, Paul must surely have been saying that appropriate worship is proper behavior in church and society. It is a liturgy of life! Such a sacrifice is of course a living one, offered by one who is "alive to God in Christ Jesus" (6:11) and who walks in "newness of life" (6:4). It is holy, devoted to God without spot or blemish. It is pleasing to God, that is, acceptable. This was certainly how Chrysostom read Paul at this point.

> And how is the body, it may be said, to become a sacrifice? Let the eye look at no evil thing, and it has become a sacrifice; let thy tongue speak nothing filthy, and it has become an offering; let thine hand do no lawless deed, and it has become a whole burnt offering.10

Remembering what God had done, Paul appealed to the Roman Christians: as you are enabled by God's mercies, present yourselves as sacrifices to God in a liturgy of righteous living. The true worship for which the apostle called embraces the whole of believers' lives from day to day.[11]

Verse 2 is a parallel exhortation to v. 1. If the first focused on our selves as "bodies," the second concerns our selves as "minds." Taken together, the emphasis is on the total self given to God. A negative begins the exhortation. "Do not be conformed to this world (= the present evil age with its distorted values)." A positive follows. "Be transformed by the renewing of your minds" (cf. Col 3:10; Eph 4:23). The verbs are passive: "be conformed, be transformed." The self is caught between cosmic powers that struggle for control of life: sin and God. Now that they have died with Christ, Christians are freed from the power of sin. Sin is still possible, but

Sacrifice in War

German artist Kaethe Kollwitz is renowned for her deeply expressionistic prints depicting the human suffering and sacrifice that comes out of war, poverty, and social injustice. This woodcut print titled *The Sacrifice* is part of a series of seven prints created from 1922–23. The entire series was titled *War* and represents the traumatic experiences of World War I between 1914 and 1918.

In this print, a visceral sense of separation and vulnerability is communicated as a baby son is sacrificed to the forces of wartime chaos outside the sphere of a mother's nurturing domain. Like animal sacrifice, this variety of sacrifice to the forces of a greater power was not that about which Paul spoke.

Kaethe Kollwitz. 1867–1945. *The Sacrifice.* Kunsthalle. Bremen, Germany. (Credit: Erich Lessing/Art Resource, NY/©2002 ARS, NY/VG Bild-Kunst, Bonn)

it is not necessary! Now that they have received the Holy Spirit, Christians possess an enabling power that makes righteousness (= faithfulness) possible. Only because of this deliverance and enabling power is an exhortation possible. People who are in bondage to sin cannot respond to an exhortation; they are prisoners with no freedom to do anything except sin. Those who have been set free and granted God's own enabling presence, however, are capable of a response to "Do not be conformed" and "Be transformed." It is a response that resists sin and allows God to change one's mind (cf. 2 Cor 3:18). With a transformed mind one is able to discern God's will, recognizing it as good, acceptable, and perfect. Only such a transformed mind has the capacity of forming the correct Christian ethical judgment at each given moment (cf. Phil 1:9-10; contrast Rom 1:28, 32).

"B," 12:3-13, in the pattern of Romans 12–13 deals with spiritual gifts within the Christian community. Paul believed that all Christians receive the Spirit when they die with Christ to sin (1 Cor 12:12-13). He understood the Spirit as God's presence, personal presence, personal presence experienced as power. This divine presence indwelling Christians, he believed, manifested itself in two ways: fruit and gifts. On the one hand, in Galatians 5:22-23 the apostle spoke about the fruit of the Spirit: love, joy, peace, patience, kindness, generosity, faithfulness, gentleness, self-control. These are not so much virtues for which one strives as fruit that manifests itself naturally in the personality that is being changed by the indwelling Spirit. On the other hand, in 1 Corinthians 12–14 and Romans 12:6-8 (cf. Eph 4:11-12) Paul treated the gifts of the Spirit. In these texts the lists of gifts vary (cf. 1 Cor 12:8-10 and 12:28 with Rom 12:6-8). In all cases, however, gifts of the Spirit refer to ministries with which Christians are gifted by the Spirit for the good of the believing community.

In Romans 12:6-8 there are seven gifts mentioned. The number seven probably indicates these seven are symbolic of the totality of God-given charisms. They are: (1) prophecy (1 Cor 12:10, 28; 14:1; 1 Thess 5:19-20), (2) ministry/service (*diakonia*; Acts 6:2; 1 Pet 4:10), (3) teaching (1 Cor 12:28; Jas 3:1; Heb 5:12), (4) exhortation (1 Thess 4:18; 5:11, 14), (5) generous giving (Eph 4:28; Acts 2:45; 4:34-37), (6) diligence in leading (1 Thess 5:12; 1 Tim 5:15, 17), and (7) cheerful compassion (Tob 1:3; 4:7; 9:6; Sir 7:10; 35:2).

The problem with spiritual gifts in the Pauline communities was that those so gifted often viewed their empowered actions as grounds for personal pride rather as ministries for mutual upbuilding. It is for this reason that Paul gave his exhortation in vv. 3-4: "not to think of yourself more highly that you ought to think, but to think . . . each according to the measure of faith (= the trust, cf. 1 Cor 12:7; 1 Pet 4:10; *pistis* is so used in Polybius 5.41.2— "This Hermeias was a Carian who had been set over the affairs of Seleucus, Antiochus's brother, who had committed this trust [*pistis*/responsibility] into his hands") that God has assigned." What would it mean to think of oneself in terms of one's own responsibility? It would mean to recognize that one's gift is only part of the Spirit's arsenal. Others have different gifts; yet we are all part of the same community. "For as in one body we have many members, and not all the members have the same function, so we, who are many, are one body in Christ, and individually we are members of one another" (vv. 4-5; cf. 1 Cor 12:14-27). There is a variety of gifts, and each is important to the community. Gennadius of Constantinople, in his *Pauline Commentary from the Greek Church*, said in this regard:

> God did not give us His gift in order that we should hate each other or that spiritual things should become an excuse for warfare, but so that we should enjoy harmony and friendship and the common salvation of all.[12]

The important thing for Paul was that the motive for the employment of spiritual gifts be right. That motive is love. In 1 Corinthians 12–14, chapters 12 and 14, which discuss spiritual gifts, are separated by chapter 13, which is devoted to love. Love is not there regarded as the supreme spiritual gift. For Paul love was a fruit of the Spirit (Gal 5:22-23). So 1 Corinthians 12:31 should probably be translated: "But you are striving for the greater gifts" (= a conclusion to chapter 12, observing that the Corinthians were indeed striving for the superior gifts for status sake). "And I will show you a still more excellent way" (= an introduction to chapter 13, where love is displayed as the proper motivation for use of spiritual gifts). Likewise in Romans 12 the section on spiritual gifts contains the Pauline emphasis on love. So v. 9a goes with vv. 3-8. It is an exhortation for proper motivation in the use of spiritual gifts. Just as in 1 Corinthians 13, there is then a sketch of what love looks like in Romans 12:9b-13.

Verses 9-13 have numerous parallels with other writings. A chart shows this:

Romans 12:9a—cf. 2 Cor 6:6; 1 Pet 1:22
12:9b—cf. 1 Thess 5:22
12:9c—cf. 1 Thess 5:21b; *T. Asher* 3:1; *T. Benj* 8:1
12:10a—cf. Col 3:14; 1 Thess 4:9-10; Heb 13:1; 1 Pet 1:22
12:10b—cf. Phil 2:3
12:11a—cf. 1 Thess 5:14b
12:11b—cf. 1 Thess 5:19; Acts 18:25
12: 12a—cf. Phil 4:4-5; 1 Thess 5:16
12:12b—cf. 1 Pet 2:20; Jas 1:12; Heb 10:32; Mark 13:13
12:12c—cf. 1 Thess 5:17; Col 4:2; Eph 6:18; Luke 18:1
12:13a—cf. Rom 12:8b; 15:27; Phil 2:25; Acts 11:27-30; 12:25
12:13b—cf. 1 Tim 3:2; Titus 1:8; Heb 13:2; 1 Pet 4:9; *T. Job* 10:1-
      3; 53:3; Philo, *Abraham* 107-114

These verses may very well have come to Paul as a piece of a larger oral tradition on the Two Ways. The contents are traditional; the

Eucharistic Banquet

The coming together of brotherly love into an agape community is suggested through several catacomb paintings that fill the walls in the burial tunnels of Rome. In one such painting, the emphasis is upon the celestial banquet in the Kingdom of God—a celebration that accompanies the resurrection of the Christian community. It is no accident that this painting is located directly over the tomb remains of a Christian buried in the catacombs. Framed by baskets brimming with bread, this community is partaking, collectively, in the Body of Christ.

Eucharistic Banquet. Crypt of the Sacraments. Early Christian Fresco. c. AD 225. Catacomb of Saint Callisto. Rome, Italy. (Credit: Scala/Art Resource, NY)

structure is symmetrical; the content is relevant to the context only in the first two and the last two injunctions. The central six are concerned with the vertical dimension rather than the horizontal. The introductory statement looks like the introduction to a Two Ways teaching.

Verses 9b-13 begin with an exhortation: "Hate what is evil, hold fast to what is good" (vv. 9b,c). What follows is a bracketed unit of ten injunctions following the pattern: 2,3,3,2. In English form the unit looks like this:

With brotherly love (*philadelphia*) love one another; in honor preferring one another.

In zeal not lagging; in spirit being ardent; serving the Lord.

In hope rejoicing; in tribulation patient; in prayer persevering. Contribute to the needs of the saints; extend hospitality (*philoxenian*) to strangers.

The first two and the final two of these ten strokes give content to Paul's exhortation that love be genuine. The little unit opens and closes with a term for love (*phil-*). If the manifestation of the Spirit's presence in the lives of Roman Christians in the form of gifts is controlled by the manifestation of the Spirit in their lives in the form of the fruit of the Spirit (love), then their lives will be a sacrifice to God arising out of a renewed mind. There will be no grasping for individual status but rather a commitment to the welfare of the whole community. [Pursue Hospitality]

 **Pursue Hospitality**

- Hospitality was important to the early church, especially that offered to traveling fellow Christians (e.g., Rom 12:13; 16:1-2, 23; 1 Cor 16:6,10-12; 2 Cor 1:16; Col 4:10; Titus 3:13; Philm 22; Heb 13:2; 1 Pet 4:9; 2 John 10-11; 3 John 5-8,10; *Didache* 12; *Herm, Mand*, 8.10).
- The Jewish Scriptures offered numerous examples of such behavior.
  - God (Ps 23:5-6)
  - Abraham (Gen 18:1-33)
  - Lot (Gen 19:1-3)
  - Rahab (Josh 2:1-21)
  - Samuel (1 Sam 9:18-27)
  - The woman who cared for Elisha (2 Kgs 4:8-36)
  - Job (Job 31:32)
- Romans 12:13's "pursue hospitality" reflects the same type of values as that ascribed to Abraham in postbiblical Judaism. Abraham is portrayed as one who would run out of his house to beg strangers to stay with him because he wanted to extend hospitality to them (Philo, *Abr* 107, 109) or who would build his house at a major thoroughfare in order to be able to extend hospitality to everyone passing by (*T. Abr* 1:1-2). Paul was eager, then, to urge his readers to extend generous hospitality to fellow Christians.

"C," 12:14-21, in the pattern of Romans 12–13 consists of another section of teaching that may be traditional. It focuses on nonretaliation and extends such behavior both to the Christian community and to outsiders. It is held together by an inclusion (v. 14 and v. 20-21). Inside of the frame are two parallel units (vv. 15-17 and vv. 18-19), the first dealing with relations within the community and the second with relations to those outside. The pattern looks like this:

A—12:14: Bless those who persecute you
  B—12:15-16: Live in harmony with one another
    C—12:17: Repay no one evil for evil
  B'—12:18: Live peaceably with all
    C'—12:19: Never avenge yourselves; leave it to God's wrath
A'—12:20-21: Overcome evil with good

The teaching in vv. 14-21 has parallels with numerous other sources. A chart shows this clearly.

Rom 12:14—cf. 1 Cor 4:12b; Matt 5:44; Luke 6:27-28; *T. Jos* 18:2; 1QapGen 20:28
12:15a—cf. Epictetus 2.5.23
12:15b—cf. Sir 7:34; *T. Iss* 7:4-5; *T. Zeb* 6:5; 7:34; *T. Jos* 17:7
12:16a—cf. 2 Cor 13:11; 1 Thess 5:13b; Rom 15:5
12:16b—cf. Gal 6:3; *T. Jos* 17:8; *m. 'Abot* 1:10; 6:5
12:16c—cf. LXX Prov 3:7

12:17a—cf. 1 Thess 5:15a; 1 Pet 3:9; Matt 5:38-42; *Joseph and Aseneth* 23:9; 28:5, 14; 29:3; Prov 20:22

12:17b—cf. 2 Cor 8:21; LXX Prov 3:4

12: 18—cf. 2 Cor 13:11; 1 Thess 5:13b; Heb 12:14; 1 Pet 3:10-12 (Ps 34:14-15); Mark 9:50; Matt 5:9; Sir 6:6; *m. 'Abot* 1:12; Epictetus 4.5.24

12:19a—Matt 5:44; Lev 19:18; *T. Gad* 6:7; 1 QS 10:17-18; CD 9:2-5; Sir 28:1-7; *2 Enoch* 50:3-4; Seneca, *De Ira* 3.12.39; Iamblichus, *Life of Pythagoras* 155, 179

12:19b—cf. Deut 32:35 (Heb 10:30)

12:20—LXX Prov 25:21-22

12:21—*T. Benj* 4:3; 1 QS 10:17-18

The teaching of these verses is focused on (a) nonretaliation and (b) a response to evil with good. Nonretaliation is found in vv. 17 ("Do not repay anyone evil for evil") and 19 ("Never avenge yourselves"). The exhortation to return good for evil comes in vv. 14 ("Bless those who persecute you") and 20-21 ("Overcome evil with good").

This two sided teaching is found elsewhere in the New Testament. (1) 1 Thessalonians 5:15 has both components: (a) See that none repays evil for evil, and (b) seek to do good to all. (2) 1 Peter 3:9 has the same two components: (a) Do not return evil for evil, and (b) bless. (3) Matthew 5:43-48 focuses on (b) love your enemies and pray for your persecutors. The nonretaliation (a) is found in 5:39's turn the other cheek. (4) Luke 6:27-36 has both (a) turn the other cheek and (b) do good to one's enemies.

In the early noncanonical Christian tradition the two emphases continue.[13] (1) Polycarp, *To the Philippians* 2:2-3, had (a) do not render evil for evil and 12:3 has (b) pray for those who persecute you. (2) *Didache* 1:1-3 focuses on the (b) component bless them that curse you; 1:4 on (a) turn the other cheek. (3) *2 Clement* 13:4 also focuses on the (b) component: love your enemies and those that hate you. (4) Justin Martyr in two different sources emphasized the (b) component: pray for your enemies (*1 Apology* 14:3; 15:9-10; *Dialogue* 35:8; 133:6) and love them that hate you (*1 Apology* 15:9-10; *Dialogue* 96:3; 133:6). (5) Epistle of the Apostles has the (b) component: love your enemies. (6) Irenaeus, *Against Heresies* 3.5 focused on the (b) component: love your enemies, bless them, pray for them. (7) Clement of Alexandria, *Instructor* 1.8 had both (a) do not take revenge and (b) pray for them. The (b) component is found also in *Miscellanies* 4:13-14 and 7:14: love your enemies, bless them, pray for them. (8) Tertullian,

Nonretaliation

(From a letter by Gandhi, January 25, 1920)
In the application of Satyagraha, I discovered, in the earliest stages, that pursuit of Truth did not admit of violence being inflicted on one's opponent, but that he must be weaned from error by patience and sympathy. For, what appears to be truth to the one may appear to be error to the other. And patience means self-suffering. So the doctrine came to mean vindication of Truth, not by infliction of suffering on the opponent but one's own self.

Satyagraha and its off-shoots, non-co-operation and civil resistance, are nothing but new names for the law of suffering. With *satya* combined with *ahimsa*, you can bring the world to your feet. *Satyagraha* in its essence is nothing but the introduction of truth and gentleness in the political, i.e., the national life.
Satyagraha is utter self-effacement, greatest humiliation, greatest patience and brightest faith. It is its own reward.

Satyagraha is a relentless search for truth and a determination to reach truth.
It is a force that works silently and apparently slowly. In reality, there is no force in the world that is so direct or so swift in working.
Satyagraha literally means insistence on truth. This insistence arms the votary with matchless power. This power or force is connoted by the word satyagraha. *Satyagraha*, to be genuine, may be offered against parents, against one's wife or one's children, against rulers, against fellow-citizens, even against the whole world.

Such a universal force necessarily makes no distinction between kinsmen and strangers, young and old, man and woman, friend and foe. The force to be so applied can never be physical. There is in it no room for violence. The only force of universal aplication can, therefore, be that of ahimsa or love. In other words, it is soul-force. Love does not burn others, it burns itself. Therefore, a *satyagrahi*, i.e., a civil resister, will joyfully suffer even unto death.

repeatedly talked about (b): *Apology* 31: pray for enemies; *On Prayer* 3: pray for them; *On Patience* 6: love your enemies, bless them, pray for them. In his *On Idolatry* he had both (a) do not return a curse and (b) bless them. (9) Ps-Clementine, *Homilies* 12:32-33 had both (a) do not punish those who do you wrong and (b) love your enemies, bless them, pray for them. (10) Origen, *Against Celsus* 8.35 had both (a) do not harm any, and (b) love and pray for enemies. (11) Cyprian, *Treatises* 9:5 and 10:15 had the (b) component: love your enemies and pray for them. (12) Lactantius,

Divine Institutes also had both (a) never avenge yourself and (b) rather bless them. These sources outside the canon combined with those within the New Testament bear witness to a dominant theme in early Christianity. It is a two sided coin: both nonretaliation and the returning of good for evil.

The Mediterranean world's values in this regard were mixed. In the pagan world several pieces of evidence illustrate the reigning rule of reciprocity. Xenophon's Socrates counted benefiting friends and defeating enemies as one of the things that bring the greatest pleasure (*Memorabilia* 4.5.10). In Achilles Tatius's novel *Leucippe and Clitophon* 7.6, we hear a character verbalize: "Nothing is shameful that hurts your enemy." Heliodorus, *Ethiopian Story* 1.16, spoke of "vengeance on a hated foe" as the norm. At the same time, the Stoics did not advocate retaliation. Seneca, *De Ira* 2.34.5 advised that if someone strikes you, step back, for by striking back you will give him both the opportunity and excuse to repeat his blow (cf. *De Ira* 2.32.1). Epictetus, *Encheiridion* 42, argued that if someone treats you badly, you should be gentle with the one who reviles you. In *Discourses* 3.22.54, he said that if the Cynic is flogged, he must love the men who flog him! The ground of these arguments is usually the Stoic desire to maintain the serenity of the individual. A Pythagorean maxim recorded by Iamblichus in his *Life of Pythagoras* 155, 179, runs: "It is much more pious to suffer injustice than to kill a person; for judgment is ordained in Hades."

The Old Testament's dominant attitude towards the enemies of Israel is well known: annihilate them. What is often overlooked, however, is the other side of the coin in ancient Judaism. Leviticus 19:18 says one should not take vengeance. Proverbs 20:22 advises one not to say, "I will repay evil." Exodus 23:4-5 urges the Israelite, if he sees his enemy's ox or ass going astray, to bring it back. The *Epistle of Aristeas* 225, 227 advises one not only to be generous to friends but to show liberal charity to opponents. *T. Benjamin* 4:2-3 says to love those who wrong you. *T. Joseph* 18:2 urges the readers that if anyone wishes to do you harm, then pray for him and do good to him. *Joseph and Aseneth* 23:9 says it does not befit us to repay evil for evil. *Second Enoch* 50:3-4 teaches that we are not to take vengeance for the Lord is the one who takes vengeance. At Qumran, 1 QS 10.17-20 says "I will pay to no man the reward of evil; I will pursue him with goodness. For judgment of all is with God and it is He who will render to man his reward." In 1 QapGen 20.28-29 Abraham prays for the healing of the king of Egypt, the very king who has taken Abraham's wife. Josephus,

Conversion of St. Augustine

The towering figure of early Christian theology, Augustine of Hippo, was converted to the Faith in July of 386. According to Augustine, his long movement toward Christianity ended in a garden in Milan when he seemed to hear a voice saying, "Tolle lege, tolle lege (Pick up, read it)." His eyes fell on Paul's words in Rom 13:13, and all his previous resistance to conversion was overcome.

Fra Angelico. 1387–1455. *The Conversion of St. Augustine.* Tempra on wood panel. Musee Thomas Henry. Cherbourg, France. (Credit: Giraudon/Art Resource, NY)

Against Apion 2.211-12, said Moses required Jews to "show consideration even to declared enemies."

This evidence shows that both pagans and Jews had mixed teaching about the treatment of enemies. The early Christians, however, perceived their professed attitude of love towards enemies to be distinctive (e.g., Athenagoras, *Plea* 11; Ps-Clementine *Homilies* 12.32-33; Origen, *Against Celsus* 8.35). The unanimity of the Christian voice was distinctive and the motivation of the Christian stance was unique (love your enemies because Christ did and taught us to do so and because Christ lives in and through believers).

It was doubtless this focused tradition of returning good for evil that influenced certain of the early fathers in their interpretation of Romans 12:20: "If you enemies are hungry, feed them; if they are thirsty, give them something to drink; for by doing this you will heap burning coals on their heads." Instead of reading v. 20's burning coals as a reference to judgment, Origen, in his *Commentary of the Epistle to the Romans*, said LXX Isaiah 47:14 refers to burning coals as a means of warmth. So, he said, coals are heaped for the benefit of the wrong doer, that is, his repentance.[14] Jerome, *Against the Pelagians* 1.30, also argued that v. 20 taught:

Let the enemy be softened by the fire of charity.[15] God at the last judgment (and the State in this present evil age—13:4) exercises judgment; the disciples of Jesus, who are enabled by his power, return good for evil.

Romans 13:1-7, C' in the pattern, is linked with 12:14-21 by the key phrases "the wrath of God" and "servant of God to execute wrath" (12:19; 13:4). Logically, 13:1-7 follows naturally on 12:14-21. If Jesus' disciples are never to avenge themselves, it is because they are to leave such to God. This divine judgment on wrongdoing comes at the last judgment directly from God. In this present evil age, the State is God's servant to administer wrath on wrongdoers.

The text, 13:1-7, falls into two parts. The first deals with rulers; the second with rulers' dues. Each part is symmetrically organized. We begin with vv. 1-5 which look like this:

A—vv. 1-2: Exhortation: be subject because . . .
  B—v. 3a: The role of rulers (a terror to bad conduct)
    C—vv. 3b-4a: Appropriate behavior receives approval
    C'—v. 4b: Inappropriate behavior faces the sword
  B'—v. 4c: The role of rulers (execute wrath of wrongdoers)
A'—v. 5: Exhortation: be subject because . . .

This text asserts that there is no authority except from God, a Jewish conviction (e.g., 2 Sam 12:8; Jer 27:5-7; Prov 8:15-16; Dan 2:21, 37-38; 4:17, 25, 32; 5:21; Wis 6:3; *Ep Arist* 224; Sir 10:4; 17:17; *1 Enoch* 46:5; *2 Bar* 82:9). Early Christians endorsed it (e.g., John 19:11—"You would have no power over me unless it had been given you from above"; Luke 4:6—"To you I will give their glory and all this authority; for it has been given over to me, and I give it to anyone I please"). If Rome rules, it is because God has authorized it. If it bears the sword, it is because God has allowed it. Jesus' disciples are, therefore, called upon to be subject to the governing authorities who restrain the flood waters of evil behavior and reward good behavior. Jewish tradition regarded this restraint of evil as good. Rabbi Hanina said: "Pray for the peace of the ruling power, since but for fear of it men would have swallowed up each other alive" (*m. 'Abot* 3.2).

What form does Christian submission to the ruling powers take? Verses 6-7 make that clear. Here one finds an ABA' pattern that looks like this:

A—v. 6a: Pay taxes (*phorous* = direct taxes)

  B—v. 6b: for rulers are servants of God

A'—v. 7: Give to all their due: direct taxes (*phoron*), indirect taxes
    (*telos*), respect (*phobon*), honor (*timēn*)

The same theme runs through this segment on rulers' dues. They are God's servants. So give them their due, both monetary and attitudinal. The point of the passage as a whole seems clear.

This text, however, must be located in its larger context to become intelligible. In antiquity there were multiple perspectives on the State. (1) The dominant one was pro-Roman, whether one was Roman, non-Christian Jewish, or Christian. (a) Greco-Roman—In Tacitus, *Histories* 4.74, Cerialis gives a rousing pro-Roman speech. Plutarch, *To An Uneducated Ruler* 3, said "rulers serve God for the care and preservation of men." (b) Non-Christian Jewish—*Epistle of Aristeas* 45 urges one to obey those in power. Josephus, *JW* 5.366-68, said the universe is subject to the Romans by God's act. God is on the Roman side. In 2.390, Josephus said that God is on the side of the Romans for without God's aid so vast an empire could never have been built up. In 5.378 he said to the Jews: You are warring not against the Romans only but also against God. (c) Early Christian—Titus 3:1 says: "be subject to rulers and authorities." 1 Peter 2:13-14 urges: "For the Lord's sake accept the authority of every human institution, whether of the emperor as supreme, or of governors, as sent by him to punish those who do wrong and to praise those who do right." *First Clement* 60:4 prays that we may be obedient to our rulers and governors on earth; 61:1 offers the explanation why: God has given the power of sovereignty to them. So we should be subject to them, in nothing resisting God's will. The *Martyrdom of Polycarp* 10:2 tells us that Christians were taught to render suitable honor to the authorities appointed by God. This is the stance reflected in Romans 13:1-7.

It must be understood against the background of Israel in the exile. Israel in exile was told to respect the governing authorities. Jeremiah 29:7 called the Jews to seek the welfare of the city to which God had exiled them and to pray for it. Baruch 1:11 called on the exiles to pray for the life of Nebuchadnezzar, king of Babylon. As citizens of heaven living as resident aliens in this present evil age (Phil 1:27; 3:20; 1 Pet 1:1; 2:11; *Diog* 5), Christian messianists are to respect the governing authorities.

Circumstances, moreover, would have conditioned Paul's attitude expressed in Romans 13:1-7. He would have known of Claudius's decree in AD 49 that expelled Jews and Jewish Christians from Rome because of disturbances in the synagogues (Suetonius, "Claudius," 25.4). He wanted no repeat of that. Priscilla and Aquila had only recently returned to Rome (Acts 18:1-2; Rom 16:3). He and his readers were living in the early years of Nero's reign when the young emperor behaved properly. There had been no persecutions of Christians in Rome to date. This led to a generally positive attitude toward imperial power. By this time, moreover, there were likely the beginnings of disturbances about taxes in Rome. In Judea, Zealots were advocating nonpayment of taxes to Rome (Josephus, *JW* 2.118). Elsewhere, Romans in AD 57 or 58 were complaining about the shameless and extortionary practices of the tax collectors (Tacitus, *Annals* 13.50-51; Suetonius, "Nero," 10.1). Paul would not have wanted Christians to become involved in such matters for their own safety's sake.

Paul's teaching in Romans 13:1-7 looks like parenesis for a specific time and situation, not a general teaching for all times and places.[16] It is not a complete statement about the Christians and government (1 Cor 6:1-8 expresses reserve about involvement with Roman courts; cf. 1 Tim 2:1-2 whose exhortation to pray for rulers assumes that they need changing). It is not a call for absolute obedience to the State. The verb *hypotassestho*, 13:1, should be translated as a middle imperative (= subject yourselves). The reason given is: for God's sake. Taken together, these words imply a Christian decision to be subject (i.e., it is not a given) and a higher loyalty than the State (= God!). All that is asked of the readers is that they "do good," "pay taxes," and "honor and respect those in power." All that is legitimately ascribed to the authorities is punishing the evil and rewarding the good. This limited homage is far from an enthusiastic endorsement of the empire.

(2) There was also a negative attitude toward the Roman State present among some non-Christian Jews (e.g., *Pss Sol* 1:4-25; 17; *Sib Or* 5:155-178). It was also found among some early Christians. In Revelation 13, 17 one encounters a view of Roman imperial power as demonic. Rome is the servant of Satan; Rome demands worship of the emperor and persecutes those who will not do this idolatrous thing. Rome will be judged by God, thrown down and destroyed. Christians in the Revelation of John are called upon to resist. This is not armed but passive resistance. One remains faithful to Jesus, refusing to worship the emperor, even if it costs one's life. God will take care of Rome (14:8) and anyone worshipping the emperor will share in Rome's judgment (14:9-11). This negative attitude is found also in the *Epistle of Barnabas* (2:1—the

worker of evil is in power; 4:3—the final stumbling block is at hand; 4:4-5—the Roman king is the fourth beast of Daniel) and in *Sibylline Oracles* 8.65-72. In these instances, the attitude toward the State is determined by the context. John the prophet saw the incompatibility of the ethos of Roman imperial power and that of the Christian communities and visualized a future when Rome's persecution of Christians would constitute the tribulation of the last days. Rome, having overstepped its bounds and asked for that which belongs only to God, was viewed as a demonic State. The attitude growing out of such a situation was that of passive resistance, involving a readiness to accept martyrdom, combined with a theoretical opposition to the persecuting powers that are under the wrath of God.[17] It seems clear that this stance is also conditioned by circumstances and is not a general teaching for all times and places.

There was, as well, a mediating position found in Luke-Acts that had affinities with both positive and negative positions described. (1) In Luke, Jesus' parents are described as obedient to the State (Luke 2:1-5). Jesus' words do not call for revolt against the State but for limited subservience (Luke 20:25). In Acts, Paul relies upon the State to protect himself in his missionary work (Acts 16:37-39; 18:12-17; 22:24-29, etc). Throughout, the disciples are portrayed as politically innocent. (2) Acts 12, however, does have words to say about rulers who step out of bounds. In 12:1-9 the point is that bad rulers cannot stop the progress of the gospel. In 12:20-23 the point is that rulers who exalt themselves into the place of God will be judged harshly by God. (3) In Acts 5:29, moreover, we hear the words of the apostles spoken in a situation when the rulers' demands run counter to their commission. "We must obey God rather than man." There is in Luke-Acts, then, a nuanced position about Jewish rulers and Roman imperial power. This position shares some of the positive attitude of Romans 13; it partakes of some of the reserve about the State characteristic of Revelation; and it calls for the same resistance to the State when its demands run counter to allegiance to God.

It is arguable that the three Christian perspectives surveyed can all be rooted in the logion attributed to Jesus. Mark 12:17's form reads: "Give to the emperor the things that are the emperor's, and to God the things that are God's." This saying almost certainly means that the political realm is legitimate and hence taxes are to be paid; nevertheless, the priority of God shatters all pretensions to divine rights of secular structures and authorities. The Markan Jesus, in this view, is neither a revolutionary (Zealot) nor a servile

Tribute Money

This Baroque painting clearly shows a split of allegiance to the state and to God (the Roman government and Christ). As if double checking the acceptability and appropriateness of this moment, one of the disciples looks back at Christ as the other disciples and tax officials are exclusively focusing upon the tribute. Christ does not resist the payment, yet he makes a distinction between the two worlds as he points toward himself.

Mattia Preti. 1613–1699. *Tribute Money.* Galleria Doria Pamphili. Rome, Italy. (Credit: Scala/Art Resource, NY)

subject of those who rule. At the same time that there is no overt hostility towards rulers *per se*, there is a critical distancing. How a disciple of Jesus relates to the State depends, in this frame of reference, on the circumstances, namely, in large measure the attitude of the State.

Romans 13:8-10, B' in the pattern, returns to the theme of love for one another. It is linked to 13:1-7 through a key word ("what is due" [*opheilas*], v. 7; "owe" [*opheilete*], v. 8).So if 13:1-7 spoke of what was owed to rulers, 13:8-10 speaks about what is owed to all. These verses are in the form of an injunction (v. 8a) followed by its basis (vv. 8b-10).

Injunction (13:8a):
Negative—Owe no one anything
Positive—except to love one another.

Basis (13:8b-10):
General principle—for the one who loves another has fulfilled the
            law (v. 8b).
Explanation—The commandments against adultery, murder,
            stealing, and coveting are summed up in "Love your
            neighbor as yourself" (v. 9).

Restatement of the principle—Love does not wrong a neighbor,
that is why it fulfills the law (v. 10).

When Paul spoke about loving one another, he usually referred to
other believers (1 Thess 5:15 where a distinction is drawn between
one another and all). But when he said "owe no one," he seemed to
refer to all. So Paul here was likely addressing believers' relations
with both other believers and nonbelievers. What is owed is love.
The content of this love is spelled out. It does not do wrong to a
neighbor (v. 10). Wrong is spelled out as well. It involves adultery,
murder, stealing, coveting, and any other commandment. Love,
then, is not a sentimental feeling for another; it is action that does
not harm the other!

Paul made two separate statements about love in relation to the
law. First, he said all the commandments are summed up
(*anakephalaioutai*) in Leviticus 19:18's "Love your neighbor as
yourself." The idea that the law could be summed up in a general
principle was widespread in ancient Judaism. For example, (1)
b. Makkot 23b-24a—The 613 precepts communicated to Moses
were reduced to one principle by Habakkuk: But the righteous
shall live by faith; (2) *b. Berakot* 63a—Bar Kappara expounded:
What short text is there upon which all the essential principles of
the Torah depend? "In all thy ways acknowledge Him and He will
direct thy paths"; (3) *b. Sabbat* 31a—A heathen came to Hillel.
Hillel said: "What is hateful to you, do not do to your neighbor":
that is the whole Torah, while the rest is commentary thereon; go
and learn it; (4) Philo, *Decalogue* 18-19, said that the Decalogue is
the "head of the laws"; (5) *Sifra on Lev* 19:18—"Thou shalt love
thy neighbor as thyself." R. Akiba said: That is the greatest principle in the Law; (6) Jesus, in Matthew 22:40, says of the two great
commandments, love God and love your neighbor: On these two
commandments hang all the law and the prophets. Paul's claim is
that the Decalogue is summed up in Leviticus 19:18: Love your
neighbor as yourself (cf. Gal 5:14). In so doing he acts like so many
teachers within Middle Judaism. In focusing on love of the
neighbor he shares a common perspective with Akiba and Jesus.

The second thing Paul asserted about love and the law is that
loving the neighbor fulfills the law. Origen, *Commentary on the
Epistle to the Romans*, said: "If you love somebody, you will not kill
him. Nor will you commit adultery, steal from him or bear false
witness against him. It is the same with all the other commands of
the law: love ensures that they are kept."[18] One cannot read this
text without recalling Romans 8:4. God acted in Jesus Christ "so

that the just requirement of the law might be fulfilled in us, who walk not according to the flesh but according to the Spirit." If Jesus' disciples love one another, it is only because they are enabled by the Spirit to do what they are here being told to do.

Romans 13:11-14, A' in the pattern, lays out an eschatological foundation for Christian conduct. Why let righteousness rule in your members? Because of the time! The paragraph is composed of two bases and two summons. They look like this.

> A—Basis (13:11a): You know what time (*hōra* = hour) it is; it is now the moment.
>   B—Summons (13:11b): Wake from sleep.
> A'—Basis (13:11c-12a): Salvation is nearer; the night is far gone, the day is near.
>   B'—Summons (13:12b-14): Lay aside; put on.

The statements about the time seem to be eschatological. The End is nearer! A Roman pagan might very well have agreed. Pliny the Elder, *Natural History* 7.16.73, for example, commented:

> You can almost see that the stature of the whole human race is decreasing daily, with few men taller than their fathers, as the final conflagration . . . is approaching. (cf. *Lucretius, De rerum natura* 2.1150-53)

A non-Christian apocalyptic Jew would have agreed. 4 Ezra 4:26 says that "our age is hastening swiftly to its end." The Pauline letters speak repeatedly about Christians waiting for the End (Rom 2:5—the day of wrath [cf. 5:9]; Rom 2:16—the day of judgment; 1 Cor 1:7—waiting for Christ; 1:8—the day of the Lord Jesus Christ; 7:29—the time is short; 10:11—the ends of the world have come; 16:22—our Lord, come!; Phil 4:5—the Lord is at hand; 2:16—the day of the Lord; 1 Thess 1:9-10—wait for His Son from heaven; 4:15—the coming of the Lord Jesus; 5:2—day of the Lord Jesus Christ; 5:23—the coming of the Lord Jesus; [2 Thess 2:1—the coming of the Lord Jesus; 3:5—waiting for Christ; Eph 4:30—day of redemption.]). Sometimes Paul spoke about the End being near (1 Thess 4:17; 1 Cor 15:51; Phil 4:7). In this he shared a common belief of early Christians (Matt 10:23; Mark 9:1; 14:62; Heb 10:25, 37; Jas 5:8; 1 Pet 4:17; Rev 1:1, 3; 22:7, 10, 12, 20). It is no surprise, then, to hear the apostle refer to the End and to speak about it as nearer than when his readers believed. Judgment Day is near. Because of this, you need to act in certain ways.

The appropriate action in light of a nearing End is described in terms of two metaphors: first, waking from sleep, and second, the putting off and putting on of garments. Sleep is used in Mark 13:35-36 and 1 Thessalonians 5:6 for moral and spiritual laxness; in Revelation 3:1b-2 for spiritual death. Waking up is used in Revelation 3:2-3 for spiritual revival leading to preparedness; staying awake is used in 1 Thessalonians 5:6 for spiritual alertness. A summons to awaken would likely be heard as a call to spiritual preparedness in view of the judgment which is near.

The second metaphor is that of putting off dirty garments and putting on clean ones. Paul called for a laying aside of the works of darkness: "not in reveling and drunkenness, not in debauchery and licentiousness, not in quarreling and jealousy" (vv. 12b,13b). He called for a putting on of the armor of light (v. 12) and putting on the Lord Jesus Christ (v. 14; cf. Gal 3:27). The language of putting off and putting on is found elsewhere in the New Testament. Ephesians 4:22, 25 and Colossians 3:8, 12 have both. First Thessalonians 5:8 and Ephesians 6:11-17 have the putting on; James 1:21 and 1 Peter 2:1 have the putting off.

To wear the garments of darkness is to behave as people do in the darkness. Ancient novels illustrate such behavior. In Petronius's *Satyricon* there is an account of Trimalchio's nighttime banquet that provides evidence of vice associated with nighttime revelry. In Achilles Tatius's *Leucippe and Clitophon* 6.3, we hear: "It was the festival of Artemis, and drunken people were roaming everywhere, so that all night long a crowd filled the entire agora." The Pauline corpus echoes such behavior's association with nighttime (1 Thess 5:7—"those who are drunk get drunk at night"; Eph 5:11-12— "Take no part in the unfruitful works of darkness, but instead expose them. For it is shameful even to mention what such people do secretly").

To put off the old ways is to renounce vice. Plutarch, "Agis," 6.1-2 referred to the response of youth to the king's exhortations.

> The young men . . . quickly . . . gave ear to him, and stripped themselves for the contest in behalf of virtue, like him casting aside their old ways of living as worn-out garments in order to obtain liberty (= from vice; cf. Heb 12:1-2).

By putting on the armor of light or the Lord Jesus Christ Paul meant that Christians "make no provision for the flesh (= the orientation of life that absolutizes something God has made instead of the God who made it), to gratify its desires" (cf. Gal 5:24—"those

Virtue and Vanity

Though not directly paralleled to the Paul verse (Rom 13:14), this painting focuses upon the juxtaposition of virtue and vanity and subtly points to the limits of living by the flesh while extolling the virtuous living by the spirit. The skull in the lower left of the painting and the mirrored reflection of the figure of vanity on the right point to the transience of our creatureliness, while the dove of the Holy Spirit and the upward pointing of the figure on the left refer to the virtue of inspiration and the realm of the invisible.

Francesco Rustici. 1595–1626. *Virtue and Vanity.* Coll. Monte dei Paschi. Siena, Italy. (Credit: Scala/Art Resource)

who belong to Christ have crucified the flesh with its passions and desires").

The image of putting on certain garments is one way the ancients spoke about divine empowerment of humans. (1) Originally, the practice of putting on another's actual garments was thought to transfer that person's power to oneself. In *Ps-Philo*, Joshua is told by God to take Moses' garments and to clothe himself with them. He is promised that if he does so he will be "changed and become another man." When Joshua does so, "his mind was afire and his spirit was moved" (*Bib.Ant.* 20:2-3). In LXX 4 Kings 2:13-15 we hear that when Elijah was taken up into heaven his mantle fell from off him upon Elisha. When this happened Elisha possessed the powers of Elijah. The sons of the prophets recognize that the spirit of Elijah rests upon Elisha. In both of these instances, being clothed with the garments of another facilitates the empowering of the one so clothed. (2) The metaphorical use of this image was widespread. Only a few examples may be cited. (a) Sometimes we hear about being clothed with righteousness. In Job 29:14-16, Job says that he put on the robe of righteousness; as a result he was eyes to the blind, feet to the lame, father to the needy, and champion of the stranger. To put on the robe of righteousness meant to be empowered to be righteous. *T. Levi* 18:14 says that in the golden future "all the saints will be clothed with righteousness." This is associated with a time when sin will be conquered. In *Hermas, Parable*, 6.1.4, exhorts Hermas to put on righteousness so he will be able to keep the commands given him. In each of these three cases, the clothing is associated with empowerment. (b) On other occasions one hears of people being clothed with the spirit. *Ps-Philo* 27:9-10 tells of Kenaz being clothed with the spirit of the Lord/the spirit of power "and was changed into another man." LXX Judges 6:34 says that the spirit of the Lord clothed Gideon. He then became a savior of Israel. *Ps-Philo* 36:2 says Gideon "put on the Spirit of the Lord and was strengthened." LXX 2 Chronicles 24:20 tells how the spirit of God clothed Zechariah with the result that he stood up and addressed the people about their transgressions. In Luke 24:49 the risen Christ tells his disciples to stay in Jerusalem "until you have been clothed with power from on high." *Hermas, Parable*, 9.24.2, speaks about those who were clothed in the Holy Spirit and always felt compassion for every person and provided for others from their labors. In these instances as well, the notion of being clothed is a way of speaking about divine empowerment of humans. (c) On other occasions an eschatological note is sounded. In *2 Enoch* 22:8-10, Enoch is clothed in glory and becomes, as a result, like one of the angels. Clothing again has transformative power. In 1 Corinthians 15:53-55, Paul spoke about this perishable body putting on imperishability and this mortal body putting on immortality. This is similar to 2 Corinthians 5:2-4 where he refers to being further clothed with our heavenly dwelling. In both Pauline texts, the image of clothing is associated with the transformation of a person into immortal life. (d) In Christian circles there was the notion of one's being clothed with Christ. Galatians 3:27 (cf. Col 3:10; Eph 4:24) associates it with baptism. "As many of you as were baptized into Christ have clothed yourselves with Christ." Romans 13:14 associates it with spiritual alertness. "Put on the Lord Jesus Christ and make no provision for the flesh" (cf. Col 3:12). *Odes of Solomon* 33:12 has Christ say: "And they who have put me on . . . will possess incorruption in the new world." Here being clothed with Christ yields eschatological salvation. In these examples also, the image of clothing is used to speak of human transformation by divine agency. To put on Christ means to be empowered by Christ! The Jewish and Christian ways of speaking would have been understood by a Roman pagan. *Ps-Crates* 23 exhorts the readers to put on the weapons of Diogenes with which he drove away those who had designs on him.

The two metaphors, awakening from sleep and the putting off-putting on, are alternative ways of saying what was said earlier in 12:1-2 with two different metaphors: present your bodies a sacrifice and allow your mind to be transformed.

CONNECTIONS

How Distinctive Was Paul's Parenesis?

In Romans 12:9-21 Paul's teaching has parallels with numerous other sources. Peter Stuhlmacher has put the problem plainly. He said:

> Whenever the Pauline *Paraklēsis* is surveyed in detail it is repeatedly confirmed that linguistically and in terms of content it runs parallel to exhortations being given in contemporary popular philosophy and in the synagogues in which Greek-speaking Jews came together. On the basis of such parallels scholars have repeatedly concluded that apart from the love command there is hardly anything specifically Christian in the Pauline *Paraklēsis*. Even the love command itself, in reality, is seen to be nothing more than just good Jewish tradition (cf. Lev 19:18 and *T. Gad* 6:1).[19]

Stuhlmacher has also offered his response. "As correct as these observations are, the conclusion drawn from them is just as wrong."[20] How can we understand his reservations?

The basic issue is: how are non-Christian sources to be used in Christian ethical teaching? Bruce C. Birch and Larry L. Rasmussen, in their *Bible and Ethics in the Christian Life*, lend us assistance.[21] They argue that biblical norms rule some other norms out, confirm or authorize others, and influence the boundaries for all proposed norms from whatever source. For our purposes, this says that Paul's

Christian theological center functioned as a filter for everything that
was included in his ethical teaching. If
there was teaching that came from
another source, it was excluded or
included in terms of whether or not it
was compatible with Paul's Christian
center. Furthermore, when a piece of
teaching was included, it became a
part of a larger Christian whole that
shaped the way it was to be understood and used. Even though its
origins may have been outside the
Christian circle, it was only taken into
the Christian circle if it was deemed
compatible with the Christian center
and by being included subsequently
became subordinated to the ethos
emanating from that Christian center.

John Calvin

Flemish School. *Jean Calvin as a Young Man.* c. 1500. Bibliotheque Publique et
Universitaire. Geneva, Switzerland. (Credit: Erich Lessing/Art Resource, NY)

What was Paul's Christian center? It
does not seem to have been the sayings
of Jesus. He quoted very few (e.g.,
1 Cor 7:10-11; 1 Cor 9:14; 1 Cor
11:23-25). It does not seem to have been the events in Jesus'
earthly life. He cited virtually none (except for birth, death, resurrection, and appearances). Yet he could say: "Be imitators of me, as
I am of Christ" (1 Cor 11:1). What about Christ did he imitate?
Three examples give assistance. (1) In Philippians 2:1-11 Paul
called for Christians to "do nothing from selfish ambition or
conceit, but in humility (to) regard others as better than yourselves" (v. 3) and grounded that in the mind of Christ who
"humbled himself" (v. 8). (2) In 2 Corinthians 8–9 Paul was
attempting to complete the collection in Corinth. He was calling
for Corinthian generosity and grounded it in the example of
Christ. "For you know the generous act of our Lord Jesus Christ,
that though he was rich, yet for our sakes he became poor, so that
by his poverty you might become rich." (3) In Romans 14:1–15:13
Paul was dealing with the struggles between the weak and the
strong. While he established certain principles as fixed, he also
called for the strong to consider the effects of their behavior on the
weak. To ground this he referred to the example of Christ. "For
Christ did not please himself" (15:3). He concluded: "Welcome
one another, therefore, just as Christ has welcomed you. . . . For I

tell you that Christ has become a servant of the circumcised . . . in order that he might confirm the promises given to the patriarchs, and in order that the Gentiles might glorify God for His mercy" (15:7-9). In each of these cases, the pattern of the Christ-event as a whole, not specific sayings or events, is the religious center that served as Paul's ultimate criterion of ethical practice.[22]

In following this practice, Paul was acting in accord with cultural conventions. Ancient Mediterranean peoples expected a king to legislate not merely through his written or spoken laws but even more through his lifestyle. By living out an example of ideal law before the people the king personified a law higher than the written laws of the land because he lived his life in accord with the Law of God. Thus an ideal king would be living law, having the authority and ability to legislate out of his person. Isocrates, *To Demonicus* 36, said one should "pattern after the character of kings, and follow closely their ways," going beyond obedience to their written laws, considering "their manner of life your highest law." Paul, in line with this advice, focused not so much on what Jesus taught (his spoken/written legislation) but on the character of the Christ-event taken as a whole, how Christ acted overall: for example, in humility, in generosity, not to please himself, with care for both Jew and Gentile.

James Dunn has summarized well when he said that while the material in Romans 12 is largely traditional, Paul would be the first to say that the motivation for such a lifestyle comes from the example of Christ and its enabling from the spirit of Christ.[23]

It is important, moreover, to take Michael Thompson's observation about imitation seriously. He said:

> The example of Christ does not signify for Paul any kind of mechanical reproduction of Jesus' life and deeds, any more than the teachings of Jesus constituted a new Torah. Imitation means Spirit-enabled following of Jesus' spirit and attitude as exemplified and characterized on the cross.[24]

One need only qualify this by adding that Paul saw the incarnation of the preexistent one as testimony to his humility and self-giving. It is important to clarify that in antiquity's view imitation meant the past was to be repeated but in a non-identical, new way which is faithful both to the ancient example and the present task.

How Should Christians Relate to the State?

An absolutizing of Romans 13:1-7 has caused severe problems in the past. For example, this text, taken as a general prescription for all times and places, undercut German Christian resistance to the Nazi regime. Also, an absolutizing reading of Romans 13 served the apartheid policies in South Africa. Allan A. Boesak has given his personal experience.[25]

> On 19 October 1977, I was visited for the first time by the South African Security Police. They stayed from 3:30 A.M. till 7:00 A.M. At one point I was challenged by the Security Police captain (who assured me that he was a Christian and, in fact, an elder of the white Dutch Reformed Church), on my persistent resistance to the government. "How can you do what you are doing," he asked, "while you know what Romans thirteen says?" In the hour-long conversation that followed, I could not convince him. For him, as for millions of other Christians in South Africa and across the world, Romans 13 is an unequivocal, unrelenting call for blind, unquestioning obedience to the state.

The necessary balance required in a reading of Romans 13 was supplied by Augustine, *On Romans* 72. He said:

> If anyone thinks that because he is a Christian he does not have to pay taxes or tribute nor show the proper respect to the authorities, . . . he is in very great error. Likewise, if anyone thinks that he ought to submit to the point where he accepts that someone who is his superior in temporal affairs should have authority even over his faith, he falls into an even greater error.26{End quote}

Basil, *The Morals* 79.1, had the same outlook. He said: "It is right to submit to higher authority whenever a command of God is not violated thereby."[27] Both of these fathers were aware that the authorities themselves might do bad. When this happens, Romans 13's call for submission is relativized. Revelation and/or Acts 5:29 come into play.

John Calvin released the fifth edition of his *Institutes* in August 1559. An intriguing addition appeared in it. Here he suggested that if magistrates commanded anything of their subjects contrary to the commands of God, the biblical injunction, "We ought to obey God rather than men," comes into play. Interpreting Daniel 6:22, Calvin explained Daniel's praying to the God of Israel in spite of the king's edict against such: "For the king had exceeded his limits, and had not only been a wrong-doer against men, but, in lifting up his horns against God, had himself abrogated his power." Appealing to Hosea 5:11-13, Calvin also noted the censure upon Israel for complying with the decrees of ungodly kings.[28] In the fifth edition, Calvin clearly did not take Rom 13 as an absolute.

Karl Barth, *Church and State*,[29] argued that the State is responsible for granting the church freedom to proclaim the gospel. The church acknowledges the divine ordination of the state and its rightful sphere of authority and jurisdiction. If the church's freedom is restricted by an evil state, the church serves the state through passive and active resistance rather than through obedience. The Christian's necessary allegiance to the state precludes making an oath of absolute loyalty to a totalitarian state and its claims. Responsible Christian citizenship today entails prayer for the state, political action, and political struggle. Such action is responsible for the rise of the democratic state. Although the state serves the reign of justice, peace, and concern for human welfare, it is neither called nor able to usher in the kingdom of God.

John Stott has put it well for contemporaries: "Whenever laws are enacted which contradict God's Law, civil disobedience becomes a Christian duty."[30] When this occurs, however, the purpose is to demonstrate Christians' submission to God, not their defiance of government. This perspective has been likewise voiced by Douglas Moo.

> But perhaps our submission to government is compatible with disobedience to government in certain exceptional circumstances. For heading the hierarchy of relations in which Christians find themselves is God; and all subordinate "submissions" must always be measured in relationship to our all-embracing submission to Him.[31]

Taking the several perspectives on the State found in the New Testament into consideration, it seems that a Christian's stance with reference to the State will shift depending upon the State's own posture. Three options are possible.[32]

• A critical-constructive stance = cooperation by neighbors. This is appropriate when the powers that be are attempting to achieve justice. Christians can then work side by side with the State.
• A critical-transformative stance = constant tension, uneasy peace between neighbors. This is appropriate when authority errs but can be realistically moved to salutary change.
• A critically resistive stance = courageous opposition to particular governments that are corrupt and idolatrous. This is appropriate

when the powers are responsible for demonic injustice or idolatry and refuse to be responsible to change. This may (e.g., Bonhoeffer) or may not (e.g., even Revelation does not call for violent resistance) involve violence.

Walter Wink's observations are similar. He has said that:

God at one and the same time *upholds* a given political or economic system, since some such system is required to support human life; *condemns* that system insofar as it is destructive of full human actualization; and *presses for its transformation* into a more humane order.[33]

NOTES

[1] Seneca, *Epistle* 64.8.

[2] Walter T. Wilson, *The Mysteries of Righteousness: The Literary Composition and Genre of the Sentences of Pseudo-Phocylides* (Tübingen: Mohr [Siebeck], 1994), 102, 82.

[3] Victor Paul Furnish, *Theology and Ethics in Paul* (Nashville: Abingdon, 1968), 215-16.

[4] John Murray, *The Epistle to the Romans, 9–16* (Grand Rapids: Eerdmans, 1965), 109.

[5] Peter Stuhlmacher, *Paul's Letter to the Romans* (Louisville: Westminster John Knox, 1994), 186.

[6] Diodorus Siculus 5.49.5-6.

[7] Brendan Byrne, "Living Out the Righteousness of God: The Contribution of Romans 6:1–8:13 to an Understanding of Paul's Ethical Presuppositions," *CBQ* 43 (1981): 557-81, especially p. 575.

[8] Ben Witherington III, *Paul's Narrative Thought World* (Louisville: Westminster John Knox, 1994), 339.

[9] H. Wenschkewitz, "Die Spiritualisierung der Kultus Begriffe Temple, Priester, und Opfer im Neuen Testament," *Angelos* 4 (1932): 71-230.

[10] Douglas J. Moo, *The Epistle to the Romans* (Grand Rapids: Eerdmans, 1996), 754.

[11] R. J. Daly, "The New Testament Concept of Christian Sacrificial Activity," *Biblical Theology Bulletin* 8 (1978): 99-107.

[12] Cited in Gerald Bray, *Romans* (*ACCS;* Downer's Grove IL: InterVarsity, 1998), 310.

[13] Scott M. Kyles, "Love Your Enemies and Pray for Those Who Persecute You: The Love/Prayer for Enemies Parenesis in Pre-Nicaean Christianity," MA Thesis, Wake Forest University, 1994.

[14] Cited in Bray, *Romans*, 321.

[15] Ibid., 322.

[16] Richard J. Cassidy, *Christians and Roman Rule in the New Testament* (New York: Crossroad, 2001), makes this case for all teaching about the State in the NT.

[17] L. C. A. Alexander, "Rome, Early Christian Attitudes to," *ABD* 5.835-39.

[18] Cited in Bray, *Romans*, 331.

[19] Peter Stuhlmacher, *Paul's Letter to the Romans* (Louisville: Westminster John Knox, 1994), 216-17.

[20] Ibid., 217.

[21] Bruce C. Birch and Larry L. Rasmussen, *Bible and Ethics in the Christian Life* (Minneapolis: Augsburg, 1976), 114-117.

[22] Michael Thompson, *Clothed with Christ: The Example and Teaching of Jesus in Romans 12:1–15:13* (Sheffield: JSOT, 1991), 240, ends his study with the conclusion that the example of Jesus carries more significance for Paul than dominical logia.

[23] James D. G. Dunn, *Romans 9–16* (WBC; Dallas: Word, 1988), 752.

[24] Michael Thompson, *Clothed with Christ*, 239.

[25] Allan A. Boesak, "What Belongs to Caesar? Once Again Romans 13," in *When Prayer Makes News*, ed. A. A. Boesak and C. Villa-Vicencio (Philadelphia: Westminster, 1986), 138-57.

[26] Cited in Bray, *Romans*, 325.

[27] Ibid., 326.

[28] John T. McNeill, ed., *Institutes of the Christian Religion* by John Calvin, 2 volumes (Philadelphia: Westminster, 1960), 1.520.

[29] Greenville S C: Smyth & Helwys, 1991.

[30] John Stott, *Romans*, 342.

[31] Douglas J. Moo, *The Epistle to the Romans*, 797.

[32] Walter E. Pilgrim, *Uneasy Neighbors: Church and State in the New Testament* (Minneapolis: Fortress, 1999), 192.

[33] Walter Wink, *Engaging the Powers* (Minneapolis: Fortress, 1992), 67.

HOW SLAVES OF RIGHTEOUSNESS BEHAVE, PART TWO

14:1–15:13

COMMENTARY

The second part of the parenetic section of Romans (12:1–15:13) is 14:1–15:13. It is held together by an inclusion (14:1—welcome; 15:7—welcome). Romans 14:1–15:13 sounds, on first reading, very much like 1 Corinthians 8–10. The correspondences are many. For example:

• The problem over eating certain foods	1 Cor 8:1	Rom 14:2-3
• One side feels free to eat	1 Cor 8:4-6, 8; 10:23, 29b-30	Rom 14:2, 6, 14
• Another side feels it is wrong to eat	1 Cor 8:7	Rom 14:2
• One side's exercise of freedom hurts the other	1 Cor 8:9-11	Rom 14:13
• One side is called the weak	1 Cor 8:7, 9, 11-12	Rom 14:1; 15:1
• Do not harm one for whom Christ died	1 Cor 8:11	Rom 14:15
• Do not eat meat if it causes another believer to stumble	1 Cor 8:13	Rom 14:21
• (Imitate me as I) imitate Christ	1 Cor 11:1	Rom 15:3, 8.

The differences are just as striking, however. For example:

• In 1 Corinthians the issue is meat polluted by idols. In Romans the issue is vegetarianism (= asceticism?). Pollution by idols is not an issue.

- In 1 Corinthians the debate is limited to meat. In Romans the controversy includes also wine and days.
- In 1 Corinthians the weak are converted pagans who are having difficulty with their break from pagan ways. In Romans the weak are probably Jewish Christiansand Judaized Gentiles who are having difficulty with their break from ethnic Judaism.

Romans 14–15 seems to be a reworking of some of the same type of material found in 1 Corinthians 8–10. In Romans, however, it is applied to a new situation, one that reflects the particular circumstances of the that city's messianist congregations. This material, then, is not addressed to a typical situation but to a specific one in Rome at the time the letter was written.

The nature of the issues addressed in Romans 14:1–15:13 is different from that in chapters 12–13. In Romans 12–13 Paul spoke about behavior that, given certain circumstances, is good or bad in itself (e.g., no revenge; pay taxes; avoid vice). In Romans 14:1–15:13 the matters addressed are those that are good or bad depending upon what connotations they have for the person doing them. This latter set of issues consists of what was, in antiquity, called *adiaphora* (= matters of indifference).[1] The Stoic philosopher Epictetus (*Dissertations* 2.19.13) said: "Now the virtues and everything that shares in them are good, while vices . . . are evil, but what falls in between these . . . are indifferent (*adiaphora*)." When Paul assessed dietary rules and observance of days as irrelevant (= not of the essence of the faith), he was relegating such regulations to the ancient philosophic category of *adiaphora*.

For Epictetus (*Dissertations* 2.5.7), however, although certain matters were not inherently virtuous or inherently evil, their use is not a casual matter. He said that *adiaphora* "must be used carefully, because their use is not a matter of indifference." Likewise Paul, who regarded diet and days as inherently matters of indifference, believed how such matters were handled was not a matter of indifference. It was a vital Christian issue whether or not disagreements over such matters led to division within the congregations; likewise, it was a crucial ethical issue whether or not fellow Christians were damaged by other Christians' freedom. In this, again, Paul's thought runs parallel to that of Epictetus. The philosopher argued that one should never treat anything as a matter of one's own private profit. He said: "never exercise choice or desire in any other way but by reference to the whole" (*Dissertations* 2.10.4). Paul, similarly, argued against pleasing oneself and in favor of pleasing one's neighbor, for "the good purpose of building up the neighbor"

(15:2b). Of course, Paul's motivations were different from the Stoic's. Paul appealed to the pattern of Christ's behavior and to the words of Scripture (15:3-4). But the Christian Jew, Paul, belonged to the larger Mediterranean culture and would have been heard in such terms.

The situation in 14:1–15:13 may be summarized in several steps. First, both vegetarianism and the observance of certain days had double roots: both pagan and Jewish.[2] (1) Pagan—(a) Vegetarianism: Certain neo-Pythagoreans were vegetarians (Diogenes Laertius 8.38; Philostratus, *Life of Apollonius* 1.8). Pythagorean teachers in Rome, like Sotion and Quintus, were vegetarians (Seneca, *Epistle* 108.13-16, 17-18, 20-21). The Stoic, Musonius Rufus in the time of Nero, was provegetarian. (b) Days: Theophrastus, *Characters* 16.10, spoke of the religious/superstitious person who observes the fourth and the seventh days each month. Tacitus, *Annals* 16.21, referred to Nero's charge against Thrasea Paetus for failure to observe the Juvenalia days as a senator was expected to do. (2) Jewish—(a) Vegetarianism: Although the Scriptures did not command vegetarianism, some Jews for various reasons did not eat meat (or drink wine). [Reasons for Vegetarianism during the Hellenistic Period] For example, Daniel 1:8 (Daniel ate vegetables and drank water); Philo, *Contemplative Life* 37 (the Therpeutae were vegetarians); Josephus, *Life* 14 (some Jewish priests imprisoned in Rome ate only figs and nuts); Judith 12:2; Additions to Esther 14:17; *T. Reuben* 1:10; *T. Judah* 15:4; *Joseph and Aseneth* 8:5. Certain Jewish Christians were vegetarian: Eusebius, *Church History* 2.23.5 (James the brother of Jesus); Origen, *In Matthew* 11.12 (Ebionites).(b) Days: For Jews, Sabbath observance was rooted in creation (Gen 2:2-3), commanded in the Decalog (Exod 20:8-11), part of Israel's covenant understanding (Exod 31:16-17), required of proselytes (Isa 56:6), and protected by Roman law for Jews in Asia (Josephus, *Ant* 14.241-46, 258,263-64) and in Rome (Philo, *Legat* 155-58). Gentiles recognized Sabbath observance as a mark of Jewishness (Seneca, *Ep* 95.47; Tacitus, *Hist* 5.4; Plutarch, *Superst* 169C). For Josephus, *Antiquities* 11.346, eating unclean food and violating the Sabbath were two chief hallmarks of covenant disloyalty among Jews.

Second, The Roman congregations had members of both types: those who were vegetarians and observed certain days and those who were not and did not.

Third, Paul labeled the two types of believers: the weak and the strong. He did not call them Jewish and Gentile! This leaves open

Reasons for Vegetarianism during the Hellenistic Period

There was no one reason for vegetarianism in antiquity. The various reasons include the following. (Dombrowski)

- Belief in the transmigration of souls—Ovid, *Metamorphoses*, based his vegetarianism on a belief in transmigration of souls. He said that the soul passes from beasts into human bodies and from human bodies into beasts, never perishing (15.165-69). To kill an animal, then, is to kill a human being (15.463-67). Sotion, a Pythagorean who taught Seneca, contended that if the theory of transmigration of souls is correct, it is a mark of purity to refrain from eating flesh (Seneca, *Moral Epistles* 108.20-21).

- Belief in a Golden Age (or Age of Cronus) in which there was universal vegetarianism when humans lived according to nature—Plutarch (*Moralia* 993 ["On the Eating of Flesh," 1.1]) wondered by what accident and in what state of mind the first man who did so touched his mouth to gore and brought his lips to the flesh of a dead creature. Eating animal flesh, he thought, is contrary to nature (1.5). Musonius Rufus (18A) likewise said "meat was a less civilized kind of food and more appropriate to wild animals."

- Desire for mental enhancement—Apollonius of Tyana abstained from animal flesh because it made the mind gross. He, therefore, ate only dried fruits and vegetables (Philostratus, *Life of Apollonius of Tyana* 1.8). Plutarch (*Moralia* 132 ["Advice about Keeping Well" 18]) said: "We should use other foods and relishes which for the body are more in accord with nature and less dulling to the reasoning faculty." Musonius Rufus taught that animal flesh was "an obstacle to thinking and reasoning, since the exhalations rising from it being turbid darken the soul" (18A).

- Health concerns—Plutarch advised a vegetarian diet for health reasons. He says: "Especially to be feared are indigestions arising from meats; for they are depressing at the outset, and a pernicious residue from them remains behind. It is best to accustom the body not to require meat in addition to other food" (Plutarch, *Moralia* 132 ["Advice about Keeping Well" 18]). Seneca's teacher, Sotion, taught that eating flesh "was unsuited to our constitutions" (Seneca, *Moral Epistles* 108.18).

- The cultivation of spiritual sensitivity—Plutarch also recommended vegetarianism for spiritual reasons. "The eating of flesh . . . makes us spiritually coarse and gross by reason of satiety and surfeit. For wine and indulgence in meat make the body strong but the soul weak" (*Moralia* 995). In Daniel 10:2-3, the seer tells of his three-week period in which he abstained from meat and wine before receiving a vision (cf. 2 Esd 12:51 together with 13:1).

- Commitment to covenant faithfulness—Ancient Jews believed that some animals were unclean and should not be eaten; they believed that they should not eat flesh with the blood in it; they were convinced that they should not eat meat that had been sacrificed to idols. All of these restrictions stood in the way of Jews eating Gentile food. Such food could violate one or more of these beliefs and in doing so manifest unfaithfulness to the covenant with Yahweh. So Daniel and his friends did not eat the king's food (Dan 1:5-16); Tobit, when carried off to Nineveh, abstained from Gentile food (Tob 1:10-13); Judith, when invited to a banquet, ate Jewish food she had brought with her (Jdt 12:1-4); Esther refused to eat Gentile food (Add Esth 14:17); Judas Maccabeus and nine others who escaped to the mountains lived on what grew in the wild "so that they might not share in the defilement" (2 Macc 5:27); certain Jewish priests sent by Felix to Rome in bonds while there "supported themselves on figs and nuts" (Josephus, *Life* 14). Covenant fidelity motivated these Jews to abstain from Gentile food/meat.

It is possible that the converts to Christ in Rome may have come out of circles in which one or more of these rationales for vegetarianism would have been held. It is, nevertheless, likely that it was the last of these that was most relevant in the Roman congregations to which Paul wrote.

Daniel A. Dombrowski, *The Philosophy of Vegetarianism* (Amherst: University of Massachusetts Press, 1984). This book is devoted mostly to a survey of attitudes toward vegetarianism in the Greco-Roman period. Cf. Richard A. Young, *Is God a Vegetarian?* (Chicago: Open Court, 1999).

the possibility that the weak could be either converted pagans or converted Jews.

Fourth, the focus of the letter on Jew and Gentile issues crops up again in 15:7-12. An inclusion (14:1, welcome; 15:7, welcome) holds 15:7-13 together with 14:1-23. This leads one to take the weak-strong division as a Jew-Gentile issue. Such a conclusion must, however, be nuanced. As James D. G. Dunn has said:

> A straightforward identification of 'the weak' as Jewish Christians, and 'the strong' as Gentile Christians may not be assumed. No doubt the weak included Gentiles who had previously been attracted to Judaism, . . . and 'the strong' included Jews like Paul himself, or Prisca and Aquila.[3]

A supporting piece of evidence comes from Horace, *Satires* 1.9.65-66. There Horace indicated that Sabbath observance is *infirmus* (=weakness). In Greco-Roman moral discourse, weakness was described as an "intense belief (in which someone) regards a thing that need not be shunned as though it ought to be shunned." It was an "act of judging that one has knowledge where one has none" (Cicero, *Tusculun Disputations* 4.26). Such judging was in areas like foods and wine.

Fifth, the problem was twofold. On the one hand, the weak's list of essential marks of the people of God included items that other members of the Roman congregations regarded as matters of indifference. The weak judged these other members as deficient. On the other hand, the strong who held diet and days to be *adiaphora* (matters of indifference) put their private freedom ahead of everything else, disdaining the weak. Judgment, disdain, and division were the result. Paul had to deal with a situation where matters he and others regarded as *adiaphora* were held by some to be essential to the faith. How did he handle it?

This section of Romans consists of three parts: 14:1-12, 14:13-23, and 15:1-13. The first, 14:1-12, is addressed to both sides, weak and strong. It criticizes both the presumption of the weak and the pride of the strong. Its call is for Christians not to judge one another in matters of *adiaphora* (indifference). Its organization looks like this.

Opening exhortation (14:1): Welcome those who are weak in faith
Unit One (14:2-4)
  A—(14:2): Different opinions about foods exist
    B—(14:3a): Exhortation—Let neither side judge the other
      C—(14:3b-4): The religious basis of the exhortation (God is the Judge.)
Unit Two (14:5-9)
  A'—(14:5a): Different opinions about days exist

B'—(14:5b): Exhortation—Let all be fully convinced in their own minds

C'—(14:6-9): The religious basis of the exhortation (We are the Lord's in life and in death.)[4]

Concluding exhortation (14:10-12, [13a]): Do not judge one another; that is God's role.

When Paul, in his opening exhortation, called for his readers to welcome the weak in faith, it sounds as though he was addressing only the strong. In A (v. 2), however, he mentioned both sides' issues: both those who believe one can eat anything and those who eat only vegetables. In B (v. 3a), moreover, the exhortation addresses both sides. Those who eat should not despise those who abstain; those who abstain should not pass judgment on those who eat. The basis for this nonjudgmental posture, C (vv. 3b-4), is that both sides are servants of God. Therefore, God is the judge of both sides.

The second little unit (vv. 5-9) likewise addresses both sides. In A' (v. 5a), some are said to judge one day to be better than another; others think all days are alike. B' (v. 5b) refers to "all," thereby including both sides. C' (vv. 6-9), likewise, indicates that both sides live not for themselves but for the Lord. This would have been regarded as a good thing by the best part of the culture (e.g., Plutarch, "Cleomenes," 31—"For it is shameful to die, as well as to live, for one's sake alone").

The first part of 14:1–15:13, 14:1-12, concludes with a rhetorical question addressed to both groups. "Why do you (the weak) pass judgment on your brother and sister? Or you, why do you (the strong) despise your brother or sister" (v. 10)? We are all accountable to God and will stand before His judgment seat (vv. 10b, 12). [Christians and the Last Judgment] The point of 14:1-12 is this: in matters of *adiaphora,* Christians are not to judge/despise one another for God is our judge. "Paul *pre*scribes mutual acceptance on the principle that those whom God has accepted His people must be prepared to accept. He *pro*scribes condemning each other on the principle that God is the only competent judge of His servants."[5]

The second part, 14:13-23, is addressed to the strong. Its call is to the strong not to be stumbling blocks for the weak. Its organization looks like this.

Christians and the Last Judgment

- Paul referred to the judgment of all Christians in Rom 14:10 ("we shall all stand before the judgment seat of God") and 2 Cor 5:10 ("we must all appear before the judgment seat of Christ").
- He implied possible judgment of himself on the Last Day in 1 Cor 4:4-5. This is a possibility even though his conscience is clear.
- The apostle stated in 1 Cor 3:13-15 that judgment of a Christian's work on the Last Day results in rewards or punishments. This judgment's effects are distinct from the question of one's eternal salvation (v. 15).

Unit One (14:13-18)

   A—(14:13): Let us never put a stumbling block in the way of another.

     B—(14:14): Nothing is unclean in itself.

       C—(14:15): If another is injured by your actions, you are not walking in love.

         D—(14:16-18): Act so as to be approved by God and humans.

Unit Two (14:20-23)

   A'—(14:19-20a): Do not destroy the work of God.

     B'—(14:20b): Everything is indeed clean.

       C'—(14:20c, 21): It is wrong to make other fall by what you do.

         D'—(14:22-23): Act so as to be approved by yourself.

A, (14:13), in the first subunit (14:13-18) calls for disciples "never to put a stumbling block or hindrance in the way of another." Paul said this in spite of what he said in B (14:14): "I know and am persuaded in the Lord Jesus that nothing is unclean in itself (cf. 7:15, 18-19, 23//Matt 15:11,17,20; Acts 10:1–11:18); but it is unclean for anyone who thinks it is unclean." Paul clearly stood with the strong on the matter of principle! Paul did not mean to say thereby that nothing is wrong unless one thinks it so. He would certainly have held that moral principles are objectively valid. Some things are wrong whether one thinks so or not. The apostle would not have urged mutual tolerance and give-and-take in regard to such matters (cf. 1 Cor 5:11). This statement is contingent on its context. The context indicates that here Paul was dealing with *adiaphora*. Only in matters of indifference does the statement of v. 14 apply. This knowledge that nothing is unclean in itself does not take precedence over love, however (cf. 1 Cor 8:1). C (14:15) says: "If your brother or sister is being injured by what you eat, you are no longer walking in love." D (14:16-18) begins: "Do not let your good (= the knowledge that nothing is clean or unclean in itself and, hence, the liberty to eat all things)[6] be spoken of as evil" (v. 16), that is, by absolutizing it as though that is what Christian faith is all about. Both sides need to know that "the kingdom of God is not food and drink (i.e., either partaking or abstaining) but righteousness (= justification, cf. Rom 5:1) and peace (= with God, cf. Rom 5:1) and joy in the Holy Spirit (cf. 15:13)" (v. 17). Those who so regard the Christian life are the ones who are acceptable to God and to other Christians. [Kingdom of God in the Pauline Corpus]

Kingdom of God in the Pauline Corpus

AΩ Kingdom of God is not used as extensively in the Pauline corpus as in the Gospels and Acts. There is no difference in the meaning of the kingdom of God in the seven genuine Pauline letters and in the Deuteropaulines. They may be treated together.

• Most references to the kingdom of God refer to the eschatological kingdom, the New Age beyond the resurrection.

(1 Thess 2:12—calls you into His kingdom and glory;

2 Thess 1:5—made worthy of the kingdom of God for which you are suffering;

Gal 5:21—certain ones will not inherit the kingdom of God;

1 Cor 6:9-10—certain ones will not inherit the kingdom of God;

1 Cor 15:50—flesh and blood cannot inherit the kingdom of God;

Eph 5:5—certain people have no inheritance in the kingdom of God;

2 Tim 4:1—God's kingdom which is associated with Christ's parousia;

2 Tim 4:18—God's heavenly kingdom)

• A few references seem to speak of a present kingdom, the reign of God.

(1 Cor 4:20—the kingdom of God does not consist in talk but in power;

Rom 14:17—the kingdom of God does not mean food and drink;

1 Cor 15:24—when Christ delivers the kingdom to God the Father at the End;

Col 1:13—Christians have been transferred to the kingdom of God's son)

The first two of these present references speak about what the rule of God in the present looks like. The first says it involves power, spiritual power, probably involving miracles. The second says it is not distinguished by markers of things like diet but rather by markers like persons' having been justified, having achieved peace with God, and having a joy arising out of the presence of the Holy Spirit in their lives.

When, therefore, kingdom of God does appear in the Pauline corpus, it is used in basically the same ways that it is in the Gospels and Acts.

A' (19-20a) insists that pursuing what makes for mutual upbuilding will not, for the sake of food, destroy the work of God. Again, the apostle supportee the principle (B', 14:20b): "Everything is indeed clean." Again, in C' (v. 20b, 21), he subordinated knowledge to love. "It is wrong for you to make others fall by what you eat." If it makes a fellow Christian stumble, do not do it. Taking B' and C' together yields Luther's position of Christian freedom:

A Christian is a perfectly free lord of all, subject to none.
A Christian is a perfectly dutiful servant, subject to all.[7]

In D' (14:22-23), Paul exhorted both sides to act in ways that would allow them no self-condemnation. Origen summed up this segment of Paul's argument in these words.

Eating meat and drinking wine are matters of indifference in themselves. Even wicked people may abstain from those things, and some, idol worshippers in fact do so, for reasons which are actually evil. Likewise quite a few heretics enjoin similar practices. The only reason abstinence of this kind is good is that it may help to avoid offending a brother.[8]

This was precisely Paul's point. If in the first part (14:1-12) the apostle argued against either side's judging the other over *adiaphora*, in this second part (14:13-23) he urged the strong to sacrifice their freedom based on their correct knowledge for the sake of the weaker brother or sister. Love is to triumph (remember 13:8-10).

The third part of 14:1–15:13 is 15:1-13. Its call is to Christians to bear with one another, following Christ's example. Like the previous two parts, 14:1-12 and 14:13-23, 15:1-13 falls into two subunits: 15:1-6 and 15:7-13. The first is addressed to the strong; the second is addressed to both groups. The organization of this part looks like this.

Unit One (15:1-6)
    A—(15:1-2): What the strong should do: build up the neighbor
      B—(15:3a): What Christ did: He did not please himself.
        C—(15:3b-4): An appeal to Scripture
          D—(15:5-6): A Pauline prayer for his readers

Unit Two (15:7-13)
    A'—(15:7a): What all Christians should do: welcome one another (welcome one another [15:7] echoes welcome the weak [14:1])
      B'—(15:7b-9a): What Christ did: He acted on behalf of both sides.
        C'—(15:9b-12): An appeal to various Scriptures
          D'—(15:13): A Pauline prayer for his readers

The first of the little subunits is addressed to the strong. A (15:1-2) appeals for self sacrifice on the part of the strong in behalf of the weak. "Each of us must please our neighbor for the good purpose of building up the neighbor." Why? B (15:3a) and C (15:3b-4) provide two bases for not pleasing oneself exclusively. The first is christological. "For Christ did not please himself." This is a reference to the self-abasement of Christ on our behalf (cf. 2 Cor 8:9; Phil 2:5-8). Here again it is the overall pattern of the Christ-event to which Paul appealed. The second basis is scriptural. Psalm 69:9

Men Exist for the Sake of One Another

The title of this work by Jacob Lawrence was taken from the meditations of Marcus Aurelius Antoninus, in which he writes "men exist for the sake of one another . . . Teach them then or bear with them." Lawrence, an African-American artist of the 20th century, develops the Antoninus quote from an African-American perspective rather than from a perspective based on Roman virtue. Using flat, collage-like planes of color, Lawrence graphically shows through gesture and simple design the nurturing and life-bestowing effects of teaching the younger ones.

Jacob Lawrence. 1917–2000. *Men Exist for the Sake of One Another, Teach Them Then or Bear With Them.* 1958. Oil on fiberboard. Smithsonian American Art Museum. Washington, DC. (Credit: Smithsonian American Art Museum/ Art Resource, NY/© Gwendolyn Knight Lawrence, courtesy of the Jacob and Gwendolyn Lawrence Foundation, NY)

is cited. Then Paul said that "whatever was written in former days was written for our instruction" (cf. 1 Cor 9:10; 10:11). D (15:5-6) is a Pauline prayer for his readers.

> May the God of steadfastness and encouragement grant you to live in harmony with one another, in accordance with Christ Jesus, so that together you may with one voice glorify the God and Father of our Lord Jesus Christ.

The second subunit (15:7-13) is addressed to both persuasions, weak and strong. A', (v. 7a), "Welcome one another" echoes 14:1, the two vv. serving as a brackets around the unit as a whole. Why welcome one another? Two bases again follow the injunction. Again, the first (B') is christological (15:7b-9a): "as Christ has welcomed you. . . . For . . . Christ has become a servant of the circumcised on behalf of the truth of God (= God's covenant faithfulness) in order that he might confirm the promises given to the patriarchs, and (a servant) with respect to the Gentiles on behalf of the mercy (of God) in order to glorify God."[9] The two sides are to welcome one another because Christ has welcomed both. He has both guaranteed the continuity of God's purpose to the circumcised and opened the promises to the Gentiles. Again, the second basis (C') is scriptural. This time there is a catena of references from Paul's Bible. Verse 9b uses Psalm 18:50 ("Therefore I will confess you among the Gentiles"); v. 10 uses Deuteronomy 32:43 ("Rejoice, O Gentiles, with His people"); v. 11 employs Psalm 117:1 ("Praise the Lord, all Gentiles, and let all the peoples praise Him"); and v. 12 quotes Isaiah 11:10 ("The root of Jesse shall come, the one who rises [in Paul's context, a reference to Jesus' resurrection] to rule the Gentiles"). One needs to note that these scriptural quotations all are a support not of the fulfillment of the promises to the patriarchs but of the inclusion of the Gentiles through Christ. D' (15:13) is a Pauline prayer for his readers:

> May the God of hope fill you with all joy and peace in believing, so that you may abound in hope by the power of the Holy Spirit.

Paul's third part of 14:1–15:13 brings his argument to a climax. It affirms mutual acceptance by and of those whom Christ has accepted. Matters of indifference must not be allowed to destroy individuals or the community. Paul's aim in 14:1–15:13 was not to remove diversity but to promote harmony within diversity. Ethnicity, while not of ultimate significance, is not dismissed.[10]

CONNECTIONS

Christian Tolerance

Martin Marty has been quoted as saying: "The problem is that the civil people are not committed and the committed people aren't civil."[11] G. K. Chesterton said: "Tolerance is the virtue of the person without convictions."[12] The dilemma of tolerance/intolerance in modern society has caused some to attempt to derive a general Christian stance on social tolerance from Romans 14:1–15:13.[13] This cannot be done.

Paul here distinguished between essentials (living and dying for God; justification; peace with God; joy in the Holy Spirit) and *adiaphora* (= matters that are indifferent, like diet and days). He did not treat the two alike. For example, Paul would not advocate tolerance for "the works of darkness" (13:12-13). They are to be put off. He would advocate tolerance for *adiaphora*. So the two areas of life demand two different approaches by Christians. John Stott has put it this way. "In fundamentals . . . faith is primary, and we may not appeal to love as an excuse to deny essential faith. In nonfundamentals, however, love is primary, and we may not appeal to zeal for the faith as an excuse for failure in love."[14] He then concluded with a quotation from Rupert Meldenius (= Richard Baxter?): "In essentials unity; in nonessentials liberty; in all things charity." But if Paul was dealing with *adiaphora* in 14:1–15:13, any attempt to build a general view of Christian tolerance on the basis of this text is doomed to failure.

It is, however, possible to criticize two modern views of tolerance on the basis of Paul's thought. (1) One modern view of tolerance is based on the division between public and private spheres. So long as those who feel strongly about their religion regard their feelings/convictions/beliefs as private matters not to be brought into the public sphere, civility is preserved. Those who feel strongly do not impose their beliefs on others; those who are unconcerned allow the passionate to be so in private. Tolerance reigns so long as one side does not express its passion and the other remains unconcerned. This view is untenable because it assumes that no one who is antireligion will ever express passion in the public sphere. Even those who are unconcerned about one issue will be passionately concerned about another. Passion cannot and will not remain private, for either the religious or the nonreligious. Nor would Paul assume Christians should or would be able to remain only a conclave of private passion. (2) Tolerance in postmodernism is grounded in the alleged perceived ambiguity of all human thought and in the alleged irreconcilable pluralism of human groups. Everything, beliefs and cultures, is relative. So tolerance is the only option. As this view plays out in some interpreters, all religions are regarded as equal except Christianity, and it is viewed as the great oppressor because it believes it knows the truth about God and humankind. This stance of total relativity subverts its own assertions, which have to be taken as only relative. Paul could never have affirmed such a position. His gospel, he regarded as true in a universal sense.[Fred Craddock on Christian Judgment of Others]

Perhaps the greatest contribution of Baptists to modern life has been their emphasis on religious liberty. Historically, Baptists have combined a passion for the truth of the gospel and its propagation publicly and universally with a conviction that power should never replace persuasion in matters religious. This position transcends all versions of tolerance. It affirms liberty, not tolerance. The conscience is free and belongs to God alone. The State, or any other institution of power, has no right to interfere with this religious liberty that is inherent in our humanity. Baptists have insisted that this freedom must be available to all peoples:

Fred Craddock on Christian Judgment of Others

What the apostle Paul understood, of course, is that if you are not careful, being judgmental or critical of other people goes along with a Christian life. When you hear the gospel and embrace the gospel, it heightens your awareness of things, increases your sensitivity, makes you feel more deeply and strongly about things. You care more than you did before, and one way this caring can get expressed, not admirably of course, is by being discontent, even ill-tempered sometimes, toward people who do not measure up. When the gospel begins to go through your veins week after week after week after week, it changes you.

Fred Craddok, "Who Am I to Judge Another?" in *The Cherry Log Sermons* (Louisville: Westminster John Knox Press, 2001), 75.

Christians, Jews, Muslims, unbelievers, etc. Faith cannot be coerced! At the same time, Baptists have historically believed that all faiths, including an alleged lack of faith, have the right to compete freely in the public arena in the marketplace of ideas by means of persuasion. Restrictions on evangelism have been regarded by Baptists as as much a violation of conscience as is the use of power to coerce belief or lack of belief. This stance on religious liberty the apostle Paul would have supported.

The Role of Ethnic Distinctives in Church

Since all humans are culture-bound, any experience of Christ will be filtered through one's culture/ethnicity and one's faith with be intertwined with pieces of one's culture. Americans will find their culture filtering Christ to them; Africans, Asians, Europeans will find the same. Each person's culture is a filter. The issue is: is our ethnicity good or bad in Christ?

Every culture has some things that, when evaluated from the vantage point of Christ, are in continuity with him. Likewise, every culture will possess some things that are in discontinuity with the Lord Jesus. In addition, every culture will contain some things that are indifferent. A renewed mind (Rom 12:2) will be able to discern which is what. That which is in continuity with Christ may stay; that which is in discontinuity will have to go; and those things that are indifferent may stay or go. In Christian communities these discernments will have to be made and implemented. In these communities love will lead the way in dealing with *adiaphora* (matters of indifference).

In discussions of Christian missions, the degree of a church's absorption of a culture is often categorized loosely on a scale from 1-5 according to the measure of its contextualization. Church One (C1) congregations are those that are implanted and that bring a new use of language and worship that are completely differentiated and estranged from the local culture. Church Five (C5) congregations are at the opposite end of the spectrum. They consist of converts who have retained their cultural identities yet perceive themselves as followers of Christ. These converts may continue to pray in their former holy sites and be involved in local community life. Of course, C2-4 congregations progress along the line from one extreme (C1) to the other (C5). Missionary strategists fall into all camps on the spectrum. C1 advocates contend that C5 Christians have crossed the line of syncretism. C5 advocates argue that C1 Christians encumber the Christian message with a myriad of legal, social, and cultural issues that are not of the essence of the faith.

In some cases the issue is not difficult to adjudicate. For example, if a Muslim convert who does not eat pork or drink alcohol encounters in a congregation non-Muslim converts who believe the eating of pork and drinking of wine are matters of indifference, what will happen? Almost certainly, the former will have the same reaction as the weak of Romans 14:1–15:13. Almost certainly, the latter will react as did the strong in 14:1–15:13. In this situation, Paul's directives (don't judge one another; let the strong accommodate the weak) seem directly applicable.

The sticky part comes when one tries to sort out matters of indifference from matters of principle. Certain parts of a given culture are oftentimes so inextricably intertwined with that which is alien to Christ that conversion demands a break with at least that part of the culture. Then, it is often the case that separation from one or more parts of a culture alone seems impossible. Many of the writings of Tertullian, Clement of Alexandria and Origen near and immediately after AD 200 struggled with just this issue. It is interesting to note that their discernments differed. Tertullian was less accommodating of the pagan culture while Clement and Origen were more accepting. If faithful Christians differ, then what? A general observation helps us begin. Especially in new converts, a radical break with a mixed non-Christian past with its associated structures seems inevitable. Later on, once the Christian identity of the convert is secure, it is often possible for the convert to discern which parts of the culture to accept as compatible with Christ and which ones to continue to reject as incompatible. If the previous illustration of pork and alcohol is spoken to directly by Romans 14:1–15:13, other more complex matters must depend on the renewed mind that is able to discern God's will (Rom 12:1-2). The latter cases, as debates among current missiologists show, are not easy to decide.[15] Knowing where to draw the line between the inculturation of the gospel and the evangelization of cultures is an ongoing process.

NOTES

. [1] James L. Jaquette, "Life and Death, *Adiaphopra*, and Paul's Rhetorical Strategies," *NovT* 38 (1996): 30-54.

[2] Mark Reasoner, *The Strong and the Weak: Romans 14:1–15:13 in Context* (Cambridge: Cambridge University Press, 1999).

[3] James D. G. Dunn, *Romans 9–16* (WBC; Dallas: Word, 1988), 802.

[4] Brendan Byrne, *Romans* (Collegeville: Liturgical Press, 1996), 410, notes that vv. 7-9 have a symmetrical structure (six lines consisting of three corresponding couplets) and a hymnic ring about them, suggesting the quotation of an early Christian hymn or statement of faith.

[5] Stephen Westerholm, *Preface to the Study of Paul* (Grand Rapids: Eerdmans, 1997), 123.

[6] Robert A. J. Gagnon, "The Meaning of *humōn to agathon* in Romans 14:16," *JBL* 117 (1998): 675-89.

[7] Martin Luther, "The Freedom of a Christian" (*Luther's Works*, Vol 31 [1957], 344).

[8] Cited in Gerald Bray, *Romans* (Downers Grove: InterVarsity, 1998), 350.

[9] J. Ross Wagner, "The Christ, Servant of Jew and Gentile: A Fresh Approach to Romans 15:8-9," *JBL* 116 (1997):473-85.

[10] William S. Campbell, "The Rule of Faith in Romans 12:1–15:13," in *Pauline Theology, Vol. III: Romans*, ed. David M. Hay and E. Elizabeth Johnson (Minneapolis: Fortress, 1995), 275.

[11] Robert Jewett, *Christian Tolerance: Paul's Message to the Modern Church* (Philadelphia: Westminster Press, 1982), 9.

[12] Ibid., 38.

[13] So Jewett.

[14] John Stott, *Romans* (Downers Grove: InterVarsity, 1994), 375.

[15] Such discussions may be seen in several current articles in the same journal: e.g., Joshua Massey, "His Ways Are Not Our Ways," *Evangelical Missions Quarterly* 35 (1999): 188-97; Phil Parshall, "Danger! New Directions in Contextualization," *Evangelical Missions Quarterly* 34 (1998): 404-10; John Travis, "Must All Muslims Leave Islam to Follow Jesus?" *Evangelical Missions Quarterly* 34 (1998): 411-14. James C. Walters, *Ethnic Issues in Paul's Letter to the Romans* (Valley Forge: Trinity Press, 1993), uses Romans 14:1–15:13 as an entry into this discussion.

MAKING THE MOST
OF AN ENDING

15:14–16:27

The central argument of Romans (1:16–15:13) is set within an epistolary framework (1:1-15 and 15:14–16:27). This commentary has now reached the epistolary material at the end of the theological argument. This material is composed of two parts: first, the apostolic parousia (15:14-33), and second, the letter closing (16:1-27).

COMMENTARY

The apostolic parousia is that part of a Pauline letter that provides travel information: past, present, and future (cf. 1 Thess 2:17–3:13; 1 Cor 4:14-21; Phil 2:19-24; Phlm 21-22). It may come at any point in a Pauline letter: early, middle, or end. In Romans the apostolic parousia comes at the end so as to form, together with 1:8-15, an inclusion around the letter's theological argument. Note the similar themes in the two sections of the letter.

• Congratulations	15:14	1:8
• Ministry to the Gentiles	15:15-21	1:13b
• Hindrance in Paul's coming	15:22	1:13a
• Desire to see them for mutual benefit	15:23-24, 28-29	1:11-12
• Paul's indebtedness	15:25-27	1:14
• Prayer	15:30-32	1:9-10
• Commendation to/ thanks to God	15:33	1:8

These similarities form a frame around the theological argument of 1:16–15:13.

The apostolic parousia in Romans 15:14-33 consists of six components:

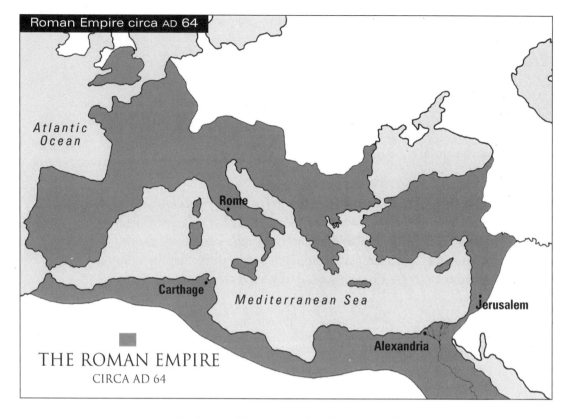

Roman Empire circa AD 64

Atlantic Ocean

Rome

Carthage

Mediterranean Sea

Jerusalem

Alexandria

THE ROMAN EMPIRE
CIRCA AD 64

15:14-16—Paul's stance with reference to the Romans
15:17-22—Paul's past record
15:23-24—Paul's future plans
15:25-29—Paul's present preoccupation
15:30-32—Paul's appeal for prayer
15:33—Paul's peace wish

Each may be examined in turn.

Romans 15:14-16 focuses on Paul's two-sided relationship with the Romans. On the one hand, the apostle said: "I myself feel confident about you, my brothers and sisters, that you yourselves are full of goodness, filled with all knowledge, and able to instruct one another" (v. 14). This is a diplomatic touch (cf. 1:8, 12). On the other hand, Paul wrote: "Nevertheless, on some points I have written to you by way of reminder" (v. 15a). The reason he has done this is "because of the grace given me by God" (v. 15b; cf. 1:5). This task given to Paul by God is described in priestly terms: "to be a minister (*leitourgon*—in the LXX and NT often used of the priest who performs service in the temple: Neh 10:40; Sir 7:30; Heb 8:2) of Christ Jesus to the Gentiles in the priestly service (*hierourgounta*—not in the LXX, but in Philo [e.g., *Leg Alleg* 3.130] and Josephus [e.g., *Ant* 5.263] it is used of the priestly offering of sacrifice) of the gospel of God, so that the offering of the Gentiles may be acceptable, sanctified (*hagiazein*—the act of setting apart, dedicating to God, so as to be His alone or to be used solely for His purposes) by the Holy Spirit (1 Cor 6:11; 2 Thess 2:13; Heb 10:29; 1 Pet 1:2)" (v. 16). In this cultic image, the god is Jesus, the priest is Paul, and the worshipers are the Gentiles. The priest's responsibility is to make sure the worshipers' offering is presentable according to the requirements of the cult. The image, then, indicates the dependence of the Gentiles on Paul in making a right response to the gospel.[1] Paul was the one whose preaching was the occasion for the Holy Spirit to fall on his Gentile hearers (cf. Gal 3:2; 1 Thess 1:4-5;1 Cor 2:4-5). Then when they present themselves to Christ (= the Gentiles are both the worshippers who present an offering and the offering presented—cf. Rom 12:1-2), the Gentiles are sanctified (holy) because of the Holy Spirit they have received.

Romans 15:17-22 turns our attention to Paul's past record. "I have reason to boast of my work in God" (v. 17). What has Christ done through Paul? He has worked to "win obedience from the Gentiles" (v. 18b; cf. 1:5; 16:26) "by word and deed, by the power of signs and wonders, by the power of the Spirit of God" (vv. 18c-19a; cf. 2 Cor 12:12; 1 Cor 4:20; cf. Heb 2:3-4; Acts 4:29-30). Paul was a miracle-working preacher. On this point the picture of Paul in the undisputed letters and the picture of Paul in Acts are agreed. Where has he worked? Two things are said. Geographically, Paul said he has preached the good news from Jerusalem to Illyricum (= modern Albania; v. 19b). Illyricum is another name for Dalmatia (cf. 2 Tim 4:10). The expression "as far around as" translates the word *mechri* which can denote simply "up to" instead of "into." If so, then Paul was saying that he has gone to the boundaries of the civilized world at this point. Demographically, he was saying that he had tried to work "not where Christ has already been named (cf. 2 Cor 10:13-16; 1 Cor 3:6, 10), so that I do not build on someone else's foundation" (v. 20), that is, his mission was to preach only in virgin territory. What has been the consequence of this ministry? "This is the reason that I have so often been hindered from coming to you" (v. 22). Preoccupation with his missionary task has prevented Paul's visiting Rome before now.

Romans 15:23-24 turns to Paul's plans for the future. Since there was no more virgin territory in the part of the world in which Paul had been working, his sights were now set on Spain. On his way to this new frontier, the apostle hoped to visit for a while with the Roman Christians. He also hoped that they would then assist him in his Spanish mission. Spain was frequently visited from Rome (Pausanias 10.4.6; cf. Cicero, *Tusc Dis* 1.45). Paul's plan to go to Spain would be different in one regard from his previous work. In the Aegean area, he had worked in and out of the Jewish synagogues. There is, however, no evidence of Jewish communities in Spain prior to the fall of Jerusalem in AD 70.[2] In Spain Paul would have to work without the support of synagogues.

Romans 15:25-29 focuses on Paul's present preoccupation. "At present I am going to Jerusalem in a ministry to the saints" (v. 25). This is a reference to the collection for the poor in Jerusalem (Gal 2:10; 1 Cor 16:1-4; 2 Cor 8–9; cf. Acts 24:17). Churches in Macedonia and Achaia had shared their resources in an offering to assist "the poor among the saints in Jerusalem" (v. 26). There have been numerous attempts to explain what such a collection meant to Paul. Some have argued that the delivery of the collection fulfilled the prophecies that Gentiles would bring their wealth to Jerusalem in the last days (Isa 2:2-3; Mic 4:1-2; Isa 45:14; 60:5-17; 61:6; Mic 4:13; Tob 13:11; 1 QM 12.13-15). Others have contended that Paul hoped that the delivery of the collection would provoke the unbelieving Jews to jealousy (cf. Rom 10–11) and thereby speed the coming of the End. Both of these explanations are possible. Neither is mentioned explicitly in the text. All that Paul said here explicitly about the collection is in terms of reciprocity, a controlling principle in almost all Mediterranean relationships. "They were pleased to do this, and indeed they owe it to them; for if the Gentiles have come to share in their spiritual blessings, they ought also to be of service to them in material things" (v. 27; cf. 2 Cor 9:13-14). In terms of the assumptions of antiquity, such reciprocity proved a relationship among equals existed. This doubtless was Paul's primary aim, whatever subsidiary goals he had as well. After completion of his delivery of the collection in Jerusalem, Paul aimed to "set out by way of you to Spain" (v. 28). The projected visit to Rome was subordinated to the apostle's missionary plans just as his earlier absence had been.

Romans 15:30-32 is an appeal for prayer. There are two specific requests. "Join me in earnest prayer to God that I may be rescued from the unbelievers in Judea" is the first (v. 31a). The second is that "my ministry to Jerusalem may be acceptable" (v. 31b). Acts 21:27-31 indicates that nonmessianic Jews were catalysts in his arrest and imprisonment in Jerusalem. According to Acts, Paul's fears were justified about the unbelievers. What about the Christian messianic Jews in Jerusalem? Acts 21:20-22 speaks about the thousands of believers among the Jews, zealous for the law, who have heard that Paul taught Jews living among the Gentiles to forsake Moses, not to circumcise their children, and not to observe the customs. If Paul's opponents in Galatia and Philippi were Jewish Christians opposing a law-free gospel, then there must have been Jewish Christian opposition to Paul in Jerusalem. Furthermore, the nationalism that led to the Jewish Revolt of AD 66–70 may have been on the rise even in the late 50s. Acts 22:21-22 seems to indicate that this was so. The very mention of Gentiles starts a riot! Such nationalism led to the later decision that the temple should accept no further gift or sacrifice from a foreigner (Josephus, *JW* 2.409-10), a prelude to war. The possibility was very real, therefore, that the Jewish Christians in Jerusalem would not accept Paul's collection from the Gentile churches in Macedonia and Achaia. Indeed, we do not know for a fact that it ever was accepted! Paul's request for the Romans to be his prayer partners was fully justified by the unbelievers and believers who opposed him. If, in fact, all worked out in Jerusalem, however, this would allow Paul to visit the Roman Christians "with joy and be refreshed in your company" (v. 32). As it turned out, according to Acts, Paul did indeed visit the Roman Christians but not because his collection visit worked out. He came to Rome as a prisoner. [Paul's Imprisonment in Rome]

Romans 15:33 is a peace wish such as can be found elsewhere in the Pauline letters (cf. 1 Thess 5:23-24; 2 Cor 13:11b; Gal 6:16; Phil 4:7-9; 2 Thess 3:16; Eph 6:23). With this the apostolic parousia segment of this letter is at an end.

What follows in Romans 16:1-27 is the closing of the letter. Contemporary research is virtually unanimous that chapter 16 is indeed an integral part of the correspondence sent to Rome. Earlier

Paul's Imprisonment in Rome
According to Acts 28:30-31, Paul lived in Rome under house arrest for two years. Church tradition holds that he was released, and then several years later was arrested again, imprisoned, and beheaded during the Neronian persecution that also claimed the life of Peter. Later church tradition identified the Mamertine Prison, located at the foot of the Capitoline Hill, as the place where Peter was imprisoned. Paul was imprisoned at about the same time, perhaps, at Mamertine also.

(Credit: Scott Nash)

doubts about the integrity of the letter were based on the fact that three different forms of Romans circulated in antiquity: in essence, Romans 1–14, Romans 1–15, and Romans 1–16. Origen's comments on 16:24 in his *Commentary on the Epistle to Romans* show how the questions have been resolved. He said:

> Marcion, who interpolated both the Gospels and the Epistles, deleted this passage (Rom 16:24) from the text, and not only this but everything (after 14:25) as well. In other manuscripts not edited by Marcion we find this passage in different places. Some have it immediately after (14:25), and others have it here, at the end of the epistle.[3]

The three forms of Romans found in the textual tradition are usually explained as follows: Romans 1–16 is the original form of the letter; Marcion shortened it to the chapter 1–14 version; then Marcion's shortened version was supplemented by the addition of chapter 15. It is this reconstruction that is assumed in this commentary.

The components of this closing section are clear:[4]

Romans 16:1-2—A letter of recommendation
16:3-16a—Greetings to Christians in Rome
16:17-20a—Hortatory section
16:20b—Grace benediction
16:16b, 21-23—Greetings from Christians outside Rome
[16:24—Not part of the text of Romans]
16:25-27—Doxology

Each of these component pieces may be examined in turn.

Romans 16:1-2 reflects the early Christian practice of using letters of recommendation (Acts 18:27; 2 Cor 3:1-3; 1 Cor 16:3). Such a letter would guarantee the person so recommended a welcome from the church addressed. It would also be a protection of the church offering hospitality against impostors. Lucian's *Peregrinus* tells how a scheming impostor made a very good thing out of the generosity of simple and credulous Christian communities. A letter of recommendation would protect against such.

The commendation has four components: (a) identification of the one commended (Phoebe); (b) credentials of the one commended (a deacon); (c) request by the commender (receive . . . assist her); and (d) credentials of the one commended (a patroness).

The person recommended here is Phoebe. She is described in three ways. First, she is "our sister" (v. 1a). This is a family term used widely by early Christians (1 Cor 7:15; 9:5; Phlm 2; Jas 2:15; Ignatius, *Polycarp* 5:1; *2 Clem* 12:5; 19:1; 20:2; *Hermas, Vis*, 2.2.3; 2.3.1). A certain view of the church (as family) is assumed. [The Church in Paul] Second, she is called "a deacon (*diakonon*) of the church at Cenchreae" (v. 1b). Deacons are mentioned in Philippians 1:1; the women in 1 Timothy 3:11 are almost certainly female deacons; Pliny, *Epistle* 10.96.8, refers to two female slaves called *ministrae* in Bithynia; a sixth-century inscription found on the Mount of Olives describes a deaconess called Sophie as the "second Phoebe."[5] The NASV's and NIV's translation as "servant" is inadequate. Phoebe was a deacon, the first deacon named in Christian history! Origen, in his *Commentary on the Epistle to the Romans*, had this to say:

> This passage teaches that there were women ordained in the church's ministry by the apostles' authority. . . . Not only that—they ought to be ordained into the ministry, because they helped in many ways and by their good services deserved the praise even of the apostle.[6]

The Church in Paul

Paul did not use the term "church" in Romans until ch. 16. The word *ekklēsia* was used in a variety of ways in antiquity. Two stand out: (1) in the LXX, it was used to designate the assembly of Yahweh, the people of God (e.g., Deut 23:1-2; Judg 20:2; 1 Sam 17:47; 1 Chr 28:18; Neh 13:1); (2) in secular settings it was used to refer to the summoned political gathering of Greek cities, the ruling body composed of every citizen who had not lost his rights (e.g., Acts 19:41, 39; Chariton, *Chaereas and Callirhoe* 8.7). Paul used the term as one of his ways of speaking about the Christian community as the people of God.

- "Church" in Paul always refers to people, never a building.
- In the undisputed Paulines, it almost always refers to a local body of believers (e.g., the church at Cenchrea [Rom 16:1]; church of the Thessalonians [1 Thess 1:1]; churches of the Gentiles [Rom 16:4]; churches of Galatia [Gal 1:2]; of Macedonia [2 Cor 8:1]; of Asia [1 Cor 16:19]; church in the house of [Rom 16:5; 1 Cor 16:19; Phlm 2]; every church [1 Cor 4:17]; all the churches [Rom 16:16; 1 Cor 7:17; 14:33].
- Sometimes it points to the worshiping people of Christ, met together (1 Cor 11:18; 14:4, 5, 12; 14:23; 4:17; 7:17).
- A few times in the undisputed Paulines "church" refers to the universal body of believers (1 Cor 12:28; Phil 3:6). In the deuteropaulines, church often refers to whole company of believers in every place and nation (Eph 3:10, 21; 1:22; 5:23-25; Col 1:18, 24).
- The community is identified by its allegiances (e.g., churches in Christ [Gal 1:22]; churches of Christ [Rom 16:16]; church of God [1 Cor 1:1; 2 Cor 1:1]; church of God in Christ [1 Thess 2:14]; church in God and the Lord Jesus Christ [1 Thess 1:1; 2 Thess 1:1]).
- "Church" is one picture among others used by Paul for God's people. Others include "body of Christ" (1 Cor 12:12, 27;12:5), "Israel of God" (Gal 6:16), "saints in Christ Jesus" (Phil 1:2), house/temple of God (1 Tim 3:15; 1 Cor 3:16-17).
- Allusions to the communities' organization are present in the undisputed letters but are rare (e.g., government, 1 Cor 12:28; those that rule, 1 Thess 5:12; Rom 12:8; rulers/bishops, Phil 1:1; deacons, Phil 1:1; Rom 16:1). This tells us that the Pauline churches were not devoid of structure. The deuteropaulines are filled with references to church organization (e.g., bishop, 1 Tim 3:1-7; deacons, 1 Tim 3:8-13; widows, 1 Tim 5:3-16; elders, 1 Tim 5:17-22; Titus 1:5-9), in a form tending toward an episcopal polity.

Geneva Bible

Romans 16:1-8 in the Geneva Bible of 1576.

(Credit: Baylor University Rare Books Collection)

Third, Phoebe is "a benefactor (*prostatis*) of many and of myself as well" (v. 2b). The term translated benefactor refers to a patron (e.g., an inscription [CIL X810] honors Eumachia, patroness to the fuller's guild, a trade association in which she could not have been a member; cf. Aristotle, *Politics* 1275A). Such a person would have been wealthy enough to care for a group and its members. Phoebe had cared for many, including Paul. So, at some level, she was Paul's social superior.[7] Within the church family Phoebe was a sister whose function was a two-sided coin: a patron and a deacon. The church at Cenchreae (= a port of Corinth on the eastern side toward the Aegean Sea, serving trade with Asia—cf. Pausanias 2.2.3; Apuleius, *Metamorphoses* 10.35; 11.8-11, 16-17) was fortunate to have both a protectoress and a servant of the needy. Phoebe's prominence should be no surprise. In the Judaism of that period women were often prominent (e.g., Judith; *T Job* 21-26, 39-40, Job's wife; *Ps-Philo* 30-33, Deborah; women with titles like *archisynagōgos* = synagogue ruler[8]). Epigraphic evidence shows that in the mid-first century AD in Greek cities of the Roman Empire women of wealth held influential positions in society. The title *prostatis* (patron) and cognate words designated such standing.[9] Paul called on the Roman congregations both to welcome her and to help her "in whatever she may require from you" (v. 2). Was this need Phoebe's personal need or her needs in order to set up a base for Paul's mission to Spain? The text is unclear on this point.

Romans 16:3-16 consists of a series of greetings sent to Christian persons in Rome (cf. Col 4:15; 2 Tim 4:19; Titus 3:15b for similar greetings to churches the canonical Paul did not himself found). Who is represented in this list of persons addressed? First, there are likely nine women: Priscilla (v. 3; cf. 1 Cor 16:19; 2 Tim 4:19; Acts 18:2,28); Mary (v. 6), Junia (v. 7); Tryphena and Tryphosa (v. 12);

Persis (v. 12); the mother of Rufus (v. 13); Julia (v. 15); and the sister of Nereus (v. 15). The only question that might be raised about this enumeration is in the case of Junia in v. 7. The Greek text has *Iounian*. Depending on its accent mark, grammatically it may be masculine (if circumflex, then Junias, so NASV, NIV, RSV, JB) or feminine (if acute, then Junian, so KJV, NRSV, REB, NABRNT) accusative. The ending is the same. Why prefer the feminine?[10] First, the masculine form is not found anywhere in the entire corpus of ancient literature, while the feminine form is repeatedly attested in ancient inscriptions. Second, the ancient fathers took it as feminine. John Chrysostom, in his *Homilies on Romans* 31, is typical. He said: "Think how great the devotion of this woman Junia must have been, that she should be worthy to be called an apostle."[11] The extant early translations (Old Latin, Vulgate, Sahidic, Boharic, Syriac) also seem to take it as feminine. Attempts to resist this reading argue that *episēmos* followed by *en* plus personal datives often connotes no more than one is known by the group.[12] In that case, Romans 16:7 would read: "Junia who was well known by the apostles." This meaning is present in antiquity but so also is the meaning "membership within the group" (e.g., Junia was a well known apostle). Since both meanings are possible, the evidence of the early Greek-speaking fathers and the ancient versions of the NT are decisive. Junia, the wife of Andronicus, was an apostle. The two, husband and wife, were apostles (cf. 1 Cor 15:5—"all the apostles"—not apostles of the churches, but apostles of Christ) prior to Paul's apostleship. This role should not surprise us. "Given the ancient societal roles and relationships, it would have been difficult to reach and address women from a missionary standpoint without the active collaboration of women."[13] Based on the evidence, *Iounian* was a woman and an apostle! She makes nine women addressed by Paul. If the others were not apostles, certain of them received praise: Prisca risked her neck for Paul and had a church in her house (vv. 4-5; cf. Acts 12:12-17 for a church in the house of the mother of John Mark; Acts 16:14-15, 40 for a church in the house of Lydia; Col 4:15 for a church in the house of Nympha); Mary had "worked very hard among you" (v. 6); Tryphaena and Tryphosa are called "workers in the Lord" (v. 12); Persis "has worked hard in the Lord" (v. 12); Rufus's mother had been a mother to Paul as well (v. 13); Julia and Nereus's sister are part of the core of a congregation (v. 15). Romans 16 shows that in the early church, women worked in similar ways to those in which men worked.[14]

House Churches

Romans 16:5 speaks about the church in the house of Prisca and Aquila (cf. Phlm 2—the church in the house of Philemon; Col 4:15—the church in the house of Nympha). This raises the question about the meeting places of early Christian congregations.

- It seems that the places where early Christians worshiped went through four stages: (1) unrenovated space—the house church (1st century); (2) specially adapted space within an existing building—house of the church (2d century); (3) larger, more regular halls of assembly—hall of the church (3rd century); (4) specialized buildings—basilicas especially but also other types of space (4th century). So there was no formal church architecture until stage four, the time after Constantine legalized the Christian movement. (White)
- This overall picture has to be modified slightly for Rome. Archaeological evidence suggests that stage (3) above belonged to the provinces rather than Rome. Large churches were not erected in Rome until the adoption of Christianity as the official religion in the early 4th century made them necessary for greatly increased congregations. (Peterson)
- All of this means that in the time of Paul Christians would have met in the house of either a Christian patron (Rom 16:5) or that of a non-Christian household (Rom 16:14, 15). There would no special space for Christian worship, even in Christian houses, until later (late 1st, 2d centuries).

Second, at least five of the people named were Jews: Prisca and Aquila (v. 3); Andronicus and Junia (v. 7); and Herodian (v. 11). Were the rest Gentiles? It seems likely that the Jew-Gentile divisions in the Roman congregations had their roots in just such distinctions as those reflected here.

Third, inscriptions indicate that Ampliatus (v. 8), Urbanus (v. 9), Hermes (v. 14), Philologus and Julia (v. 15) were common names for slaves. Prisca and Aquila were well off (vv. 3-5). It is possible that Aristobulus (v. 10) was the grandson of Herod the Great and a friend of the emperor Claudius, and that Narcissus (v. 11) was the well-known rich and powerful freedman who influenced Claudius. They were not themselves Christians but had Christians in their households. Was Rufus (v. 13) the son of Simon of Cyrene (Mark 15:21)? Although conclusions concerning some of these questions are not certain, it seems that the congregations contained slave and free, well to do and poor.

Fourth, there appear to have been at least five congregations reflected among those greeted: the church in the house of Prisca and Aquila (v. 5a); those who belong to the family of Aristobulus (v. 10b); those who belong to the family of Narcissus (v. 11); those who are with Asyncritus, Phlegon, Hermes, Patrobas, and Hermas (v. 14); those who are with Philologus, Julia, Nereus and his sister, and Olympas (v. 15).[House Churches]

Why would Paul have spent so much space passing greetings to people in Rome? It was likely because many of these were people

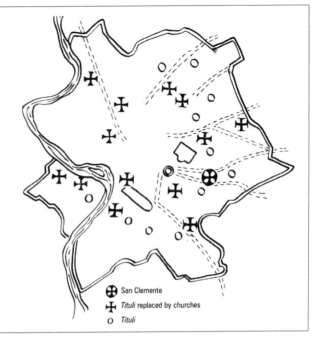

Churches in Rome

Included in this map of early Christian sites in Rome are the locations of ancient churches. According to the 6th-centruy work *Liber Pontificales*, there were 25 title churches (*tituli*) in Rome that could claim to have existed in the 1st century While the *tituli* later became the sites of basilicas dedicated to saints, they appear to have earlier been the private residences of the presbyters who presided over the churches that met in their homes. In Rom 16, Paul mentions several house churches.

⊕ San Clemente
✠ *Tituli* replaced by churches
○ *Tituli*

known to him from elsewhere who had migrated to the city. To mention them was a way of building his lines of communication with those who did not know him. Ask your brothers and sisters in Christ who know me. They will vouch for me. The greetings also give Phoebe a list of people to count on for assistance when she first arrives. [Churches in Rome]

Romans 16:17-20a is an exhortation (cf. 1 Thess 5:27; 2 Cor 13:11b; Gal 6:17; Col 4:16-17 for similar material in a similar location in letters from the Pauline corpus). It is organized as follows:

A—A Warning (v. 17): Avoid those who cause dissensions.
  B—The Reason (v. 18): They serve themselves and deceive others.
A'—An Encouragement (v. 19): Be wise; be guileless.
  B'—The Promise (v. 20a): God will shortly crush Satan under your feet.

Literarily, vv. 17-20a separate the greetings for the people in Rome (vv. 3-15) from those from the Christians in Corinth (vv. 21-23). Rhetorically, it functions to reinforce the argument of 1:16–15:13. A, v. 17, warns the congregations to avoid those who would create dissensions in spite of Paul's irenic theological stance that should enable both sides to come together in Christ. B, v. 18, impugns the motives of such people (cf. Phil 3:18-19; Gal 6:12-13; 2 Cor 11:13-15; 1 Tim 6:3-5; 2 Tim 3:1-9) and recoils in horror at the thought of their using smooth talk and flattery to deceive the simple. A', v. 19, asks for wisdom in the area of goodness and sincerity/guilelessness in the area of evil. This, of course, is only possible with a transformed mind. B', v. 20a, offers a promise that makes this possible. If God is our vindicator, then believers can be guileless in the face of evil (remember 12:19). So, the gist of the exhortation is: follow Paul's teaching about Jew-Gentile unity in Christ and avoid those who are working in another direction.

Romans 16:20b is Paul's benediction: "The grace of our Lord Jesus Christ be with you" (cf. 1 Thess 5:28; 1 Cor 16:23; 2 Thess 3:18; cf. 2 Cor 13:13).

Romans 16:21-23 consists of greetings from Christians who are at Corinth when Paul writes this letter (cf. similar greetings in 1 Cor 16:19-20a; 2 Cor 13:13; Phil 4:21b-22; Col 4:10-14; 2 Tim 4:21b; Titus 3:15a; Phlm 23-24). The greetings follow an ABA' pattern.

A—Greetings from Jewish Christians (v. 21)
  B—Greetings from the Amanuensis (v. 22)
A'—Greetings from Gentile Christians (v. 23)

The Jewish Christians are four. Timothy, Paul's coworker, sends greetings (v. 21a; cf. Acts 16:1; 2 Tim 3:15). Paul's relatives (*syggeneis*), Lucius, Jason, and Sosipater, send greetings (v. 21b).

Erastus Inscription

Mid-1st-century inscription from Corinth, discovered in 1929. In return for his aedileship, Erastus laid the pavement at his own expense.

[E]RASTUS PRO AEDILIT [AT] E
S P STRAVIT

(Credit: Sharyn Dowd)

The writer of the letter, Tertius, sent his greetings as well (v. 22). The Gentile Christians are three: Gaius, "who is host to me and to the whole church, greets you" (v. 23a; cf. 1 Cor 1:14—one of the few Paul baptized in Corinth); Erastus, "the city treasurer" (v. 23b; Acts 19:22; 2 Tim 4:20); and Quartus, our brother (v. 23c). An inscription found at Corinth mentions an Erastus as a city official.[15] Since the inscription dates from the mid-first century AD, many have identified the Erastus of the inscription with the Erastus of Romans 16:23. On the basis of this identification they have then argued for the spread of the new faith among socially powerful people. This is possible, but since Erastus was a common name, the identification cannot be certain.[16]

Romans 16:25-27 is a concluding doxology. Six forms of the use of it are found in Greek manuscripts, ancient versions, and the early fathers.

1. It is omitted entirely (e.g., F, G, 629; Marcion, Jerome).
2. It is added after 14:23 (e.g., L, 181, 326; Harclean Syriac, Cyril, Theodoret).
3. It is added after 15:33 (only in P46).
4. It is added after 16:23-24 (e.g., P61, Sinaiticus, Vaticanus, D, 81; Peshitta, Vulgate, Coptic).
5. It is added after both 14:23 and 16:23-24 (e.g., A, P, 5, 33; Armenian).
6. It is added after both 14:23 and 15:33 (1506).

The unit begins and ends with praise: "Now to God who is able to strengthen you (v. 25a) . . . to the only wise God, through Jesus Christ, to whom be the glory forever. Amen" (v. 27). What comes in between, the basis for the praise, focuses on the gospel: "my gospel . . . , the mystery (cf. Col 1:26-27; 2:2; 4:3; Eph 1:9; 3:3-4, 9; 6:19) that was kept secret for long ages but is now disclosed, and through the prophetic writings is made known to all the Gentiles . . . , to bring about the obedience of faith" (vv. 25b-26). Doxologies in antiquity often concluded religious texts (4 Macc 18:24; *1 Clem* 64:2; *2 Clem* 20:5), letters (Phil 4:20; 1 Tim 6:16; 2 Tim 4:18; Heb 13:21; 1 Pet 5:11; 2 Pet 3:18; Jude 24-25; *1 Clem* 65:2), and liturgies (Rev 4:9; 5:13-14; 7:12; 19:1; *1 Enoch* 39:10, 13; *Didache* 8:2; 9:2, 3, 4). Here the doxology concludes a letter that is a religious text and does so in a way that may reflect the letter's liturgical use.[17] Many scholars regard the doxology as non-Pauline, as an editorial addition, perhaps added when Paul's letters were collected at the end of the first century. If so, it certainly functions well in its present location, giving a fitting climax to a majestic epistle. [Paul's Burial in Rome]

Paul's Burial in Rome

According to church tradition, after Paul was executed during Nero's reign, his body was recovered and buried in a vineyard by a Roman matron named Lucina. A small shrine dedicated to the apostle as a martyr existed on the site at least as early as the period of Constantine's rule (306–337 AD). In the late 4th century, a large basilica was built here and came to be known as the Church of Saint Paul outside the Walls.

(Credit: Scott Nash)

CONNECTIONS

Egalitarianism in Christian Communities?

The evidence for a woman deacon (Phoebe, Rom 16:1-2), a woman apostle (Junia, Rom 16:7), and various female laborers for the Christian cause (Rom 16:6, Mary who has worked very hard among you; 16:12a, Tryphaena and Tryphosa, workers in the Lord; 16:12b, Persis, who has worked hard in the Lord; 16:13, Rufus's mother who has been a mother to Paul; cf. Phil 4:2-3, Euodia and Syntyche who have struggled beside Paul in the work of the gospel; 1 Cor 11:4, women pray and prophesy in church) in the time of Paul raises the question about the role of women in Christian ministry.

Certain Christians are willing to grant the evidence even for a woman deacon and a woman apostle but then offer qualifiers. Thomas R. Schreiner is an example.[18] About Phoebe, he has said:

> The office of deacon, however, must be distinguished from that of overseer/elder. . . . One should not conclude from Phoebe's role as a deacon that she functioned as a leader of the congregation.[19]

Regarding Junia, he has argued:

> One should scarcely conclude from the reference to Junia and the other women coworkers named here that women exercised authority over men contrary to the Pauline admonition in 1 Timothy 2:12. We

see evidence that women functioned as early Christian missionaries, and it may have been the case that they concentrated especially on other women, given the patriarchal nature of the Greco-Roman world. The Pauline pattern prescribed in 1 Timothy 2:11-15 was the apostolic pattern in the early Christian mission, and the vibrant ministry of Christian women did not contradict the admonitions delivered in 1 Timothy 2.[20]

Two questions must be raised about such a position. First, in Acts 18:26 we hear that Priscilla and Aquila took Apollos aside and explained the Way to him more accurately. Here a woman is a teacher of a male preacher, behavior that is approved of by the author of Acts. Moreover, the fact that she is mentioned first in the best manuscripts indicates that she is regarded as the dominant authority (cf. Acts 13:2, Barnabas and Saul; 13:13, Paul and his companions, etc.). So, in a document from the Pauline wing of the church, in the same geographical area as the Pastorals, from about the same time as the Pastorals, we have a woman's teaching and having authority over a male preacher approved. How, then, should one read 1 Timothy's rejection of women's teaching?

Second, it is necessary to ask about the historical occasion of the Pastoral epistles. They were written to counteract heresy in the churches addressed by these three little letters. The technique used to protect against heresy was the principle of succession. God gave the true tradition to Paul (2 Tim 1:11-12). Paul delivered it to Timothy (2 Tim 1:13-14) before many witnesses (2 Tim 2:2a). Timothy is to entrust this tradition to "faithful men" (contra NRSV's "faithful people"; 2 Tim 2:2b) who will be able to teach others also. The author believed that if the churches listen only to authorized teachers, those who received their teaching from Timothy who got it from Paul who received it from God, they will be protected against the false teaching circulating in the communities addressed. Who were the members most susceptible to the false teaching? In this particular case it was the women (2 Tim 3:6-7). In such a situation, using such a technique, those most susceptible to heresy would hardly be entrusted with the task of teaching. In this case, the women members were like Eve who had been deceived by Satan. In this case, only men could teach. Read in this way, it is clear that the issue is not gender but orthodoxy and heresy. The women are not prohibited from teaching because they are women but because they are caught up in heresy. Viewed in such a light, the differences between Acts 18 and the Pastoral epistles become clear. When women are teaching the true Pauline tradition (like Priscilla is doing), they can teach; when women are espousing heresy (like the women referred to in the Pastorals), they may not teach. Who teaches does not depend upon gender but on orthodoxy! If women (or men!) are involved in heresy they should not teach. If they are devotees of true Christian doctrine, they may teach! The emphasis in 2 Timothy 2:2's "faithful men" is on faithful rather than men.

Given the line of reasoning just outlined, it seems possible to say that the Pauline corpus reflects women apostles, prophets, teachers, and deacons, as well as female patrons of Christian communities. Such involvement of women in ministry in the early churches was in spite of the patriarchal structures of Mediterranean society generally.

At the same time that one acknowledges the involvement of women in ministry in earliest Christianity, it is important to note that for Paul the opposite of patriarchy was not egalitarianism but something else! Paul's vision was of a society of siblings in which only God was called Father, in which there were differences among members and in which each family member used his or her strengths to enrich the quality of life in the family of God.[21] Within such a family, contributions were not determined by one's sex, one's economic status, or one's race. They were determined by the "measure of faith/responsibility/trust" (Rom 12:3b) God assigned to each. Within such a family, the measure of responsibility assigned by God to each one regardless of sex, class, or race was not one's right to be claimed but a grace to be received. Within such a family, the measure of responsibility assigned by God as a gift of grace was not aimed to enhance the recipient's status but to build up the community. Egalitarianism is based on rights possessed, just deserts to be received, and aims at the enhancement of the status of the one who possesses such rights and who is granted such just deserts. The family of God is based on God's gracious gifts to each of His children regardless of sex, status, or race, which gifts are to be used for the enhancement of others. Egalitarianism is based on power! Christian community is based on human transformation by divine agency: on God's enablement of our transcending our Adamic nature.

NOTES

[1] D. W. B. Robinson, "The Priesthood of Paul in the Gospel of Hope," in *Reconciliation and Hope*, ed. R. Banks (Grand Rapids: Eerdmans, 1974), 231-45.

[2] J. P. Bowers, "Jewish Communities in Spain in the Time of Paul the Apostle," *JTS* 26 (1975): 395-402.

[3] Cited in Gerald Bray, *Romans* (*ACCS*; (Downers Grove: InterVarsity, 1998), 379-80.

[4] Jeffrey A. D. Weima, *Neglected Endings: The Significance of the Pauline Letter Closings* (Sheffield, UK: Sheffield Academic Press, 1994), 222.

[5] James D. G. Dunn, *Romans 9–16* (WBC; Dallas: Word, 1988), 887.

[6] Cited in Bray, *Romans*, 369.

[7] Caroline F. Whelan, "Amica Pauli: The Role of Phoebe in the Early Church," *JSNT* 49 (1993): 67-85.

[8] Paul R. Trebilco, *Jewish Communities in Asia Minor* (Cambridge: Cambridge University Press, 1991), highlights the prominence of women in synagogues.

[9] R. A. Kearsley, "Women in Public Life in the Roman East," *Tyndale Bulletin* 50 (1999): 189-211. Eldon Jay Epp, "Text-Critical, Exegetical, and Socio-Cultural Factors Affecting the Junia/Junias Variation in Romans 16:7," *New Testament Textual Criticism and Exegesis: Festschrift J. Delobel*, ed. A. Denaux (Leuven: Leuven University Press, 2002) 227-91.

[10] John Thorley, "Junia, a Woman Apostle," *NovT* 38 (1996): 18-29; Richard S. Cervin, "A Note Regarding the Name 'Junia(s)' in Romans 16:7," *NTS* 40 (1994): 464-70.

[11] Cited in Bray, *Romans*, 372.

[12] M. H. Burer and D. B. Wallace, "Was Junia Really an Apostle? A Re-examination of Romans 16:7," *NTS* 47 (2000): 76-91. Although Burer and Wallace oppose reading Junia as an apostle, they provide linguistic data for both sides of the argument.

[13] Peter Stuhlmacher, *Paul's Letter to the Romans* (Louisville: Westminster/John Knox, 1994), 249.

[14] R. L. Omanson, "Who's Who in Romans 16?" *The Bible Translator* 49 (1998): 430-36.

[15] J. H. Kent, *Inscriptions 1926–1950: Corinth VIII. Part Three* (Princeton: American School of Classical Studies at Athens, 1966), 99.

[16] Justin Meggett, "The Social Status of Erastus (Rom 16:23)," *NovT* 38 (1996): 218-23.

[17] G. J. Cuming, "Service-Endings in the Epistles," *NTS* 22 (1975), 110-113.

[18] Thomas R. Schreiner, *Romans* (Grand Rapids: Baker, 1998).

[19] Ibid., 787, n.4.

[20] Ibid., 797.

[21] Scott Bartchy, "Undermining Ancient Patriarchy: The Apostle Paul's Vision of a Society of Siblings," *Biblical Theology Bulletin* 29 (1999): 77.

BIBLIOGRAPHY

Bibliographies

Mills, Watson E. *Bibliographies for Biblical Research: Romans.* Mellen, 1996.

Wagner, Günther. *An Exegetical Bibliography of the New Testament: Romans and Galatians.* Macon: Mercer University Press, 1996.

Collections of Essays

Donfried, Karl P., ed. *The Romans Debate: Revised and Expanded Edition.* Peabody MA: Hendrickson, 1991.

Hay, David M. and E. Elizabeth Johnson, eds. *Pauline Theology, Volume III: Romans.* Minneapolis: Fortress, 1995.

Soderlund, Svend K. and N.T. Wright, eds. *Romans and the People of God.* Grand Rapids: Eerdmans, 1999.

Commentaries

Augustine. *Augustine on Romans.* Ed. Paula Friedriksen Landes. Atlanta: Scholars Press, 1982.

Byrne, Brendan. *Romans.* Sacra Pagina 6. Collegeville: Liturgical Press, 1996.

Calvin, John. *Commentary on the Epistle of Paul the Apostle to the Romans.* Grand Rapids: Eerdmans, 1948.

Cranfield, C. E. B. *A Critical and Exegetical Commentary on the Epistle to the Romans.* 2 volumes. Edinburgh: T. & T. Clark, 1975-79.

Dunn, James D. G. *Romans.* Word Biblical Commentary. 2 volumes. Dallas: Word, 1988.

Fitzmyer, Joseph A. *Romans.* Anchor Bible 33. NY: Doubleday, 1993.

Johnson, Luke T. *Reading Romans.* Reading the New Testament. Macon: Smyth & Helwys, 1997.

Käsemann, Ernst. *Commentary on Romans.* Grand Rapids: Eerdmans, 1980.

Luther, Martin. *Commentary on the Epistle to the Romans.* Grand Rapids: Zondervan, 1954.

Moo, Douglas J. *The Epistle to the Romans.* New International Commentary on the New Testament. Grand Rapids: Eerdmans, 1996.

Schreiner, Thomas R. *Romans: Exegetical Commentary on the New Testament.* Grand Rapids: Baker, 1998.

Stott, John. *Romans.* Downers Grove, Ill.: InterVarsity, 1994.

Stuhlmacher, Peter Stuhlmacher. *Paul's Letter to the Romans.* Louisville, KY: Westminster/John Knox, 1994.

Wesley, John. *Explanatory Notes upon the New Testament.* London: Epworth, 1950.

INDEX OF MODERN AUTHORS

INDEX OF SIDEBARS

Illustration Sidebars

INDEX OF SCRIPTURES

INDEX OF TOPICS